D0023059

Managing Hotels Effectively
Lessons From Outstanding General Managers

Eddystone C. Nebel III
C. B. Smith Professor of Hotel Management
Purdue University

Professor Emeritus
University of New Orleans

JOHN WILEY & SONS, INC.

New York • Chichester • Weinheim • Brisbane • Singapore • Toronto

A NOTE TO THE READER
This book has been electronically reproduced from
digital information stored at John Wiley & Sons, Inc.
We are pleased that the use of this new technology
will enable us to keep works of enduring scholarly
value in print as long as there is a reasonable demand
for them. The content of this book is identical to
previous printings.

This book is printed on acid-free paper. ☺

Copyright © 1991 by John Wiley & Sons, Inc. All rights reserved.

Published simultaneously in Canada

No part of this publication may be reproduced, stored in a retrieval system or transmitted
in any form or by any means, electronic, mechanical, photocopying, recording, scanning
or otherwise, except as permitted under Sections 107 or 108 of the 1976 United States
Copyright Act, without either the prior written permission of the Publisher, or
authorization through payment of the appropriate per-copy fee to the Copyright
Clearance Center, 222 Rosewood Drive, Danvers, MA 01923, (978) 750-8400, fax
(978) 750-4470. Requests to the Publisher for permission should be addressed to the
Permissions Department, John Wiley & Sons, Inc., 111 River Street, Hoboken, NJ 07030,
(201) 748-6011, fax (201) 748-6008.

This publication is designed to provide accurate and authoritative information in regard to the
subject matter covered. It is sold with the understanding that the publisher is not engaged in
rendering professional services. If professional advice or other expert assistance is required, the
services of a competent professional person should be sought.

Library of Congress Cataloging-in-Publication Data:

Nebel, Eddystone C.
    Managing hotels effectively : lessons from outstanding general
  managers / Eddystone C. Nebel, III
      p. cm.
    Includes bibliographical references and index.
    ISBN 0-471-28909-4
    1. Hotel management. I. Title.
TX911.3.M27N43 1991
647.94'068—dc20   91-8078

Printed in the United States of America

To My Wife, Dorothy Fox Nebel

CONTENTS

PREFACE   **xvii**

ACKNOWLEDGMENTS   **xxi**

INTRODUCTION   **xxiii**

      THE GM RESEARCH   xxiii

      THE GMs   xxiv

      UNIFYING THEME   xxvii

      REFERENCES   xxviii

CHAPTER 1   **The Environment of The Hotel Business**   **1**

      THE GLAMOUR OF IT ALL   2

        The Hotel as History   3

        The Hotel as Excitement   4

        The Hotel as Theater   7

        A City Within a City   8

        A Vocation   8

      THE PACE OF A HOTEL   9

        Hotel Cycles   10

        Open for Business 8,760 Hours per Year   10

Scope of Operations   12

The Unpredictability of Problems   14

The Immediacy of Problems   16

The Need for Dedication   18

THE COMPETITIVE ENVIRONMENT   18

Hotels Are Commodities   19

Permanent Overbuilding   20

Rooms Are Perishable Products   21

Forecasting Demand   22

CONCLUSION   24

REFERENCES   26

QUESTIONS   26

CHAPTER 2   Service, People, and Profits in the Hotel Business   28

SERVICE COUNTS   28

Service Is Intangible   31

Setting Service Standards   32

Service Consistency   35

Attitudes Toward Service   36

PEOPLE SERVING PEOPLE   36

Guests   37

Employees   39

Managers   46

OWNERS, PROFITS, AND MANAGERS   48

Absentee Owners   48

Corporate Input   50

Profits Versus Service   50

Profits During Good Times and Bad   52

CONCLUSION   53

REFERENCES   55

FURTHER READING   55

QUESTIONS   55

CHAPTER 3   An Overview of Strategic Planning   57

THE NATURE OF STRATEGIC PLANNING   57

Strategic Planning Defined   57

Distinguishing Characteristics of Strategic Planning   58

THE STRATEGIC PLANNING HIERARCHY   59

Strategic Planning and the Corporate Organization   60

Corporate-Level Strategic Planning   61

Business-Level Strategic Planning   61

Functional Level Strategic Planning   62

Strategic Planning and the Individual Hotel   62

THE STRATEGIC PLANNING PROCESS   63

Overview of the Strategic Planning Process   64

Setting Organizational Goals   66

Formulating a Strategic Plan   70

Strategy Implementation   76

Evaluating the Strategic Plan   78

The Time Horizon of Strategic Planning   79

CONCLUSION   80

REFERENCES   82

QUESTIONS   82

CHAPTER 4   Planning in Hotels   84

THE HOTEL PLANNING CONTEXT   84

The Hotel Planning Time Horizon   86

The GM's Role in Strategic Planning   87

SETTING HOTEL GOALS AND OBJECTIVES   89

Determining Markets to Serve   90

Setting Service and Quality Standards   91

Other Goals and Objectives   93

Productivity Goals   93

Human Resource Goals   95

Profitability Goals   95

Developing a Hotel's Culture   97

FORMULATING A STRATEGIC PLAN   98

    An Aggressive Strategic Plan   100

    A Time for Retrenchment and Turnaround   105

CONCLUSION   109

REFERENCES   109

QUESTIONS ·   110

CHAPTER 5   Hotel Organization   111

AN OVERVIEW OF ORGANIZATIONAL DESIGN   111

    The Elements Of Organizational Structure   112

        Specialization   112

        Departmentalization   115

        Authority   118

        Line Versus Staff Authority   118

        Span of Control   119

        Coordination of Activities   122

    Static Principles of Organizational Design   125

        Chain of Command   125

        Unity of Command   127

        Delegation   128

THE HOTEL FUNCTIONAL ORGANIZATIONAL
DESIGN   130

    A Mid-Sized Hotel's Organizational Design   130

        The Rooms Department   130

        The Food and Beverage Department   133

        Sales and Marketing   134

        Personnel   135

        Accounting   135

    A Large Hotel's Organizational Design   137

    Strengths of the Functional Organization   139

    Weaknesses of the Functional Organization   139

CONCLUSION   141

REFERENCES   142

QUESTIONS   142

CHAPTER 6   Coordinating the Activities of a Hotel   144

THE NEED FOR INTERDEPARTMENTAL
    COORDINATION   144

THE EXECUTIVE OPERATING COMMITTEE   146

OTHER HOTEL COMMITTEES AND MEETINGS   150

The Variety of Hotel Committees and Meetings   151

Meetings and Communications   151

CONCLUSION   156

REFERENCES   156

QUESTIONS   157

CHAPTER 7   Hotel Staffing   157

THE HOTEL STAFFING SYSTEM   159

Job Design   159

Employee Selection   160

Training and Development   165

Performance Appraisal   168

Employee Compensation   170

CONCLUSION   170

REFERENCES   171

QUESTIONS   171

CHAPTER 8   Motivation   173

UNDERSTANDING PEOPLE   173

MOTIVATION AND WORK   175

Assumptions About People   176

A Changing View of Workers   177

The Motivational Process   179

INDIVIDUAL NEEDS   180

Theory X and Theory Y 180

A Needs Hierarchy   182

The Need for Achievement   185

Worker Satisfaction and Dissatisfaction   187

MOTIVATIONAL PROCESS   189

An Expectancy Theory of Motivation   190

Goal Setting and Management by Objectives   195

Equity as Part of the Motivational Process   198

Behavior Modification   200

JOB SATISFACTION AND JOB PERFORMANCE   201

Does Satisfaction Lead to Performance?   202

Does Performance Lead to Satisfaction?   202

Some Practical Considerations   203

Views of Hotel GMs   205

CONCLUSION   205

REFERENCES   207

QUESTIONS   208

CHAPTER 9   Communication in Hotels   210

THE INTENSITY OF COMMUNICATIONS
    IN HOTELS   210

THE KEY ROLE PLAYED BY COMMUNICATIONS   213

TIPS FOR BETTER COMMUNICATION   216

It's Easy to Get into Trouble   217

Misunderstanding Slow Service   219

GMs CAUGHT IN THE ACT OF COMMUNICATING   220

Putting Yourself in the Other Person's Shoes   221

Rushing to Judgment   221

No Such Thing as an Interruption   221

You Can Learn Only When Someone Else Is Talking   224

If You Do All the Talking You'll Also Have
    to Do All the Thinking   226

CONCLUSION   226

REFERENCES   227

QUESTIONS   228

CHAPTER 10   Leading People   229

THE IMPORTANCE OF LEADERSHIP   229

Leadership in Hotels   230

What Is Leadership?   232

LEADERSHIP TRAITS AND SOURCES OF POWER   233

Leadership Traits   233

Sources of Leader Power   234

LEADER BEHAVIOR   236

Authoritarian Versus Participative Leadership   237

Pros and Cons of Authoritarian and Participative Leadership   238

Factors Affecting Leadership Style   239

GM Leadership Behavior: Authoritarian Versus Participative   240

Consideration and Initiating Structure   243

The Management Grid   243

Factors Affecting Leadership Style   244

GM Leadership Behavior: Task Versus People   245

GMs Attention to Detail and Follow-up as a Leadership Trait   248

CHOOSING A LEADERSHIP STYLE   248

How Follower Maturity Affects Initiating Structure and Consideration   249

Choosing a Leadership Style   249

How GMs Act   250

How to Choose Between an Authoritarian and a Participative Leadership Style   251

Choosing a Decision-Making Leadership Style   251

GMs and Decision Making   254

CONCLUSION   256

REFERENCES   258

FURTHER READING   259

QUESTIONS   259

CHAPTER 11 Leading Organizations   261

AMERICAN DOMINANCE CHALLENGED   261

CHARACTERISTICS OF A JAPANESE BUSINESS   263

Theory Z   265

TYPE Z ORGANIZATIONS   265

Why Type Z Firms Are Top Performers   267

THE ART OF JAPANESE MANAGEMENT   268

Interdependence and Junior–Senior Relationships   268

An American Example of Japanese Management   268

Superordinate Goals   269

JAPANESE MANAGEMENT IN THE
HOTEL BUSINESS   271

Turnover and Its Consequences   271

Specialized Career Paths   272

Holistic Relations and Trust   273

Collective Decision Making and Collective Responsibility   273

IN SEARCH OF (AMERICAN) EXCELLENCE   276

Attitudes Toward People   277

Values and Meaning   278

Management by Wandering Around   281

Hotel GMs Searching for Managerial Excellence   282

SOME THOUGHTS ABOUT AMERICAN LEADERS   285

Strategy 1: Attention Through Vision   286

Strategy 2: Meaning Through Communication   286

Strategy 3: Trust Through Positioning   287

Strategy 4: Self-development   289

CONCLUSION   291

REFERENCES   292

FURTHER READINGS   292

QUESTIONS   293

CHAPTER 12 An Overview of Controlling Hotel Operations   294

FEEDBACK CONTROL   295

Simple Feedback-Control Process   295

Where Feedback Control Cannot Be Used   296

Feedback Control in Hotels   296

CONTROL TACTICS   298

Results Accountability Controls   298

Specific-Action Controls   299

Personnel Control   300

CHOOSING THE RIGHT CONTROL STRATEGY   301

Specific-Action Controls   301

Results Control   304

Personnel Control   305

CONCLUSION   307

REFERENCES   307

QUESTIONS   308

CHAPTER 13 Controlling Results: Hotel Revenues and Costs   309

THE BEGINNING FORECAST   311

Occupancy Forecast   311

Departmental Forecasts   314

FORGING THE ANNUAL BUSINESS PLAN   317

Group Consensus at The Regal Hotel   317

Making Difficult Choices at The St. Charles Hotel   322

The Final Business Plan   323

THE MONTHLY CONTROL CYCLE   323

The Thirty- To Ninety-Day Forecast   323

The Monthly Forecast   324

The Profit and Loss Forecast   329

The Ten-Day Planning and Control Cycle   331

CONCLUSION   336

REFERENCES   337

QUESTIONS   337

CHAPTER 14 Control: Getting Employees To Do Things Right and To Do the Right Things   338

SPECIFIC-ACTION CONTROLS: GETTING EMPLOYEES TO DO THINGS RIGHT   338

Introductory Training: The "Dos" and "Don'ts" of Working for a
    Living   339

Doing Things Right on the Job: Housekeeping
    Room Attendants   341

Specific-Action Controls for Managers   343

Systems of Specific-Action Controls   346

Direct Supervision as a Form of Specific-Action Controls   348

PERSONNEL CONTROL: GETTING PEOPLE TO DO THE
    RIGHT THINGS   349

Telephone Training: Simple Training for a Critical Skill   349

Guest-Relations Training   350

Total Employee Training   354

Employee Relations Programs   356

    Employee Programs   356

    Employee Surveys   359

    Employee Turnover   360

CONCLUSION   361

REFERENCES   364

QUESTIONS   364

CHAPTER 15   The GMs' Background
             and Personal Characteristics   366

The GMs' Backgrounds   367

    Formal Education   367

    Strengths and Weaknesses of the GMs' Formal Education   370

    Choice of a Hotel Career   371

    Types of Experience and Career Progression   372

    Major Career-Decision Points   375

    Future Ambitions   378

PERSONAL CHARACTERISTICS OF THE GM   378

    GMs' Outlook About Their Jobs   379

    Tough Job Decisions   379

    Recent High and Low Points in the GMs' Lives   381

    Likes and Dislikes of Being a GM   382

    Views About Family   383

Self-evaluation   383

Others' Evaluation's   384

PERSONAL CHARACTERISTICS OF THE IDEAL GM   385

Needs and Drives   386

Attitudes and Values   387

Interpersonal Orientation   388

Temperament   389

Cognitive Orientation   390

CONCLUSION   392

REFERENCES   395

FURTHER READINGS   395

QUESTIONS   396

CHAPTER 16 The Day-to-Day Activities of Outstanding
Hotel Managers   397

THE CHALLENGES OF THE GM'S JOB   398

Job Demands and Relationship Demands   398

Short Run Demands   398

Intermediate-Run Demands   399

Long-Run Demands   400

The Roles a GM Must Play   401

Managerial Roles as Operational Controller   402

Managerial Roles as Organizational Developer   404

Managerial Roles as Business Maintainer   405

The GM as Information Focal Point   405

WATCHING A HOTEL GM MANAGE   406

A Typical Day   407

Characteristics of Managerial Work   412

Hotel GMs Perform a Great Amount of Work (Mintzberg's number
1/Kotter's number 1)   413

Hotel GMs Perform a Wide Variety of Activities (Mintzberg's
number 2/Kotter's number 2, 3, 4)   413

Hotel GMs Make Many Small Decisions on Current Issues
(Mintzberg's number 3/Kotter's number 5)   415

Hotel GMs Have Extensive Dealings With the Outside World
(Mintzberg's number 4/Kotter's number 6 and 7)   416

Hotel GMs Spend Their Work Days in Intensive Verbal
Communication (Mintzberg's number 5
/ Kotter's number 8)   417

Hotel GMs Allocate Their Time by Reacting to the Events That
Take Place Around Them (Mintzberg's number 6/Kotter's
number 9)   418

Additional Aspects of Managerial Work   423

CONCLUSION   425

REFERENCES   427

FURTHER READINGS   427

QUESTIONS   428

APPENDIX   429

GENERAL MANAGER QUESTIONS   429

DIVISIONAL HEAD QUESTIONS   430

INDEX   433

PREFACE

This book is an outgrowth of research into hotel general manager (GM) effectiveness begun in 1987 while on sabbatical leave from the University of New Orleans. During the research, I interviewed ten outstanding GMs and their key subordinates: fifty-three hotel division heads. I also talked informally to at least twice that number of other hotel executives. I was asked over and over again if I was going to write a book about what I was finding. These hotel executives were genuinely interested in what I was doing. They wanted to become better managers, so they wanted to learn what successful GMs did to be effective. Their interest in becoming better hotel managers, more than anything else, encouraged me to write a book on my findings that would be broadly available to serious young hotel executives.

Why study hotel GMs? Legend has it that when Conrad Hilton was asked how many people were needed to run a quality hotel he replied, tongue in cheek, "Just one, the general manager." While it takes more than just one person to run a hotel, the GM is undoubtedly the key executive in the hotel industry. An effective GM can surmount many obstacles and still turn a profit; it's impossible, however, to overcome the burden of an ineffective GM. A hotel company can only be as strong as its individual hotels, each of which is a separate profit center. If the individual hotels are badly managed and unprofitable, the entire company is unprofitable.

A hotel's GM is the chief executive officer of its business. The GM gets the credit if the hotel is successful and the blame if it is not. No hotel executive position below the GM has such broad business responsibility. If you are preparing for or have begun a career in the hotel business it would be quite normal for you to set your sights on becoming a hotel GM. And why not! This is the executive, after all, who has the total responsibility for the success or the failure of the business. This is the person who has risen to the top executive position in the hotel and who is in charge of the entire business.

But what if your career goals at this time are to specialize in a functional area of hotel operations such as sales, food and beverage, or rooms? Why study hotel management from the prospective of the GM? One reason is that to be effective in any area of hotel operations, it's vitally important that you understand the larger perspective of the total business. That larger perspective, of course, is the one that must be taken by the hotel's chief executive, the GM. Another reason, is that as your career progresses you may decide to change your goals and strive for the top job. In either case, your knowledge of how hotels should be managed will be enhanced by a careful reading of this book.

One reason for conducting this particular study was to address specific curriculum issues for hotel administration students. Many hotel administration courses cover topics relating to specific functional areas within a hotel. Examples would be courses in front office operations, food and beverage cost control, hotel sales and marketing, and hotel accounting. All of these courses are certainly important. Each, however, approaches its subject from its own narrow functional perspective. A course in *hotel management*, however, must approach its topic from the perspective of the entire business. This is exactly the perspective that the GM, as the chief executive of the individual hotel, must take. Thus, understanding how effective hotel GMs manage their hotels fits in quite nicely with understanding hotel management. For these reasons, I decided to conduct extensive field research about hotel GMs.

The best known recent research on the nature of managerial work has been conducted by Mintzberg (1973) and Kotter (1982) using observational research methods where the researcher actually records what the executive is doing while on the job. These two researchers studied the nature of managerial work among executives, but not hotel executives. Furthermore, the managers studied by Kotter and Mintzberg typically held higher positions in their companies' organizational hierarchy than do hotel GMs. Only Ley (1978) has studied hotel GMs using observational research methods. For his doctoral dissertation, he studied seven GMs of 140- to 170-room hotels. While other GM research has been conducted and will be referred to throughout the book, there are still many unanswered questions concerning what GMs do to be effective. Therefore, I decided to conduct a study of hotel GM effectiveness generally following Kotter's (1982) approach.

You will learn, when reading this book, that outstanding hotel GMs possess a variety of personal qualities. Included among these qualities are attention to detail, obsessiveness for task completion, abundant people skills, patience, and an action orientation. Each of the GMs studied was a hard-working, responsible person. Each had overcome difficulties and challenges to get to where he was. Each had made sacrifices to become successful. Each was also extremely happy doing what he did. Frank Anderson, really by chance, found his way into a hotel sales job. He knew, almost immediately, that he "had been made for the hotel business." Henri LeSassier had been fascinated by the organized precision of a well-managed kitchen ever since he was a twelve-year-old oyster shucker in a restaurant in France. Curtis Samuels realized while watching the movie, "Hotel," in Vietnam that hotel management was the career for him. Matthew Fox said that as soon as someone suggested he apply for a hotel job he realized that he had always been intrigued and fascinated by hotels.

Bruce Warren said that he disliked nothing about his job and that every day was wonderful!

The book is comprised of sixteen chapters. The first two discuss key characteristics of hotels that influence how they should be managed. These characteristics were derived from detailed discussions with the ten GMs and their 53 key subordinates about the challenges of managing hotels. Understanding the issues raised in Chapter One, "The Environment of the Hotel Business," and Chapter Two, "Service, People, and Profits in the Hotel Business," is very important to fully appreciating why outstanding hotel GMs manage as they do.

Chapters Three through Fourteen discuss the four basic management functions of planning, organizing, directing, and controlling. Chapters Three and Four discuss the *planning* function of management. Chapter Three, "An Overview of Strategic Planning," gives an overview of the modern principles of strategic planning. In Chapter Four, "Planning in Hotels," these principles are applied to planning in hotels. Chapter Four includes numerous examples of the ten GMs' strategic planning.

Chapters Five, Six, and Seven cover the *organizing* function of management. In Chapter Five, "Hotel Organization," the basic principles of organizational design are covered, including the typical functional organizational structure found in complex hotels. The strengths and weaknesses of a hotel's functional organizational structure are also discussed. This leads directly to Chapter Six, "Coordinating the Activities of a Hotel," which is a response in well-managed hotels to overcome the major weaknesses of a hotel's functional organizational structure. Chapter Seven, "Hotel Staffing," rounds out the treatment of management's organizing function with a brief discussion of some of the major personnel issues faced by hotels.

Chapters Eight, Nine, Ten, and Eleven address important issues relating to management's *directing* function. Chapter Eight, "Motivation," discussed some of the most influential concepts of human motivation as they relate to people at work. Chapter Nine, "Communication in Hotels," is devoted to verbal communications because that is primarily what takes place in hotels. The important topic of personal leadership is covered in Chapter Ten, "Leading People." Numerous examples of effective leadership from the GM research are given. Chapter Eleven, "Leading Organizations," discusses the important concept of "corporate culture." It includes some of the things American managers have recently been learning from the Japanese. As in all chapters, examples of these concepts from the GM study are presented.

Chapters Twelve, Thirteen, and Fourteen discuss the *control* function management in hotels. In Chapter Twelve, "An Overview of Controlling Hotel Operations," the various control strategies available to a manager are discussed, along with consideration of how to choose the most appropriate control strategy. Chapter Thirteen, "Controlling Results: Hotel Revenues and Costs," presents a detailed example of a results accountability control system taken from the GM research. Chapter Fourteen, "Control: Getting Employees to Do Things Right and to Do The Right Things," presents examples of both personnel and specific action control taken directly from the GM research.

Chapter Fifteen, " The GMs' Background and Personal Characteristics," discusses in detail the backgrounds of the ten GMs, how they got to their current position, and the personal traits that seem to have led to their success in the hotel business. I've gone back and forth in trying to decide where this chapter would best placed in the book. It would also fit quite nicely after Chapter Two. Should you be interested in learning more about these ten GMs sooner, rather than later, feel free to read Chapter Fifteen whenever you like, but I'd at least read Chapters One and Two first.

Chapter Sixteen, "The Day-to-Day Activities of Outstanding Hotel General Managers," is the final chapter of the book. It describes the key job challenges of hotel GMs and how these challenges affect the different managerial roles they are required to play. It also describes in some detail what outstanding hotel GMs actually do while on the job and why this kind of behavior is effective. Analyzing what successful and effective hotel GMs actually do seems a fitting way to end a book on hotel management, especially one whose unifying theme is that of the hotel general manager.

My hope is that when you finish this book you will have a better understanding of the hotel business and what it takes to be an effective hotel executive. My fondest wish is that, if you decide to make hotels your career, you will be as happy with your choices as the ten GMs I had the privilege and the pleasure of studying.

ACKNOWLEDGMENTS

The decision to write this book was the result of much encouragement by my colleagues at the University of New Orleans. Dr. Thomas J. Canan first suggested the idea to me and kindly read numerous drafts of the book's prospectus and early chapters. Dr. Jeffrey D. Schaffer, himself a former hotel GM, spent many hours discussing the project with me and carefully reviewed many of the book's chapters. Drs. G. Kent Stearns and Harsha E. Chacko generously gave their time and advice in conversations too numerous to remember.

Professor William Galle, chairman of the Department of Management at UNO deserves special thanks for the time he spent with me while planning this project and for his careful review of many of the chapters. Bill's unselfish assistance was in the best tradition of what an academic colleague should be.

I've had the good fortune of a long and fruitful professional relationship with Mr. Hans U. Wandfluh, President and General Manager of the Royal Sonesta Hotel in New Orleans, Louisiana. His insights and encouragement regarding the GM research project was particularly helpful to me, and I thank him for it.

I was very fortunate to have two bright and dedicated student research assistants during this project. Ms. Louise Blandon, an undergraduate student at UNO did an incredible job coding over 700 pages of field notes. Mr. Ju Soon Lee, a graduate student at Purdue University, has been an enormous aid during the final stages of the book. His dedication and assistance on a wide variety of jobs was invaluable to me.

A group of people who deserve particular mention are the ten outstanding hotel GMs who participated in the research project. They allowed me to share in their professional lives in a very personal and very special way. Their generosity, candor, and cooperation made the research, and subsequently the book, possible. Because of them I've been able to write a book about real people managing real hotels.

My wife, Dorothy "Sister" Fox Nebel did all the word processing and editing for the book. It could not have been written without her assistance.

INTRODUCTION

Because you are reading this book you are probably seriously considering or have already committed yourself to a career in hotel management. The choice of a career is one of the most important decisions a person can make. It's also one of the most difficult. In thinking about a career you've probably asked yourself some of the following questions. What do I know about the hotel business? What is the hotel business really like? What are the important things to know about managing hotels? Am I really suited for this kind of work? What personal traits does it take to be successful in the hotel business? What kinds of experience and career paths will lead to success in the hotel business? What do successful hotel executives actually do in their daily jobs to be effective? Will I be happy in this kind of work?

This book will help you answer some of these questions. It will not fully answer all of your questions; no book can. It will however, give you some important insights into a number of important aspects of hotels, hotel management, and hotel managers. In particular, after studying this book, you will better understand

- The key characteristics of hotels that relate to how they should be managed;
- The important management functions that must be performed to manage hotels effectively;
- What kinds of people make successful hotel GMs and what they did to become successful;
- What successful and effective hotel GMs actually do in their day-to-day jobs.

THE GM RESEARCH

Ten extremely successful GMs of some of America's largest and finest hotels agreed to participate in a study designed to research hotel GM effectiveness. My purpose was to study hotels that exhibited the full range of operational and managerial complexity. The smallest participating hotel was a world-famous luxury property of about 400 rooms and the largest was a great convention hotel of 2,000 rooms. Nine of the hotels were parts of well-known national and international hotel chains, while the tenth was a famous independent. A number of the hotels were among their companies' leading, or flagship, properties. All of the GMs were veterans, most having successfully managed two or more hotels. Some were, or soon would become, regional vice-presidents of their companies. All had been GMs for a number of years. Two graduated from U.S. hotel schools while four were Europeans who had graduated from the finest hotel schools in Europe. In other words, these ten GMs all possessed the "right stuff." Each was an experienced and successful hotel executive.

I stayed as a guest at each hotel; joined the GM as he proceeded through his normal work day; observed and recorded his every activity. I attended the meetings he did, listened in on his phone conversations, watched him do paperwork, and lunched with him. I was, in effect, his shadow. I arrived on the job when the GM did (which was 6 A.M. in one case) and returned to my room only when he had finished his day's work (which in many cases was well past eight in the evening). I also conducted extensive interviews with each GM. These interviews extended over a number of days and took between four and six hours with each GM. I conducted additional interviews of about one hour each with the GM's key division heads. I was excluded from nothing and found both the GMs and their division heads extremely open and candid. The field research was conducted during the fall of 1987. It resulted in over 700 pages of field notes. Data coding and analysis took over a year. This process was greatly aided by a 1988 Summer Research Scholar grant from the University of New Orleans.

In conducting the research, I was looking for the answers to many questions. Some important questions were: What are the key characteristics of hotels that influence how they should be managed? What is the nature of the GM's job? What do GMs do to effectively manage their hotels? How do successful GMs motivate and exert leadership? What decisions do GMs make? What are the important personal and background characteristics of successful GMs? What are the important similarities and differences in their behavior? What is their daily routine? What do they like and dislike about their job? How did they advance to their current positions? What are their future ambitions? In short, I was very interested in everything that went on in the hotels they managed.

THE GMs

When I began the research I knew only one of the GMs very well. I had known two others for some years but had not had any close relations with them. I had met a fourth GM on a few occasions. The other six were total strangers, known to me only by their reputation. It's still amazing to me that these ten busy executives would allow me to spend three full days prying into every aspect of their business lives, asking them all kinds of personal questions, and quizzing their key subordinates about their boss's effectiveness! As you will discover while reading the book, these GMs were in many ways a remarkable group of people. While all of Chapter Fifteen will be devoted to their backgrounds and personal characteristics, a brief sketch of each will be given here. To ensure that the GMs would be completely candid and forthcoming during the research, I decided before the project began not to use their real names or the names of their hotels. Other important characteristics about the GMs and the hotels they manage are factual.

Here, then, is a brief thumbnail sketch of the ten GMs you will get to know through this book.

- Frank Anderson, forty-four years old, is the GM of the 2,000-room Napoleon House Hotel. Anderson, an American, studied finance as an undergraduate. Once he got into the hotel business he realized that, "I was made for this business." Frank Anderson works at a tremendously fast pace, something he calls "warp speed." A former professional football player, Anderson, at one stage in his career, served successfully as the director of housekeeping in a large hotel. Anderson credits much of his success to his ability to be a coach and mentor to subordinates, traits he attributes to his days in athletics. He has successfully managed five different hotels over thirteen years.
- Godfrey Bier, forty-five years old, is the GM of the 800-room General Eisenhower Hotel. Bier is German and was educated in a European hotel school. His hospitality career began on a cruise ship. When he emigrated to the United States, he worked for a number of years as a manager of well-known nightclubs before moving into hotel food and beverage positions. Bier's potential to be a GM was recognized when he was a food and beverage director. He was then put through a demanding year-long corporate training program and served for a number of years as a resident manager before becoming GM of the elegant and historic General Eisenhower. He has been managing this hotel for seven years.
- Jonathan Claiborne, forty years old, is the GM of the 440-room Riviera Hotel. Claiborne is French, having finished first in his European hotel school class. While Claiborne has managed two different hotels for a total of four years, he has had to fight hard for each opportunity throughout his career. The Riviera is Claiborne's first experience managing in America. After a career spent in Asia and the Middle East, he is having difficulty adjusting to some cultural differences in America. He is also charting a bold new strategic direction for the luxurious, but unprofitable, Riviera Hotel.
- Matthew Fox, fifty-one years old, is the GM of the world-famous 400-room St. Charles Hotel. Fox is American and studied accounting as an undergraduate. The elegant St. Charles is the only hotel Fox has managed and he's done that for seventeen years. Fox has turned down numerous promotions, including the presidency of a sizable hotel chain, because of his love for the St. Charles. Fox's subordinates describe him as a "soft touch."
- Richard James, forty-two years old, is the GM of the 1,200-room Hotel Apollo. James, an American, majored in English in college, became a school teacher, and found his way into the hotel business because he wanted to make more money. James is meticulous, artistic, and detail oriented. He has brought a controlled, focused manage-

ment approach to The Hotel Apollo. James has managed three different hotels for a total of six years. He thinks that managing hotels is a "young person's business."

- Henri LeSassier, thirty-nine years old, is the GM of the 450-room Normandy Hotel. LeSassier is also French, has a European hotel school undergraduate degree, and a masters in hotel administration from a well-known American university. Extremely bright and competitive, LeSassier is in the process of rescuing The Normandy from the verge of financial collapse and turning it into a profitable business. In recognition of his tenacity, his subordinates refer to him as "the little bulldog." He likes to go into difficult situations and gets bored without challenges. He's managed three hotels for a total of five years.
- Curtis Samuels, forty years old, is the GM of the 1,000-room skyscraper Hotel Frenchman. Samuels, an American, did his undergraduate work in science but has a masters degree in hotel management. A Vietnam war veteran, Samuels' first hotel job out of school was as resident manager of a hotel. Extremely competitive, his subordinates describe him as a consummate manager and motivator. He has managed four different hotels for a total of nine years.
- William Scully, thirty-nine years old, is the GM of the 1,500-room Bourbon Hotel. An American, Scully earned an undergraduate degree in physics but made the decision early in his college career to pursue a career in hotel management. Scully has a real skill with people. He easily gets commitment and dedication from subordinates based on personal relationships he develops. He was unique among the GMs in his stated ambition to attain a high corporate office in his company. He also seemed to manage The Bourbon Hotel effortlessly. Scully has managed two different hotels for a total of six years.
- Lawrence Wagner, fifty-two years old, is the GM of the 500-room Regal Hotel. Wagner is Swiss and received a first class European hotel school education. Described by his subordinates as a "hotelman's hotelman," Wagner possesses a nearly encyclopedic knowledge of every aspect of the hotel business. Wagner has been a GM for seventeen years and The Regal is the third hotel he has managed.
- Bruce Warren, fifty-one years old, is the GM of the 700-room Vieux Carre Hotel. He manages the only independent hotel in the GM study. Warren, an American, studied accounting in college and was a practicing certified public accountant for many years. Tiring of public accounting, Warren jumped at the opportunity to become the controller of The Vieux Carre Hotel. In five years he became its GM. Since then, as he puts it, "Every day is wonderful!" In addition to running a very profitable hotel, Warren has become a civic leader in the hospitality and tourism industry in his community. He has managed this one hotel for eleven years.

This is a brief sketch of the ten GMs who took part in the research study. Each of the ten approached his job and his life a little differently. As you will learn, there were many common characteristics among these GMs. Still, each was effective managing in his own way. As your career progresses and your management skills develop, you too will find the management style that works best for you. But you will not manage by rote according to some set rules you've read in a book or heard on an audio cassette. You will develop your management style based on your knowledge, your experience, and what you learn from studying how other, more experienced, executives manage. Think of these ten outstanding and effective hotel GMs as people from whom you can learn. Pay close attention to them. They have already proven their abilities as hotel executives. Remember what they say, what they do, and how they think. They have already had successful careers in the hotel business while you are still trying to learn what it will take to be successful. By paying close attention to these ten GMs you can have ten different mentors teaching you what it will take to succeed in a career in hotel management.

UNIFYING THEME

If you really want to know what managing a hotel is all about who would you ask? A good answer would be extremely successful and experienced managers of major hotels. The book you will be reading is about managing hotels from the perspective of the GM; in other words, it deals in large part with how effective GMs manage hotels. Thus, the book's unifying theme and most important feature is the hotel GM. Understanding how effective GMs manage hotels is, of course, a way of studying hotel management.

It's important to keep in mind that hotel GMs had to excel throughout their careers to get to their current positions. The ten executives you will get to know in this book were excellent supervisors, assistant department heads, department heads, and in some cases, resident managers before they became GMs. Many of the management skills that make them effective GMs also helped them at earlier stages in their careers. Thus, much of what you learn about how GMs manage effectively will be valuable to you in lower level hotel management positions.

When writing about GM effectiveness it is necessary to ask, "Effective doing what?" The answer is effectiveness in carrying out their management functions, which are traditionally classified into planning, organizing, directing, and controlling. This book will follow this traditional approach by describing how successful and effective GMs perform these four functions while actually managing hotels.

An important feature of the book is that much of it will describe what I found observing and interviewing these ten GMs and fifty-three of their immediate subordinate executives. The book, therefore, will deal with the real world issues that hotel executives actually face. Another important feature is that the GM theme will personalize the book. Management functions don't just occur, they are performed by people. This research involved a very personal approach. Many days were spent observing how these men ran their hotels, and many hours were spent in detailed discussions with them and their key executives. As a result, I've collected numerous stories and examples of real people struggling daily to manage real hotels. These stories and examples will be used liberally throughout the book. Pay attention to these stories and examples; they will help you better understand the management principles being presented.

I believe that humanizing the study of hotel management with real life stories and quotes will make the book more informative and interesting, and possibly even exciting. My hope is that the book is as interesting and exciting to you as the research and writing was for me.

Finally, taking the GM perspective and presenting material on the personal characteristics and backgrounds of outstanding GMs provides you with a glimpse of what it takes to be successful in the hotel business. It also provides you with successful role models after which you may pattern your behavior and your careers.

REFERENCES

Kotter, John P. 1982. *The General Managers.* New York: The Free Press.

Ley, David A. 1978. *An Empirical Examination of Selected Work Activity Correlates of Mangerial Effectiveness in the Hotel Industry Using a Structured Observational Approach.* Ph.D. dissertation: Michigan State University.

Mintzberg, Henry. 1973. *The Nature of Managerial Work.* New York: Harper & Row.

CHAPTER 1

The Environment of
The Hotel Business

Although individual hotels are often part of great hotel chains, each hotel within a chain can be thought of as a separate business. Each has its own management staff and is capable of operating on its own. The individual hotel is a profit center; it must operate at a profit or it is of little use to the chain. Because the success or failure of a hotel chain depends on how well the individual hotels in it are managed, this book emphasizes managing an individual hotel.

Being successful in business depends, in part, on the kind of business one is managing and how much one knows about it. So before discussing how to manage a hotel, it is very important to understand what the hotel business is all about.

Hotels are many things. They are businesses in a very competitive industry, and this affects how they need to be managed. Some hotels are magnificent works of architecture, true landmarks in their community, but the services they provide are more important to most guests than thirty-story atriums. Hotels are labor-intensive businesses where many employees provide service for many guests, and the services provided are of a very personal nature. Hotels are fast-paced, multifaceted operations where sometimes 2,000 guests check out and 2,000 guests check in on the same day, and a banquet for 5,000 is handled with ease. This and the following chapter will discuss these and other aspects of hotels. The discussion will focus on key characteristics of hotels that influence how they should be managed. As you read these chapters, remember that what you are learning about hotels will be valuable background information for the later chapters about managing hotels.

THE GLAMOUR OF IT ALL

Who among us is so dull as to be unimpressed by the vaulted lobby of a fine hotel, the French service in one of its great restaurants, or a spectacular flaming dessert served by hundreds of waiters to thousands of banquet guests. As a young man in the U.S. Navy, I remember our ship steaming into Cannes, France, in the heart of the French Riviera. The first sight we

A glamorous resort in Cairns, Australia

Courtesy: Radisson Hotels International

saw from sea was the broad white facade of a grand European hotel dominating the skyline of the city. This was The Hotel Carlton, which faces directly onto the famed Cannes promenade—La Croisette. The Carlton was my first sightseeing stop once on shore, and I can still remember wondering what it would be like to stay in such an exciting place. The memory of first staying at The Plaza Hotel in New York City, with its grace and beauty, is still fresh in my mind. The next section discusses some of the aspects of hotels that give them their glamorous appeal in general and from the viewpoint of successful general managers (GMs) and other senior hotel executives (Vare 1986).

The Hotel as History

Some important and sometime historic things happen in hotels. Presidents and prime ministers, kings and queens, diplomats and captains of industry, in other words, the movers and shakers of the world all spend a lot of time in hotels. A McDonald's Restaurant and The Mayflower Hotel in Washington, D.C., are both in the hospitality industry, but I'd venture to say, a lot more history takes place in The Mayflower. Frank Anderson manages The Napoleon House Hotel, a great 2,000-room convention hotel that was headquarters for a national political convention. When asked what was the significance of being designated headquarters hotel, he replied that it was wonderful to be a part of history. Was he happy for the media exposure his hotel would receive, for the full house and high room rates for eight days during a usually slow month, and for millions of dollars of food and beverage sales? You bet he was! But he was really turned on because he and his hotel were going to be a part of history. What he said and how he acted made it obvious that being part of history made him proud. History is made in hotels. Not all Presidential Suites are occupied by presidents, but just naming them "Presidential" conveys a sense of history and importance.

Jonathan Claiborne, the French-born GM of the elegant 440-room Riviera Hotel, recounted having served The shah of Iran, a U.S. secretary of state, then Vice-President George Bush, and other world leaders. Mr. Claiborne kept a file containing congratulatory notes from numerous world leaders and when he recounted those memories, his pride was more than evident.

A veteran food and beverage director, when asked to describe the hotel business, said, "Nothing unimportant ever happens in a hotel." His statement, while not literally true, does convey the fact that many important things do go on in hotels and have throughout history. Not only were early American inns used by travelers, but they also served as focal points for local political debates. Much of the political discussion and debate that eventually lead to the Revolutionary War, The Constitution, and the founding of the United States took place in early American inns.

In addition to history being made, much of the world's work takes place in hotels. Great conferences on the most pressing issues of our time are held in hotels. Physicians meet seeking cures for diseases, scientists gather to discuss the origins of the universe, diplomats huddle to plan relief for flood victims, and financiers negotiate billion dollar corporate takeovers. As one hotel executive put it, "The hotel business is bringing people together to solve the world's problems." That statement pretty well conveys the sense of history and importance that surrounds hotels. Of course, history is made at the local and county level as well. So whether it's a meeting to pick a candidate for county commissioner, a strategy session to choose a Supreme Court justice, or delicate negotiations to end hostilities between two warring nations, history is always being made in hotels. The world's problems are both large and small and many of them are solved in hotels. That's a lot more exciting than thinking of hotels as a place where heads are put on beds.

The Hotel as Excitement

It is exciting to think of a hotel as a gathering place where important people make important decisions. While I was interviewing Bruce Warren, general manager of the historic 700-room Vieux Carre Hotel, he received a phone call from the Governor of the state to reserve a ballroom for a press conference. The Governor had used the Vieux Carre for numerous press conferences, meetings, and election night parties over the years, and he and Bruce were on a first name basis. Of course, in addition to the excitement of having powerful and famous people staying in his hotel, Warren pointed out that the free publicity his hotel received didn't hurt at all.

Hotels, both large and small, are exciting places. Many of the people who work in hotels are drawn to them because of this excitement and glamour (*Meetings and Conventions* 1989). It's exciting, for example, to attend a gala banquet in a fine hotel. I remember attending a testimonial dinner one evening; 400 guests, all in evening attire, were having cocktails in an area adjacent to the banquet room. When it was time to be seated, the partitioned wall separating the guests from the banquet room was retracted revealing the splendidly arranged tables. The sight was so beautiful that the 400 guests spontaneously began to applaud. Just seeing the room so beautifully set was exciting to all of us, and to the manager and staff of the hotel's catering department as well.

Excitement comes in many sizes and shapes in hotels. During the GM research, I attended the morning staff meeting of The Regal Hotel, located in the entertainment district of New Orleans' famous French Quarter. During these meetings the security officer is always asked to report on any

The Hall of Mirrors in Cincinnati's Omni Netherland Plaza Hotel in all of its French Art Deco splendor.

Courtesy: Omni Hotels

incidents that occurred during the past twenty four hours. He reported that at about 10 P.M. the evening before a person entered the hotel carrying a snake. Upon seeing this, a bellman informed the night clerk who, in turn, called the security officer. The security officer determined that the person with the snake was not a guest of the hotel and had only entered the hotel to look around. He was politely asked to leave the lobby because many guests were becoming uneasy about the snake. He did and that was the end of the incident. There were a few chuckles from the assembled executives as the security officer made his report. When he finished, GM Lawrence Wagner asked what kind and size snake had been involved. The security officer had, it turned out, saved the best for last: the hotel's unwanted visitor had walked in with a ten-foot boa constrictor draped around his neck!

Excitement comes in many forms. To Jonathan Claiborne it was serving heads of state like the shah of Iran or the vice-president of the United States. To Frank Anderson, a man who had played professional football in his younger days, it was having sports figures such as Joe Namath and Bear Bryant as guests at his hotel. Hotels regularly play host to sports heroes, movie stars, corporate presidents, famous surgeons, diplomats, governors, mayors, judges—all successful, powerful, and important people. Many of the GMs and executives I interviewed mentioned that part of the excitement of hotels resulted from being able to serve these types of people.

An exciting hotel incident, but one quite different from those previously described, occurred while I was studying the day-to-day activities of Matthew Fox, the GM of the famous and truly luxurious St. Charles Hotel. It was budget preparation time and Matt had spent many hours that day in meetings with department heads trying to pare down expenses in order to meet corporate expectations. His day had been spent with spread sheets covering his desk and in endless negotiations with his executives, who were not particularly enthusiastic about seeing their budgets cut. Matt's frustrations had been amplified, it turned out, because new corporate budget preparation instructions were written in a difficult to understand bureaucratese. Throughout a day of haggling and tedium, he remained quite cheerful. By about 5 P.M., however, it was clear that his patience was beginning to wear thin. He continued to forge on until, at 6:30 P.M., he ran into more bureaucratic obstacles from corporate headquarters. After ten hours of this he took off his glasses, laughed, and suggested we take a tour of the hotel.

After a day spent on budgets, touring the hotel was indeed refreshing. Matt spent the next 20 minutes looking things over, talking to employees and, as he said, "just getting a feel for how things were going in the hotel." By the end of the tour he had a spring in his step and had cast off the ill effects of a day doing paperwork. The hotel was full that evening and the lobby was packed. He suggested we have a cocktail in the elegant Mardi Gras Lounge just off the lobby. It was quite a sight. Well-dressed men and women packed every table, the room was beautiful, and by the sound of the conversation, the guests were having a fine time. As we relaxed Matthew Fox let his experienced eye wander over the lounge and the lobby. He told me that he had managed that hotel for eighteen years, and it was nights like these that really were exciting for him. There was a full house, the hotel was beautiful, the staff was functioning smoothly, and the guests were well cared for and having a great time. To Fox, just realizing that he had played a major role in making that magical night happen for the hotel's 700 guests was exciting. I could hear it in his voice and see it in his eyes. Refreshed, he returned to his office at eight that evening for another two hours of budget grinding. But, all in all, the half-hour in the lounge that evening made his day, and mine, exciting.

The Hotel as Theater

When asked to describe hotels, the conservative-looking department head of a major hotel responded uncharacteristically by saying, "Hotels must work like magic for the guests." After interviewing ten outstanding GMs and fifty-three of their key executives, the idea that hotels work like magic, or the theatrical aspects of the hotel business, had been expressed in various ways by many of these so called hardheaded business people. Hoteliers, after all, invite people to stay in their "house" and to partake in their "hospitality." As the dictionary tells us, hospitality means "a friendly reception, and the generous treatment of guests or strangers." Hotels offer the traveler a home away from home. Without hospitality hotels have little to offer. George Bernard Shaw tells us that, "The great advantage of a hotel is that it's a refuge from home life." What better way to make a hotel "a refuge from home life" than to make it work like magic for a guest (Kryzanek 1987).

Magic, make believe, and theater are all ingredients that make hotels truly a refuge from home life. The assistant GM of the luxurious 450-room Normandy Hotel referred to the hotel business as theater and the GM as the director. The Normandy's general manager, Henri LeSassier, when asked to recount a particularly good learning experience when coming up in the hotel business, first reminisced about working with what he described as a "particularly creative banquet manager." Henri recounted an incident when the banquet manager had decorated a luncheon banquet for a convention in a gay and festive pink-elephant theme. The group was thrilled by the effect but were overwhelmed when, for their banquet that evening, the same room was completely redone in a sky theme, including simulated clouds with the moon shining through. LeSassier likened the banquet manager to the set director of an opera company. Even hard-nosed, bottom line–oriented Frank Anderson described a key characteristic of the hotel business as, "show business."

The best description of hotels as theater, however, comes from Lawrence Wagner. Wagner is a seasoned GM in his fifties who is practical, demanding, dedicated, and without question, profit oriented. When asked to describe the key characteristics of the hotel business, he began his remarks as follows:

"It's a stage play called 'Hotel.' The GM goes on stage as soon as he arrives at the hotel each morning and is on stage until he goes home at night. All the hotel's employees, but especially those with guest contact, are performers—they must, like the theater, be both creative and professional and have pride in what they are creating. The GM must disguise his true feelings when he goes on stage to play his part.

Like the theater, there is glamour in the hotel business such that still, after all these years, I must remind myself that it's necessary to make money in the business.

Just like acting, once you are hooked it's impossible to get out of the hotel business. I'd rather do the job right than go fishing—like acting, it's a total commitment.

Some GMs have large egos, like actors, and their egos are often fulfilled through their hotels. I don't have a large ego, and I'm not working for riches. The job itself is the thing, and that's satisfying guests. GMs also have great power within their hotels, but this characteristic is secondary to service."

A stage play, actors, magic, theater, these are part of what hotels are all about. You feel it when you enter a hotel and the people who work in and manage hotels feel it also—it's an important part of their glamour.

A City Within a City

The larger hotels get, the more awesome they become. Hotels, in fact, resemble a small city. Like a city, people live, eat, exercise, entertain, work and play, get married, have children, get sick, and die in hotels. Most of the services that must be provided to citizens of a city must be provided to guests in a hotel. In a large hotel one might easily find butchers, bakers and barbers, doctors and nurses, electricians and carpenters, plasterers and painters, computer experts and accountants, machinists and masons, tennis pros and lifeguards, detectives and horticulturists, maids and dishwashers, chefs and bartenders, salesmen and secretaries, engineers and elevator operators. (Of course, smaller hotels do not employ the full variety of individuals listed, but rather contract for some of these services.) Hotels employ all kinds of people—from manual workers to skilled professionals.

Hotels are similar to great ships in that both have a need to be self-sufficient; both must provide basic human services to large numbers of people. A large hotel may be the best place to ride out a hurricane. Even if a hotel lost electricity during the storm, its emergency generators could provide enough electricity for vital services. So like a ship, part of the glamour and excitement of hotels relates to the complexity of their operations and diversity of talents and skills of the people they must employ in order to fulfill their mission. Hotels are complex multidimensional organizations that take a lot of managing. Hotels provide the people who manage them with a never ending variety of challenges. That's what Richard James, GM of the 1,200-room Hotel Apollo, says he likes most; the never ending variety of tasks he faces.

A Vocation

Since hotels offer history, excitement, theater, and variety, they tend to get under people's skin. As Lawrence Wagner said, "Once you are hooked you can't get out." It's often said that there's high turnover, both among hourly employees and management, in the hotel business. While the statement is true, it may actually mask the process that is going on. At the management level, those who leave often do so because of a realization that there is a mismatch between their personalities and the hotel business. This mismatch is not necessarily a lack of brains, knowledge, or ambition as much as, it often seems, simply a lack of compatibility (Miller 1990). Executives who leave the hotel business don't, if you will, have a true calling. The thirty-four-year-old food and beverage director of a 1,200-room convention hotel told me exactly that. To him a person had to be either all the way in the hotel business or all the way out. "Why would I spend so much time here at the hotel and away from my wife and family?" he asked. He answered his own question by saying "Without love, one must be out of the business." He made this statement after relating for ten minutes the difficulties of his job. It was something like listening to an all-pro linebacker discuss how tough it is playing all season with nagging and painful injuries and then swearing that he loved every minute of it!

Love, devotion, and commitment are the kinds of words that successful GMs and other top hotel executives use to describe their jobs. Without exception, the ten GMs felt extremely fortunate to be doing what they do. One, Frank Anderson, had worked in sales for about seven years before finding his way into the hotel business. He soon discovered that, "I had been made for the hotel business." His only regret was that he had not discovered hotels sooner.

Two extremely successful GMs told stories of turning down higher paying executive positions in order to continue managing hotels. Matthew Fox had been offered the GM's job in a much larger hotel but turned it down without a second thought because it was not a "quality" property. He also turned down the presidency of a hotel chain because it would remove him from hotel operations. Lawrence Wagner tells a similar story. Moving up to the presidency of a chain held little interest for him. The extra money, which was considerable, was insufficient compensation for what he would be losing. What they were losing was the closeness to what hotels are all about. Such closeness is not, of course, possible from an executive suite at corporate headquarters. As Henri LeSassier said, "It's not a business like others, it touches you personally because you are constantly dealing with people and guests. It's a vocation, the feeling and the love of service."

Hall of Fame baseball star Willie Mays is supposed to have said that he loved baseball so much he would have happily played for nothing. The hotel executives we've been quoting may not go as far as Willie Mays, but it's certain that their work is more a calling than a job.

THE PACE OF A HOTEL

To say that the hotel business is fast paced is something like saying that football is a contact sport. Hotels really are fast-paced businesses, and this section discusses some of the aspects of this speed. Remember, the pace of a business has implications as to how it must be managed, so understanding in what ways hotels are fast paced will be helpful when discussing what GMs do and how hotels are managed.

Hotel Cycles

Before discussing the day-to-day aspects of hotels that make them fast-paced businesses, it's important to appreciate that hotels exhibit cyclical characteristics that affect their operation and their management. The demand for hotel rooms varies from day to day. This variation takes many forms depending on the type of hotel and the markets it serves. For example, a transient hotel that caters mostly to business travelers will run high occupancy levels on weekdays and lower occupancies on weekends. Resort hotels, and those that cater to pleasure or vacation travelers, often exhibit large seasonal variations in occupancy. During the high, or busy, season a hotel will run very high occupancies; during the off-season it may have half or less the business it enjoyed during the high season. Convention hotels may be 100 percent occupied when groups are booked but virtually empty during other periods. Another example of cyclical demand is the low occupancies many hotels face during holidays like Thanksgiving and Christmas.

The cyclical nature of demand causes hotels problems. When demand is high and all or most of its rooms are occupied, hotels can keep their room prices high and are very profitable businesses. During slack periods, however, rates tend to be driven down and hotels often operate at a loss. The cyclical nature of the hotel business is a characteristic that must be accepted. Often, little can be done to dampen hotels' revenue cycles and fluctuations. Since revenues vary in a cyclical fashion, the only way a hotel can hope to maintain some level of profits (or minimize its losses) during a down cycle is to control its costs. As pointed out in Chapter Two, one of a hotel's major costs is its people—both its hourly staff and its management. Thus, adjusting staffing levels to coincide with cyclical swings in occupancy is one way a hotel tries to maintain profits or minimize losses. The challenge hotels face is to maintain service standards and quality while expanding and contracting staff to coincide with fluctuations in occupancy. (Hotel executives and GMs generally agree that service is a key ingredient to a hotel's success.) Frequent staff fluctuations, necessitated by cyclical demand, makes it particularly difficult for hotels to maintain service standards.

Open for Business 8,760 Hours per Year

There are 8,760 hours in a year. Hotels are open for business every hour of every day of every year. That's really something! Colleges are pretty

Getting ready for the next banquet at the Bethesda Marriott.

Courtesy: Marriott Hotels, Resorts and Suites

busy places, but they are open, including summer school, only about forty weeks out of each year, and then only five days each week and usually no more than fourteen hours a day. That adds up to 2,800 hours, which is less than one-third the number of hours a hotel is open. Excluding about five holidays, a bank is usually open 9 A.M.–5 P.M., five days per week, Saturday until noon, fifty-two weeks per year. That's a total of 2,196 hours per year, or just one-fourth that of a hotel. A neighborhood restaurant may be open six days a week, fifty-two weeks per year from 11 A.M. till 11 P.M. These are long hours, 3,744 hours in a year, but that's only about 43 percent of that of a hotel.

There are other businesses that run around the clock each day of the year. Some gas stations and convenience stores are examples of rather uncomplicated businesses that are always open. Hospitals are an example of a complex service that is provided around the clock. There are, however, few examples of retail businesses that operate at the level and pace of a hotel throughout a twenty-four hour day. A hotel's kitchen can be finishing up a banquet at 10 P.M. one evening and preparing for a large breakfast meeting at 7 A.M. the next morning. Night clubs stay open late into the evening, public spaces must be cleaned and maintained after midnight to be ready for the morning traffic, maids must sometimes clean every room in the hotel if it experiences a heavy checkout and checkin on the same day. Vital equipment must be repaired without loss of guest service. Room service and restaurant service must be available, in many hotels, twenty-four hours a day. Each guest's bill must be updated every day. Hospitals often provide only emergency services in the evening. Incredibly, many hotels are capable of providing nearly all guest services twenty-four hours of each day.

It's no wonder that people who work in hotels usually describe them as twenty-four-hour-a-day businesses! One long-time executive called them "little worlds that never close. Only certain kinds of dedicated people can survive in this business." Another characterized the hotel business as "relentless" while a third said it was "not for the faint of heart."

Scope of Operations

The controller of a large hotel described its scope by saying that, "Hotels are many different businesses under one roof, each with its own knowledge base." The knowledge needed to run different hotel departments really does vary dramatically. The manager of the most lodging-related department, the rooms division, must understand the mechanics of guest checkin and checkout and, today, the intricacies of computerized reservation, phone, and guest accounting systems. The director of the food and beverage department works with a completely separate knowledge base founded in the culinary arts. The world of the accounting department revolves around revenues and costs, cash management, payroll, and computer systems. Sales and marketing operates in a separate world of its own not directly involved with daily operational problems. Engineering departments employ many people who would be as at home working in an oil refinery as in a hotel. Hotels are an amalgam of different businesses performing different functions, different knowledge bases, different viewpoints, different kinds of people—all working under the same roof, hopefully, with a common purpose.

These examples demonstrate that the scope of a hotel's operations is broad and diverse. Furthermore, the purpose of these broadly based activities all revolve around providing basic human services to people away from their homes. An important aspect about providing human services is that it takes a lot of little things to keep people going. Put another way, many different services must be performed in a hotel in order to satisfy guest needs. Failure to provide even a seemingly inconsequential service, or failure to maintain the standards of the services that are provided, can often result in a dissatisfied or, just as bad, an indifferent guest. When dealing with people, as the old song says, "Little things mean a lot." That's all the more important when providing people with personal things, such as beds, bathrooms, and food. Thus, one of the essential characteristics about the scope of hotel operations is that hotels must get a lot of little things right most of the time. Furthermore, hotels need the cooperation of a large and diverse group of people to do it. For hotels to run properly, everyone had better keep close track of all the details. Godfrey Bier, the German-born GM of the elegant 800-room General Eisenhower Hotel, calls it a business of details. Matthew Fox's warning is, "If you ignore the little stuff it will become big stuff." Frank Anderson describes the hotel business as "having one hundred different things to do at the same time." Lawrence Wagner says that, "Most problems in hotels and most decisions are small ones and not really that tough." Although they may not be tough decisions, many decisions must be made each day. The food and beverage director of a large hotel put it well when he said, "The pace of a hotel is hectic. The coordination and solution of daily problems are continuous. There is a never ending need to coordinate short-term problems on every shift."

As hotels get larger, the scope of their operating problems expand accordingly. Where roadside motels may be run with a GM, department heads and supervisors, very large hotels will sometimes have two additional layers of management between the GM and the hourly employee who actually serves the guests. We all make fun of large bureaucratic organizations because of their seeming inability to get things done quickly. This malady can develop in any organization as it gets larger and executives of large hotels are acutely aware of it. It's interesting how GMs and senior executives refer to large hotels, especially great, 1,000-plus-room convention hotels. During the GM research a number of executives used the same analogy, calling very large hotels battleships, aircraft carriers, or supertankers. This analogy refers to the fact that operating problems are compounded by size.

Richard James said, "It's like a battleship; you cannot know all that is going on in it." The executive assistant GM of a 1,000-room property likened it to a supertanker that, she felt, could only be turned slowly. Curtis Samuels, who had managed a mid-sized hotel before being promoted to run the 1,000-room Hotel Frenchman, called it "an aircraft carrier; it must be turned slowly or it might crash." All of these descriptions relate to the increased complexity in the scope of operations of large hotels. They speak volumes about keeping such an enterprise under control and managing it properly to provide the variety of services guests need.

The Unpredictability of Problems

It's been said that if businesses had no problems there would be little need for managers. The previous section discussed the pace and scope of the hotel business, but there is another trait of hotels that influences how they should be managed. Certain things about hotels tend to be inherently unpredictable, adding to the difficulty of managing a hotel efficiently and profitably (O'Dwyer 1989). Two unpredictable elements of hotel management are uncertainty caused by guests and uncertainty caused by employees.

A major uncertainty guests cause is that it is difficult to predict just how many will show up on any given night, and it is also difficult to be sure when guests already in the hotel will leave. What problems does this cause? For one, employee staffing depends on hotel occupancy. The optimum number of maids, bellpersons, front desk clerks, waiters, and kitchen workers depends on the number of guests in the hotel. If the actual occupancy on Wednesday is less than the forecast, the hotel may be overstaffed and thus labor costs will be high. If occupancy exceeds forecast, the hotel may be understaffed and service will suffer.

A manufacturing business faced with a situation where production exceeds demand can produce to inventory. As inventories continue to build, the manufacturer may cut back on production, possibly by eliminating a shift or by shutting down one of its production lines. Exactly the opposite response would be called for if demand exceeded production. By producing to inventory a manufacturer is able to vary its level of production in as efficient a manner as possible, because finished product inventories act as a buffer between fluctuations in demand and the efficient manufacture of products.

Unlike a manufacturer, a hotel has little flexibility in handling this problem. If occupancy is forecasted too high, more employees are scheduled than needed and labor costs exceed budget. If forecasted too low, too few employees are scheduled for the number of guests and service suffers. In the first incident, short-term profits suffer because of excessive labor costs; in the second, long-term revenues and profits may suffer because of poor service, which affects repeat business. In both cases the problem is caused by the inherent difficulty of predicting room demand and the inability of hotels to inventory their product.

Uncertainty in forecasting occupancy occurs for a variety of reasons: guests with advance reservations simply do not show up or cancel late on the day of their arrival; travelers, called "walk-ins," arrive at the hotel looking for a place to stay; guests already in the hotel decide to leave a day or so early or stay over an extra night; at the last minute the rooms actually booked for a convention either exceed or fall short of the forecasted number. Whatever the reason, the effects of unanticipated fluctuations in occupancy reverberate throughout a hotel, affecting staffing, purchasing, and hotel op-

An enchanting setting for a poolside party at the Hyatt Regency Grand Caymen Resort.

Courtesy: Hyatt Hotels Corporation

erations in general. The important thing to understand is that this is a day-to-day problem that must either be attended to on that day or the moment is lost. Money spent today for unneeded staff or perishable products is simply gone. Poor service today, because of understaffing, cannot be made up for tomorrow. Uncertain demand thus requires that hotels be constantly on guard to be properly staffed and supplied to provide cost-effective service each day.

Many things are unpredictable in the normal course of a hotel's daily operations. I recently attended a convention at a lovely resort hotel located on a point of land overlooking a beautiful bay. The main banquet of the convention was to be held in an open-air pavilion located directly on the water. The weather was mild and the moon was full as the 200 guests gathered that evening. The pavilion was beautifully decorated and we were all looking forward to a wonderful evening. Then it began to rain. And rain it did! Within ten minutes we were all inside the hotel, the table settings at the pavilion had been ruined, and people were beginning to wonder what the hotel would, or could, do about the banquet. To our delight, the hotel staff quickly readied an inside banquet facility for our group. The staff was not only efficient but also their positive "can do" attitude quickly allayed our fears, and the evening was saved.

Guests become ill and must be cared for; robberies take place, accidents take place, employees call in sick, elevators malfunction, electrical power outages occur, bathtubs overflow, boisterous parties disturb other guests. These events are, to some degree, unpredictable; however, they occur all the time! Thus, it's very important that a hotel's management and staff be trained to cope daily with a wide variety of unpredictable events. Effective management means being able to change plans, reassign staff, and redirect efforts to cope with a situation that had not been expected. In effect, one attribute of effective hotel management is the ability to anticipate and react to uncertainty. The division head of a large convention hotel aptly described uncertainty when he said, "You must take a 1,200-room hotel on its own terms. The hotel dictates your time, you don't dictate its. Plan as you might, anticipate as best you can, but remember that adjusting to unanticipated events is part of the challenge of running a hotel."

The Immediacy of Problems

One of the central features of hotels is that many of their operating problems must be solved quickly—really quickly. All businesses, of course, face deadlines. Car repairs that drag on for a week inconvenience customers; a two-hour wait in a doctor's office is aggravating; long lines at a supermarket checkout counter are a pain. Today, more and more, consumers are demanding prompt service as a condition of their continued patronage. In hotels the response time for many services is measured not in weeks or days, but in hours or even minutes.

Richard James' Hotel Apollo is known for its spectacular architecture and elegance. He describes the hotel business as "quality service delivered on time." He feels that "hotel executives at all levels must be time conscious." Richard had been GM of this hotel for about six months when I spent time interviewing him. He was not satisfied with its level of service. James toured the hotel each morning at 6 A.M. to see firsthand how the day was getting started. At 7:15 A.M. one morning, he discovered that a function room scheduled to be used for a 7:30 A.M. breakfast meeting had not been cleaned. The hotel had fifteen minutes to clean the room or face a service breakdown and possibly lose future business with this group. The next day, a seminar in progress was disturbed by the noise of a jackhammer being used on a construction site outside the hotel. That problem didn't even have fifteen minutes in which to be solved!

The Hotel Apollo, which is thirty stories high, had an elevator system just barely adequate when all 1,200 rooms were occupied. With a 950-room convention checkin anticipated for Sunday, one of the hotel's elevators malfunctioned on Saturday. The key repairman for the firm that held the elevator maintenance contract was out of town until Monday. The hotel's chief engineer accepted these circumstances as inevitable. Richard James did not. He had visions of hundreds of tired conventioneers checking into his hotel on Sunday night and waiting thirty minutes or more for an elevator. To him, the immediacy of the problem was obvious, and he personally found a way to get the elevator repaired before Sunday's checkin.

All of the GMs and their key executives in the study agree on this point. Jonathan Claiborne feels that, "A GM must be able to make quick decisions." Henri LeSassier who holds degrees in hotel administration from world class schools in both Switzerland and the United States stated, "There is a true immediacy with respect to problems in hotels. You often have a short time span for getting things done."

Small problems or large problems, most of them must be solved quickly—or the damage is done. A tired guest with a guaranteed reservation is inadvertently checked into a dirty room. How much time does the hotel have to move the guest into a clean room before the guest forms an unchangeable negative impression? The answer, of course, depends on a number of circumstances, not the least of which is how the hotel's staff responds to the problem. Put yourself into the guest's shoes. You've traveled all day and you're upset to start with, when ushered into a dirty room. Would a ten minute wait be "acceptable?" Is thirty minutes too long? Would you be fuming after forty-five minutes? Whatever your answer, that's the amount of time this hotel has to solve your problem.

Of course, a hotel's problems can affect more than one guest. Had that elevator not been repaired, at The Hotel Apollo, hundreds of guests would have been affected. On the first day of a major convention, a kitchen mix-up caused 4,000 delegates to be served one hour late at a large breakfast meeting. What a way to start a convention! The hotel, of course, viewed this service breakdown as a major blunder. Frank Anderson vividly describes this aspect of the hotel business, "Hotel managers are in a combat situation and must be able to make quick decisions." The food and beverage director of a 1,200-room convention hotel said that hotels are "a real-time, on-line business where executives must be willing to confront issues and make decisions, even if wrong." In a somewhat more humorous vein, he illustrated the point by recounting the time an elevator got stuck while transporting an ice carving to a cocktail reception. With skill, and a little bit of luck, the staff was able to get the ice carving out, before it melted, through the escape hatch. More importantly, the rescue was effected in time for the reception. Melting ice may be a pretty good metaphor for the immediacy of problems in hotels.

Effective hotel executives seem to instinctively understand the need for quick action and immediate attention. In well-run hotels there's a sense of urgency. Procrastination often means that the human needs of guests go unattended. In hotels, problems solved slowly are not really solved. In hotels, service that is not timely is not really service.

The Need for Dedication

Owning a barber shop is few people's idea of excitement. It sure is a placid business. Hours are from 9 till 6, the scope of operation is narrow and predictable, and seldom is there a true immediacy of need for the service. Barbers, at least regarding their profession, should be able to sleep the sleep of the truly content. Not so the hotel executive.

A price must be paid for the glamour and excitement that hotels offer. In contrast to the barber shop business, hotels are diverse and multifaceted, there is a certain amount of unpredictability in the problems that develop, and there is a true immediacy to the many problems that arise. In other words, hotels are fast-paced businesses; they really hop. The people that run them effectively also really hop. Why does Curtis Samuels begin his day at 4 A.M. doing paperwork in his hotel suite? It's so he can arrive in his office at 7:30 A.M. and really get involved with running the hotel. Does he like things to hop? In his words, "I can't tell you how much I love the action of a hotel." A dedicated hotel GM? Yes. A person who loves what he is doing? Absolutely.

Henri LeSassier calls working in hotels "a vocation." Frank Anderson says hotels are "a constant challenge" extracting "heavy demands" and are often "physically demanding." The way he puts it, "I don't go at supersonic speed, around here it's warp speed."

The pace of hotels require constant, not sporadic attention. Each day brings new guests, different luncheons, and the next convention. Each day a hotel has to prove itself over again to a new set of clients. No wonder, when describing the characteristics of a good hotel executive, Frank Anderson said, "There is no such thing as a one-time author." Jonathan Claiborne said that executives, "must be dedicated, loyal and dependable, especially when young," if they want to succeed in the hotel business. That's a pretty good prescription for success no matter what the business.

THE COMPETITIVE ENVIRONMENT

Various economic conditions influence the amount of competition a business faces. Some services, like electric power, are called natural monopolies because it only makes sense to have one company supplying a community's electricity needs. Thus, there is no direct competition for an electric utility. Some companies, for example Xerox, are protected for a time from competitors because of patents held on their products. Other businesses, like automobile manufacturing, require such massive sums of capital to start that competition is limited to only a few companies. Generally speaking, the fewer barriers to entering a particular industry the more businesses will do so and the greater will be the level of competition. Also, competition will be greater among firms in an industry the more the product or service they sell tends to be the same. Hotels fall into the category of industries that are considered very competitive. In this section some of the reasons for the highly competitive nature of the hotel industry will be discussed.

Hotels Are Commodities

The physical appearance and layout of guest rooms and public spaces of most competing hotels are similar enough so that the average guest finds it hard to choose one hotel over another. We know, of course, that this is not entirely true: architectural and location differences can give some hotels distinct and, in a few cases, even lasting advantages over their competition. In most circumstances, however, this is not the case. One characteristic of commodities is that they engender little or no brand loyalty. Since each producer of a commodity (like wheat) is producing essentially the same thing, consumers have little incentive to choose one producer's product from another's—except for price. Thus, relatively small price differences cause consumers to switch from one producer to another. If large numbers of consumers are indifferent to one hotel (or chain of hotels) over another, then the competitors have little choice but to compete for the consumer's business on the basis of price. In such a competition the competitor who wins will be the lowest-cost, most-efficiently-run hotel.

To compete on the basis of price does not mean that prices need be low. Hotels are designed to appeal to certain market segments (for example business travelers, vacationers, or conventioneers). Within each market segment a certain pricing structure exists. While the roadside budget inn's market may dictate a $25 to $30 per night room rate, the downtown transient business hotel may need a room rate of $90 to $110 to break even. The point is, within each hotel market segment, there may be many guests who see little difference between competing hotels and will choose one over the other mostly on the basis of price. Thus, hotel executives must find ways to differentiate their hotel from the competition in ways other than ruinous price competition.

This Embassy Suites atrium affords guests extra security because all suites open into it, thus guests don't face long walks down dark halls.

Courtesy: Embassy Suites, Inc.

Permanent Overbuilding

There has, in the past, been a tendency for overbuilding in the hotel industry. Put simply, this means that many geographic markets in the United States have a greater hotel room inventory than individual competing hotels would like to see. Overcapacity in the hotel business, as in any other, has a depressing impact on prices and profit margins. When a hotel is half full, as are its competitors, there is quite a bit of pressure to try to steal business by cutting prices.

There are, it turns out, few barriers to entering the hotel business that would tend to forestall overbuilding. Although not inexpensive, the capital required to build a hotel is by no means a deterrent to investors. No patents or secret operating processes bar entry. In fact, the large number of hotel franchise systems and hotel management companies makes it easy for investors and developers with no hotel operating experience to get into the business. Although zoning and environmental restrictions may preclude hotel development in a few locations, generally speaking this is not a major deterrent. Thus, there's been a tendency, whenever an area's occupancy and room rates begin to increase, for new hotel developments to pop up. New hotels are often built when credit is readily available, so there are often cycles of new hotel building with a number of new properties being developed in an area at the same time. With room supply increasing sharply, area occupancy falls, resulting in pressure on room prices. Profits for all the area's hotels are depressed, sometimes for a number of years (Anthony 1987).

When overcapacity occurs, high-cost, ineffective hotels often begin to suffer losses, and some are forced into bankruptcy. In time, room supply either shrinks as marginal operators close down or room demand begins to grow. As hotel occupancies and room rates rise to profitable levels, the building cycle repeats itself as developers and entrepreneurs see the opportunity to make profits by building new hotels. It's an old story, and one with which hotel executives have to live. It's one of the reasons that GMs stress the need to be able to make money in good times and in bad. It's also why Matthew Fox says that, "Anyone can make money when times are good."

Rooms Are Perishable Products

The problem of predicting occupancy was previously discussed. It's difficult to do, and as Bruce Warren, a GM with a strong accounting background, puts its, "You can't inventory a hotel room, it's a leased space." If that hotel room isn't rented today, it can't be rented twice tomorrow. Once a hotel is built, its room supply is fixed for all time.

One might be tempted to say, "Well, that's the way things are; this is just a situation we have to live with." True, but it's a problem that doesn't have to be taken passively. Outstanding hotel managers realize that if they cannot vary supply they need to concentrate on demand. Hotels attempt to make demand conform to their fixed supply of rooms. Instead of turning guests away when they are full, hotels would like to induce them to stay at another time when they are not full. They also want to be sure that when demand is high they get the highest possible room rates, and when demand is low ways are found to induce price-conscious travelers into hotels with "specials."

In its extreme form, the problem faced by a fixed-supply, variable-demand business like a hotel is as follows: if today twice as many people want rooms as can be accommodated, and tomorrow no one wants a room, then a hotel's occupancy today is 100 percent and tomorrow 0 percent. Its average occupancy for the two days is 50 percent, which isn't particularly good. If a way can be found to induce half of today's potential guests to stay in the hotel tomorrow, its occupancy for both days would be 100 percent! A hotel's ability to manipulate demand will often determine its financial success or failure. Dealing with a fixed supply and variable demand is one of the central features of the hotel business.

Forecasting Demand

If supply can't be changed, hotels had better know as much as possible about demand if they are to be successful. An example will show the importance of forecasting demand. Consider a 1,000-room hotel that caters both to conventions and business travelers. Average room rates for business travelers are one hundred dollars per night, while convention rates are discounted to seventy dollars per night. The hotel has booked a convention that anticipates using 800 rooms for three nights at seventy dollars per night, and it has set aside, or blocked, 800 rooms for the three nights of the convention. Management is not certain how many rooms will be occupied by the convention but based on past convention attendance settles on 800. The hotel has, in effect, obligated itself to having 800 rooms available for the convention. If less than 800 rooms are used by the group the hotel is free to sell them to anyone. If convention delegates want more than 800 rooms, the hotel is not obliged to have them available if they have already been rented to individual business travelers. For the weeks preceding the convention, the hotel receives reservations from conventioneers. At the same time, business travelers are making reservations for the same kind of room but at one hundred dollars per night rather than the convention rate of seventy dollars.

The hotel faces two forecasting problems and two important decisions. It must forecast room demand for both conventioneers and business guests for the three-day period. These forecasts can be correct, high or low, so there are quite a few possible outcomes. Suppose that two weeks before the convention 200 business and 725 convention reservations have been made. Based on past history, the hotel forecasts 800 rooms by the time of the convention. Facing the possibility of 100 percent occupancy, and not wanting to "overbook" (that is, take more reservations than it has rooms available), management decides to stop taking business reservations in anticipation of convention reservations building up to 800 during the remaining two weeks. Instead, convention bookings build up only to 750 rooms during the next two weeks, and during the interim the hotel turns down fifty business reservations. By the time of the convention, 950 of the 1,000 rooms are occupied: 750 by conventioneers and 200 by business travelers. To an outside observer this seems to be quite good, but because of our inside knowledge we know differently. Had the hotel forecasted convention demand accurately it could have continued accepting reservations from individual business travelers and filled those fifty vacant rooms at one hundred dollars each. That's $5,000 per day in lost revenue, or $15,000 during the three day convention, resulting from a forecasting error. Since a hotel's added costs associated with renting a few more rooms are quite small, most of the $15,000 represents lost profits!

There is an alternate outcome. Two weeks before the convention 700 convention and 225 business rooms are actually booked. This time, management forecasts 750 convention and 250 business bookings during the three-day convention. Again, forecasted occupancy is 1,000 total rooms, or 100 percent. In this case the hotel continues to accept both convention and business reservations for the next two weeks. However, in one week business reservations quickly build from 225 to 300 while convention reservations build slowly to 725. The hotel has now booked 1,025 rooms while only 1,000 are available. It quickly cuts off business reservations but continues to accept convention reservations since it is obligated to have 800 rooms available for this purpose. At the same time, management begins to pray that some reservations are canceled. Unfortunately, convention bookings build to 800 by the start of the convention and there are no business cancellations. The hotel is faced with 800 reserved convention rooms and 300 reserved business rooms. It must dishonor, or walk, the guests who would occupy one hundred rooms.

Both problems were caused by forecasting errors and both were costly to the hotel: one in terms of lost revenue, the other in terms of ill will caused by overbooking. In a real situation, a greater number of variables would be involved, thus causing a more complicated problem than this simple example. The task of forecasting is, therefore, quite difficult. An experienced rooms division manager of the 800-room General Eisenhower Hotel, who was responsible for forecasting occupancy, said "All other problems pale in comparison to occupancy forecasting." Extending these two examples for a full year will help clarify her point. Suppose the hotel in the example anticipates selling out, (that is, running a 100 percent occupancy) fifty times a year. If, because of conservative forecasting, it ends up with fifty unsold rooms each time it will have lost $250,000 in revenues for the year ($100/room x 50 rooms/night x 50 nights per year). That's, as they say, serious money! If, on the other hand, aggressive forecasting resulted in one hundred guests being walked fifty times each year, that's 5,000 unhappy guests and a ruined reputation. It's no wonder that the executive quoted felt that all her other problems "pale in comparison" to forecasting demand. As an experienced marketing director put it, his job involved "selling the right person the right room at the right price at the right time."

CONCLUSION

Your ability to succeed in the hotel business will depend on many factors, not the least of which is how well you are suited to it. Just as not everyone is suited to be a general or surgeon or college professor, not everyone is suited to be a hotel executive. While nothing beats actually working in a hotel to discover what they are like, this chapter touched on a number of aspects of the hotel business that successful hotel executives feel are important.

This chapter discussed the glamour of the hotel business because it's important for people to be excited about what they do. Most successful people really enjoy what they do and truly look forward to going to work. Successful hotel GMs are having a great time doing what they do. After many days of extremely close contact, I cannot report one statement from these GMs that could be interpreted as regret about their career choice or dissatisfaction with their jobs. Each of them mentioned some aspect of glamour as an important characteristic of the hotel business to them.

Although successful hotel executives think of themselves as working in a glamorous industry, it's important to keep in mind exactly what aspect of the hotel business they find most alluring and fascinating. To them, it's providing great service to guests that accounts for the glamour of their jobs. Lawrence Wagner says, "The job itself is the thing, and that's satisfying guests." Jonathan Claiborne tells stories of serving world leaders. Matthew Fox was happiest when he saw his guests happy. More than one spoke of the need to have a "service phobia" to be successful in the hotel business.

In addition to their natural allure, hotels are also fast-paced businesses that present executives with a wide variety of challenges. Hotel guests demand prompt service because hotels satisfy so many of their basic human needs. In many cases, service not provided promptly cannot be considered good service at all. Thus, constant attention to detail, and follow-through are required to ensure that on-time service is provided to guests. That's why happy hotel executives are people with a service phobia. In other words, they are dedicated to providing service and through service find true enjoyment in their jobs. For people like this, the hotel business is one grand game that's fun to play. For people without this kind of mind set, it's a grinding, never-ending series of unpredictable yet critical problems requiring immediate response.

The last characteristic of hotels discussed in this chapter dealt with various aspects of the competitiveness of the hotel business. The glamour of hotels and the desire to provide great service are important motivators for being in the business, but unless a hotel makes a profit it's a failure as a business. This is often not easy because of the tendency in the hotel industry toward overbuilding, the perishability of a hotel room, and most importantly, the fact that there are certain characteristics of hotels that cause them to resemble commodities. Hotels may be thought of somewhat like a commodity whenever they are indistinguishable one from the other in the minds of potential guests. Consumers will have no particular loyalty to use one hotel rather than another and will usually choose based on price. Although a hotel developer will be able to use location and architectural design as distinguishing features to differentiate his or her hotel from the competition, the managers of existing hotels have little or no ability to manipulate these variables. Generally speaking, outstanding hotel managers use service as a

The Embassy Suites hotel, Palm Beach Shores, houses the Jupiter Crab Company, a popular seafood restaurant, as a way of differentiating itself from the competition.

Courtesy: Embassy Suites, Inc.

primary competitive strategy to differentiate their hotels from the competition, thus lifting it out of the category of a commodity. Finally, excellent hotel managers must know how to make profits when times are good and occupancies and revenues are high and also when times are bad and costs must be controled closely.

It's important to remember that the characteristics of hotels discussed in this chapter were enumerated by outstanding hotel GMs and their key executives. Put another way, these are the things about hotels that are important to the successful men and women who manage them. Successful and happy hotel executives think of themselves as working in a glamorous, fast-paced, and competitive environment, and they love every minute of it. They want their hotels to function "as if by magic," they are willing to work at "warp speed" to see that they do, and they love "the action" of their jobs and the challenge of making money in good times and in bad.

REFERENCES

Anthony, Carmen. June 1987. "The Experts' Views on Overbuilding." *Hotel & Resort Industry* 10(6):32–38.

Anon. Downtown Hotels. 1989. *Meetings and Conventions* (Advertising Supplement):149–172.

Kryzanek, Michael R. November 2, 1987. "Bad Experience Can Have 'Cascade' Effect on Business." *Hotel & Motel Management* 202(16):32.

Miller, Griffin. March 1990. "New Challenges For a Marketing Virtuoso." *Hotel & Resort Industry* 13(3):22–29.

O'Dwyer, Christine. October 1989. "With Nothing to Guide Him, GM Faces Suicidal Guest." *Lodging* 15(2):85–86.

Vare, Ethlie Ann. June 1986. "The Allure of Big City Hotels." *Meetings & Conventions* 21:78–83.

QUESTIONS

1-1. In what ways are hotels glamorous and exciting businesses? Describe five different aspects of their glamour that appeals to you.

1-2. Discuss whether you think that different businesses require managers to have different success traits.

1-3. How is being a hotel GM like being an actor? How is being a manager and a leader like playing a role?

1-4. What makes major hotels the complex organizations they are?

1-5. Describe five aspects of the hotel business, other than glamour and excitement, that might draw you toward a hotel management career.

1-6. Explain why hotels usually experience cyclical swings in occupancy.

1-7. Why is it so important to get the "little things" right for hotel guests?

1-8. Why are so many of the challenges found in hotels somewhat unpredictable?

1-9. Give five examples of problems that must be solved quickly in hotels. Estimate how quickly each must be solved.

1-10. What does it mean when it is stated that a hotel is a fixed-supply, variable-demand business?

1-11. Explain why a hotel room is referred to as a perishable product.

1-12. Why is forecasting room occupancy for a hotel extremely important?

CHAPTER 2

Service, People, and Profits in the Hotel Business

This Chapter is a continuation of the discussion from Chapter One on key characteristics of hotels that influence how they should be managed. In this chapter discussion centers around various aspects of service, people, and profits.

SERVICE COUNTS

In recent years American business has awakened to the importance of service.[1] There are many reasons for this interest, not the least of which is the fact that the service sector now dominates the U.S. economy. During the last quarter century, the U.S. economy has moved from one that was production oriented to one that is service oriented. This massive shift has caused a reexamination of the differences between goods-producing businesses and service-producing businesses. The motive for this reexamination is, of course, profits. Understanding how service businesses differ from goods-producing businesses helps executives manage better. An important by-product of this reexamination has been a better understanding of the

---

[1]The further reading section to this chapter lists some of the important articles and books that have explored the role of service in American business. A reading of these works would certainly benefit anyone who is serious about a career in the hotel business.

importance of service in businesses that traditionally have been thought of as producers of goods. What has become clear is that service can be a powerful competitive strategy that goods-producing companies can use to differentiate themselves from their competition. Because of these trends, service management has become one of the most discussed topics in American business.

Hotels provide both a product and a service. Hotels vary architecturally from modest functional economy to some of the most spectacular structures built by a society. Great hotels, like other great structures, are in a way symbols of the society that produces them. All hotels, whether great or modest, reflect the purpose and function they were designed to perform. But there is much more to the hotel business than just what meets the eye. A physical product, once in the possession of a consumer, is used without the need for continued participation on the part of the business that provided the product. A fountain pen, clothing, furniture, simple household tools, food, and houses are examples of products that have a very small service component associated with them. A product has a small service component if the consumer uses it without any need for further contact with the business that produces it. This, of course, is not the case in most hotels.

The physical aspects of a hotel do, of course, contribute to its ability to provide service. A hotel's central location is a convenience to its guests; spacious, comfortable rooms are important to a good night's rest; attractive lobbies and public areas add to the ambiance of the building; efficient elevators save time. These physical features are all part of the "services" that hotels provide. However, the physical product, no matter how expensive or beautiful, is incapable of providing for the needs of its guests without the ongoing and active participation of the hotel's staff. The facility, in other words, cannot stand on its own. In hotels, the building and the service are intimately connected. Thought of in this way, it is clear that the product a hotel sells is a combination of its physical facility and its staff's services, each of which is essential and indispensable to the guest.

Because this is a book about hotel management and not hotel architecture, our attention will focus on the services a hotel's staff provides its guests. Outstanding GMs and high-level hotel executives all agree that guest service is critical to a hotel's success. The thoughts of two top GMs illustrate how strongly they feel. William Scully and Curtis Samuels manage large convention hotels that are located within one hundred yards of each other. When asked to discuss key characteristics of the hotel business, Curtis Samuels said:

> "Hotels themselves are commodities; there is nothing that's unique physically one from the other. Except for a very few physically unique hotels, con-

The elegant lobby of the Four Seasons Hotel in Washington, D.C.

Courtesy: Four Seasons Hotels and Resorts

sumers are often indifferent with regard to one hotel versus another and, in consequence, are quite price sensitive. To compete a hotel must be aggressive in its ability to provide services."

William Scully, when asked the same question, responded as follows:

"A hotel's physical plant is an expected standard on the part of the guest. You must provide a certain level of physical amenities to be in business. It's guest service that differentiates one hotel from another and, therefore, successful from unsuccessful hotels. Guest service determines revisits."

These two GMs were among the very best in their respective companies, each having received numerous awards for the outstanding performance of their hotels. Their backgrounds and education, however, were quite different. Nevertheless, their statements regarding service are so similar that they seem to be reading from the same book. The great football coach, Vince Lombardi, once said that winning isn't everything, it's the only thing. In the hotel business, Bill and Curtis would probably agree that "Service isn't everything, it's the only thing."

Service Is Intangible

A person buying a ball-point pen can look at it, hold it, and write with it; it's a physical object that can easily be tested and experienced. The same is true for a set of golf clubs. It's fairly easy to judge these products in a tangible way, before purchasing them. Services, however, are different. The term "service" is defined as a helpful act; being useful to others. Personal services involve people doing things for other people. The bellperson who carries luggage to a guest's room has performed a helpful act, but the guest's evaluation of the service may depend as much on the bellperson's attitude as on the act of delivering the luggage. A waiter's personality, as well as skill, plays a role in a customer's dining experience. One person's idea of fast service will differ from another's. One person's idea of courteous service will differ from another's. One's own standard of fast or courteous service will often vary depending on a variety of factors. Tastes, state of mind, and past experiences all bear on service evaluation. Because people are subjective, service is evaluated subjectively. Unable to evaluate a physician's professional credentials, patients often equate "bedside manner" with caring and competence. With personal services, it's not only what service is performed but also how it is performed that makes a difference.

It's important to remember also that the kinds of services a hotel provides are quite personal in nature. Putting a new set of tires on the family car is an important service, but few customers are that concerned about the mechanic's friendly attitude during the process. It's quite different in hotels. Because hotels provide a home away from home, the degree of hospitality required when delivering service is much greater.

The intangibility of hotel services extends beyond personal services to include guest perceptions of all aspects of the hotel. Is the lobby too large or too small? Is the room's color scheme pleasant or disagreeable? Is the mattress too hard or too soft? Is the food too spicy or too bland? It's all a matter of guest's tastes and perceptions. Matthew Fox feels strongly about this aspect of hotels. In his view, to manage a hotel successfully:

"One must understand the subjectivity of the product. What is clean? What is attractive? Standards cannot be easily written. What is 'fresh food?' What's a

good receipt? Two percent of our guests will not like anything! There are no absolutes, all is perception."

That's quite a sensitive, even abstract, expression of what a hotel's
product really is. It's all the more interesting that it comes from Matthew,
a hard-nosed, bottom-line-oriented executive with an accounting background!

When Bob DeSilva was the resident manager of the giant Napoleon
House Hotel he expressed the intangible nature of hotel services a little
differently. To him, "You are dealing with two intangibles, the hotel's staff
and the hotel's guests. The GM of a hotel must listen to the grumblings
of both guests and staff and perform a balancing act to ensure good guest
service." Bob is now the GM of his own 400-room hotel, performing, I'm
sure, his own delicate balancing act.

Intangibles, no absolutes, perceptions, and balancing acts—it's all a little
reminiscent of the hotel as theater, isn't it? That's why Jonathan Claiborne,
when he came to the United States to manage The Riviera Hotel, was
shocked to find no flowers in the lobby and why he thinks it's important
to personally oversee the placing of flowers in the lobby.

Setting Service Standards

Even though many hotel services have intangible aspects, service standards
must be set. There are, certainly, numerous cases where objective criteria
can be adopted when it comes to the quality of a hotel's services. The
purchase specifications of the food it serves and the goods (bath towels,
dinner china, bed sheets, and so forth) it provides to guests are part of a
hotel's service standards because these physical objects affect guest perceptions. Other objective service standards relating to physical aspects of
services include the temperature of the hot water in guest rooms, the lighting
level in bathrooms and corridors, and the temperature in public areas.

Conscious decisions must also be made concerning exactly which services will be provided: room turndown service, concierge service, twenty-
four-hour room service, express checkin and checkout, secretarial
assistance, a health club, and a courtesy van to the airport are all examples
of specific services a hotel may or may not choose to offer its guests. These
are important decisions. The total package of services offered by a hotel,
along with the physical facility itself, constitutes the product it offers to
its guests.

Service standards also relate to the time required for their delivery. When
discussing the pace of a hotel, the immediacy of many of its problems was
emphasized. Hotel services face time deadlines that affect their acceptance
by guests. Richard James referred to it as "on-time" service. Timeliness is
truly one of the abiding challenges of the hotel business. How long should

The rich wood paneling in the Philadelphia Four Seasons Hotel meeting room sets a mood.

Courtesy: Four Seasons Hotels and Resorts

it take to check into a hotel? When check-in lines get "too long" at The Hotel Frenchman, GM Curtis Samuels reallocates front office personnel from other functions to help out. If the wait is still unacceptable, he has the food and beverage department take drink orders from waiting guests. He even provides music when lines get too long. Although the best situation would be no waiting at all, Samuels has set standards and devised strategies to compensate when things go wrong.

Jonathan Claiborne has set ten minutes as a service goal for delivering morning room service at The Riviera Hotel. In his view "getting morning coffee to a guest in ten minutes is more important than how it tastes." Hotels have developed systems whereby guest participation can improve service. By placing room service orders the night before, guests can increase their chances of timely service the next morning. One hotel's strategy is to provide a self-service continental breakfast on each floor as an alternative to room service. If accepted by the guests, this form of "room service" has the added advantage of being less labor-intensive.

It all boils down to the need to set service standards that themselves are somewhat subjective. Jonathan Claiborne feels that Americans are most interested in quick checkins and clean rooms and beds. On the other hand, he feels that Europeans insist on good restaurants without waits. One may or may not agree with his assessment of American and European tastes, but his desire to understand the wants and needs of the guests he serves and to set the standards of his hotel accordingly should be applauded. Matt Fox brings up another interesting aspect of service standards. As he sees it, "A GM must have his own standards, and he must also set standards for his guests."

All companies, whether they produce goods or services, attempt, in one way or another, to impress their standards of quality and service on their customers. The more subjective the product or service, the more important the task becomes. The more subjective the product or service, the more symbols become important. Two quite different examples will be used to illustrate this point. The rich wood paneling of a law office is meant to convey stability, dependability, and trust. This symbol is important because many of the services provided by attorneys are quite intangible. The wood paneling and, in fact, all of the interior decorations of law offices are meant to convey an impression about the quality of services a client can expect. A quite different example is the paper lid often found on the glasses in a hotel's bathroom. These modest paper lids are also symbols. They are placed there to convey the hotel's concern with cleanliness. As modest a symbol as they may be, they represent a hotel's attempt to convey its standards to its guests. Subjectivity is never very far from the surface when Godfrey Bier, GM of the 800-room General Eisenhower Hotel, worried that he would have to cut his staff of 700 employees, therefore harming service. Matthew Fox, faced with a similar problem, stated, "The employee–guest ratio does not necessarily mean anything" when it comes to acceptable service standards.

Finally, service standards must be tempered by financial realities. Even Lawrence Wagner, who romantically likens hotels to the theater, understands that "service levels must be realistic" and responsive to financial considerations.

This section illustrates that setting service standards in hotels is a much more subtle and complex process than first meets the eye. As in any subtle and complex situation, it should be understood that the process of setting and maintaining service standards in hotels requires management's continual attention.

Service Consistency

Hotel services have an inherent tendency to be inconsistent or variable. This is a result of the nature of personal services and of the hotel business. Service quality varies because it is intangible and because the consumer is present when the service is being performed. By its very nature, the service provided by a waiter varies not only from day to day but also from table to table on the same day. The same holds true for most of a hotel's "front of the house" employees (that is, those who have direct contacts with guests). The service quality of "back of the house" employees can also vary. The quality of food produced in a hotel's kitchen is always a concern, as are the politeness of its telephone staff and the efficiency of its house-keeping department. Part of the reason for inconsistency in a hotel's service is because so many of its services are performed by people rather than machines, and people are not as consistent as machines.

Another reason why hotel service is inconsistent is because hotels are cyclical businesses, as was discussed in Chapter One. In some locations there are definitely high and low seasons with substantial occupancy swings. Many hotels exhibit weekly cycles of higher occupancy on week nights due to business travel followed by lower weekend occupancy when most guests are traveling for pleasure. The ever-growing importance of conventions and special events also contributes to wide variations in occupancy as large groups check into and out of hotels within a matter of days. Severe occupancy fluctuations make it difficult to maintain a uniform service standard. As discussed in Chapter One, to keep labor costs down, hotels usually vary their staffing levels with anticipated occupancy. Service consistency, of course, is more difficult when staffing fluctuations are greater.

Another cause of service inconsistency is employee turnover. Turnover in hotels is quite high compared to many other businesses. Rapid turnover, of course, compounds a hotel's problem of providing a uniform level of guest service because of the continual influx of new workers (Russ 1988).

The importance of service consistency cannot be overestimated. Most of the services provided by hotels are viewed by guests as rather straightforward, everyday things. Hot water for a shower, breakfast served efficiently, messages delivered promptly and wake-up calls at the correct time are examples of what might be called "low tech" as opposed to "high tech" services that guests have come to take for granted. When a service breakdown occurs, guests are all the more irritated because of a hotel's inability to provide even these "simple" services. It's the old complaint: "If we can put men on the moon why can't I get the coffee delivered to the conference room on time." If guests take most of a hotel's services for granted, one service breakdown can cloud a guest's opinion of a hotel. Put another way, the goodwill built up by three days of successful service encounters can be wiped out by a single service failure! In today's competitive world, the admonition, "What have you done for me lately?" really does apply to the hotel business. But wait; it's even tougher than that.

Attitudes Toward Service

If hotel guests expect good service for the money they spend, then good service alone will not ensure guest loyalty or repeat business. A service level about equal to the competition will result in customers being more or less indifferent to one hotel over another. Guest loyalty, and therefore repeat business, requires a level of service that exceeds that provided by the competition. If a hotel cannot provide exceptional service it will be thought of as a commodity that can only be differentiated from other hotels on the basis of price. Relying solely on price as a competitive strategy is often a last resort, and is not always the most desirable competitive strategy in the hotel business.

Excellent GMs understand this. They seem to instinctively know that, as Jonathan Claiborne says, "You must get the basics right or you are out of business." Lawrence Wagner commented on the great power GMs have in their hotels. He quickly let it be known, however, that it wasn't power but service that really counted. Claiborne goes on to note that good hotel executives "must have a service phobia." Each of the ten outstanding GMs studied, in his own way, had a service phobia. Godfrey Bier displayed it in his personal involvement with individual guests; Curtis Samuels, with his system of measuring guest satisfaction; and Richard James, in his concern for service delivered on time. Effective GMs all live with a service phobia. The following quote by William Scully about guest service is a good summary of how successful hotel GMs feel: "Guest service differentiates one hotel from another and successful from unsuccessful hotels." That's a pretty strong statement, and it's one to which most successful hotel executives would subscribe.

In addition to their own personal commitment to quality service, each GM worked continuously to foster this attitude in employees throughout his hotel. This is essential because good service in hotels takes place when people are serving people (Lieberman 1989).

PEOPLE SERVING PEOPLE

Hotels are always described as "people intensive" businesses, but often the description ends right there. But there's more to it than that. One of the truly striking features of the hotel business is the sheer numbers of people that are involved. A 1,000-room hotel is likely to employ 700 to 1,100 people, depending on the level of service it provides. On a night when all 1,000 rooms are fully occupied, the hotel will house between 1,500 and 2,000 guests, each of which is a separate customer. The total capital investment in such a business might be 100 to 200 million dollars. A chemical plant costing about the same can be run by a work force of 25! Moreover, its entire output might be sold to two or three customers thousands of miles away! Hotels, on the other hand, must be able to deal effectively with large numbers of guests and a large work force. In this section some of the characteristics of each will be discussed.

Guests

Businesses exist to satisfy customer needs. This can't be done properly without a clear understanding of these needs (Barrington and Olsen 1987). Hotels cater to a variety of guest types. On any given night a hotel may be accommodating individual business travelers, a group in town for a school reunion, a convention of civil engineers, a regional sales meeting, individual pleasure travelers in town for a concert, a motor coach tour of senior citizens, and a couple on a honeymoon.

Different types of guests have different needs; sometimes these differences are minor, sometimes great. Some guests are experienced travelers who have stayed at the hotel many times. Other guests travel infrequently and may be new to the city. Some require only the basic necessities while others need the full resources of the hotel. Some guests are extremely demanding while others are not. Whatever the case, successful hotels have one thing in common: they are all customer driven. Understanding guests' needs ranks high on outstanding GMs' priority lists. In fact, they often referred to understanding guests' needs as their number-one priority.

Curtis Samuels tries very hard to communicate what is important to his employees. He's developed a series of sayings to help guide the thinking and actions of the entire hotel staff. His very first saying, which he preaches with missionary zeal to his staff of 850 employees and executives is, "Talk to the guests." Talking to the guest is meant to convey a number of things. It means that a pleasant hello from all of the staff is a sign of hospitality, even in a 1,000-room hotel. But talking to the guests means much more; it means finding out from the guests if things are going well or if they need anything. In short, "talk to the guests" means constant and total communication, one-on-one, between as many employees and as many guests as possible. How is your stay? What do you need? Are there any problems? How can I help? These are the kinds of questions his staff is continuously asking guests. Curtis' goal is to not only talk to the guest but also to get the guest talking. I've seen him greet guests in elevators

A chef at The Ritz-Carlton, Buckhead, chatting with dinner guests at The Cafe.

Courtesy: The Ritz-Carlton Hotel Company

and in no time have them talking about their stay in the hotel. I've seen his executives mingle with guests every evening during a cocktail hour on the VIP floor. Most impressively, however, I've personally experienced this attitude from bellpersons, desk clerks, waitresses, and housekeeping maids while I was a guest of the hotel. Guests get the impression that there are a lot of people willing to do whatever it takes to make their stay a success.

A very successful convention services manager of the 1,500-room Bourbon Hotel feels that his job is to anticipate the needs of the groups in his hotel. To do that, he needs to understand both the group's strengths and its weaknesses. Godfrey Bier manages a really elegant hotel known for its traditional approach and attention to detail. His view of guest satisfaction is, "You must constantly be on guard about guests because you are their home away from home." He understands, as does Curtis Samuel, that most dissatisfied guests do not fill out negative guest comment cards, they just check out and don't return. Godfrey strives, as he puts it, to constantly find ways of providing "the finer touches to get our guests back."

Understanding guest needs and reacting quickly to their problems is one of the keys to effective hotel management. Although this is the ideal, in the real world it's not always possible. Mistakes are made, and from time to time guests are unhappy. For this reason, outstanding GMs pay extremely close attention to the negative comments on guest comment cards, even though these cards are usually received after the guest has left the hotel. Since complaints often represent the "tip of the iceberg," it is not unusual to find top-notch GMs reviewing each guest comment card the hotel receives. If trends are spotted, action is swift to remedy the cause of the problem. Of equal importance is the lengths to which outstanding GMs and other high-level hotel executives go to remedy a guest problem. "To turn," as Godfrey Bier puts it, "a negative into a positive."

Charles Eddystone is now the GM of a midsized hotel. At the time I interviewed him he was resident manager of a large convention hotel. He related a story of something good coming from a guest complaint. It seems that a guest felt he had been overcharged sixty dollars on his bill, but let it go while checking out because he had to make a plane connection. Soon, however, the hotel received an angry letter from him. On checking into the case, Charles found that the hotel had indeed made a mistake. He called the guest long-distance to apologize and to tell him that the hotel was not only refunding the sixty dollars but also one night's room rent as a token of its good will. The man was genuinely impressed. As fate would have it, he was responsible for choosing the headquarters hotel for a large convention to be held in that city the next year. Charles' sympathetic follow-up to the man's complaint not only turned a dissatisfied guest into a happy one, but also landed Charles' hotel an 1,800 room-night convention at ninety dollars per room. Charles' concern for guest satisfaction turned a negative into a positive and brought in over $200,000 in revenue!

Successful hotel executives know that guests' needs must be satisfied, one at a time. If this can be accomplished, most other problems will take care of themselves.

Employees

The people who actually serve guests are a hotel's employees. These are the workers, not the hotel's supervisors, managers, department heads, or executives. These are the people who answer the phones, clean the rooms, checkin the guests, cook and serve the food, and repair the air-conditioners. A hotel's employees perform nearly all guest services. They also do nearly all the interacting with the guests. Just think about it; a traveler can check into an expensive hotel, stay three or four nights, spend 1,000 dollars or more, and never have contacts with any member of the hotel's management staff. In fact, that guest may never have contacts with anyone earning more than six dollars per hour![2] There is something of a paradox to this. Henri LeSassier refers to it as "the employee–guest dichotomy." As he puts it, it's possible to "have the least educated employees dealing with the most educated guests. Some employees go from the ghetto to luxury and back in the same day." This contrast is not lost on Godfrey Bier, who sees it as "a dichotomy between the two kinds of people a GM must deal with—hotel staff and guests." The reasons for this dichotomy are not hard to find.

Many hotel jobs deal with basic domestic chores such as cleaning, carrying, and serving. These jobs, while vitally important to the hotel's mission, require employees with relatively few skills. In consequence, the jobs are low paying.

There is another aspect of hotel jobs that keeps wages down: the average productivity of hotel employees. Because they employ relatively large numbers of workers to satisfy guest needs, hotels are characterized as labor-intensive. In contrast, the chemical plant discussed earlier, with 25 employees and a large physical facility, is classified as capital-intensive. The few chemical workers, because they have so much productive machinery to work with, are more "productive" than hotel workers because a chemical plant's sales per employee is much greater than a hotel's. Also, labor costs for a hotel, as a percentage of revenues, will be much greater than for a chemical plant. The combination of low-skilled jobs and relative labor-intensiveness results in large numbers of low-paying jobs in hotels. This is a fact of life, the basic economics of the hotel business. Attempts to pay significantly higher wages would fail; the added wage costs would have to be passed on to guests in the form of higher room rates, and the hotel would become noncompetitive (Meyer and Schroeder 1989).

Hotels are forced to pay relatively low wages and, therefore, cannot compete in the labor market on the basis of price. In consequence, skilled and experienced workers often overlook hotels for better paying jobs elsewhere. Hotels, therefore, must often hire less-qualified workers. Hotels attract many young employees who have just entered the labor force. They are inexperienced both with regard to basic skills and work habits. Many hotel employees may have little formal education, thus making their training and development more difficult. Still others are attracted to hotel work as a part-time or temporary job—not as a career. Students, for example, often work in hotels part-time. Minorities and immigrants, groups with few job alternatives, often find their way into the work force through ho-

---

[2]Of course, many tipped employees, who earn minimum wage or less, actually have a greater take-home pay because of tips.

tels. Being able to shape such a diverse group of people into an effective team is one of the greatest challenges in the hotel business.

It's not surprising that employee attitude ranks high on the list of management concerns. Since much of the service provided by hotels has important intangible components, how people perform their tasks is often as important as what they do. Like the old adage, "It's not what you say, but how you say it." Thus, Jonathan Claiborne feels that his hotel's staff is the key to its success and a "yes, positive attitude is needed by all." In fact, the number-one job concern voiced by the hotel department heads interviewed during the GM research was employee problems. And the number-one employee problem they face is how to motivate employees and keep up their morale. These experienced executives expressed concern with so-called "attitude" problems in a variety of ways. One said that although the hotel had cut its staff recently because of falling occupancy, maintaining a "family atmosphere" among the staff was his number-one priority. Another alluded to the difficulty of motivating the "wide variety" of people who work in hotels. A third felt it was important to keep employees "thinking" and not relying only on the system to get things done. However they put it, it all revolved around the importance of morale, motivation, and attitude.

A story told by Richard James illustrates the importance of attitude. He had been managing The Hotel Apollo for about three months and was concerned about poor employee attitude. During a tour of the hotel he noticed that empty styrofoam coffee cups had been left by guests on the ledge of a flower planter in the lobby. The cups were in full view of the hotel's bellmen who usually congregated around the bell stand when they were not busy. In full view of the bellmen, James picked up the cups from the planter and dropped them in a trash receptacle. He said nothing to the bellmen other than his usual good morning—hoping, of course, that his example and initiative would motivate the bellmen to do the same. To his disappointment, he found empty coffee cups on the same planter the very next morning with the same bellmen still standing around. Richard again picked up the cups, but this time he discussed the first and second incidents with the bellmen to impress upon them the importance of taking initiative. To his dismay, he found the same situation within a week of the second incident. Needless to say, his approach to the problem the third time was much less subtle than the first and much less gentle than the second!

A small incident? Yes, but this outstanding GM felt that it was important. It symbolized the employees' negative attitude. Whether it is called attitude, motivation, or morale, Richard James saw it as one of the hotel's great obstacles to being excellent, and he was determined to do whatever it took to change these attitudes. Frank Anderson and all of his key executives express the importance of employee attitude in the following way:

"If you can improve employee attitude you will improve guest satisfaction, which will result in increased hotel profits." It's an elementary and straightforward statement. There are only two tricks; one is truly believing it, and the second is making it happen.

Employees must be trained as well as motivated, so training is a key issue in the hotel business (Russ 1988). Certain characteristics of hotels affect the kind of training that should take place. Few jobs in hotels are what might be called "machine driven" in that the pace of the worker is determined by the pace of the machine. Assembly lines are designed to

Waiter properly presenting a wine selection to guests at the Le Meridien San Diego's Marius Restaurant.

Courtesy: Le Meridien Hotels, Inc., and Edward Gohlich, photographer.

allow machines to dictate a worker's pace. Jobs are broken down into simple repetitive steps and workers are trained to perform these tasks. As employees on a production line get more proficient, the line's speed is increased. In this way the machine (the production line in this example) dictates the employee's work pace. In effect, employees are "motivated" to perform by the pace of the line. There are a few jobs in hotels that lend themselves to this kind of pacing. Examples would include the number of rooms a maid is required to clean during an eight-hour shift or the number of tables assigned to a waiter. The analogy, however, is far from perfect; the quality of the production line's product can more easily be measured than the quality of the maid's or waiter's work in a hotel. It's easy enough to check if a worker has installed the rear tires on an automobile as the assembly line's speed is increased. It's quite another thing to be certain that a waiter's "service" is unchanged when he is assigned an additional two tables.

Many jobs in hotels are relatively uncomplicated and can be taught to inexperienced, new employees in a matter of days (Meyer and Schroeder 1989). Consequently training often takes place on the job, where more experienced workers "break in" new employees. This can be an effective training method, providing management properly controls the process. There are obvious pitfalls to this method if it is poorly designed and supervised. New workers can be taught bad habits as easily as good habits, and new employees can be left to learn on their own if management is lax. Keys to effective training in well-managed hotels will be discussed in more detail in later chapters. Suffice it to say that effective hotel executives are keenly aware of the need to properly train their staff. As Matthew Fox puts it, "All that is done in hotels is done through people. To manage people you must be fair and you must train them!"

A not so obvious aspect of employee training results from the fact that many hotel employees are new entrants into the work force. In addition to acquiring basic job skills, many employees need to be taught what can be called good work habits. An experienced personnel director at the 2,000-room Napoleon House Hotel puts it this way:

> "Many new employees, although quite willing to work, don't understand the importance of good work habits. For example, they sometimes don't realize the hardships they cause the hotel because of tardiness and absenteeism and, therefore, don't make the extra effort required to avoid these problems. It's our job, when new employees are hired, to instill them with good work habits as well as train them in job skills."

Although skills training is important, employee development is more important. Work habits and attitudes must be molded if a hotel is to provide effective service. This is all the more important because of two additional characteristics of the hotel business: the employee-guest encounter and the level of employee turnover.

Managers are usually not present when employees are serving guests. In other words, most employee-guest encounters in a hotel are unsupervised by management. The sheer numbers of employees and guests, and the number and different places where encounters take place in a day, make close management supervision impossible. Thus, the employee is often on his or her own when serving a guest, and the quality of the guest encounter depends entirely on the training, attitude, and judgment of the employee. Jan Carlzon, president of Scandinavian Airlines, has called such service encounters, which take place by the thousands each day, the individual moments of truth for a service-oriented business. The skill with which each employee-guest encounter is handled truly determines a hotel's effectiveness, and most of these moments of truth take place away from the watchful eye of management! Since employee-guest encounters are not usually monitored, it is all the more important that a hotel's staff be properly trained and motivated so that these moments of truth are properly carried out.

A humorous example of a service encounter that went astray was related to me by a businessman who travels extensively and stays in many hotels. On a recent trip he decided to go to the hotel's lounge to watch the Monday Night NFL football game. It was ten minutes before a waitress arrived to take his order, and he was then served a different brand of beer than he had ordered. When he pointed this out, the waitress cheerfully returned with the correct brand but forgot to bring a bowl of pretzels, as was provided to guests at other tables. It took another five minutes to get the pretzels. He was, by then, a little annoyed and gently chided the waitress about the slow service. Watching an NFL game without beer and pretzels was, after all, a heavy burden to bear. She cheerfully responded that the delay couldn't be helped because of the number of tables she had to serve and wished him "better luck next time." While returning to his $150 a night room he chuckled about her "better luck next time" remark. On reflection, however, he decided to try another hotel chain on his next business trip to see if his luck might be a bit better. This particular moment of truth was, of course, a failure. The extent of the failure can be better understood by the fact that this businessman spends about one hundred nights each year in hotels. His allegiance, or lack of it, to a particular hotel chain in his case means $15,000 in rooms revenue annually. This employee-guest encounter was, without a doubt, a moment of truth.

Another reason why training is so important relates to the relatively high level of employee turnover in hotels. For reasons previously discussed (cyclical business, low wage rates, part-time work, new entrants into the labor force, high stress levels, and so forth), hotels experience fairly substantial turnover rates. Although certain positions turn over more rapidly than others, it is not uncommon to find employee turnover rates of 50 percent annually, and sometimes much more. Percentages don't fully convey the extent of this problem. A hotel with 500 employees and a 50 percent annual turnover rate must hire and train 250 new employees each year, or one-half of its total staff! Thus, a fact of life in the hotel business is a never-ending cycle of interviewing, hiring, training, and terminating significant numbers of its staff. This process is expensive. It means that hotels must always contend with maintaining service standards with significant numbers of fairly new employees. Well-managed hotels understand this problem and have devised methods of dealing with it (DeMicco and Giridharan 1987).

Quality banquets at The Ritz-Cartlon in Naples, Florida, help build its reputation.

Courtesy: The Ritz-Carlton Hotel Company

Managers

Hotels require a lot of managing; it's one of the key characteristics of the business. Because of their pace, diversity, and service orientation, large hotels need large numbers of supervisory and management personnel. There are certain characteristics of management jobs in hotels that distinguish them from many other kinds of businesses.

As discussed hotels are fast-paced businesses that are always open, and there is a true immediacy to most hotel problems, as well as an element of unpredictability. These characteristics mean that much effort must be put into ensuring the smooth day-to-day functioning of hotels. This puts considerable pressures on young, inexperienced managers. A concern for young hotel managers is usually a concern of hotel department heads. Even more so than GMs, it's the department heads who wrestle with the day-to-day problems faced by their junior managers. It's no wonder that after employee concerns, department heads rank management problems as their second most pressing concern. Job pressures result from the service imperative faced by hotels: banquet guests must be served on time, arriving guests must be checked in quickly, work schedules must be changed because of absenteeism. Junior managers must cope with most of the deadline-oriented problems faced by hotels. When things don't work, managers know it quickly because they are confronted by angry guests, frustrated employees, or both.

Management pressures also derive from hotels' profit orientation. Experienced department heads often comment that it is difficult to teach young managers "how to balance the need for profits with maintaining service standards." Indeed, learning how to do this is one of the secrets to success in the hotel business. Nearly anyone can provide excellent service if money is no object. The trick is to provide excellent service and also stay in budget. As Lawrence Wagner puts it, "One's ability to provide service must be realistic." It's really a very tricky proposition. John Kemp has been catering manager at the four-star General Eisenhower Hotel for over thirty years. His department may be the principal reason the hotel has consistently won Holiday Awards for its excellent handling of conventions and business meetings. The oil and gas industry was one of the principal markets served by this hotel, but decreases in oil prices depressed the industry for a number of years. As Kemp put it, "Catering was a lot more fun when the client didn't ask what the function would cost. Now, things are quite different. Clients are very concerned about costs and business is won or lost on the basis of price." However, even when functions are booked at lower prices, John notes that clients still expect the same high-quality service for which his hotel is famous! His challenge now is to compete on the basis of price, maintain the high service standards that built his hotel's reputation, and make a profit to boot! That's the kind of balancing act that

The elegant Ritz-Carlton in Naples, Florida

Courtesy: Ritz-Carlton Hotel Company

distinguishes excellent managers from average managers in the hotel business.

These factors, combined with long hours, result in considerable job pressures for managers. In consequence, management turnover, especially at the lower and mid-management levels, tends to be fairly high. Turnover occurs not only for negative reasons but also for positive ones. Good managers are in great demand and move up quickly, thus causing vacancies in the ranks. Therefore, a common problem in the hotel business is a lack of good, effective, experienced managers at the entry and middle management levels. It's the exception rather than the rule to find the same management team together for a number of years. For this reason many hotels find it difficult to maintain management consistency.

Excellent hotels understand the nature of this problem and work to overcome it. Outstanding GMs and department heads realize that their effectiveness depends on their ability to train and develop the managers under them. They realize that they must find a way to provide this training and development, not withstanding the day-to-day job pressures of their positions. Although formal training and development programs are useful and can be effective, much of the management training and development that takes place in hotels takes the form of coaching between superior and subordinate managers. In the course of supervising subordinate activities, excellent managers are able to teach, motivate, and direct subordinates in a way far superior to anything possible in formal training. The fine line between profits and quality service can only be taught while on the job. The important lessons of how to set priorities and goals often come from effective coaching. Certainly, the practical lessons and skills of managing people are best learned by trial and error with the help of an experienced and sympathetic superior.

Given the job pressures and high employee/management turnover, it would be very easy for a hotel's top management to accept the inevitable and live passively with the problem. The easy road would be to hope that the organization could be sustained through good recruitment alone. Excellent hotels, like excellent football teams, realize that good draft choices alone will not result in a winning team. Excellent hotel managers find the time amid their many day-to-day operating demands to train, coach, and develop young management talent, which leads to greater organizational effectiveness.

OWNERS, PROFITS, AND MANAGERS

Hotels may be exciting and glamorous, but ultimately they are businesses owned by people who are very interested in making money. Certain aspects of hotel ownership are somewhat unique to the business and, in consequence, affect how they are managed.

Absentee Owners

There is a general misconception by the public that most hotels are owned by the chains whose name appears over the marquee. In fact, many of the most recognized hotel chains in America own only a small percentage of the hotels that carry their names. The actual owners are local real estate developers, wealthy business and professional people, and large institutional investors such as insurance companies and pension funds. These owners develop hotels like any other real estate investment. They often don't know how to manage a hotel, and for this reason, enter into contracts with hotel companies such as Holiday Inns, Hilton, or Sheraton to manage the hotel. The building's owners and a hotel or management company enter into what is called a management contract. The GM, executives, and employees of the hotel work for the hotel company. The hotel must be managed, however, in such a way that will satisfy both the hotel company and the hotel's owners.

The owner of a business who does not also participate in its day-to-day management is called an absentee owner. Since there is no day-to-day management involvement, it's fair to say that an absentee owner derives little pleasure from actually running the business, as might an owner who also manages it. Rather, it's the bottom-line profit that is of utmost importance to owners. The business is not a career, it's just an investment. In addition, absentee owners who know little about the hotel business may be unsympathetic to its operational problems. The reason for investing is profit, and the more profits the better.

The tendency toward hotel overbuilding was discussed in Chapter One. When overbuilding occurs, profits fall and losses may occur. Also, developers sometimes make poor initial investment decisions relating to location, facilities, or financing. In either case, a hotel's chances of making a profit may be severely impaired no matter how well it is managed. For these reasons, as Lawrence Wagner says, "One must be very selective and careful as to where, and for whom, he works."

It should be obvious from this discussion of absentee ownership that, as many seasoned hotel managers put it, "There is incredible pressure to perform" in the hotel business. What this often translates into is pressure to show short-run (a month, quarter, or year) profits or to avoid short-run losses. It's a question of owners looking for an adequate return at all times on their money, no matter what the circumstances. Having little sentimental attachment to a hotel, and often little knowledge of the difficulties of managing it, absentee owners' interests often settle on the bottom line: short-run profits and little else.

Owners of valuable assets want to look after them rather closely. Monthly owners' meetings with the GM and other key hotel executives are common. A highlight of these meetings is naturally a review of the monthly profit and loss statement. Additionally, more frequent contact usually occurs between the principal partners and the GM to monitor programs during the month and to make decisions that cannot wait for the owners' meetings.

Corporate Input

In America today, with the exception of the many small "Mom and Pop" hotels and motels, most hotel executives work for corporations that manage more than one, and often a substantial number of hotels. Well-known companies such as Marriott, Westin, Ramada, Sheraton, and Hilton are examples. There are less well-known companies, however, that manage large numbers of hotels. The following independent hotel management companies are less well known but manage quite a few hotels: AIRCOLA (131 hotels), VMS Realty Partners (fifty-six hotels), The Continental Companies (fifty-eight hotels), Servico (fifty-two hotels), and Larken, Inc. (seventy-two hotels). Thus, hotel executives, and especially GMs, must understand how to interact with the corporate hierarchy above the individual unit level.

It is important to understand that each individual hotel in a chain is a profit center. The profitability of the company depends solely on the profitability of each of the hotels in the company. Thus, the primary purpose of a hotel company's management hierarchy above the unit level is to monitor the performances of its individual hotels, to oversee the decisions they make, and to help them be as profitable as possible. The corporate hierarchy cannot run the individual hotels, but it certainly can keep close tabs on what is happening. Corporate gets involved in certain decisions of individual units, ensures that policies and procedures are being carried out, and provides help to individual hotels to ensure their profitability. Of course, all of these functions require a close working relationship between the individual hotel GM and corporate-level executives.

Corporate executives, though of course interested in the operational details of their hotels, are also very bottom-line or profit driven. If the corporation owns its hotels, its interest in profits is the same as any owner. If, instead, the hotel company manages hotels owned by others, its interest is to maintain its management contracts, which can be accomplished only by managing profitable hotels. As Jonathan Claiborne said, "We only have two years remaining on our management contract. If we don't show a profit, we will be gone."

Profits Versus Service

Service is what often differentiates one hotel from another in the minds of consumers. It's impossible to underestimate the importance of service to guest satisfaction, repeat business, and a hotel's reputation. At the same time, the previous section makes it clear that to a hotel owner, great service without profit is charity. The dilemma is simple. It often costs money to improve a hotel's service. Improved services make for more satisfied guests, which should lead to repeat business, a better reputation, higher revenues, and greater profits. However, it takes time for the benefits of improved service to be felt, and it is not always easy to measure the effects of good service on revenues and profits. Although everyone agrees that the effect will be positive and in the hotel's long-run interest, it's hard to prove. On the other hand, it's very easy to see how increased spending on service impacts a hotel's bottom-line: every additional dollar spent on service immediately reduces pretax profits by a dollar!

For these reasons there exists a natural and inevitable tension in hotels between service and profits. It's a dilemma that all businesses face: how to ensure the long-term profitability of the business and, at the same time, make acceptable profit levels this month or quarter or year. Effective GMs and senior hotel executives understand this problem. They must because they are faced with it daily. Understanding the dilemma does not make it any less difficult to deal with. Owners and corporate executives exert pressure for increased short-run profits. Hotel managers understand the importance of this but, at the same time, realize that the long-run viability of their hotel demands that sufficient funds be invested now.

A hotel's GM and executives are operationally oriented managers who are constantly on the firing line trying to provide quality guest service. They are reminded daily how fragile guest satisfaction can be and how much it costs to maintain a hotel's service standards. It is normal, therefore, that hotel executives incline toward the maintenance of standards to ensure long-term viability. It's equally understandable that owners and corporate executives, being removed from daily operating problems, tend to look at the hotel as an investment that should produce a short-run return as well as a long-run return.

This is as it should be. The tug-of-war that exists between the two competing goals of short-run profit and long-run viability, although frustrating, is healthy. Hotels are businesses that must make profits to survive. Thus, when Godfrey Bier complains that, "Guest services and profits are sometimes in conflict," you can bet he speaks from experience! Other managers insist that you can't make short-run profits a hotel's number-one objective. They argue that guest satisfaction must be the number one objective and that if this is accomplished, profits will follow "in the long run." However, as a famous economist once said, "In the long run we are all dead!" If your money were invested in a hotel project, it's likely you would expect both short-run profits and the long-run viability of your investment. Hotel managers must, therefore, walk a fine line between service and profit. It's worth repeating Lawrence Wagner's statement: "One's ability to provide service must be realistic." Experienced and effective hotel managers have little praise for managers who are extreme at either end of the service-profit spectrum. They realize that by spending large sums of money nearly any manager can provide high–quality service. Conversely, it takes little skill to drastically reduce costs (and service) to ensure short-run profits.

The skill comes in learning how to accomplish both conflicting goals. Learning how to stay in budget and provide quality service, at any management level in a hotel, is the essence of effective management. It's not easy to learn how to do this, but it's a skill all managers are looking for in their subordinates. Once learned, it's a skill that surely leads to rapid success in the hotel business.

Profits During Good Times and Bad

As discussed, there are seasonal cycles and weekly cycles in the hotel business. There are also business cycles where room demand and occupancy increase for a number of years followed by periods of overbuilding and recession that result in falling occupancies and profits. An individual hotel usually cannot expand it's room supply during good times nor decrease it during bad. It must, nevertheless, be prepared for good times and bad, and know how to change with changing conditions. Experienced GMs often say that hotel managers are not really proven until they have managed in both good times and bad.

Of course, it's more fun to manage a hotel during good times. Even though Matthew Fox says that, "Anyone can make a profit when demand exceeds supply," it does not follow that a hotel has made all the profit it could have or that the quality of its guest service was as high as it should be. Good times and rising profits often tend to make people lazy because they don't have to try very hard to show improved results. Opportunities for even greater profits are sometimes missed, payrolls become inflated, costs are not as carefully watched; in other words, management becomes sloppy! When Lawrence Wagner took over as GM of The Regal Hotel, his predecessor had been considered one of the real stars of the company. The Regal's sales and profits had been increasing for five straight years, and it was generally felt that Lawrence would do well just to keep things where they were. In fact, sharp-eyed Wagner realized that the hotel's potential had not nearly been reached. Management had, in effect, become lazy. He tightened controls, reorganized operations and took advantage of market opportunities that had been neglected. In one year he was able to double the hotel's profitability. This accomplishment, needless to say, "made" his career. He became recognized as a manager who could be relied on to make as much money as was possible under the circumstances. He has always maintained this reputation, and it was never more important to him than when the hotel had to face hard times.

Bad times follow good, and managing a hotel during downturns has both its challenges and rewards. Simply put, the challenge a hotel faces is to get through the bad times with a minimum of financial loss while still remaining viable for the long run. During bad times the importance of attending to details is magnified. Booking a twenty-room-night piece of business becomes cause for joy; seeing that the housekeeping department is never overstaffed takes on a high priority, controlling food costs becomes an hour-by-hour concern, and justifying capital expenditures becomes more difficult. Attending to details and focusing on critical issues make the difference. Saving a few dollars here or fractionally increasing revenues there often spells the difference between profits and losses. It's during such times that being effective is often synonymous with being efficient.

At the same time, a hotel's management must prepare for the return of good times. The economizing measures taken during bad times must do as little damage as possible to the hotel's reputation and long-run profitability. During bad times, attending to details and economizing must be balanced with a vision of the future. Numerous examples of this kind of vision will be given throughout this book. Incidents of forward-thinking GMs arguing for millions in capital improvements, while the hotel is losing money, are common. These executives knew what was needed to keep things together during temporary downturns. They also knew that even in bad times money sometimes must be spent to ensure long-run success. It takes guts to make these kinds of decisions because a manager's job and career often hinges on being right. Nevertheless, fluctuations in business activity are a reality of the hotel business, and a hotel executive's ability to manage in both good times and bad is the true measure of his or her effectiveness.

CONCLUSION

The U.S. economy is being increasingly dominated by service-oriented businesses. Hotels, no matter how good their location, how beautiful their architecture, or how efficient their national reservation system, can only truly differentiate themselves from their competitors by superior service. Guest loyalty and repeat business can only be earned by consistent, superior service. Anything else quickly relegates a hotel into the dreaded classification of an undifferentiated commodity. In that unpleasant world, customers think that all hotels are just about the same and will, therefore, quickly switch from one to another based on price.

The fact that many of a hotel's services are intangible complicates management's job. Although easily recognized, it's hard to define friendly service. To one person the bathtub is clean, to another the mildew between two tiles stands out like a beacon. And who can explain the subjectivity of people's tastes in food! Thus, hotel managers must constantly involve themselves in the subtle process of understanding the needs and expectations of their guests and translating these needs and expectations into service standards for the hotel's employees.

The more guests expect good service, the less tolerant they are of lapses, and the more likely they will switch their patronage to another hotel. Outstanding hotels try to deliver close to zero-defect service and when mistakes are made try extra hard to turn an unhappy guest into a happy one. It is especially difficult for hotels to provide consistently exceptional service because of great variations in occupancy and high employee turnover. Outstanding hotel managers nevertheless succeed by instilling a "service phobia" in employees throughout their hotel.

Guests come in all shapes and sizes and with all kinds of needs. They also come in large numbers, sometimes by the thousands. Outstanding hotel managers realize that it takes an all-team effort of both managers and employees talking and working with guests, all the time, to be sure that guest services are being effectively delivered. Outstanding managers stay close to their guests and they regard negative guest comments as a valuable early warning system to detect potential major guest service problems.

It's not an exaggeration to say that when a member of middle or upper management gets directly involved with a guest it's usually to remedy a problem. Most guests only have contact with a hotel's hourly or tipped employees, and most employee guest contacts take place out of the watchful eye of management. Furthermore, the economics of the hotel business dictate relatively low wages. Thus, guests are provided quite personal service by hotel employees who are often unskilled, new to the workforce, and consider their hotel jobs as temporary. These factors, along with employee turnover rates of 50 percent or more, make it obvious that concerns over employee morale and motivation rank at the very top of the list for hotel department heads. For each employee–guest moment of truth to go off properly it's also important that rapid and efficient employee training systems be developed. The training and development of young hotel managers is equally important. Because they face the majority of a hotel's day-to-day operational problems, their jobs are quite stressful and their turnover is high. Excellent managers find the time to provide the supervision, coaching, and training young managers need to succeed. Young managers especially need to learn how to balance a hotel's need for short-run profits against the need to provide exceptional service that will ensure long-run profitability.

Balancing short-run profits and service quality is especially important in the hotel business because so many hotels are financed by absentee owners who are sometimes unfamiliar and unsympathetic with hotel operational problems. Their concern with making a return on their investment leads to a desire for profitable operations each quarter and, consequently, puts performance pressure on hotel managers. Finally, hotel managers must learn how to make the maximum profits possible when times are good and occupancy and room rates are high, and they must learn to minimize losses or make whatever small profits they can during bad times when rates and occupancies are low. Many excellent hotel GMs feel that the true test of a GM is being versatile enough to make money both in good times and in bad.

REFERENCES

Barrington, Melvin N. and Michael D. Olsen. 1987. "Concept of Service in the Hospitality Industry." *International Journal of Hospitality Management* 6(3):131–138.

DeMicco, Fred J. and Jiri Giridharan. Fall 1987. "Managing Employee Turnover in the Hospitality Industry." *FIU Hospitality Review* 5(2):26–32.

Lieberman, Gregg. September 1989. Service Picks Up. *Meetings & Conventions* 24(10):40–47.

Meyer, Robert A. and John J. Schroeder. Spring 1989. "Rewarding Non-Productivity in the Hospitality Industry." *FIU Hospitality Review* 7(1):1–12.

Russ, Stephan P. October 17, 1988. "Training, Consistency Keys to Business Service." *Hotel & Motel Management* 203(15):24ff.

FURTHER READING

Albrecht, Karl and Ron Zemke. 1985. *Service America: Doing Business in the New Economy*. Homewood, Il: Dow Jones-Irwin.

Heskett, James L. 1986. *Managing in the Service Economy*. Boston: Harvard Business School Press.

Ultimate Service: "Going Far Beyond the Call of Duty." April 1988. *Hotel & Resort Industry*:36–42.

Koepper, Ken. December 1988. "Management Effectiveness: A Hotel Industry Appraisal." *Lodging* 14(4):53–57.

Sasser, W. Earl, R. Paul Olsen, and D. Daryl Wyckoff. 1978. *Management of Service Operations*. Boston: Allyn& Bacon, Inc.

Tas, Richard F. August 1988. "Teaching Future Managers." *Cornell Hotel and Restaurant Administration Quarterly* 29(2):41–43.

QUESTIONS

2-1. Why do some hotel GMs refer to hotels as commodities?

2-2. List and explain seven intangible services provided by hotels? How does a hotel ensure that these services are being properly provided to guests?

2-3. How would you set service standards for intangible services?

2-4. Give examples of how the size of a hotel's staff affects guests service levels.

2-5. How can a hotel differentiate itself from its competition on the basis of service?

2-6. Explain why employee wages are relatively low in the hotel business.

2-7. What are some of the key challenges young managers face in the hotel business?

2-8. What challenges does absentee ownership pose for hotel managers?

2-9. What should be a hotel managers goal, profits or outstanding guest service?

2-10. How does managing a hotel differ during good times and bad times?

CHAPTER 3

An Overview of Strategic Planning

All successful businesses plan for the future, and excellently managed hotels are no exception. This chapter will describe the planning process used by most well-run businesses today, and these principles will be applied to hotels in Chapter Four.

THE NATURE OF STRATEGIC PLANNING

The term strategic planning is used in a special way in business today, so a precise definition of it is needed.

Strategic Planning Defined

A strategy is nothing more than a business's method of competing (Aldag and Stearns 1987). Even a casual reading of business publications such as *The Wall Street Journal*, *Business Week*, or a newspaper's business section will reveal many references to business strategies. Read just one copy of *Business Week* and it will become apparent that a business's strategy relates to how it competes in the marketplace for its products or services. Thus, when a hotel's strategy is discussed in this chapter it will refer to how it competes; in other words, strategy and competitive strategy will be used synonymously. Military strategies are plans devised to win wars against competing armies. Similarly, business strategies are plans devised to win in the competitive struggle for profits. Within this context of businesses competing against each other, strategic planning can be defined as "the set of decisions and actions resulting in formulation and implementation of strategies designed to achieve the objectives of the organization" (Pearce and Robinson 1988, 6). A hotel's strategic plan can be thought of as a blueprint or a game plan that it follows in its competitive struggle. The process of formulating and implementing a strategic plan is called strategic management.

Distinguishing Characteristics of Strategic Planning

It's important to make a distinction between strategic planning and other kinds of planning that go on all the time in businesses. When a hotel's food and beverage manager plans the menu for a banquet or a rooms manager schedules a certain number of front desk clerks for a heavy check-in, they are performing important managerial tasks, but they are not engaged in strategic planning. These tasks represent important operational matters that contribute to a smoothly running, efficient hotel, but they are not strategic in the sense that they relate to the way in which the hotel competes. Strategic planning is different in that it helps a hotel answer three important questions: (1) What will we do and for whom will we do it, (2) what goals do we want to achieve, and (3) how are we going to manage the organization's activities to achieve the chosen goals (Aldag and Stearns 1987, 204)? These are really fundamental questions. Answers to them will, without doubt, set the course for all of a hotel's future activities.

If all decisions hotel executives make are not strategic, what issues do require strategic thinking? Pearce and Robinson (1988) identify six dimensions that distinguish strategic issues from other issues facing a business.

- *Strategic Issues Require Top-Management Decisions* because decisions affect several areas of a firm's operation.
- *Strategic Issues Involve the Allocation of Relatively Large Amounts of Resources* that must be redirected from other internal uses or secured from outside the business. Either way, the business has committed to a series of actions involving substantial resources.
- *Strategic Issues Are Likely to Impact the Long-Term Prosperity of a Business.* Strategic decisions commit a business to particular markets, products and services, and technologies. Once these critical decisions are made they are not easily reversed.
- *Strategic Issues Are Future Oriented.* They are based on what a business anticipates will happen in the future.
- *Strategic Issues Usually Have Major Multifunctional Consequences* that must be closely coordinated. For example, decisions regarding changes in a hotel's guest mix, service level or organization structure usually affect more than one operating department with respect to resource allocation and areas of responsibility.

• *Strategic Issues Require Consideration of a Business's External Environment.* Strategic issues relate to how the business faces its competitors in the markets in which it competes. More broadly, strategic issues relate to all external factors that bear on a firm's performance.

THE STRATEGIC PLANNING HIERARCHY

Today, many major U.S. hotels are individual operating units of much larger companies, such as Hilton, Omni, and Ramada, whose primary business is lodging. Other hotels are parts of corporations, such as Holiday Corporation and Marriott, that are in the lodging business and also other related businesses. Finally hotels, such as Sheratons and Hyatts, are part of hotel companies that are just one business in a much larger corporate conglomerate comprised of many different kinds of businesses.

Embassy Suites hotel's new "Cycle Suites" featuring computerized Schwinn Air-Dyne exercise cycles.

Courtesy: Embassy Suites, Inc.

Strategic Planning and the Corporate Organization

This book's focus is on managing hotels at the individual unit level. Consequently, discussion will emphasize the kinds of strategic decisions individual hotels usually make. Because most major hotels are part of larger organizations, it is important to understand the overall context, or organizational hierarchy, in which they operate, and the strategic decisions that are made at different levels within that hierarchy.

It is perhaps easiest to grasp the hierarchy of strategic decision making by taking a look at a typical organization chart for a hotel company. Figure 3-1 depicts such an organization chart along with the kinds of strategic decisions that are usually made at various levels within the organization. At the top of the management pyramid is the Board of Directors, and the chief executive officer (CEO), who is responsible to the Board of Directors for the overall performance of the company. At this level within a hotel company, *business-level* strategic decisions are made. If this business were part of a larger conglomerate, *corporate-level* strategic decisions would be made at an even higher level. If the company is not part of a larger

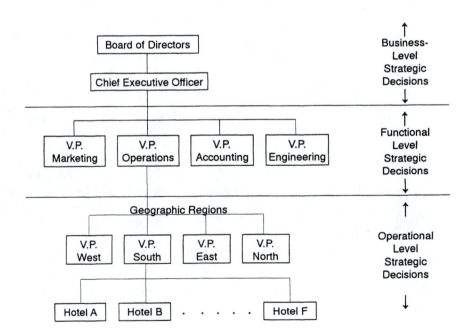

FIGURE 3-1.   Strategic Decisions in a Hotel Corporation

corporation, corporate and business-level decisions are one and the same and are made by the Board of Directors and the CEO.

Directly below the CEO are the functional executives of the hotel company, so named because each is responsible for a particular specialized aspect, or function, of the business such as marketing, accounting, personnel, and food and beverage. Included at this level is a vice-president of operations who has overall responsibility for the operational activities of the company's hotels. *Functional level* strategic decisions are made at this level in the management structure.

In a relatively small hotel company, the individual hotel managers report directly to the vice-president of hotel operations. In larger companies, regional vice-presidents oversee the operations of individual hotels in various geographic regions. They in turn report to the V.P. of hotel operations. At the regional and individual hotel level, operational level strategic decisions are made.

Corporate-Level Strategic Planning

Strategic planning takes place at each level within a modern business; the corporate level, the business level, and the functional or operational level (Pearce and Robinson 1988, 8–11). Many corporations are involved in more than one, and sometimes many, separate businesses. For example, International Telephone and Telegraph (ITT) is a giant corporate conglomerate engaged in literally hundreds of different businesses ranging from telephone exchanges to electronics components to the lodging business through its wholly owned subsidiary, Sheraton. Corporate-level strategic plans deal with issues such as the types of businesses in which ITT should be, overall financial performance and dividend policy of the corporation, the allocation of corporate capital to individual business units, social responsibility, and stockholder relations.

Business-Level Strategic Planning

A second level of strategic planning takes place in individual business units, an example of which would be Sheraton Hotels within ITT. Strategy at this level deals concretely with how best to compete in a particular market area. For example, although Sheraton competes in the lodging industry, it has chosen to limit its activities to only certain market segments within the total lodging market and not to compete in all submarkets of the lodging industry. Examples of strategic decisions on the part of Sheraton would include determining markets in which to compete, geographic expansion plans, and franchising strategy. Since the industry has already been chosen (that is, the lodging industry), business-level strategic managers "strive to identify and secure the most promising market segment. This market segment is the fairly unique piece of the total market that the business can claim and defend because of competitive advantage" (Pearce and Robinson 1988, 8). Such a business-level strategy, for example, led Holiday Inns, during the 1950s and 1960s, to develop a network of roadside inns catering primarily to individual business travelers and families traveling by automobile. Everything about these motels—their location, architecture, services, amenities, financing, reservation system, and management were designed with one thought in mind: to capture and defend a significant share of that segment of the lodging market. Each hotel company, by its business-level strategic decisions, tries to do the same thing.

Functional Level Strategic Planning

The next level of strategic planning takes place at the functional level. Functional level strategic planning is done by the vice-presidents at Sheraton who oversee the operations, marketing, accounting, personnel, and food and beverage functions of the company's individual hotels. Functional level managers carry out, or implement, the business level strategies of the firm. Business level strategies often have a multiple year time frame (for example, it might take three to four years to develop twenty new hotels in major markets west of the Mississippi). Functional level strategies are usually characterized by annual objectives and short-term strategies (for example, next year's advertising budget, installation of a new national 800-number reservation system, or development of a quality assurance program).

Strategic Planning and the Individual Hotel

Most of the strategic planning done at the business and the functional levels is intended to impact the individual hotels within a hotel company. Profits are made and losses incurred at the individual hotel level. Individual hotels are the unique businesses upon whose collective health the overall health of the company relies. In short, the individual hotel within a hotel company is the critical point of action around which all other activities revolve. Because of this, certain aspects of how they fit into the management and planning hierarchy of a company must be discussed (Olsen and Dev 1989).

Reference to Figure 3-1 makes it clear that the individual hotel is at the bottom of both the managerial and the strategic planning hierarchy of a hotel company. As such, many strategic decisions have already been made at both the business and the functional levels that, in effect, limit the flexibility of strategic decision making at the hotel level. Decisions regarding which market segments the company seeks to serve have already been made at the business level, as have basic plans for geographic growth. At the functional level, even more decisions affecting individual hotels have already been made. Examples included the exact location, architecture, size, and basic facilities of each hotel. Additionally, functional strategic decisions may have been made concerning specific financial control and reporting procedures, companywide personnel policies, energy conservation programs, and companywide advertising and marketing programs.[1]

One might be led to conclude that the managers of individual hotels have little discretion with regard to strategic issues; that the managers of individual hotels are responsible only for efficiently operating their hotel in accordance with the strategic plans imposed above. This is often true for limited service budget motels and hotels. However, as a hotel increases in size and complexity, the amount of strategic planning and decision making that occurs at the local level also increases.

In one sense the GM of a hotel is at the bottom of the managerial hierarchy of a hotel company. On the other hand, a GM is also at the top of the management hierarchy of a sizable business that could employ over a thousand workers and generate tens of millions of dollars in annual revenues. The GM of a medium-sized to large hotel has reporting to him or her functional specialists in most of the same areas as the functional corporate vice-presidents shown in Figure 3-1. Since an individual hotel is itself a profit center, the GM can be thought of as its CEO. So within the context of the broad business-level and functional level strategic plans set by the company, individual managers of most medium-sized and larger hotels have ample opportunity to engage in a variety of strategic decisions affecting the profitability of their hotels. The nature and scope of hotel-level strategic planning will be discussed in detail in Chapter Four.

THE STRATEGIC PLANNING PROCESS

A hotel's strategic plan is the specific actions or initiatives it intends to follow in order to compete. The plan will include its strategies regarding pricing, service levels, personnel, renovations, marketing, and a variety of other issues that affect its competitive position. Once developed, a strategic plan may remain in place for some time or, depending on circumstances, could be revised quite often. In either case, a clear distinction must be

---

[1]The extent to which strategic decisions are made at the functional or business level will, of course, vary from company to company. In some cases fairly tight control will be imposed from above. The author is familiar with one case where extremely elaborate instructions were issued from corporate headquarters regarding the precise use of the corporate logo throughout each hotel. In other companies, the local management at each hotel will be given wider authority with regard to strategic decision making.

made between the strategic plan itself and the process a hotel follows to develop a strategic plan—the strategic planning process rather than the specific strategies. Strategies differ with circumstances so what's good strategy for one hotel may be bad for another. By understanding process, one will be able to develop a strategic plan to fit whatever circumstances a hotel faces.

Overview of the Strategic Planning Process

The strategic planning process can be divided into four basic steps:

1. Setting organizational goals and objectives,
2. Choosing the proper strategic plan,
3. Implementing a strategic plan, and
4. Evaluating the strategic plan.

Figure 3-2 shows the steps involved in the strategic planning process and the manner in which each step relates to the other.

Note in Figure 3-2 that there is a left to right flow of the dark arrows from goal setting to strategy formulating to implementing and finally to evaluating of results. There is, of course, a straightforward and powerful logic involved here. Setting goals and objectives is the first step in the strategic planning process. Goals give purpose to activity. There is an old saying, "If you don't know where you are going you will never know when you get there." Setting goals resolves this dilemma by defining what success

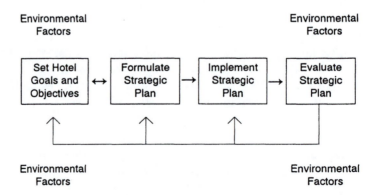

FIGURE 3-2.   The Strategic Planning Process in Hotels

is! Setting organizational goals must also precede the formulation of specific strategic plans because, to some degree, the choice of strategy depends on a firm's goals and objectives. Another expression captures the nature of this argument: "If you don't know where you are going, any road will take you there." Note in Figure 3-2 that the goals and strategic options of a hotel are affected by external factors as well as internal conditions. That is to say, external and internal circumstances limit the range of actions that can practically be taken by a hotel. It can happen that the strategic choices open to a hotel will not allow it to achieve certain goals and objectives. For example, a goal to increase room revenues by 10 percent next year may be impossible to achieve in light of new competition and a recession in the local economy. There is no strategy the hotel can follow to achieve that particular objective. Therefore, there exists a two-way interaction between goal setting and the choice of a strategic plan: (1) strategic plans must be chosen in such a way as to meet goals and objectives, but (2) the limitations that circumstances place on strategic options must be taken into consideration when setting goals and objectives. This two-way interaction between goal setting and strategy formulation is indicated in Figure 3-2 by the two-headed arrow between the squares representing these two steps in the strategic planning process.

Once a hotel chooses an overall, or grand, strategic plan, it must be implemented. This requires formulating detailed long-term and annual objectives. It also requires operational strategies that follow from the grand strategy. At this point in the strategic planning process, much of the decision making and strategic thinking has been done and the actual work of implementing a strategic plan begins. It is during this phase that a hotel formulates annual budgets and detailed action plans. Detailed action plans and budgets are the guideposts that direct a hotel's activities; action plans are the final result of strategic planning. A hotel's success or failure for the next quarter or year depends on successfully meeting the objectives and budgets it has set for itself through the strategic planning process.

In real life, of course, things do not always go according to plan. Thus, an important part of the strategic planning process is evaluation. Evaluation is an ongoing activity where comparisons are made between anticipated and actual outcomes. An important aspect of evaluation is management's ability to take corrective actions to keep the hotel moving toward its goals and objectives. Note in Figure 3-2 that arrows from the evaluation step of the strategic planning process return back to each of the other three major steps. It's never possible to predict the future with certainty: conditions in the local economy change, thus invalidating basic assumptions—a new hotel service is not well received by guests, labor costs increase because minimum wages go up. Thus, changes may be needed in operating strategies, sometimes grand strategies need to be rethought, and it can even happen that basic goals and objectives must be reviewed as underlying conditions change. The importance of the evaluation step is that it provides feedback to the other parts of the strategic planning process. Feedback gives management the necessary information to take whatever corrective action is appropriate to the circumstances.

Strategic planning is not a management exercise that, once accomplished, remains in place for the life of a hotel. Although plans usually have a specific time frame, strategic planning is best thought of as an ongoing process. As action plans are completed, results are evaluated against objectives and corrective action, if necessary, is taken. As environmental conditions change, basic assumptions and strategies must be reassessed. Although it is possible for certain goals and strategies to remain unchanged for many years, strategies at the individual hotel level often must be reassessed and adjusted more frequently. Examples of strategy changes will be given in Chapter Four. The following discussion details the four major steps in the strategic planning process.

Setting Organizational Goals

The strategic planning process takes place throughout an organization's management hierarchy—from top management down to operational managers. Running parallel to a business's organizational hierarchy are the types of goals that it usually sets. A business's goals can be divided into *official goals*, *operative goals*, and *operational goals* (Aldag and Stearns 1987). As Table 3-1 shows, official goals are made by top management, tend to be somewhat abstract, and are open-ended with regard to their completion. Official goals often form an important part of a company's mission statement and are articulated throughout the company in its annual report and its policy manual.

A good example of official goals is the Hilton Hotel Corporation's Corporate Mission Statement, which is reproduced in Exhibit 3-1. Note that much of Hilton's Corporate Mission deals in generalities. Hilton strives to be the "best" but does not define what constitutes being the best. Hilton also strives to "improve," to "prosper," to provide "superior" quality, to charge "fair" prices, to make an unspecified level of "profits," to be "innovative" and also "efficient."

At first glance official goals like Hilton's might seem to be nothing more

TABLE 3-1.   Organizational Goals in the Management Hierarchy

Goal Type	Made By	Degree of Abstraction	Time for Completion
Official	Top Management	Abstract	Long Run
Operative	Middle Management	Mixed	Intermediate
Operational	Operational Management	Concrete	Short Run

Hilton's Corporate Mission

To be recognized as the world's best first-class hotel organization, to constantly strive to improve, allowing us to prosper as a business for the benefit of our shareholders, our guests, and our employees.

Fundamental to the success of our mission are these values:

People

Our most important asset. Involvement, teamwork, and commitment are the values that govern their work.

Product

Our programs, services, and facilities. They must be designed and operated with superior quality, to satisfy the needs and desires of our guests.

Profit

The ultimate measure of our success—the gauge for how well and how efficiently we serve our guests. Profits are required for us to survive and grow.

With these values come certain guiding principles:

Quality Comes First

The quality of our product and service creates guest satisfaction, our No. 1 priority.

Value

Our guests deserve quality products at a fair price. That is how to build business.

Continuous Improvement

Never standing on past accomplishments, but always striving—through innovation—to improve our product and service, to increase our efficiency, and profitability.

Teamwork

A tradition at Hilton that gets things done . . . now!

Integrity

We will never compromise our code of conduct—we will be socially responsible—we are committed to Hilton's high standards of fairness and integrity.

EXHIBIT 3-1.

than a public relations statement that bears little relation to how a company is actually managed. This need not be the case. The author once asked a top Hilton GM to describe his job. The first thing he did was to hand me a copy of Hilton's Corporate Mission and say that his job was to carry out and achieve the goals set forth in it! A closer look reveals that this Mission

Statement says quite a bit about Hilton as a company and provides vital information to its managers regarding what the company considers important. To start with, Hilton strives to be "the world's best" hotel company. That's quite a lofty goal, no matter how being the world's best is measured. Striving to be the world's best sets high performance standards and acts as a motivating incentive for all who work for Hilton. Hilton's Mission Statement is also quite specific with regard to what it considers important when it speaks of values. Only three things are listed: (1) involved, committed employees who can work as a team, (2) superior quality facilities and services, and (3) profits for survival, growth, and as a measure of the company's success. Any number of different values could have been stated but were not. Hilton could, for example, value being the largest hotel company in the world; it could have included a statement regarding promotion from within; or that it valued expansion into nonlodging but hospitality-related businesses. The three it chose are meant to be a guide for its executives and managers.

Hilton's Mission Statement goes on to enumerate five guiding principles that are meant to aid its executives, managers, and employees in the execution of their jobs. It's clear that guest satisfaction, through the provision of quality products and services, takes precedence over all other aspects of the business. In fact, guest satisfaction is specifically called "our No. 1 priority." This is a clear and powerful guideline for Hilton managers; it says that, first and foremost, quality standards will be maintained. It says that when in doubt always come down on the side of maintaining superior product and service quality because that is what creates guest satisfaction. The other guiding principles are also intended to aid Hilton's people with their responsibilities. For example, teamwork is again stressed as it is under values, but this time an action-oriented imperative is added. Hilton expects "that things get done . . . now!" It's pretty clear that indecision or delay will not be tolerated and that deadlines had better be met; in fact, it's considered a "tradition" at Hilton. Official goals, therefore, can be of considerable value to an organization because they clarify what the organization is about, what it values, and the guiding principles that should be followed by its management and staff.

Official goals are usually open-ended and imprecise. For example, a goal of continually improving profits and efficiency does not tell us what level of improvement is acceptable, nor do we know over what period of time this improvement should be measured. Operative goals are meant to be more specific and closed-ended and to relate directly to the operating policies of the organization. Peter Drucker (1954, 63) lists eight specific operative goals found in most organizations: market standing; innovation; productivity; physical and financial resources; profitability; management performance and development; worker performance and attitude; and public responsibility. Operative goals are much more concrete and specific

Staffing a major hotel like The New Orleans Hilton Riverside and Towers is a challenging job.

Courtesy: Hilton Hotel Riverside and Towers New Orleans

than official goals. Here are some examples of operative goals: deciding to cater to a new travel market segment (that is, senior citizens), developing and testing a new phone system for the company's hotels, increasing return on investment of company-owned hotels, constructing additional meeting rooms at certain convention hotels, and initiating a safety training program in all company hotels. Operative goals are usually specified on an annual basis and are specific in that individual projects and initiatives are identified. Based on an analysis of external and internal factors, management makes choices that result in specific action plans that in turn form the basis for operative goals.

Still, there is a lack of completeness to operative goals. It is operational goals that provide the needed completeness by including detailed and specific performance criteria, completion times, and action steps for each operative goal. An operational goal for breaking into the senior citizen travel market might read something like this: "To increase senior citizen room-nights by 15 percent next year, the company will institute a senior citizen 10 percent room-rate discount program, hire two new sales representatives to call on tour wholesalers who specialize in this market, and initiate a $500,000 advertising campaign aimed specifically at senior citizens." Note how specific each of these goals is. Room-nights must increase by 15 percent, not 8 percent or 10 percent, if the goal is to be met. Room-rates will be discounted by exactly 10 percent. Exactly two, not one or three, new sales representatives will be hired and their duties are also outlined. Finally, the specific amount of $500,000 has been allocated for an advertising campaign. At the operational goals level, management is quite specific about how its initiatives will be carried out, as well as what constitutes success.

It's probably occurred to you while reading this section that much thought had to take place before operative and operational goals could be completely specified. The previous section discussed the two-way interaction between goal setting and the final choice of a strategic plan. An example of this interaction is that of an ambitious student who would like to set a goal of earning straight A's in school. At the same time, however, she must work twenty five hours per week to help with college costs. Because the option of not working is denied to her, study time is severely reduced. Thus, the initial goal of straight A's may have to be lowered given her limited set of strategic choices. With this relationship between goals and strategic choices in mind, the following section discusses the process of formulating a strategic plan.

Formulating a Strategic Plan

A strategic plan is based on an internal analysis of the business itself and an external analysis of the environment in which it operates. Figure 3-3 illustrates this process. The purpose of an internal analysis is to objectively profile the capabilities of the firm. One way to think of a company profile is to view it as a ledger listing the firm's strengths on one side and its weaknesses on the other. Various categories of strengths and weaknesses should be considered. A business's internal strengths might include financial stability, a particular management capability, and a cost advantage over its competitors. Internal weaknesses might include obsolete facilities, high employee turnover, the lack of a certain management capability, and high debt costs.

A straightforward approach to considering strengths and weaknesses is to organize them around the major functions of the business. For example,

FIGURE 3-3.   The Process of Formulating a Strategic Plan

a hotel company may consider its major functions to be marketing, accounting and finance, hotel operations, hotel development, personnel, and food and beverage. It would then develop a company profile of strengths and weaknesses within each of these functions (Tse 1988).

How does a company determine which factors to include as strengths? Are strengths everything a firm does well (that is, competencies)? A list of competencies would tend to become long and unfocused. Instead, firms should develop relatively short lists of strengths based on their importance to influence the competitive environment. A strength should be judged in relation to its ability to improve a firm's competitive position. A strength gives a business some kind of competitive advantage. For example, a professionally competent executive chef should only be listed as a hotel's strength if his or her presence allows the hotel to gain an advantage over its competitors. On the other hand, a weakness is something that a firm does poorly that could be a competitive disadvantage. It can also be something that a firm is incapable of doing that its competitors can do (Haywood 1986).

Finally, a listing of strengths and weaknesses should be limited to those key factors that determine success or failure in a particular business. All aspects of what a hotel company or an individual hotel does are not equally important in its competitive struggle. Internal strengths and weaknesses should be limited to those areas that are critical to success or failure in the hotel business.

A firm's strategy must be based on external as well as internal factors. Changes in the external environment, such as the development of interstate highways during the 1960s, had a profound effect on the lodging industry. As we know, Holiday Inns devised a strategy based in part on this development and became the largest lodging company in the world as a result. At the local level, construction of a new competing hotel is a common example of an external change that might affect the strategy of an existing hotel. The external environment can be divided into two parts: the remote environment and the operating environment.

The remote environment consists of factors that may affect a firm but over which it has no control. These factors include economic, social, political, and technological developments. Remote factors such as an economic expansion or recession, deregulation of the airline industry, increased female business travel, breakthroughs in teleconferencing technologies, and higher gasoline prices will, in varying degrees, affect the hotel business. Understanding and anticipating such trends plays a role in a firm's ultimate choice of strategies.

The operating environment of a firm relates to factors such as competitive forces in its industry, its customers, suppliers, creditors, and the labor market in which it operates (Porter 1980). Factors in the operating environment directly influence how a business operates, and changes in these factors have an immediate impact on the firm. Also, actions of the firm may have an impact on its operating environment where they would have none on its remote environment.

Of particular importance to a hotel's strategic planning are competitive forces, customers, and labor markets. Assessing a hotel's competitive position requires analysis of factors such as location, market share, pricing, age and quality of facilities, competitor's actions, service levels, and marketing strategies. The end result of this exercise is a *competitive profile* of one hotel relative to its competition.

A customer profile is an indispensable aid to a hotel and an integral part of its operating environment. Hotels, like all businesses, need to know as much as possible about their customers. As a beginning, guests are often classified into market segments based on their travel motives. Such classifications are important because the advertising and sales methods used to attract each category of guest varies greatly as does the services and facilities required by each. A simple classification would be individual transient guests traveling for business; groups of guests on business; individual transient guests traveling for pleasure; groups traveling for pleasure; and other. Of course, further subdivision of these broad market segments is sometimes useful. For example, the group, business market, may be further subdivided into conventions and business meetings. In turn, the convention market may be subdivided into business, professional, educational, fraternal, and special interest groups. The object of each further subdivision is to better understand the needs and wants of specific groups of customers that they can be marketed to and served more efficiently.

Guests are also classified according to geographic, demographic, buying behavior and sometimes even personality and life-style characteristics. A geographic classification divides guests in terms of their place of residence. It is indispensable to a well-planned sales and advertising campaign. Demographic information includes age, sex, income, family size, education, and occupation. It is most akin to census-type information and is commonly used to differentiate one type of customer from another. Buying behavior includes such factors as frequency of stay, method of making a reservation (that is, through a travel agent, direct call to hotel, through a reservation system, part of a package), and whether the guest has responded to a special promotion such as reduced weekend rates. Finally, personality and life-style characteristics can be useful in understanding buying behavior. Traits, such as leisure-time activities, compulsiveness, gregariousness, and status needs can be important clues to the kinds of services and amenities guests seek while traveling. The importance of characteristics, especially to resort hotels, is fairly obvious. The trend toward elaborate hotel fitness centers, even in central city transient hotels, is an example of a response to a rather pervasive health and fitness-oriented life-style change.

A view of The Ritz-Carlton Buckhead lap pool in their Swimming and Fitness Center.

Courtesy: The Ritz-Carlton Hotel Company

The reason for developing a company profile and conducting an external analysis is to put a hotel in a position to:

1 Analyze its internal Strengths and Weaknesses, and
2. Analyze its external Opportunities and Threats.

The process of analyzing internal *Strengths* and *Weaknesses* and external *Opportunities* and *Threats* is referred to as SWOT analysis. SWOT analysis allows a business to systematically study its options as part of the process of clarifying the strategic choices open to it. Pearce and Robinson (1988, 292–93) define the four SWOT variables as follows:

Strengths—A resource, skill, or other advantage relative to competitors and the needs of the markets a firm serves or anticipates serving.
Weaknesses—A limitation or deficiency in resources, skills, and capabilities that seriously impede effective performance.
Opportunities—A major, favorable opportunity in a firm's environment.
Threats—A major, unfavorable situation in a firm's environment.

SWOT analysis provides a systematic way of focusing on a firm's situation. Analyzing external opportunities and threats is a way to clarify and understand what a firm is really facing. Similarly, analyzing internal strengths and weaknesses, especially in light of external opportunities and threats, helps bring into focus the strategic choices open to a firm. Most businesses face both external threats and opportunities. At the same time, they usually possess some internal strengths and have some internal weaknesses. The process of classifying each of these four factors and analyzing how they relate to each other helps the strategist reach conclusions about whether the firm is operating from a position of relative strength or relative weakness and, in consequence, what types of strategies are most appropriate.

A good way to understand SWOT analysis is to depict these four factors in a diagram such as that shown in Figure 3-4. The vertical axis of the SWOT diagram portrays major external opportunities at the top and threats at the bottom. Likewise, the horizontal axis depicts internal weaknesses on the left and internal strengths on the right. These two axes divide Figure 3-4 into four separate quadrants. Quadrant one is, of course, ideal. A firm faces major external opportunities and, at the same time, possesses substantial internal strengths. Such a favorable situation calls for an aggressive expansion strategy oriented toward growth. Consider an established and profitable convention hotel located near a large convention center. If the convention center announced plans for a major expansion, the hotel will likely consider an aggressive strategy that might include a substantial in-

Major External Opportunities

Quadrant two
(Turnaround)

Quadrant one
(Aggressive expansion)

Internal
Weaknesses

Internal
Strengths

Quadrant three
(Retrenchment)

Quadrant four
(Diversification)

Major External Threats

FIGURE 3-4.   SWOT Diagram

crease in rooms and facilities in anticipation of more convention business. Quadrant two depicts a situation where a firm sees major external opportunities but is saddled with internal weaknesses that prevent it from capitalizing on them. In such a case a business must concentrate on overcoming its internal deficiencies in order to take advantage of external opportunities. This case warrants an internal *turnaround* strategy. An example would be a hotel that is missing out on a rapidly growing convention market because of weaknesses in its banquet and catering department. Its strategy must be to first bolster this department and then aggressively pursue the major market opportunity open to it (Prevette and Giudice 1989).

In Quadrants three and four a business faces major external threats. In Quadrant four, however, it possesses substantial internal strengths with which to meet its challenge. For example, a hotel may lose a major part of its transient business market to a new competitor with a better location. If this hotel's strength includes a strong and innovative sales and marketing department, it might decide to pursue an aggressive strategy of developing new markets to replace the one it has lost. Quadrant three confronts the firm with a difficult set of circumstances. It not only faces a severe external threat but, at the same time, possesses internal weaknesses that make the external problem all the more serious. Clearly a firm must adopt a defensive strategy in such circumstances. One such strategy, known as retrenchment, often results in belt-tightening and cost reduction. Management feels the firm can survive (or else a strategy to sell the business, or its liquidation, would be appropriate) but only if costs are cut. At the same time, most firms also initiate a strategy intended to overcome the critical internal weaknesses that contributed to its predicament. Desperate times often call for desperate measures; retrenchment and turnaround strategies usually result in drastic cost cutting, employee layoffs, and replacement of key executives as the business struggles to survive. An older hotel, whose physical and service standards have slipped over time, may face a crisis situation when new hotels are built that compete directly for the same market segments. The strategic response is often to bring in a new GM and department heads who drastically cut costs in an attempt to keep the hotel afloat financially until turnaround strategies can be implemented.

Strategy Implementation

Techniques like SWOT analysis are useful for choosing the most appropriate strategy (Tse 1988). It takes more than a strategy, however, to be successful; plans must be executed and results must be monitored and controled. A useful way to view strategy implementation is shown in Figure 3-5 which depicts plans being developed as a consequence of strategy formulation and goal setting (Aldag and Stearns 1987, 256). Strategic plans are implemented through *action plans, operating plans*, and *standing plans*.

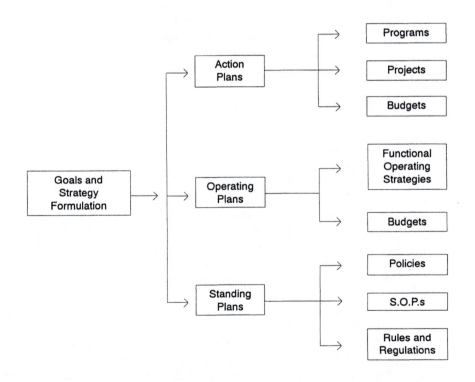

FIGURE 3-5   How Plans Follow Goals and Strategy

Action plans are detailed, step-by-step procedures that are necessary to meet the operational goals of a business. A *program* is an action plan that coordinates a variety of activities toward a common goal. A hotel's strategy might include a decision to develop a program to improve employee–guest contact skills. The entire program is to be the responsibility of the resident manager. Such a program might entail a number of activities. For example, the personnel department may be asked to develop an in-house training film on guest courtesy. Another activity might be a hotel fact sheet of guest services. Those responsible for the film and the fact sheet are involved in specific *projects* that are more limited in scope than the overall action program. This particular program, and the individual projects that are part of it, are part of an overall strategic plan to improve guest satisfaction, repeat business and hotel occupancy. An action plan must contain clearly stated goals, detailed steps, assignment of individual responsibility, time schedules, and budgets. Finally, a well-thought-out action plan will include a method for measuring results (Shriver 1988).

Action plans are usually associated with special nonrecurring projects. However, much of the activity of a hotel is routine. Thus, an important part of managing a hotel is the development of annual *operating plans* that set goals for the day-by-day and month-by-month management of the business. This is usually accomplished by the process of developing *annual operating budgets* and *functional operating strategies* to guide the various departments of a hotel. Each department will usually have annual functional strategies along with its annual operating budget, which give direction to its activities throughout the year. The food and beverage department may have adopted an annual budget that includes a 3 percent reduction in food costs. Its functional strategies to accomplish this might include more competitive bids from food vendors; greater controls over receiving, storing, and issuing to cut down on pilferage; and additional training in portion control for food production workers. Hotels measure their financial results on an annual basis. In consequence, they prepare annual budgets prior to the beginning of each fiscal year. These annual operating budgets, and the functional operating strategies and detailed action plans a hotel makes, constitute what it wishes to accomplish in the coming year. Meeting budget goals and successfully accomplishing action and operating plans define success for most hotels.

In any ongoing business there are numerous situations that occur over and over again that can be handled in a routine, standard fashion. *Standing plans* are developed to ensure uniform treatment of routine matters. Standing plans may be further divided into *policies, standard operating procedures*, and *rules and regulations*.

Policies are general guidelines for managerial decision making. For example, a policy that hotel employees caught fighting or stealing will be dismissed, regardless of years of service, is intended to relieve managers of discretion in an area where the company has already established a policy. Another example would be a hotel's policy to pay for two nights lodging at comparable accommodations if a guest with a confirmed reservation cannot be accommodated.

Standard operating procedures (SOPs) are similar to policies except that they usually cover more detailed and/or procedural matters. Standard operating procedures might include the steps taken in response to a guest complaint, the procedures to follow in case of an accident or when a guest cannot pay his bill. Finally, rules and regulations refer to specifically allowed or prohibited behavior. Examples would include designated nonsmoking areas, personal hygiene requirements of food servers, prohibitions regarding the use of alcohol or drugs, and rules regarding lunch and rest breaks.

Evaluating the Strategic Plan

The final step in the strategic planning process is control and feedback. If the preceding steps are properly performed (that is, if goals are properly set), if strategies are intelligently chosen, and if implementation steps and budgets are well planned and documented, the control step is made easier. Remember that a strategic plan deals with how a firm competes in its chosen market. Thus, control must be concerned both with monitoring conditions in the external environment as well as the internal actions and initiatives a business undertakes to implement its strategic plan. Monitoring environmental factors means keeping track of developments in the remote and the operating environments to ensure that the factors upon which a strategic plan is based have not changed. A hotel's marketing strategy will, for example, be based in part on local economic conditions. As local economic conditions change strategies may also have to change.

Action and operating plans must be controled. The most obvious and, in many ways, effective method to do this is through controling budgets. As Figure 3-5 showed, budgets are prepared for operating plans and for action plans. Budgets reflect how resources will be used. Budgets also anticipate operating results in terms of revenues and costs. Finally, since budgets "embody" action and operating plans, they reflect how well these plans have been implemented. Budget reviews do more than just ensure that a department is staying within its budget. Reviews also probe into how well operating and action plans are being implemented. This is particularly true when budget projections are not being met.

An effective way to exercise control over operations is to identify the *key success factors* of a business and to keep particularly close track of them. Curtis Samuels refers to success factors as the "key indicators of the hotel business." There are, of course, numerous ratios and statistics that hotel executives regularly review to assess their hotel's progress: percent occupancy, average room-rate, percent double occupancy, labor and food costs, food and beverage revenues per occupied room, and profit before fixed changes are all examples of operating statistics and ratios that are closely watched. Each represents a key success factor for most hotels. Additionally, the particular strategic plan a hotel is following may require it to track other, less traditional, success factors. A success factor might be the percentage of female guests staying in a hotel because of a strategy to penetrate this growing market; the average productivity of food preparation workers might be a success factor because of a hotel's strategy to redesign and reequip its kitchen areas; average room-rates for rooms booked through the hotel's reservation system could be a key factor that tracks the success of an action project to train reservationists to sell higher priced rooms first. The point is that thought must be given to the choice of variables that management seeks to control *based on its strategic plans*. It should also be noted that outstanding hotels measure a variety of variables in addition to traditional financial and operating statistics. There is an adage in business that "you can control only what you measure"; so deciding what to measure is an important part of the strategic management process.

Things rarely go completely according to plan. A well-conceived control process gives managers the ability not only to monitor but also take action when things are not going according to plan. Thus, in Figure 3-2, the evaluation phase of the strategic planning process has arrows from it returning to the other three major steps in the process, reflecting that evaluation and feedback may result in alterations to goals, plans, and implementation (Haywood 1988).

The Time Horizon of Strategic Planning

A final note regarding strategic planning deals with time. How frequently should strategic planning take place and how far into the future should plans be made? Regarding planning frequency, firms in very stable environments may be able to operate with the same basic strategic plan for years. On the other hand, any major change in a firm's external environment or internal profile will usually necessitate a thorough review of its strategic plans. Examples of changing external factors that would call for review of a hotel's strategic plan would be changing competitive forces in the form of additional competition, the location of major new industries in the area, increased attempts at employee unionization, the development of new visitor attractions in the area, and technological advances in telecommunications that might affect how guests make reservations. Internal factors that would call for a reassessment of strategy would include selling a hotel to new owners, unanticipated key management personnel turnover, building and equipment aging and obsolescence, or an unexpected deterioration in employee productivity. Any of these changes, either external or internal, bring into question past assumptions and strategies. It would be a mistake for management to continue with a "business as usual" attitude. Conditions have changed, and it's time to reassess the situation. It may be that a new strategy is in order.

Finally, how far into the future do businesses usually plan? The strategic planning time horizon generally varies with the level within the organization where plans are being made. The higher within an organization, the longer into the future plans are made. As a general rule, top management is usually involved in *long-range* strategic planning, which might look five or more years into the future (Morrison 1989). Middle managers are responsible for implementing top management plans. Middle managers deal with *intermediate range* planning horizons ranging from one to three years. First-line operational managers are concerned with *short-range* plans of from less than a year to two to three years. The individual hotel GM is a first-line operational manager in the management hierarchy of a hotel company. Thus, the planning horizon at this level is typically restricted to one to three years, with much of it focused on annual plans.

CONCLUSION

People who don't learn and grow from their experiences are usually ineffective managers. They learn one way of doing things during their early, formative years and continue doing things the same way throughout their careers. It's often said of older executives with this failing that they really don't have thirty years of business experience; they have one year of experience repeated thirty times! Although it's sad to accuse someone of standing still intellectually for thirty years, it's a very human failing. Who among us would not find it difficult to change a business strategy that had proven to be successful over a number of years? Wouldn't it be natural just to try harder at what had always worked in the past? Of course it would. It turns out that the process of change and adaptation in business is something of a paradox. The world may be experiencing accelerated change, but people often resist change with all their might. The fact is, change is difficult, both for individuals and for businesses.

Strategic planning can be thought of as a method of coping with the problem of and the necessity for businesses to adapt to changing conditions. The strategic planning process forces businesses to make decisions and take actions that result in competitive strategies designed to achieve the business' goals and objectives. Strategic decisions are the really big, fundamental decisions a business must make, such as (1) What will we do and for whom will we do it, (2) what goals do we want to achieve, and (3) how are we going to achieve these goals?

Within large businesses, strategic planning takes place at the corporate, business, and functional level. While individual hotels are functional units at the bottom of the corporate organization chart, hotels are also the individual profit centers on which the success or failure of the entire business depends. Even though many strategic decisions have already been made at the business unit level, there are a variety of hotel-level strategic decisions that are made by hotel GMs that have a great affect on the hotel's profitability.

Strategic planning is an interactive process in which a business sets its goals and objectives, analyzes its internal strengths and weaknesses, assesses its external environment, and chooses the most appropriate strategic plan. A planning technique called SWOT analysis is a method by which a business analyzes its internal strengths and weaknesses as well as its external opportunities and threats in order to clarify exactly what it faces. The result of a SWOT analysis helps a firm decide if its strategy should be aggressive and expansionary or defensive and cautious, depending on the combination of external forces and internal conditions.

Once the most appropriate business strategy is chosen, it must be implemented at the functional level by a series of action plans, operating plans, budgets, and standing plans. It is through these detailed steps and procedures that a business finally implements its strategy. As the process of "working the plan" takes place, management must evaluate the results of their strategic decisions and operational plans in light of the official, operative, and operational goals they have set. This important evaluation step in strategic management is accomplished by careful review of budgets and close attention to the key success factors of the business. Evaluation allows for adjustments in action plans, strategies, or even goals and objectives, if results and conditions so warrant.

Of course, a strategic plan may continue in place for quite some time. On the other hand, major changes in the external environment or in internal conditions can easily bring into question the assumptions on which businesses' strategic decisions are based. Whenever this happens it becomes necessary to begin again the strategic planning process. In fact, successful businesses are in a way continually testing the validity of their current strategic plans through the process of evaluating action and operating plans against operative and operational goals. These companies manage strategically by assessing plans and actions based on the changing realities of the external environment, the circumstances they find within the firm, and their overriding goals and objectives. Strategic planning gives businesses and managers a way to accept and to adapt to change. It keeps management from falling victim to repeating one year's experience thirty times.

This chapter has been a brief overview of the strategic planning process. Although examples from hotels have been used to illustrate certain points, the treatment was intentionally broad in order to present the basics of strategic planning. With this general background, Chapter four will focus on strategic planning in individual hotels.

REFERENCES

Aldag, Raymond J. and Timothy M. Stearns. 1987. *Management*. Cincinnati: South-Western Publishing Co.

Drucker, Peter F. 1954. *The Practice of Management*. New York: Harper & Row, Publishers.

Haywood, K. Michael. Nov. 1986. "Scouting Competition For Survival and Success: 'Putting The Book' on Your Competition is a Sound Business Strategy." *Cornell Hotel and Restaurant Administration Quarterly* 27:80ff.

Haywood, K. Michael. Fall 1988. "Managing Strategic Change." *FIU Hospitality Review* 6(2):1–7.

Morrison, Jerry. June 1989. "Long-Range Plan: A Critical Need: Resorts Must Project Programs over 3 to 5 Years." *Hotel & Resort Industry* 12(6):35–39.

Olsen, Michael D. and Chekitan S. Dev. 1989. "Environmental Uncertainty, Business Strategy, and Financial Performance: A Empirical Study of the U.S. Lodging Industry." *Hospitality Education & Research Journal* 13(3):171–186.

Pearce, John A., II and Richard B. Robinson, Jr. 1988. *Strategic Management*. Homewood, Il.: Richard D. Irwin, Inc.

Porter, Michael E. 1980. *Competitive Strategy: Techniques for Analyzing Industries and Competitors*. New York: Free Press.

Prevette, L. K. and Joseph Giudice. November 1989. "Anatomy of a Turnaround: The Los Angeles Biltmore." *The Cornell Hotel and Restaurant Administration Quarterly*: 30–35.

Shriver, Stephen J. October 1988. "Operations Planning: It's Not Just for Management Anymore." *Lodging*: 34–38.

Tse, Eliza Ching-Yick. 1988. "Defining Corporate Strengths and Weaknesses:Is It Essential for Successful Strategy Implementation?" *Hospitality Education & Research Journal* 12(2):57–72.

QUESTIONS

3-1. What specific dimensions distinguish strategic issues from other issues in a hotel?

3-2. What are the differences between corporate, business, and functional level strategic planning?

3-3. What kind of strategic planning goes on at the individual hotel level?

3-4. Describe the major steps a hotel should follow in the strategic planning process.

3-5. Develop a complete set of organizational goals (official, operative, and operational) for the luxury guest house in San Francisco that you have just purchased.

3-6. Visit the GM of a hotel in your community. Get the manager to agree to let you conduct a brief SWOT analysis of his or her hotel. Make a report of your findings.

3-7. Describe some of the various strategic choices open to an individual hotel in each of the four quadrants of a SWOT diagram.

3-8. Distinguish between strategic plans, action plans, operating plans, and standing plans.

CHAPTER 4

Planning in Hotels

The previous chapter discussed how businesses plan strategically, touching briefly on all organizational levels within the firm. This chapter concentrates on only one level—the individual hotel. This chapter begins by examining the business and organizational context in which planning at the individual hotel level takes place.

THE HOTEL PLANNING CONTEXT

The Scope of Hotel Planning

It was pointed out in Chapter Three that individual hotels are often part of larger hotel chains, consequently certain strategic decisions have already been made at higher levels in the management hierarchy. It was noted, however, that there is still considerable latitude for strategic planning and decision making for midsized and larger hotels. There are two fundamental reasons for this. The first is that local conditions surrounding individual hotels will often vary widely across the country. Conditions can also vary within a small geographic area (Dev 1989). For example, the circumstances faced by the Hyatt Hotel at O'Hare Airport in Chicago vary considerably from those faced by the Hyatt's downtown Chicago property.

Some of the factors that vary from one hotel to another within the same hotel company include the hotel's size, age and physical condition, types of markets served, location advantage relative to its competitors, the degree of local unionization, differences in local economic conditions, differences in ownership structure, and differences in local labor markets. It should be clear that the strategies required in 1985 for a hotel in San Francisco, which was experiencing strong economic growth are very different from those

The Hyatt Regency O'Hare Airport, Chicago

Courtesy: Hyatt Hotels Corporation

needed for a "similar" hotel in Houston, which was in the midst of a severe business recession. Thus, differences in the local external environment necessitate that a certain amount of strategic planning take place at the individual hotel level.

The second reason why certain strategic decisions must be made at the individual hotel level relates to the organizational and operational complexity found among midsize and larger hotels, even within the same chain. Observation leads to the conclusion that there is a striking similarity of design and operation in all McDonald's Restaurants and most other fast-food stores. One could correctly conclude that managing one McDonald's store is probably very much like managing another. A high degree of operational standardization gives managers of these outlets very little discretion with regard to either *what* is done or *how* it is done. Similar observations of no-frills, economy motels, such as Motel 6 or Econolodge, would lead one to the same conclusion: management's primary task at the local operating level is to carry out corporate plans, procedures, rules, and regulations. Local management's job is to efficiently execute the corporate plan, and the chain's success is determined in large part by unit-level managers being able to execute the corporate plan efficiently.

However, as hotels grow in size things start to change. To begin with, they become more complex; more restaurants are added and possibly a lounge; nightclub, catering, and banquet functions expand; recreational facilities become common. Greater size also results in more diversity in architecture, design, and function. One could usually identify a McDonald's even if the name and golden arches were absent, but it would be difficult to identify a Westin, Sonesta, or Omni Hotel without its name over the door! As a hotel's size, complexity, and diversity increases, standardization becomes less possible (or desirable). Thus, local managers of complex hotels are responsible for developing and implementing many of the strategies and plans necessary for their business' success. Whereas managers of fast-food stores need only concern themselves with "doing things right" (that is, being efficient), managers of complex hotels must be concerned also with "doing the right things" (that is, being effective). We can put this into perspective by noting that the average successful McDonald's will have annual sales of about $900,000 and that a one hundred-unit budget motel will have sales of about $750,000. According to *Lodging-Hospitality Magazine* (1988), The Four Seasons Hotel in Washington, D.C., a medium-sized hotel with 197 rooms and suites, had revenues of $22.5 million in 1987; the Ritz-Carlton Hotel in Chicago, with 437 rooms, had revenues of $40 million; and the New York Hilton and Towers, with 2,100 rooms, had revenues of $120 million! It takes more than just following standard operating procedures to run businesses of that size.

The Hotel Planning Time Horizon

As discussed in Chapter Three, a strategy is a method of competing. Barring severe financial losses it can be assumed that a hotel will continue as an ongoing business for the foreseeable future. Thus, a certain amount of planning must take place simply to maintain a hotel's long-term viability. This constitutes one obvious type of strategic planning. Strategic planning at the hotel level does not concern itself with questions such as what businesses should the company be in, horizontal integration, vertical integration, or other business- or corporate-level strategies. With the exception of decisions to maintain building and equipment, the time horizon of most hotel-level strategic decisions is determined by factors in the markets in which it competes. The planning horizon could be as short as a few months if a hotel is revising its advertising and pricing strategies during its slow season. The planning horizon could be as long as a couple of years if the decision concerns building new meeting facilities to compete in the business meetings market. A six- to twelve-month time horizon might be required to perfect a new restaurant concept. Generally speaking, most strategic planning at the individual hotel level seldom exceeds a time horizon of more than a few years. This is not to say that GMs do not think about the long-term future of their hotels. They do indeed. What it does mean is that most of the *strategic decisions* that an individual hotel must make (that is, those that affect its competitive position) will seldom have time horizons of more than two years. In many cases the time horizon for individual hotels will be much less than that.

Here's what the excellent GMs felt about their hotel's planning horizon. At one extreme Frank Anderson described his time horizon as "ninety-day decision making." He did, of course, make many strategic decisions that affected the Napoleon House Hotel's longer term future. Frank, nevertheless, is making an important point. As an *operations manager* he expects to begin seeing the results of his decisions rather quickly. A similar sentiment was expressed by Jonathan Claiborne. When asked about his planning horizon, he said he liked to stay three to six months ahead of his staff. Henri LeSassier describes his job as being "visionary." To him, a visionary is one who plans six months to two years into the future. Though only 42, LeSassier has already managed three hotels. In his opinion, changing market conditions make it impossible to plan any more than two years into the future. William Scully, whose company is noted for its systematic planning, considers the "long-run" for a hotel to be a vision that looks three to five years down the road. These managers all expect their hotels to be viable businesses for many years to come. Bruce Warren, for example, spoke of his hotel's viability through the remainder of the century! Still, most of the strategic decisions they make have fairly short-run time horizons.

The GM's Role in Strategic Planning

A hotel GM plays a crucial role in strategic planning. Figure 4-1 shows the organizational structure both above and below the GM's level in many hotel companies. When a hotel is owned by a group of investors but managed by a hotel company, a GM has two bosses: his or her immediate hotel-company superior (often a regional V.P.) and the investor group that owns the hotel. It's not uncommon for a regional V.P. to be an experienced GM who, in addition to having responsibility for a number of hotels in the region, also manages a hotel. Regional V.P.s are, without a doubt, busy people. What with managing their own hotels, keeping tabs on the hotels under their supervision, and reporting up the corporate ladder to senior management, their days are full and their travel schedules are often extensive. Regional V.P.s don't have time to have in-depth knowledge about each hotel reporting to them or to have detailed knowledge about each

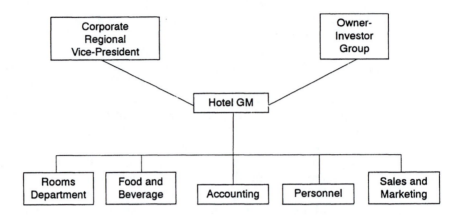

FIGURE 4-1.   Organization Structure Above and Below the GM

hotel's local environment. Regional V.P.s must, to be sure, approve major initiatives and strategies initiated by the GMs they supervise, but it is unlikely that regional V.P.s can initiate the strategic plans for the hotels under them.

Owners are usually real estate developers, successful business people, or large institutional investors such as insurance companies and pension funds. These groups usually have diverse business interests and often little detailed knowledge of hotel operations. For this reason, hotel companies contract with owners to manage their hotels. Often, investor groups cannot be expected to be the initiators of strategic operating plans. They are, to be sure, intimately involved in the strategic decision-making process but more often in a ratifying role rather than an initiating role.

Therefore the individual hotel's GM plays a central role in evaluating a hotel's strategic options. The local GM must understand and rationalize the goals of both the hotel company and the hotel's owners. The GM is given responsibility for the total business success of the hotel. Of all the hotel's executive staff, the GM brings the most hotel experience to the job of formulating a strategic plan. Strategic planning is a process that involves input from all of a hotel's key executives. A hotel's department heads, and especially its executive operating committee members, play a vital role in this process. These executives, however, are fully engaged with the day-to-day management of their divisions. It requires strong GM leadership to ensure that a hotel's department heads engage in meaningful hotelwide strategic planning.

This section and Chapter Three covered the general setting in which hotel strategic planning takes place and, with some exceptions, the central role played by the GM. It's possible that a strong-willed regional V.P. or owner will make all the strategic decisions for a hotel. Individual department heads can also exert influence disproportionate to their level in the organization. Strategic planning could end up being a *joint process* involving owners, regional V.P.s, division heads, and the GM. Finally, it is possible (though hardly desirable) for a hotel to operate without a strategic operating plan—in which case local management is relegated primarily to a role of day-to-day operational control.

To be effective, a strong and competent GM should take a leadership role in developing a hotel's strategic plan. Such a role, of course, includes full consultation and concurrence from upper management, owners, and key hotel department heads. A GM must be convincing and persistent when presenting ideas up the line. Regional V.P.s and owners will naturally question any and all plans, especially if ill conceived. Effective strategic planning also requires input and agreement from department heads. They must be part of the process if they are to truly "buy into" a hotel's plans.

The GM is at the center of the strategic planning process. He or she is the key to effective strategic planning at the individual hotel level. William Scully, of The Bourbon Hotel, works for a well-known hotel company that prides itself on its ability to develop and implement strategic plans. He feels that his company gives its individual hotel managers "all the responsibility they want and are capable of handling." That pretty well sums up the way effective, well-managed hotels operate and plan.

SETTING HOTEL GOALS AND OBJECTIVES

There are so many day-to-day things that must be done at a hotel: guests must be checked-in, rooms cleaned, meals cooked, phones answered. Each activity is an important part of a hotel's overriding goal of good guest service. However, the daily routine of doing the things that must get done is not the same as a hotel working toward a set of goals that everyone in a hotel understands and accepts. Ordinary hotels "go through the motions" of performing required duties. Excellent hotels seem to be doing much more than executing the various technical steps required to house and feed guests. The management and staff of excellent hotels understand why they are doing things in a certain way as well as for whom they are doing them.

James Heskett (1986) believes all successful service firms have developed what he calls a *strategic service vision*. Firms with a strategic service vision have: (1) a targeted market, (2) a well-defined service concept, (3) a focused operating strategy, and (4) a well-designed service delivery system. A targeted market means that a service business has clearly identified the group(s) of customers it intends to serve. Knowledge of one's customers means not only knowing who they are but also their needs. A well-defined service concept refers to how a business's services are perceived by its customers and its employees. Since many hotel services are intangible, guests' perceptions are important. A service concept is concerned with the way guests view the services a hotel provides and also with the way in which employees view the kind of services they are providing. To be effective, a hotel must be sure that both groups are in correspondence with regard to this vital question. A focused operating strategy sets forth the service elements that are of strategic importance for carrying out the service concept. Hotels, like people, cannot usually be good at everything. They therefore need to focus on the important things that they must do well. The management of a successful hotel has thought long and hard about which service elements must be stressed, where management's efforts should be directed, and which investments should be made. Finally, a well-designed service delivery system brings together all of the management procedures, systems, and physical facilities necessary to actually deliver key services to a specific target market. The service delivery system puts together people, facilities, and technology to carry out the hotel's strategic service vision.

Determining Markets to Serve

Each of the ten GMs stated that marketing considerations were among the factors they took into account in their strategic planning. Nine GMs made specific reference to having considered particular target markets in their strategic planning deliberations. Godfrey Bier sounded like he was quoting from a textbook when he said, "Choosing target markets is an essential element of planning." He also echoed Heskett by pointing out that a hotel must decide on a proper "service level" for each market segment it chooses to target. Jonathan Claiborne felt that good hotel planning results in "a product well positioned in the marketplace and a good service delivery system."

Frank Anderson talked at length about the "new marketing programs" he introduced to increase the number of markets The Napoleon House Hotel served. For William Scully of The Bourbon Hotel, it meant a detailed "revaluation of our marketing position." These GMs were talking about existing hotels, not new hotels in the development phase. The world is always changing, if not always in revolutionary ways then at least in evolutionary ways. Things do not stay the same in the lodging marketplace. Recessions and boom times affect business travel, as do changes in the tax laws that relate to business entertainment. New local industries emerge and older ones die, thus changing local travel patterns. Tourist destinations go through cycles of discovery, growth, saturation, and decline. Foreign travel increases or declines with currency fluctuations. New hotels are built, thus changing competitive conditions. For many reasons, the lodging market is far from static these days, and competition is keen. Effective hotel managers keep a close eye on market conditions and often begin their strategic planning with a thorough review of the markets their hotel is currently serving and those it may wish to serve in the future (Haywood 1986).

Setting Service and Quality Standards

When Lawrence Wagner took over as GM of The Regal Hotel, his review of the markets it was then serving revealed a startling possibility. It appeared to him that the hotel was targeting the right markets, but that it might be charging too little for its services. With some service upgrades and a renovation program beginning with guest rooms, the hotel could move up a notch relative to its competition. Lawrence felt that the guests The Regal Hotel was currently serving would be willing to pay higher room rates for improved services and upgraded quality. It turned out that he was right! With improved services and freshly renovated guest rooms he raised room rates and, low and behold, occupancy increased! This was all the more remarkable because it was accomplished during a period of falling citywide occupancies. Wagner had not changed the hotel's target markets. He just seemed to understand them better than his predecessor. He understood that his guests were willing and able to pay more for an enhanced level of service and quality. This story points out an important aspect of goal setting in hotels: determining service levels and quality standards. Knowing who a hotel intends to serve helps management determine the most appropriate service and quality levels and, as Heskett would put it, develop a focused operating strategy.

Two important variables that affect service levels and quality goals in hotels are: (1) staffing levels, and (2) capital expenditure decisions. There is a relationship, though not a direct one, between a hotel's level of guest service and its number of employees. Higher service levels often mean more employees (and, of course, higher labor costs). For example, the ultraluxurious Ritz-Carlton Hotel in downtown Chicago is reported to have 630 employees for its 437 guest rooms. On the other hand, The Roosevelt Hotel in New York City employs 500 people for its 1,070 rooms (*Lodging Hospitality* 1988). Both hotels are quite successful. Both hotels are quite different. They cater, of course, to different market segments, provide different levels of service, and employ vastly different staffing levels in relation to the number of guests they serve.

Certain hotel capital expenditures are dictated solely by physical considerations. When heating systems fail they must be replaced, when roofs leak they must be repaired. But capital expenditures are also driven by the types

A standard guest room at a Le Meridien hotel.

Courtesy: Le Meridien Hotels, Inc.

of markets a hotel wishes to serve. Hotels "wear out" quickly from intensive use. It's easy, in pursuit of short-run profits, to put off replacing corridor carpets, repainting a ballroom, or modernizing guest bathrooms. Such decisions, however, may be inconsistent with a hotel's long-term goal of catering to certain market segments. Thus, unless a hotel makes a conscious decision to refocus its attention to a less demanding or less quality-conscious type of guest, capital expenditure levels must be maintained, sometimes even in the face of falling short-term profits.

William Scully made the strategic decision to argue with his corporate bosses for $11 million to refurbish and modernize the public spaces and rooms of the hotel even though it had just gone through three years of disappointing financial performance. His request, as he put it, did not "sit well" at the corporate level. Although ultimately approved, he was on the hot seat to show improved operating results in order to justify such a major expenditure of funds. However difficult it was to make the decision, not approving these expenditures would have been contrary to corporate goals because the hotel's quality level would have fallen below company standards. In time The Bourbon Hotel would have lost the traditional market segments it served. The same reasoning must be followed when considering the kinds of facilities and services a hotel should provide. The Bourbon Hotel, for example, continued to operate an up-scale signature restaurant that could not be justified on financial grounds. It did so because Scully felt that the segment of the market it served would expect such a restaurant. In other words, this unprofitable restaurant had to be kept open because it represented an important part of the hotel's "service concept." Excellent GMs like William Scully understand the relationship between marketing goals, service strategies and capital expenditures. Lawrence Wagner, for example, recently spent $400,000 on his meeting space just to "freshen them up and have them in step with today's most popular decorating trends." All ten GMs studied made reference to the fact that capital expenditure and facility goals must be coordinated to their hotels' strategic service vision.

Other Goals and Objectives

As previously noted, Drucker (1954) identified eight goals found in most businesses. Three that are of particular importance to hotels are productivity goals, human resource goals, and profitability goals. Each will be discussed in this section.

Productivity Goals

Productivity refers to the amount of labor it takes to produce a certain level of output. In manufacturing businesses it's often expressed as the number of man-hours required to produce a physical unit of output (for example, the man-hours required to produce a Ford Escort car). Hotels don't produce physical products, they provide services to guests. In the hotel business productivity is usually measured in terms of labor costs. These costs often are expressed as a percentage of revenues. Thus, the percentage of labor cost in a food and beverage department is calculated by dividing total labor costs by food and beverage revenue, multiplied by one hundred. Labor costs for the rooms division are calculated similarly. By calculating labor costs as a percentage of revenues it is possible to compare labor productivity for similar hotels. All other things being equal, the hotel with a lower labor cost percentage is more productive or efficient than one with a higher labor cost. Hotels, therefore, will set labor cost percentage goals as a reflection of how productive they intend to be.[1]

It is certainly convenient to measure labor productivity in relation to revenues, especially because annual budgets are expressed in dollars. This process, however, somewhat masks the true meaning of labor productivity in hotels. Fundamentally, labor productivity can be defined as the number of man-hours required to provide a certain level of services to a guest. An increase in productivity would occur when (1) more guests are served at a given quality level by a fixed number of employees, (2) fewer employees are required to serve a fixed number of guests, or (3) the same number of employees deliver more services to a fixed number of guests. A true labor productivity goal would be to improve any one of the above three measures (Macaulay and Cullen 1988).

On the other hand, labor cost percentages could show apparent productivity increases (or decreases) when none has occurred, or in fact, the reverse has happened. Suppose last year that a hotel employed 200 people, had labor costs of $3 million and generated $10 million in annual revenues. Its overall labor cost percentage is $3 million divided by $10 million, or 30 percent. Let *nothing* change next year except a 10 percent increase in the prices the hotel charges. What will happen to labor cost percentages? They go from 30 percent ($3 million in wages divided by $10 million revenues) to 27.27 percent ($3 million in wages divided by $11 million in revenues). Occupancy, the number of guests served, and the number of hotel employees all remain unchanged. It appears, however, that the hotel has become more productive because revenues have increased while wages have remained the same. In fact, any time a hotel's prices go up faster than its wage rates the effect, other things being equal, will be to cause labor cost percentages to fall. There is the appearance of greater labor productivity when none has really taken place.

Just the opposite happens when wages increase faster than revenues; labor percentages go up making it appear that productivity has fallen. For example, suppose a hotel experiences a 10 percent increase in wage rates because of a new union contract and no corresponding increases in revenues. Its labor cost percentage will rise from 30 percent to 33 percent ($3.3 million in wages divided by $10 million in revenues). This would occur even as the same number of guests are being served by the same number of employees. Thus, it appears that productivity has decreased when really it has

---

[1] The labor costs of nonrevenue-producing departments, such as accounting, security, or engineering, must be expressed absolutely. Meaningful comparisons of how productive these departments are relative to other hotels will require that their costs be compared in some way to their output. One way would be to relate labor costs in these departments either to number of rooms or to total hotel revenues.

not. In the interest of lowering its costs, this hotel might decide to decrease the size of its staff and the level of its guest services. Having done this the hotel would appear to have increased its labor productivity when labor cost percentages are recalculated. In reality this calculation is illusory because a different level of services is now being provided. Labor has not become more "productive." All that has happened is that fewer people are employed and guest services have been cut back!

It is the underlying efficiency of a hotel's service delivery systems that ultimately determines its labor productivity. The design of these systems is an important management responsibility. Efficient systems, equipment and procedures, and well-trained and motivated employees ultimately determine how many man-hours are required to provide various levels of services. Thus, effective hotel executives look beyond labor percentages and concentrate on their ultimate productivity goals. It is through the design of an efficient service delivery system that productivity is ultimately increased.

Human Resource Goals

The ultimate concern of human resource goals is efficient guest service. Employee goals may not always be stated or measured directly in these terms, but the desired end result is always customer related. Examples of human resource goals would include: (1) to decrease employee absenteeism next year by 15 percent, (2) to decrease employee turnover by 20 percent, (3) to institute a ten-hour safety training program for food and beverage workers with the goal of reducing accidents by 25 percent, (4) to train front desk clerks in guest contact skills, and (5) to conduct wine appreciation seminars for the hotel's waiters. The ultimate goal of these programs is more efficient, effective, and productive employees; employees who, in one way or another, will be able to provide better guest services more efficiently (*Lodging* 1989).

Profitability Goals

Last but not least, hotels must set profitability goals. Hotels are businesses and the ultimate measure of their performance is profits. No matter what other goals a hotel may set for itself, making a profit is the acid test of effectiveness. It is quite common for outstanding GMs to argue that profits occur as a result of good staff development, great guest service, and forward-thinking capital expenditures. Still, the need to meet or exceed specific numerical profit goals is never very far from their consciousness. Annual budgets are detailed projections of revenues and expenses. The difference between revenues and expenses is, of course, operating profits or losses. As Chapter Thirteen will describe in detail, budgets are arrived at

through a complex process of proposal, evaluation, discussion, and nego-
tiation between a hotel's managers, its owners, and the hotel company's
corporate executives. A good budget and profit goal is set neither too low
so as to be unchallenging, nor is it set too high so as to be unattainable.
At its best, it should be demanding, motivating, and attainable. Meeting
budgets is a serious business. Raises, bonuses, and promotions are often
based on the ability of GMs and department heads to meet or exceed budget and profit goals. Company executives and owners are more likely to
overlook other shortcomings as long as a GM is meeting budgets and making a profit.

Outstanding GMs need little reminder that profits, or the lack of them,
are the ultimate measure of success. Jonathan Claiborne was brought in to
manage the four-year-old Riviera Hotel, a property that had never earned
one dollar's profits for its owners. His office, which was quite large, had
only one picture on its walls. It was a picture of a lifelike, smiling hotel
handing over its first dollar of profit to GM Claiborne. The picture was
prominently situated so that all of the hotel's executives who attended
meetings in his office could easily see it. This picture was a symbol of the
most important challenge The Riviera Hotel faced—making a profit.

Setting profit goals is a must. Outstanding GMs use profit goals as a
galvanizing force to move their hotels forward. Henri LeSassier tells about
taking over The Normandy Hotel when it was in serious financial trouble.
It was losing millions annually, and its owners were considering bankruptcy.
The reasons for despair were many. Among them was the "official" long-
range forecast of the previous manager, who predicted operating losses for
the next five years! This meant that the hotel's previous management was
operating on the premise of trying to minimize losses rather than making
a profit. The hotel's owners had reluctantly gone along with this goal. Upon
becoming GM, LeSassier argued to the owners that continuing to operate
the hotel under this set of assumptions and goals was futile. It would be
better all around to declare bankruptcy now, thereby avoiding the next five
years of losses, frustration, sleepless nights, and worry. He argued instead
that new goals should be set. In fact, he boldly stated that the hotel's goal
should be to produce an operating profit the very next year! There had
been no changes in the external environment that would indicate such a
reversal of fortune was possible. What LeSassier was saying was that the
previous goal was simply unacceptable. In his view the only acceptable
goal was a positive operating profit. The hotel, its management, and its
staff would simply have to find a way to meet this goal. In this example
goal setting became a powerful, motivating force for The Normandy. Everyone working in the hotel was re-educated to a simple but powerful fact.
They were not working to minimize losses but to find a way, any way, to
make a profit.

Developing a Hotel's Culture

During the course of the GM research, I spent time with the executives and staff of ten outstanding, excellently managed hotels. It was rather remarkable to discover that the management and staff of these hotels felt that their hotel was by far the best in the city! The reasons they gave for being the best, to be sure, varied from one hotel to another. Still, this feeling of

Magnificent lobby and glass elevator in the Omni Biltmore, Providence, R.I.

Courtesy: Omni Hotels

being the best was widespread among the management and staff and un-mistakable in each hotel. The GMs of these hotels had developed among their management and staff a self-concept, or culture, that said a lot about how that organization felt the hotel should be run. Call it an operating phi-losophy, a self-concept, or a culture: whatever it is called, it's quite clear that developing the right kind of culture is an important goal for all well-managed hotels.

Peters and Waterman (1982), in their best selling book on management excellence, refer to an organization's culture as its shared values. They consider shared values crucial to an organization's effectiveness. Further discussion appears later in this book on how hotel managers shape values in their hotels. It's important here simply to note that the goal-setting pro-cess needs to include consideration of what we refer to as culture. The previous section discussed Henri LeSassier's campaign to set a positive profit goal at The Normandy Hotel. Profits, of course, can be stated quan-titatively. Of equal importance, in his mind, was the need to set attitude goals for the hotel; to change, if you will, the hotel's self-concept. As he put it, "making people believe they can win" and "getting people to try and to gamble" were among the most difficult things he had to accomplish. After posting losses for four straight years it's easy to see how people can begin to think of themselves as losers. LeSassier's goal, though hardly quantifiable like a profit goal, was to make these same people think of themselves as winners.

FORMULATING A STRATEGIC PLAN

Once goals are set, a hotel must actually fashion a strategic plan to follow. The previous chapter introduced a planning technique called SWOT anal-ysis, which stands for the analysis of a business's internal *S*trengths and *W*eaknesses and its external *O*pportunities and *T*hreats. SWOT analysis is useful in formulating strategic plans because it forces hotel managers to view the business relative to both internal and external factors. By doing so SWOT analysis helps resolve a fundamental strategic question: "Will our strategy be one that takes advantage of a relatively strong position or will it attempt to overcome a relatively weak position?" If this basic ques-tion can be resolved the GM has gone a long way toward isolating the strategic choices open to the hotel.

The remainder of this chapter will demonstrate the use of SWOT analysis in hotels. The examples are actual situations drawn from hotels that took part in the GM research. The hotels' internal strengths and weaknesses, and their external opportunities and threats, were determined from conversations and meetings with the GMs and their key senior executives. So what you will be reading are real situations as well as the actual strategies each hotel formulated. To my knowledge, the hotels in question did not engage in a formal SWOT analysis in arriving at their strategies.[2] However, it was obvious that the thought process of the GMs followed logically along the lines of a SWOT analysis. One could clearly see these outstanding GMs assessing the external conditions in which they found their hotels and comparing various external conditions to the internal strengths and weaknesses of their hotels. Although some of the GMs may have never heard of SWOT analysis, they were surely following a reasoning process that was analogous to it.

Incidents from each of the ten hotels could have been given, but I've decided to concentrate on two real-world examples of strategic planning in hotels. The examples have been chosen to illustrate hotels in two different quadrants of a SWOT diagram, which is reproduced in Figure 4-2. Recall that in Quadrant one a hotel is in a very strong position. It faces external opportunities while possessing substantial internal strengths. Under these circumstances an aggressive strategy is called for to take advantage of these favorable conditions. In Quadrant two, a hotel faces a number of external opportunities but, because of internal weaknesses, is unable to exploit them.

---

[2]Many businesses, however, do engage in formal strategic planning techniques such as SWOT analysis. A good example is Chrysler Corporation's use of SWOT analyses after Lee Iococca took command and that company's subsequent dramatic turnaround from the brink of bankruptcy.

FIGURE 4-2.   SWOT Diagram

In Quadrant four an internally strong hotel faces an external threat. In such circumstances a hotel should employ some of its strengths in a way that redirects its efforts toward new opportunities, thus mitigating the threats it faces. Finally, in Quadrant three a hotel's internal weaknesses are compounded by threats in its external environment. Under such dire circumstances a hotel must resort to survival strategies such as retrenchment and turnaround.

The first example is a hotel that is strong internally and that faces a number of interesting external opportunities.

An Aggressive Strategic Plan

The hotel in this discussion is best characterized as being in Quadrant one of a SWOT diagram; it has substantial internal strengths and also faces a number of external opportunities. In the real world, businesses always have some internal weaknesses and usually face some external threats. The practical question that must be answered is whether, on balance, the business is operating from a position of internal strength in an environment that offers opportunities, or whether the reverse is the case?

When William Scully took over as GM of The Bourbon Hotel, it might at first glance have appeared that his hotel's operating environment was one of numerous external threats and few opportunities. To begin with, the local hotel market was overbuilt. Over the past four years eight new hotels within a mile of The Bourbon Hotel had added 4,500 new hotel rooms to the city's inventory. All except one of these hotels competed directly with Bill's hotel. At the same time there had been a serious downturn in one of the area's major industries, thus causing a substantial drop in business travel. In consequence, citywide hotel occupancy had fallen by 20 percent and most of the city's hotel executives were "singing the blues." There were additional external factors that looked like threats. Although the city was a major tourist destination, there were no advertising funds available to promote tourism that might make up for the fall in business travel. The city's convention center, while quite large, was currently operating close to capacity and could not be counted on to further boost business. Finally, The Bourbon's major competitor had a better location, was larger, and had facilities superior to Bill's hotel. Although his hotel was not losing money, both occupancy and average room rate had fallen from previous levels, as had profits.

A pessimist would surely have cause to view this external environment with some alarm. But William Scully is an optimist, so he chose to look at other factors and also to interpret existing conditions differently. Here are some other things he discovered in the external environment facing his hotel. Although the city was overbuilt with hotels, things had stabilized; there were no new hotels planned, and a few older, less-competitive properties were in financial difficulties. So, it was possible that the city's hotel inventory might fall slightly over the next few years. While not growing rapidly, the city's convention business was quite large and healthy. It represented a stable core business for Scully's hotel. Although far from a certainty, it seemed likely that the city's convention center, then operating at close to capacity, would be doubled in size within the next five years. While the city had little money to advertise, it was a nationally recognized tourist destination with considerable appeal and potential.

Being new to the city, Bill wondered if business travel had really fallen as much as most locals thought. Could it be that the expansion of hotel rooms just spread the existing business around and made it appear to have decreased drastically? These were his preliminary thoughts about the operating environment facing his hotel. The only major remote environmental factor of note was the fact that the U.S. economy was expanding briskly and inflation was low, an encouraging sign for pleasure travel. On the international scene the dollar had fallen in value thus stimulating foreign travel to the United States and discouraging U.S. travel abroad. All things considered, the remote environment looked favorable for the next few years.

Scully next took stock of his hotel's internal situation and found that The Bourbon Hotel possessed considerable strengths. To start with, it had a very good location: it was within walking distance of the convention center, the central business district, major shopping areas, and the city's entertainment and dining district. Its good location meant that it could effectively serve the business, convention, and pleasure travel markets. The hotel's basic design and maintenance were also quite good. It was a modern facility only a decade old. Bill was also fortunate to have taken over a hotel that was basically well managed, was operating smoothly, and was delivering quality guest services. Although he did institute some important management changes and began working on a few facility deficiencies, these were not glaring weaknesses. Finally, he had an advantage in that the parent hotel company was well managed and highly regarded in the markets in which it competed.

Scully's internal analysis did reveal one rather substantial weakness. Although only about a decade old, the hotel had already begun to look a little worn and dated. Physical upkeep had been neglected during the past three years of declining revenues and profits. The hotel needed a general refurbishing to bring its "look" up to the standards of the eight new competing hotels. Money needed to be spent to make the hotel look fresh again.

These were his preliminary findings concerning external opportunities and threats, and internal strengths and weaknesses. Scully kept asking questions. He found that his marketing staff was of the opinion that there were few individual business or pleasure travelers likely to opt for their hotel.

The fresh, contemporary look of The Le Meridien San Diego lobby.

Courtesy: Le Meridien Hotels, Inc., and Edward Gohlich, photographer.

In other words, his sales staff felt that the individual transient market, whether the pleasure or business traveler, had dried up for The Bourbon Hotel. His sales staff did feel that the group-pleasure market held promise, and they were devoting resources to it.

This left conventions and meetings as the primary market for The Bourbon Hotel. The facts bore this out. In 1985, 82 percent of the hotel's total room-nights had come from group business, and 90 percent of that was convention and business meetings. This was not unusual. After all, The Bourbon is a large convention hotel. In order to protect its dominant market, the hotel had a policy of not accepting individual transient reservations through its corporate reservation system more than two weeks into the future. By so doing they felt they were guarding against overbooking transient guests at the expense of their dominant convention business. Since transient reservations had not been accepted more than two weeks into the future, there was the possibility of a substantial number of reservation turndowns of people who tried to book more than two weeks in advance. Scully decided to analyze transient turndowns in the reservation system in some detail. He concluded from this analysis that there was a small but consistent base of transient business travelers of which his hotel was not taking full advantage.

Bill also studied the results of an aggressive advertising campaign the hotel had conducted a few years earlier. The campaign, conducted during a major city festival, was aimed at pleasure travelers. High occupancies had occurred during the normally slow summer months of that year, but management had attributed this increase more to the appeal of the one-time festival than to the appeal of the city. Bill wondered if the same sort of results were possible based only on the city's appeal, especially if low, off-season, room-rates were offered. Finally, in analyzing the hotel's group business over the past few years, it became apparent that there was significant business in some markets that had simply never been solicited. The hotel had never solicited business in a number of important geographic markets. Summing up the positives, Scully concluded that his hotel faced a variety of interesting external market opportunities, which included:

1. A small but consistent transient business base;
2. A possibly large, but price-sensitive, off-season pleasure market;
3. A number of neglected geographic markets for group business;
4. A large and stable convention and group base;
5. A possible doubling of the city's convention center; and
6. A modestly growing group-pleasure segment.

On balance, Bill felt that most of his external threats were behind him. Problems in the external environment had already occurred and his hotel's position was unlikely to erode further over the next few years. On the other hand, it appeared that most of his external opportunities were still in the future. He judged the opportunities to be significant, if not unlimited, so his outlook could be described as hopefully optimistic if not wildly enthusiastic. Still, when coupled with his assessment of the hotel's strength, he placed himself within Quadrant one of the SWOT diagram. Point "a" of Figure 4-3 would be a good representation of his assessment. If the market opportunities he identified were to materialize, if the convention center expansion became a reality, and if the local economy rebounded somewhat, his situation would improve dramatically. If, at the same time, he could overcome his one major internal weakness through an aggressive renovation program, then the future might indeed look bright! This condition could be depicted as point "b" in Figure 4-3, which calls for an aggressive strategy.

Based on this kind of thinking Scully formulated an aggressive strategic plan. The major elements of this plan were:

- The hotel embarked on an aggressive forty-nine dollars per room summer rate advertising campaign. Ads were placed in major metropolitan markets within a 500-mile radius and were intended to appeal to the transient pleasure market.
- Transient rooms were made available through the company's national reservation system six months in advance, but without any price discount. This was a move to increase transient business travel but only at favorable room-rates.
- Rooms were discounted through the reservation system only when the hotel had fewer than 950 group-rooms booked. In this way he was able to keep the average room-rate for transient business high when the hotel had few individual rooms available because of heavy convention bookings.
- He canceled most of the hotel's forty dollars per room contracts with airline crews in anticipation of increased occupancy and higher room-rates.
- He assigned sales representatives to New York City and Washington, D.C., to developing new group business that had never before been solicited.

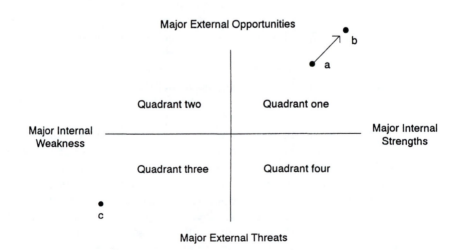

FIGURE 4-3.   SWOT Analysis

• He won approval from corporate for an $11 million renovation and refurbishing program for the hotel to bring it up to the standards of its newer competitors.

These strategies were aggressive, bold moves on William Scully's part. They were instituted during a period of depressed citywide occupancies and room-rates. His company went along with the $11 million renovation program, but high-level executives expressed their "apprehension and concern" about it. This would translate into "I told you so" at the corporate level if the other strategic moves failed to result in increased revenues and profits. One example of the boldness of Scully's strategy was that the forty-nine dollar summer room-rate marked the first time that a major hotel in that city had aggressively advertised low off-season rates.

As it turned out, Bill's assessment of conditions was quite accurate and his aggressive strategic plan proved to be successful. The advertising campaign added 36,000 room-nights during the next summer, saving the hotel from a disastrous summer. Transient business travel did increase when the reservation system was opened six months in advance and these bookings were predominately at high rates. Group business increased from the New York and Washington, D. C. markets. Finally, the renovations kept the hotel at a quality level comparable to its competitors, thus making unnecessary the discounting of room-rates in order to compete. Over the first two years of this strategy occupancies increased by more than 15 percent and average room-rates rose by over 10 percent. The resulting revenues and profits were more than adequate to justify the $11 million renovation as well as the other expenditures related to the hotel's new strategic plan.

As a final footnote it turned out that the city's convention center was, in fact, doubled in size. By pursuing an aggressive strategy, Scully has a newly renovated, profitable hotel ideally positioned to benefit from additional convention business. There were, of course, other elements to his strategic plan, including a number of internal changes. However, because the hotel was basically internally strong, we have focused mostly on the strategic moves that related to its external environment. Different external and internal circumstances will call for a hotel to react with different strategies. The second example is a hotel that had to fashion a very different strategy in order to survive.

A Time for Retrenchment and Turnaround

Henri LeSassier is French. He received a first-class European hotel school education and also graduated from one of the best U.S. hotel schools. In his twenty years in the hotel business, he has worked for two different international hotel companies in Europe, South America, Africa, the Middle East, and now the United States. He expresses concern about one day accepting a position to manage a hotel in such financial difficulties that it

Greenery adds warmth to the space age design of The Hyatt Regency O'Hare lobby, Chicago.

Courtesy: Hyatt Hotels Corporation

just might be impossible to pull it through. Appropriately, he refers to this kind of hotel as a "dead duck." When I interviewed LeSassier he had nearly run into his proverbial "dead duck" and was in the process of implementing a strategy to save the dying bird.

The hotel he managed faced major external threats. It also had a number of internal weaknesses, which made the situation quite precarious. The hotel was losing a lot of money and its owners were seriously considering bankruptcy. Here's the situation he faced. The hotel was a four-year-old luxury property built to cater to affluent business travelers and to relatively small, upscale business meetings and conventions. Its preconstruction feasibility study envisioned about 50 percent of its occupancy from individual transient business guests, 40 percent from small up-scale group business, and 10 percent from individual pleasure travel. From the day of its opening, radical changes in local business conditions resulted in most of the transient business travel market being lost, with little likelihood of its return. For the first three years of operation this hotel suffered from low occupancies and heavy losses.

Compounding these threatening external conditions were severe internal weaknesses. As losses mounted, the GM who had opened the hotel seemed unable to cope with the situation. More and more, the hotel was allowed to just run itself with little direction from above. Management and staff turnover was high, morale was nonexistent, and the hotel was suffering operating losses of half a million dollars each month. When Henri LeSassier took over as GM of the Normandy Hotel, occupancy the previous year was 30 percent and a "realistic" occupancy goal for the next year had been set at 40 percent. If this hotel was not a "dead duck" it was certainly a crippled one! Henri LeSassier's situation corresponded to something like point "c" in Quadrant three of Figure 4-3. His hotel had serious internal weaknesses and faced ominous external threats.

The strategy LeSassier chose to follow was a combination of both retrenchment and turnaround. To begin with, he needed to quickly cut costs. Previous management had done little in this regard, even in the face of low revenues and huge losses. One of LeSassier's first moves to forestall bankruptcy was to slash the hotel's staff by 120 people, a 30 percent reduction. He economized in every other way possible. In his words, it was imperative to "bring costs into line with low occupancy levels." These were extremely difficult decisions, but in desperate circumstances extreme measures are often required. What he did is a classic example of a retrenchment strategy designed to keep a business alive while a turnaround strategy can be derived.

Because of the many internal problems his hotel faced, LeSassier's turnaround strategy had to focus on internal issues. Although many things had to be done, the most important, he felt, was to rekindle a winning feeling among his management and staff. While it was understandable that after three years of heavy losses attitudes had turned negative, a continuation of a negative mind-set would keep a turnaround from ever occurring. LeSassier first turned to goals and objectives as the place to begin. The hotel's previous occupancy goal for the next year had been set at 40 percent. At this occupancy the hotel would continue to lose large sums of money and, in all likelihood, be thrown into bankruptcy before the end of the year.

Working toward a 40 percent occupancy goal was a futile effort. Even if reached it would not avert bankruptcy. However, a 60 percent occupancy, given the large labor saving LeSassier had already accomplished, would result in a positive cash flow that would keep the hotel going. Thus, in the fall he announced to his executive staff that the hotel's occupancy goal for the coming year had been raised from 40 percent to 60 percent and that he had every intention of meeting this goal. This was a stunning statement for the hotel's executives. They knew that the hotel would probably finish the current year with an average occupancy of only 25 percent! Henri didn't give them much time to think about this. At the same time he announced the new occupancy goal, he initiated a series of changes which included:

- Spending $60,000 on guest room rehabilitation.
- Adding $60,000 to the hotel's employee training budget.
- Relocating the catering department so that its offices were adjacent to the sales department. He also began an extensive upgrade of both departments' physical appearance.
- Constructing a VIP lounge adjacent to the main lobby.
- Initiating a number of ambitious civic projects requiring the active participation of most key executives.
- Embarking upon a complete reorganization of the hotel to make it more responsive to the guests' needs.
- Increasing the number and quality of the hotel's sales managers in order to concentrate on the small convention and business-meetings market.
- Increasing the secretarial and support services of the sales department.

In addition to these initiatives, his management style consisted of an aggressive, hands-on involvement in every aspect of the hotel's operation. He also exerted constant pressure on key executives to produce results. To his way of thinking he had "eliminated the excuses and then demanded results." Some thought of him as a tyrant, others as a genius. He was trusted by some of the staff and not by others. No matter what their individual feelings, by the end of one year there was a unanimous feeling that his strategies and personal involvement in the hotel's management had saved the hotel from bankruptcy. As it turned out, the hotel did meet its 60 percent occupancy goal, a result thought completely unattainable just 15 months earlier. The hotel also accomplished most of the other initiatives LeSassier had forced on it.

Henri LeSassier's first year at The Normandy Hotel had been one of long hours, hard work, and constant agitation. But it was also one during which things started to get done, victories were won, and people accustomed to failure began to experience success. Through all the hardships there was, as his staff called him, this "little bulldog of a GM" constantly prodding, pushing, and challenging all of them to reach goals and to achieve results they had previously considered unattainable. His turnaround strategy transformed a losing team into a winner. Internal weaknesses were overcome, and the hotel was repositioned into the small convention and business-meetings markets. The Normandy was saved from the brink of bankruptcy and is now a viable business with a future. A strategy of retrenchment and turnaround, born out of desperation, worked.

CONCLUSION

These two examples of strategic planning in hotels illustrate the kind of planning decisions that are typically made at the individual hotel level. Except for the most basic budget motel chains, it's probably fair to say that individual hotel GMs and key department heads play a significant role in their property's strategic planning and decision making. Certainly, as hotels grow in size and complexity, the amount of strategic planning and decision making at an individual hotel level increases accordingly.

This conclusion should be extremely good news for aspiring hotel executives. It means that as your career progresses you can anticipate being involved in strategic decision making. In all likelihood this should happen by the time you become a hotel department head. If you aspire to be a hotel GM, this chapter amply illustrates the variety and scope of the strategic planning in which you will be engaged. The message from these examples and from others throughout this book, is that hotel executives exercise considerable discretion and influence with regard to their hotel's strategic decisions. Although the individual hotel appears to be at the bottom of a hotel chain's organizational chart, there is still a lot of room at the unit level for exciting and imaginative strategic decisions.

Hotel executives at the individual hotel level must, of course, be great hotel operators. Young managers will not progress unless they acquire the operational skills required to serve banquets, purchase liquor, prepare guest folios, and supervise room maids. But in addition to being great at operations, one of the characteristics that distinguishes outstanding hotel managers is that they have the ability to think, to plan, and to manage strategically. By so doing, they are able to influence the direction and profitability of the hotels they manage.

REFERENCES

Anon. August 1988. "Lodging Hospitality's Top 400 Performers." *Lodging Hospitality Magazine* 44(9): 50-53.
Anon. September 1989. "The New York Show: Productivity." *Lodging* 15(1):30.

Dev, Chekitan S. Aug. 1989. "Operating Environment and Strategy: The Profitable Connection." *Cornell Hotel and Restaurant Administration Quarterly* 30(2):8–13.

Drucker, Peter F. 1954. *Management: Tasks, Responsibilities, Practices*. New York:Harper & Row Publishers.

Haywood, K. Michael. Nov. 1986. "Scouting The Competition For Survival and Success." *Cornell Hotel and Restaurant Administration Quarterly* 27:80ff.

Heskett, James L. 1986. *Managing in the Service Economy*. Boston: Harvard Business School Press.

Macaulay, James and Thomas P. Cullen. 1988. "The Three M's of Service Industry Productivity: Misunderstood, Miscalculated and Mismanaged." *Hospitality Education and Research Journal* 12(2):443–452.

Peters, Thomas J. and Robert H. Waterman, Jr. 1982. *In Search of Excellence: Lessons From America's Best Run Companies*. New York: Harper & Row Publishers.

QUESTIONS

4-1. What type of strategic planning decisions can be made by GMs at the individual hotel level?

4-2. Explain the four quadrants of a SWOT diagram and relate how this technique of strategic planning can be used in hotels.

4-3. Could the principles of strategic planning be used at the departmental level in a hotel? Give some examples of how strategic planning might be used in the rooms, food and beverage, personnel and controllers departments. You may want to read Chapter Five on hotel organization before answering this question.

CHAPTER 5

Hotel Organization

The cartoon pictured two men lounging casually in reclining chairs on a beach, each with a cold drink in his hand. As they languidly looked out to sea, one turned to the other and said, "One of these days we've got to get organized." From the looks of those two guys, their prospects for getting organized didn't seem very promising. Unfortunately, the same is true of many businesses, schools, clubs, cities, hospitals, and hotels. Many organizations, it turns out, are rather unorganized. If you've held even a few jobs, it's impossible not to have encountered some examples of badly organized, poorly managed businesses. Workers and customers see it every day. It's sometimes amazing that businesses do such stupid things. Often, the reason for this seeming lack of care and intelligence is a lack of organization.

This chapter will discuss many of the important issues that must be taken into account in order to develop an effective organization for a hotel.

AN OVERVIEW OF ORGANIZATIONAL DESIGN

This section will review some of the general management principles of organizational design. Some of the common terms used to describe these principles sound rather theoretical. To some, that might imply that they are of no practical use. Be assured that nothing could be further from the truth. The principles herein reviewed are of considerable practical value to managers at all levels within a hotel's organizational structure. Understanding them will aid not only new managers but also experienced higher level executives. Remember, as you study this chapter, that as a manager one of your primary responsibilities will be to organize the employees who work for you into an effective team and that there are proven principles that can help you in that task.

The Elements Of Organizational Structure

If the efforts of people in organizations are to be channeled toward productive ends, structure must be given to their activities. Aldag and Stearns (1987) list five ways by which managers give structure to organizations:

a. Work specialization,
b. Departmentalization,
c. Patterns of authority,
d. Spans of control, and
e. Methods of coordination.

Whenever a hotel manager decides to make an organizational change, he or she will usually have to take these five elements into account.

Specialization

If there is more than one way to accomplish something, management must make a conscious decision about how to divide tasks among workers. One extreme is the case of little or no specialization where an individual worker is responsible for all of the tasks required to complete a job. An example is the skilled furniture maker who performs all the carpentry required to make a fine chest of drawers. The chef in a small country restaurant who single-handedly prepares an entire meal for twenty guests would be another. For most of history, much of civilization's work took place in this manner. There is, to be sure, much to recommend this method of work. In the restaurant example the chef gets to choose the menu, decide on food preparation methods, purchase the ingredients, cook the entire meal, and in all likelihood, observe the guests enjoying it. It's rewarding to have total control over a project from beginning to end. Most people find it motivating to see the results of their efforts. The problem, however, is that as the demand for additional products or services increases, it becomes more and more difficult for individuals or small groups to increase their output without changing the way they are organized.

Suppose that the country chef, Heidi Baine, can prepare a meal for a maximum of twenty guests while following these traditional work methods. Should she want to expand the restaurant to accommodate sixty guests some changes would be required. One option might be to keep the method of production and organization the same and simply hire more workers to produce the additional output. This approach would require hiring two additional chefs to accommodate the sixty guests. Each chef, working independently, would prepare 20 meals. Similarly, if one furniture maker can produce one chest per week then three, each working more or less independently, can produce three per week. This is a perfectly logical solution to increases in demand. It was, in fact, the usual method by which production was increased in European craft guilds during the Middle Ages. To modern business people, however, such a solution seems impractical, even bordering on the comical. One can envision difficulties as the country restaurant expands first from twenty to sixty seats. But it's hard to envision what would happen in the kitchen if it expanded to 120 seats! Two chefs might be able to coexist in the same kitchen, possibly even three. But the thought of six chefs all working in the same space is a vista hard to contemplate. Surely, the saying "too many cooks spoil the broth" would apply long before a 120-seat restaurant is envisioned, and the scene in the kitchen becomes worthy material for a Mel Brooks movie.

The restaurant's owner–chef, Heidi Baine, would soon find she had lost

Some of the banquet staff at the Radisson Plaza Hotel in Southfield, Michigan

Courtesy: Radisson Hotels International

control of her organization when each chef was responsible for the preparation of a complete meal. It would also become apparent that each chef's meal would look and taste a little differently. Finally, every time one wanted to serve an extra twenty people a new chef would have to be hired! Modern business people understand instinctively that hiring more chefs is not the solution to the problem of increased demand. Rather, Chef Heidi should hire additional kitchen workers capable of performing certain specialized culinary functions under her overall guidance. As business increased from twenty to thirty customers, her first new employee might be an assistant to help with simple slicing, chopping, and fetching chores around the kitchen. She would soon learn, however, that as the demand for meals continued to increase, it would become necessary to break kitchen tasks into more specialized functions. As business grew it might be smart to employ someone who only prepared salads and someone else who specialized in making desserts. Additional growth might require the services of a cook especially skilled in broiling and roasting and even a culinarian skilled in preparing sauces. Specialization in food preparation subtasks would allow employees to gain great skill and speed in their work. Also, control over output quality and consistency would become easier as tasks were specialized. Finally, Chef Heidi would find, to her great delight, that the number of meals served from a kitchen organized around task specialization will far exceed one in which each person performed all tasks. The economist, Adam Smith, when describing what was happening in manufacturing processes in Scotland over 200 years ago, observed that the degree of specialization depended on the size of one's market and that "factories" engaged in specialization produced significantly higher levels of output per worker than individuals producing products alone. The same principle holds true in many aspects of the hotel and restaurant business.

Thus, one of management's primary organizational tasks is to determine the extent to which work and jobs should be specialized. As a general rule, specialization holds out the possibility of greater worker productivity and managerial control over tasks. On the other hand, dividing complete jobs into smaller subunits tends to increase the need for coordinating the activities of numerous workers, each involved in separate, specialized tasks. Thus, Heidi Baine can only ensure consistent quality and high output if she is able to coordinate the activities of the kitchen's different culinary specialists. Examples throughout this book will illustrate that one of the really crucial elements of hotel management is coordinating the many specialized functions within hotels.

Finally, although task specialization often does lead to greater efficiency and productivity, overspecialization can also lead to problems. Overspecialization results in workers performing more and more repetitive, minute tasks. A point can be reached where the degree of specialization so narrows a job's scope that the average worker finds little joy or satisfaction in it. Interest is lost, motivation drops, error rates increase, and quality suffers. Overspecialization can so trivialize a job that the productivity gains resulting from specialization are offset by employee apathy and boredom. It is management's responsibility to structure jobs in such a way as to reap the benefits of specialization while avoiding its pitfalls.

Departmentalization

As organizations begin to grow in size, managers are faced with the need to group certain jobs together in order to ensure efficient coordination and control of activities. These job groupings are usually called departments. When Chef Heidi was cooking for only twenty guests, it would have been possible (and probable) that she and two or three helpers both prepared and served the food. Under these circumstances her restaurant would be made up of only one department, food preparation and service. Figure 5-1 depicts the organization of the Country Gourmet Restaurant. It seems hardly worth dignifying such a simple organization with an organizational chart. Still, Chef Heidi did have to make a conscious decision to organize her restaurant so that one department was responsible for two functions: food preparation and service.

The Country Gourmet Restaurant has prospered and grown. As Chef Heidi added seats to accommodate the hordes of hungry guests, she also realized that worker specialization would increase productivity. But while figuring out the best way to specialize her staff, she ran headlong into a departmentalization issue; is it better to have the same workers responsible for both food preparation and service? Or does it make more sense to divide them into two separate groups: one involved in preparation only and the other responsible only for service?

Most restaurants have chosen to departmentalize with food preparation and food service as separate functional departments. This is a very logical and practical solution to Heidi's organizational problem. There are distinctly different kinds of work performed in preparing and serving food:

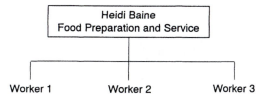

FIGURE 5-1.   Country Gourmet Restaurant Single-Department Organizational Chart

both the process and the function of the two activities are different. Chef Heidi has decided to divide the responsibilities of her workers according to functions: those who prepare food and those who serve food. Where before there was one department, now there are two. Although she retains the overall menu and recipe control, Heidi decides to hire a working chef, or *sous chef,* to supervise day-to-day kitchen operations. She also decides to employ a dining room manager. Figure 5-2 depicts this new organization. Chef Heidi, not unlike the president of Holiday Inns, has made a major organizational decision. She has chosen to organize her business along functional lines by forming two separate departments based on a criterion of common work process and function. Additionally, she has relieved herself from the direct supervision of her employees and hired two middle-level managers: a *sous chef* and a dining room manager. Forming departments along functional lines is the most common method of organizing a business. If the Country Gourmet Restaurant continued to grow a number of other specialized departments might be formed (for example, a purchasing/storage department, an accounting department and, possibly, a separate sales and marketing department).

Other criteria can be used for departmentalization. Time can be a criterion if an organization operates more than one shift of workers throughout the day. The Country Gourmet Restaurant could, for example, be open for breakfast, lunch, and dinner. In this case two different shifts (one for breakfast and lunch, and another for dinner) with a manager for each shift might be required. Organizations also form departments based on customers, service, and products. One of Chef Heidi's customers might ask her to cater a party at home. If this leads to numerous catering contracts, she might decide to set up a separate department within her restaurant to handle off-premises events. Thus, a catering department will come into being

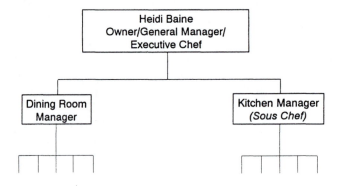

FIGURE 5-2.   Country Gourmet Restaurant Two-Department Organizational Chart

based on the criterion that it provides a different service to customers with distinctly different needs. Note that it is proper to think of a catering customer and a restaurant guest as two separate types of customers even if they are one and the same person. As Chef Heidi's restaurant becomes famous, she decides to expand into the sale of specially prepared spices and seasonings. At first she sells them directly to restaurant guests, but as orders begin to pour in she sets up a mail-order business to handle this new product. As this business prospers she decides to form a separate department with responsibility over spices and seasonings. In other words, she now uses a product criterion to further departmentalize. Business is really booming now and Heidi decides to open yet another restaurant in an adjoining county. Her business organization is further complicated by the addition of a separate restaurant with its own manager. She now uses a location criterion to further departmentalize her business.

What a great success story! With hard work and organizational genius Heidi, in the course of a few pages, has come a long way. She has been forced to leave the kitchen and hire another chef to take her place. The business is growing and she is becoming a manager. She forms a corporation called Country Gourmet Enterprises, Inc., of which she is president. With two restaurants, each with their own catering business, and a mail-order seasonings business, she decides to add three additional functional departments: accounting, personnel, and marketing. Although not revenue producers, these new staff departments are responsible for assisting the restaurants and the mail-order business in their accounting, personnel, and marketing specialties. Heidi's business is now divided departmentally as shown in Figure 5-3. She has used various criteria in determining Country

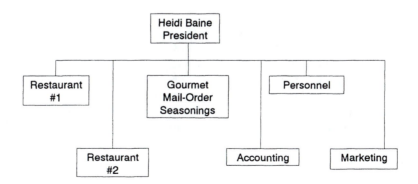

FIGURE 5-3.   Country Gourmet Enterprises, Inc. Organizational Chart

Gourmet Enterprises, Inc.'s departmentalization, including *function*, *customer*, *product*, *location*, and *time*. Each decision Heidi had to make was an important one. In fact, how she organizes her business is one of the critical management skills she has to master. Each time she groups workers into departments certain consequences follow: (1) patterns of supervision are determined because each department is usually staffed by a separate manager responsible for coordination and control, (2) resources are usually allocated to each department, (3) performance measures must be set for each department to determine if resources are being used wisely, and (4) departmentalization brings employees within each department closer together thus encouraging communication and coordination of activity.

Authority

Every time Heidi restructures a job or groups workers together into different departments, she is faced with the question of how much decision-making authority to grant individual workers, managers, or departments. If she does not think through each of these problems beforehand, it won't be long before she is confronted with issues relating to authority. For example, when opening a second restaurant she must decide whether to centralize decision-making authority and make most decisions herself or decentralize authority and allow most of the decisions to be made by the restaurant's manager. These are important, practical concerns. Does she design the menu, hire the chef, and set prices, or does she allow the restaurant manager to make all of these decisions—or some of these decisions? If she does allow him to make some of the decisions, just how far does she go, and under what circumstances will she overrule him?

Organizations are never totally centralized or decentralized with regard to decision making. Rather, they tend toward one direction or the other. A number of factors must be taken into account when deciding the pattern of authority that is best for an organization. Heidi Baine must take into consideration the experience and personality of her department heads, the environment in which they are working (Is it stable or rapidly changing?), the business strategy she wants to follow, and the management style with which she feels most comfortable. These important questions will be further explored in Chapter 10, "leadership." At this point it is sufficient to point out that the issue of how much decision-making authority to delegate is central to effective organizational design.

Line Versus Staff Authority

In the military, line officers are the ones who actually command troops in battle. Staff officers are in charge of support functions such as supply, logistics, and intelligence. Traditionally, line officers make the strategic and tactical battle decisions while staff officers only provide assistance and advice. In business, the distinction between line and staff relates not to military warfare but rather to economic warfare between competitors. Line executives are those who have responsibility over business units that actually provide products or services to customers and account for the revenues of the business. In hotels it's the rooms, and food and beverage departments that account for most of the business revenue.

On the other hand, staff departments are set up because the principles of work specialization and departmentalization suggest efficiencies in such an organizational design. The personnel and engineering departments of a hotel are examples of staff units. Once set up, however, staff departments sometimes cause organizational problems. A personnel department will, for example, have certain responsibilities pertaining to the hotel's staffing. To discharge its responsibility personnel might develop a set of minimum educational achievement standards as a screening device for prospective employees. The employees that personnel screens, however, will eventually be placed in other functional departments of the hotel such as the rooms or the food and beverage department. These screening standards (set up by personnel) may be inappropriate for the hotel's local labor market. They may be too high, especially if the local labor market is very tight, resulting in a shortage of prospective employees for the hotel's various departments. Or they may be too low, resulting in underqualified employees being referred to other departments. If either were to happen, a clash would develop between the policies of one staff department (personnel) and the other departments of the hotel. The line executives of the hotel might insist that personnel adjust its screening standards because the standards are adversely affecting their ability to carry out their functional responsibilities.

The basic issue raised in this example is how much authority should functional staff executives have over line executives? At one extreme, line executives could be given total authority. At the other extreme, staff executives, in their areas of expertise, could be granted authority over line executives. Between these two extremes the relationship between line and staff may vary. Two examples would be: (1) line executives would be required to "consult" with staff specialists before making a decision, and (2) line and staff executives would be required to make "joint" decisions. Whatever the situation, hotel GMs must arbitrate disputes when they develop.

Span of Control

Span of control relates to the number of subordinates reporting to a supervisor. In Figure 5-3 Heidi Baine organized Country Gourmet Enterprises, Inc., so that six department heads would report directly to her. In the past, some management scholars advocated an "ideal" span of control of exactly seven subordinates. That simplistic view is no longer held. Rather, the ideal span of control is now thought to depend on a number of factors and can be quite narrow (three or four) or very broad (fifty or more).

When Heidi Baine owned only one restaurant, her organization chart, as shown in Figure 5-2, consisted of two departments: the dining room and the kitchen. She had a very narrow span of control. The managers of these two departments, in turn, supervised the employees under them. Figure 5-4 depicts this organizational design under the heading, Narrow Span of Control. Under this organizational scheme Heidi can closely supervise her subordinates since she only has two. She will also have time to pursue other business interests because the restaurant can be easily managed in her absence. A disadvantage, however, is that this narrow span of control results in a layer of middle managers between Heidi and the first-line employees

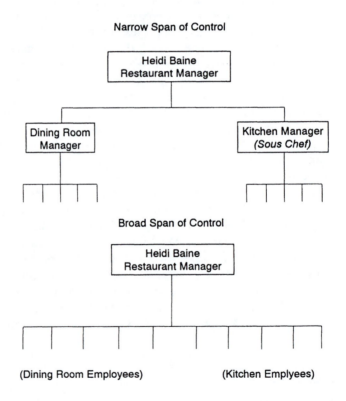

FIGURE 5-4. Two Different Restaurant Organizational Designs

who actually prepare the food and serve the guests. These two middle managers cost money. Heidi can economize by eliminating these two supervisory positions and managing all the employees herself. This would be the Broad Span of Control case in Figure 5-4. In it Heidi Baine has ten employees reporting directly to her, and in addition, she assumes the duties of chef. Clearly she cannot supervise the activities of ten 'employees as closely as she can supervise two. With no other management help, she will find it more difficult to pursue other business interests. She does, however, save considerable money by wiping out an entire level of middle management in her business. Faced with intense foreign competition American corporations, for a number of years, have been aggressively eliminating entire layers of middle managers in order to trim costs. One effect, of course, is to broaden the remaining managers' spans of control.

A number of factors must be considered when choosing the most appropriate span of control for a business (Aldag and Stearns 1987, 290-91).

- Task Similarity—The more similar the tasks of subordinates, the wider the span of control can be; the less similar the tasks, the narrower the span. Dissimilar tasks require a supervisor to pay more attention to each subordinate in order to keep abreast of the different types of problems that arise. Thus, dissimilar subordinate tasks would suggest a narrow span of control while similar tasks make possible a wider span.
- Training and Professionalism—The more trained and skilled a subordinate, the more that person can perform his or her tasks with a minimum of supervision. Similarly, professionals such as attorneys and physicians require little direct supervision. Thus, the more training and professionalism subordinates acquire the greater the span of control that is possible.
- Task Certainty—The more routine and predictable work tasks are, the greater the span of control can be. Routine tasks allow management to devise standard procedures for subordinates to follow. This decreases the need for close supervision thus allowing a broader span of control. However, closer supervision and a narrower span of control is called for when tasks are ambiguous and uncertainty is great.
- Frequency of Interaction—If the supervisor-subordinate relationship requires frequent interaction, the span of control must be narrow. If interaction is infrequent, span of control can be broad.
- Task Integration—The more a supervisor must integrate and coordinate the tasks of subordinates, the narrower the span of control must be. The time required for task integration of a supervisor goes up geometrically as the number of subordinates increases, thus quickly limiting the number of subordinates one can properly supervise.
- Physical Dispersion—The more widely dispersed a group of subordinates, the more difficult it is for a manager to properly supervise them. Thus, physical dispersal tends to place limits on the span of control.

Maid cleaning a bathroom of a Best Western hotel.

Courtesy: Best Western International, Inc.

Some of these factors may work in opposite directions. For example, fast-food restaurants are operationally quite similar to each other, suggesting a broad span of control. However, their physical dispersion works in the (opposite) direction of limiting span of control.

Coordination of Activities

Problems arise when organizations do not properly coordinate their activities. In simple organizations of only a few people, coordination is usually not a major concern. It doesn't take long, however, for problems to develop as organizations grow and become more complex. As previously discussed, work specialization and departmentalization are organizational responses to a business's growth. As duties are subdivided, it becomes increasingly important to coordinate the activities of individuals and groups toward common goals. Everyday experience suggests that coordination problems develop quickly as organizations grow. When a food order is filled incorrectly at a restaurant, when a guest is checked into a room that hasn't been properly cleaned, or when the wine planned for a banquet is not ordered, it's often because of a lack of coordination within the hotel.

The kind of coordination required for a smoothly run hotel depends on how various tasks and activities within it are linked together. These linkages result in a variety of different kinds of interdependence between individuals and groups. Three forms of interdependence occur frequently in hotels: pooled, sequential, and reciprocal (Aldag and Stearns 1987). Each calls for a different coordination response.

Pooled interdependence refers to activities that can be performed with little interaction between the individuals or groups performing them. Suppose a hotel has three telephone operators. Each can usually perform the required duties independently (that is, without any interaction with the other). The same is true of room maids and the cashiers at a hotel's food outlets. Work does not flow between phone operators, room maids, or cashiers. Rather, their efforts are "pooled" together into a common result: phone calls correctly handled, rooms properly cleaned, and food revenues properly deposited. Because these workers need not interact among themselves, coordination of their activities is best accomplished by proscribing standardized rules and procedures for each to follow, by intensive individual training, and by direct supervision. The role of coordination is to ensure that each independently performed task is carried out at the same level of efficiency and quality.

Sequential interdependence occurs when one task's output becomes a second task's input. This is typical of production line operations where products are progressively assembled. Proper coordination is ensured through detailed planning, scheduling, and standardizing products or services. Coordination also requires identification of the linkages that exist between activities. Getting the system to work properly is the key to success.

An example of such a system is the guest checkin process. The "output" of a front desk becomes an "input" to the accounting department in the form of a guest billing record, or folio. A well-planned system linking the rooms department and the accounting department is needed for this activity to go smoothly. Various food preparation activities within a kitchen, which is somewhat analogous to a manufacturing plant, also fall into this category. Sequential interdependence also takes place between a hotel's food production and food service activities. The kitchen output becomes the servers' input. Coordination is achieved through a well-planned service-delivery system that includes standardized scheduling procedures and service deadlines. Service-delivery systems pay close attention to the linkages between tasks since it's at the point of linkage that many problems develop.

Still greater coordination is required in cases of reciprocal interdependence in which individual units provide each other with input. The output of Unit A is input for Unit B, and the output of Unit B is input for Unit A. Whenever there is a high level of interaction between work units they are said to exhibit reciprocal interdependence.

Reciprocal interdependence occurs frequently in hotels. A hotel's front desk and housekeeping departments are reciprocally interdependent. When a guest checks out of a hotel, part of the front desk's output is to inform housekeeping of a vacant room. In turn, when the room has been cleaned, part of housekeeping's output is to inform the front desk that the room is ready to be rented. Thus, both departments provide inputs to the other. Similarly, the sales, reservations, and rooms departments are constantly engaged in reciprocal interdependence. The output of each department, in the form of rooms booked, is informational input to the other departments. Also, the activities of each department affect the actions of the others. For example, as more rooms are booked by sales, reservations may decide to restrict the availability of discounted rooms. During the GM research I had one rooms department manager complain about this very problem. She felt that sales and marketing was forever booking group business into the hotel without properly consulting with her. The result was to fill the hotel during periods of high demand with lower priced, group business when it could easily have rented the same number of rooms to higher average rate transient guests. Additionally, this lack of coordination sometimes resulted in serious overbooking problems. She noted that while this practice made the sales department look good, it was not in the hotel's best interest.

Another example is the interdepartmental coordination needed for a hotel to host a major convention. Rooming decisions made by the front desk must be coordinated with accounting, sales, and reservations; function-room usage requires interaction between convention services, engineering, food and beverage, and accounting. Because any one department's output and activity affect numerous other departments, mutual adjustments among each are required. This kind of coordination is only possible through *direct communication* and joint decision making between the units involved. While standardized plans and procedures are helpful, they cannot possibly solve all of the problems resulting from such a high degree of departmental interaction. Direct communication and group meetings become a necessity to ensure proper coordination when activities involve reciprocal interdependence. People simply must get together and talk to solve these kinds of problems.

Pooled, sequential, and reciprocal interdependence all occur within a hotel. Management must develop rules, procedures, standards, plans, and schedules to properly coordinate activities that exhibit pooled and sequential interdependence. When reciprocal interdependence occurs, management must design an organizational structure that fosters direct communications between units in order to ensure proper coordination. Since numerous situations of reciprocal interdependence occur in a hotel, the need for direct coordination and communication to resolve problems is an extremely important issue in managing hotels effectively. Coordination in hotels is so important that it will be the topic of Chapter Six. Communications in hotels is so important that it will be the topic of Chapter Nine.

Static Principles of Organizational Design

Society has been dealing with organizational design for quite some time; large, complex organizations have existed for thousands of years. The government of Imperial Rome, for example, is considered a model of efficiency and effectiveness. The Catholic Church is a 2,000-year-old, worldwide organization. Experience has accumulated for centuries about how to organize a variety of institutions including government bureaucracies, the military, religions, large commercial trading companies, and since the industrial revolution, large manufacturing concerns. Over time, managers and executives have developed a number of principles, or guidelines, regarding how to structure organizations. Calling them principles gives the impression they are unchanging truths. Management research has discovered, however, that these principles, while often useful, do not hold in all circumstances. Still, they are important and should be learned and applied where appropriate. The principles discussed in this section are a. chain of command, b. unity of command, c. clarity of delegation, d. completeness of delegation, and e. sufficiency of delegation (Webber 1975).

Chain of Command

This principle holds that everyone in an organization should have a superior to whom he or she is responsible. A hotel's organizational chart is a graphic description of chain of command. It should be possible for any employee to trace his or her way up the organization chart's chain of command all the way to the GM. The typical pyramid shape of an organization chart is a consequence of the chain of command and the span of control concept discussed in the previous section. Chain of command is a very powerful concept. It provides structure in an organization by setting forth a system of subordinate–superior accountability for everyone. Every new employee, no matter where within the organization, knows immediately for whom and to whom he or she is responsible.

The chain of command defines employee business communication within organizations. The chain-of-command principle holds both for subordinates

General managers take a personal interest in a hotel's restaurant decor and table setting, such as The Fountain Restaurant of The Four Seasons Hotel, Philadelphia.

Courtesy: Four Seasons Hotels and Resorts

and superiors. If a GM wants to make some change in housekeeping, the change should be communicated through the rooms department manager, who in turn will speak to the director of housekeeping. The traditional chain-of-command structure in a hotel would have the baker responsible to the chef and the chef responsible to the food and beverage director. Accordingly the baker should communicate with the chef and not directly with the food and beverage director. The baker violates the chain of command by communicating directly with the food and beverage director; in effect, bypassing the chef. It's easy to see why "following the chain of command" has become something of an organizational principle. Assume the baker wants a raise and approaches the food and beverage director instead of first going to the chef. A seemingly simple transgression like this can cause all kinds of mischief. If the raise is approved by the food and beverage director, the chef's authority has been severely undercut. It's likely that the chef will have a talk with the baker about this incident. The discussion will revolve around issues of who is in charge, how upward communications are to take place, and what the consequences of repeated violation of the chain of command will be. For the chef this could represent a serious organizational issue.

While it is important to be aware of possible chain-of-command problems when managing, too strict an adherence to this principle can take much of the spontaneity out of an organization. Experienced hotel GMs often break this principle, but in a way that is not harmful to the hotel. The immediacy of some problems in hotels sometimes require hotel executives to issue orders directly to subordinates two or more levels down in the organization. On some occasions it's simply more efficient to break the chain of command. On other occasions GMs simply want to maintain personal control over some project or aspect of the hotel and choose to bypass their immediate subordinates in order to do so. This does little harm as long as everyone knows what is happening and the organizational climate is otherwise healthy and trusting. Lawrence Wagner supervised every detail of the restaurant and patio renovation at The Regal Hotel, thus bypassing both his chief engineer and food and beverage director. Matthew Fox, GM of The St. Charles Hotel, ordered coffee in his office one morning and noticed that it was served with paper napkins rather than the usual cloth napkins. He called the director of housekeeping directly rather than his resident manager, who was in a meeting, to find out if the hotel had a linen problem. While there was no emergency, he simply wanted to get on top of this problem. In the course of the next two hours he met and spoke to the director of housekeeping four times, completely bypassing his resident manager. By midmorning, however, when his resident manager was able to drop by Matt's office, Matt brought him up-to-date with the "napkin problem" and asked him to follow through with housekeeping until it was resolved. No one's feelings were hurt; Matthew built a feeling of shared responsibility among his executives while keeping the chain of command principle in its proper perspective.

Unity of Command

This principle states that each employee is responsible to one and only one superior. In other words, each person has only one boss. If unity of command is upheld, organizational charts can look like Part A in Figure 5-5 but not Part B. In Figure 5-5A, *W, X, Y,* and *Z* report directly to *U* and only to *U*. However, in Part B, *W, X, Y* and *Z* have a problem because they have two bosses, *U* and *V*. What do these subordinates do if *U* gives one order and later *V* gives a conflicting order? Which order do they follow? This is like the problem children face when Mom says one thing and Dad says something else! The principle of unity of command is used to get around this intrinsically confusing situation.

Still, the unity-of-command principle is violated quite regularly in most organizations. A hotel waitress, whose boss is the restaurant manager, might be corrected for a safety violation by a safety officer who reports to the personnel director. The waitress feels as if she has two bosses and, in effect, she does. This common problem occurs as organizations grow in size and task specialization takes place. Specialists in safety (or accounting, personnel, data processing, and so on) often do have authority, in their specialty area, over workers who do not report directly to them through the chain of command. Problems can develop because of conflicting orders from more than one boss. The solution is not necessarily to eliminate specialization and staff positions but rather to ensure, by closely coordinating activities, that order rather than confusion reigns. As will be made clear in later chapters, the GM plays a key role in affecting coordination throughout the hotel.

Delegation

Young managers often find delegation a difficult task to master. A

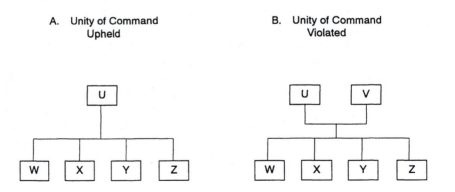

FIGURE 5-5.   Unity of Command

subordinate's ability to successfully carry out an assignment depends in part on the clarity of his or her superior's delegation instructions. Delegation can range from assigning a minor task to complete responsibility for a major undertaking. It's important for both superior and subordinate to agree on the level of responsibility, the freedom of action, and the amount of authority that goes along with a delegated task. Here's an example of limited delegation. The rooms department manager of a large hotel felt that its relationship with travel agents was not as good as it should be. He asked the reservations manager to compile data on the number of reservations made last year by travel agents in certain key geographic markets. In this example of delegation, the reservations manager was not being asked to make a decision but only to provide the rooms manager with data pertaining to the problem. Furthermore, the rooms manager also specified the exact data the reservations manager should compile, thus further delineating and clarifying the delegation of responsibility.

An example at the other extreme occurred when a highly experienced chef was brought into a hotel and given total responsibility over food production, including authority to reorganize the hotel's kitchen operations and to hire, reassign, and discharge personnel. This illustrates a principle of delegation known as *sufficiency*, which holds that the amount of authority delegated should equal one's responsibility. A person should not be made responsible for some task without being given sufficient authority to carry it out. Had the chef been made responsible for the hotel's kitchens but restricted in staffing and personnel authority, he would have complained that his "hands were being tied."

There are various levels of delegation, each of which is useful in different circumstances. Here are some examples of orders that result in different degrees of delegation:

- Gather information for my decision.
- Set out two or three alternatives; I'll then choose.
- Make a recommendation for my approval.
- Make a decision, but inform me of it before proceeding.
- Take action and inform me of the outcome.
- Take action on your own; it's not necessary to communicate with me regarding this matter.

The extent to which authority is delegated depends in part on the experience of the subordinate. Young, inexperienced subordinates can expect only limited delegation until they have proven themselves. The amount of authority delegated will usually increase as trust between superior and subordinate is built up.

It's been said that when a person becomes a manager he or she gives up earning an honest living. Hotel managers don't usually make beds, cook food, or provide service directly to guests. Rather, their job is to see to it that the organization they manage provides proper guest services. Knowing when and how to delegate responsibility and authority is one of the first skills young managers must acquire. Without this skill, confusion exists between superiors and subordinates. Without this skill, subordinates will never develop into managers. Without this skill, managers fall back to "doing it all" themselves. Without being an effective delegator it's unlikely that a person will ever progress very far up the organization chart.

THE HOTEL FUNCTIONAL ORGANIZATIONAL DESIGN

This section discusses how hotels are organized in relationship to general principles of organizational design. Individual hotels are organized along functional lines with departments grouped according to the particular work activity in which they are engaged. This section will first discuss the typical organizational structure of a mid-sized hotel of about 500 rooms and then that of a large 1,000-plus-room hotel. Departmental functions will be outlined. Authority patterns, spans of control, and line and staff relationships will be illustrated. Finally, the strengths of the hotel functional organizational design will be discussed as well as its weaknesses.

A Mid-Sized Hotel's Organizational Design

Figure 5-6 depicts a typical organization chart for a 500-room hotel. The hotel is divided along functional lines into five separate administrative departments: rooms, food and beverage, accounting, sales, and personnel. The five department heads report directly to the GM. As Figure 5-6 shows, each department is further subdivided into smaller functional units. This subdivision within the five large departments represents additional refinement of the work performed and the knowledge and skills of the people in each subunit. The function of each department and that of the subunits within each will now be discussed.

The Rooms Department

The rooms department performs the lodging function of a hotel. Reservations must be accepted, guests must be hospitably received and assigned clean rooms, the status of available and occupied rooms must be kept current, guests must receive mail and phone messages promptly, security must be maintained, public spaces such as lobbies must be kept clean, and guest questions must be answered. These are some of the more important functions of the rooms department. To do this the rooms department is divided into a number of subunits, each of which performs rather specialized tasks. In many instances, these subunits are also referred to as departments. For

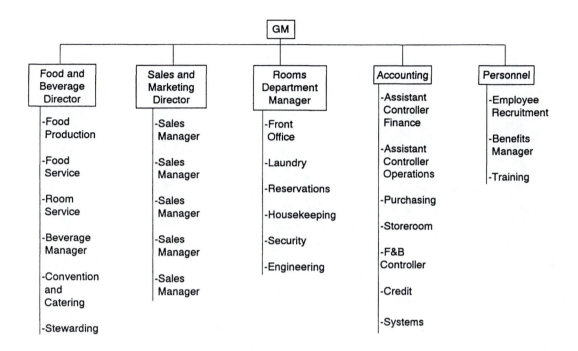

FIGURE 5-6.   Organization of a Midsize Hotel

example, the laundry department, which in a 500-room hotel is quite large, is responsible for cleaning and pressing all the hotel's linens and employee uniforms as well as guest laundry. Its function is extremely specialized. Little of the knowledge and skills required to manage a laundry operation are transferable to other areas of hotel operations.

A hotel's front office is where guests are greeted when they arrive at the hotel, where they're registered, and where they're assigned to a room. A hotel's telephone operators and other guest communications functions usually fall under the front office department. The hotel's bell staff is also part of this department. Reservations takes and keeps track of a hotel's future bookings. The housekeeping department is responsible for cleaning guest rooms and public spaces. Security is responsible for guest safety. Finally, the engineering department is responsible for the operation and maintenance of the hotel's entire physical plant, including electrical, mechanical, heating, air-conditioning and ventilation, structure, and plumbing. It also performs minor repairs and renovations.

A great deal of interdependence exists within the rooms department, thus calling for close coordination of activities between subunits. Linkages exist

Custom-designed area rugs add color and highlights to the registration desk area of The Omni Netherland Plaza, Cincinnati.

Courtesy: Omni Hotels

between the front office and the reservations department. Reservations must inform the front office of the number of presold rooms each day to ensure that a current inventory of rentable rooms is always available. Conversely, the front office must let reservations know whenever walk-in guests (those without reservations) are registered. Linkages also exist between the front office and housekeeping. Information regarding room status must flow both ways: when a guest checks out, the front office must inform housekeeping so the room may be cleaned. Once it is cleaned, housekeeping must inform the front office so that the room may be sold. These are both examples of reciprocal interdependence in which individual units provide each other with inputs. Other linkages within the rooms department are illustrative of sequential interdependence, which occurs when the output of one unit becomes the input of another. An example is housekeeping's inability to properly provision a guest room if the laundry does not supply enough clean towels or bed sheets. Another less obvious example deals with the output of information from one department to another. For example, engineering cannot replace a defective light switch in a guest room if housekeeping does not report the problem. These examples illustrate some of the many cases of reciprocal and sequential interdependence that exist between individual units within the rooms department. Effective management under these conditions calls for standardized plans, procedures, schedules, and deadlines. Coordination between units also requires frequent direct communications between executives.

The Food and Beverage Department

The primary function of the food and beverage department is, of course, to provide food and drink to a hotel's guests. In earlier times, when an inn had only one dining room, this was a much simpler task. Today, however, providing food and drink is much more complicated. The 500-room hotel in this discussion might well have a coffee shop, a gourmet restaurant, a poolside snack bar, room service, two banquet halls, and ten separate function rooms where food and beverage may be served. It might also have a piano bar and lounge, a nightclub, and a lobby bar. This adds up to nineteen separate food and beverage outlets, excluding room service! On a busy day (or night) it's quite likely that each of these outlets will have functions booked. In some cases, more than one food and beverage function will take place in an outlet during a twenty-four-hour period. There is, therefore, great diversity in the kinds of activities performed by a food and beverage department. Additionally, there is significant variety in the skills required within the department. So within the food and beverage department there are a number of functional subunits where tasks are further specialized.

To begin with, there is the food production, or kitchen, department. In a 500-room hotel this unit is headed by the executive chef, a person of great stature and authority in any first-class hotel. Under the executive chef are a variety of culinary specialists responsible for different aspects of food preparation. The larger and more complicated a hotel, the more likely its kitchen organization reflects this. The actual service of food in a hotel's restaurants is usually the responsibility of a separate department, which in a large hotel, is headed by an assistant food and beverage director. The food service department is responsible for customer service in the hotel's restaurants and food outlets. This unit contains the individual restaurant and outlet managers, maitre d's, waiters, waitresses, and bus help. Because of the special problems associated with room service, many hotels of this size have a separate subunit responsible only for room service. The high value and profit margins associated with alcoholic beverages causes hotels to form a separate department with responsibility over the bars, lounges, service bars, and other outlets where alcoholic beverages are sold. Most full-service hotels do considerable convention and catering business. The typical convention will use small function rooms for separate meetings, larger rooms for general sessions and even larger facilities for banquets. Individually catered events include local parties, wedding receptions, business meetings, and other functions held by local groups. To provide for the unique needs of these particular kinds of customers, hotels often organize separate catering and convention departments that specialize in only this kind of business. Finally, the job of cleaning the spaces of the food and beverage department, dish and ware washing, and general food and beverage expediting is often delegated to a separate subunit known as the stewarding department.

This brief description brings to light two important organizational properties of a food and beverage department: 1. the degree and variety of work specialization that exists in its different subunits, and 2. the degree of subunit interdependence. Here are some examples of the variety of specialized skills found in this department. The custodial skills required in the stewarding department are elementary when compared to the years of training required by a skilled chef. Guest contact skills are essential for a restaurant service staff; organization and efficiency are vital for a convention and catering department; control and accountability are important attributes for a beverage manager. Although there is a high degree of work specialization in each of these subunits, it is only through their continuous cooperation and coordination that a hotel's food service function can be effectively carried out. For a guest to dine in a hotel's restaurant requires the joint efforts of its kitchen, food service, beverage, and stewarding departments. A convention banquet cannot be held without the efforts of the convention and catering department along with food production, beverage, and stewarding. Even more than in the rooms department, intricate forms of sequential and reciprocal interdependence exists between the various subunits of the food and beverage department, thus placing an enormous coordinating burden on managers and employees alike.

Sales and Marketing

Problems of intradepartmental coordination are not nearly as prevalent in the sales and marketing department. In the first place, this department is quite small, thus making intradepartmental coordination much easier. Second, the department is removed from most of the day-to-day operational problems faced by other departments. Still, there is a division of work among the sales managers based usually on the type of customers a hotel is attempting to attract. Individual sales managers often specialize in corporate accounts, conventions, or tour and travel markets. Also, sales managers are sometimes further subdivided along geographical lines such as regional or national accounts. Still, the sales staff, even for a 1,000-room hotel, usually does not exceed a dozen or so. These sales managers work more or less independently in their particular market segments. For these reasons problems of intradepartmental interdependence are usually not severe (Pelletier 1988).

Personnel

A hotel's personnel department is an example of a staff organization set up to handle a specialized function. The personnel department serves no customer, books no business, and prepares no meals, yet it plays a vital role in a hotel's efficient operation. In Figure 5-6, the personnel department is subdivided into three subfunctions: employee recruitment, benefits administration, and training. The personnel director is also expected to be an expert on federal and state labor law and to advise managers in other departments on these topics. Although these three subfunctions are related to each other, there are not many problems of interdependence. Instead, the personnel department's major challenge occurs as it attempts to interact with other hotel departments. For example, although the personnel department will recruit, interview, and screen prospective employees, the final authority for hiring resides in the respective line departments and not in personnel. The same is true of promotion and disciplinary decisions, where the personnel department's input is, in most cases, limited to advice and interpretation of legal questions. As a staff department, personnel's effectiveness is largely dependent on its manager's ability to form effective working relationships with managers of other departments.

Accounting

The accounting department is an example of a department that, in many hotels, combines both staff and line functions. The accounting department's traditional role is recording financial transactions, preparing and interpreting financial statements, and providing management in other departments with timely reports of operating results. Traditional responsibilities also include payroll preparation, accounts receivable, and accounts payable. These functions are the responsibility of the assistant controller for finance. There is, however, another dimension to the accounting department that deals with various aspects of hotel operations, cost accounting, and cost control throughout the hotel. In fact, this aspect often results in the department being called the controllers department rather than the accounting department. The two areas that are the central concern of accounting control include rooms, and food and beverage. The accounting department's front office cashier is responsible for keeping track of all charges to guest accounts. Each day the night auditor must reconcile all guest bills with the charges from the various hotel departments. Although these employees work physically at the front desk and, in the case of the cashier, have direct guest contact, they are members of the accounting department and report to the assistant controller of operations.

The accounting department is also concerned with the activities of the food and beverage department. The food and beverage controller, and the food and beverage cashiers, working in the accounting department, keep track of both the revenues and expenses of the food and beverage department. The food and beverage cashiers report to the assistant controller for operations, and the food and beverage controller reports directly to the hotel controller. In effect, the food and beverage department may be responsible

An accounting analyst using state-of-the-art computer hardware at a Best Western hotel.

Courtesy: Best Western International, Inc.

for food preparation and service, but the accounting department is responsible for collecting revenues! The food and beverage controller's job is to verify the accuracy and reasonableness of all food and beverage revenues. The accounting department is responsible for keeping track of and preparing daily reports on the costs of the food and beverage used in the hotel. In many cases, as Figure 5-6 shows, the accounting department is also responsible for purchasing and storeroom operations. Finally, the director of systems is responsible for designing the accounting and control systems used throughout the hotel.

This discussion demonstrates that the accounting department is anything but a passive staff unit contending with routine record keeping. In fact, its activities in both the rooms, and the food and beverage departments represent a direct involvement in a number of day-to-day operational aspects of the hotel. This role is reinforced because the accounting department, as indicated in Figure 5-6, often has responsibility for management information systems throughout the hotel, thus increasing its interdependence with other departments of the hotel.

Two final points need to be made about the accounting department from an organizational design point of view. Accounting is responsible for collecting and reporting most of a hotel's operational and financial statistics. Through this function it plays an important hotelwide staff role as the provider of data for decision making and budget preparation purposes. Finally, the head of the accounting department has a dual responsibility not only to the hotel's GM but also to the hotel chain's financial vice-president or to the hotel's owner. The reason for this dual responsibility and reporting relationship is to afford the hotel corporation an independent (from the GM) verification of the accuracy of the financial and operating results of the hotel. Thus, the concept of unity of command is routinely violated in the case of hotel controllers.

A Large Hotel's Organizational Design

As hotels grow in size from the 500-room hotel discussed above, their organizations change somewhat. The GM of that midsize hotel had five department heads reporting directly to him (that is, the GM's span of control was five). As hotels grow, organizational units also expand. The departmental organization chart for a large, 1000-plus-room hotel will look something like Figure 5-7. It is common in large hotels for the engineering and maintenance function to be elevated to departmental status with the chief engineer reporting directly to the GM. Because really large hotels are often heavily dependent on convention and meeting business, it is not uncommon to see the convention services unit also elevated to department status with its director also reporting directly to the GM. Finally, it's common for the

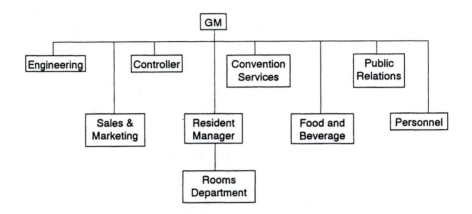

FIGURE 5-7.   Departmental Organization Chart for a 1,000-Plus-Room Hotel

director of public relations to report directly to the GM. Thus, a GM's span of control can easily increase from five to eight or more as a hotel's size increases. In addition, the extent of a GM's outside obligations seem to grow with a hotel's size. These include additional corporate-level responsibilities, civic boards and committees, and industry-related activities such as serving on the local tourist commission or hotel–motel association. The GMs of major hotels are extremely busy people who face severe demands on their time.

A typical organizational response to this problem is to promote an executive to assistant GM in order to relieve the GM of some operational duties. This is often accomplished by elevating the duties and responsibilities of one particular department head, but not relieving that person of his or her regular departmental duties! This person's title is usually resident manager. It's also quite common (and logical) for the resident manager to function as the manager of the hotel's rooms department. On the one hand the resident manager is nothing more than the rooms department manager of Figure 5-6 with a new title. On the other hand, the resident manager can be invested with additional responsibilities (and authority) by the GM that raises his or her status above that of other department heads. This added status might include serving as acting GM in the GM's absence, representing the GM as chairman on various hotel interdepartmental committees, or being given responsibility for important special projects. The resident manager's special status could, of course, have been displayed graphically in Figure 5-7 by elevating the position somewhat above that of the other department heads, which is sometimes done. Whatever the case, the resident manager's job description; his or her responsibility and authority; and the daily working relationship between the GM, the resident manager, and the other department heads will usually make the resident manager's status clear to all.

Strengths of the Functional Organization

The criterion for organizing a business along functional lines is to group together employees who perform similar tasks or who have similar skills. Thus, the most important strength of a hotel's functional organizational design is the efficiency that is possible within individual departments or subunits. The performance of common tasks allows for work specialization, which as has been shown, increases overall productivity. Since functional departments perform similar tasks, workers will more rapidly develop specialized skills and knowledge. Training will be made easier because of the similarity of tasks and the many opportunities that will present themselves for inexperienced workers to learn from experienced workers. This helps new employees quickly learn the kinds of behavior that lead to success and promotion. Finally, since functional units perform similar kinds of work, it is easier to coordinate activities within functional departments than it would be in more broadly based organizations.

A functional organization is a very logical way to organize work because it fosters efficiency, teamwork, and coordination of activities within individual units. However, the functional design's most important strength is also the source of its greatest shortcoming. This will now be discussed.

Weaknesses of the Functional Organization

The success of a hotel as a business is measured by its overall performance and not by the performance of any one department. It was pointed out in the previous section that a functional department's strength lies in its ability to focus on its own tasks and activities. Although this is surely important for departmental efficiency, it does not necessarily ensure the overall effectiveness of a hotel. Because they are specialized, it is sometimes difficult for functional departments to fully appreciate the relationship between their performance and the overall organizational goals of the hotel. It's important that all departments keep hotelwide goals of customer service and profitability in mind rather than focusing narrowly only on their own concerns. Therefore, some means must be found to coordinate the activities of individual functional departments and to set hotelwide strategies and goals. Left to themselves, it is unlikely that individual departments would be capable of doing this. Thus, specialization at the department and subdepartment levels results in the need for leadership at the top of an organization. Someone above the department head-level must set the overall strategic course of the hotel, set hotelwide goals, coordinate activities between departments, and arbitrate interdepartmental disputes. A hotel's functional organization demands strong leadership at the top.

While functional departments produce specialists within a narrow skill category they do not develop executives with broad hotel knowledge. Take, for example, the heads of a hotel's marketing department, and food and beverage department. These two executives might well have only superficial knowledge of the other's specialty. Their background, education, training, and work experience will likely be so different that either would be at a loss if placed in the other's department. The director of sales might have a marketing, general business, or liberal arts degree and have spent a career in sales-related work. The food and beverage director, on the other hand, could have a culinary diploma, extensive kitchen and food service experience in restaurants and hotels, and little knowledge or work experience in sales. Looking down the list of other department heads it is easy to see accountants running the controller's office; engineers in charge of the engineering and maintenance department; and individuals with degrees in personnel administration, business, or psychology heading the personnel department. Finally, a variety of educational backgrounds are found among rooms division managers.

Individuals educated in hotel administration are, of course, capable of filling most department head slots. But no matter what one's educational background, the longer a manager stays in one department the more specialized in training and perspective he or she becomes. Thus, while a manager may perform well within one department, he or she may be unprepared when it comes to problems that require a hotelwide knowledge and perspective. In effect, managers develop narrowly when they rise within the organizational hierarchy of one functional department. At its worst, this kind of narrow specialization can result in bias, mistrust, and friction between functional specialists and departments unless upper management takes steps to counter this tendency.

There is also a tendency, as functional units concentrate on their own activities, for new ideas and innovation to be thwarted. New initiatives in hotels often require cooperation and coordination between functional departments. New ideas tend to be stillborn if department heads lack a hotelwide perspective or have difficulty coordinating their activities toward a common objective. There is a tendency for functional specialization to concentrate on issues of efficiency; on doing things right. On the other hand, there is the need for hotels to also consider issues of effectiveness; on doing the right thing. Finally, since most of the hotelwide decision making in a functionally organized hotel must be made at the top (that is, by the GM), it is possible for a GM to be overloaded with problems and decisions. Any procrastination on the GM's part because of overload will result in decisions delayed and a drift in direction for the hotel.

This section has demonstrated the natural tendency for individual functional departments to pursue their own narrow interests rather than take the broader viewpoint of the hotel's overall goals and objectives. This is a problem inherent to all functional organizations, not just hotels (Dann and Hornsey 1986). It's a particularly important problem for hotels, however, because of the intangible nature of the services provided and because of the need for close interdepartmental cooperation in providing these services. The GM, as the chief executive of the hotel, emerges as the single person capable of providing the overall organizational direction, decision making, coordination, and arbitration needed to make a hotel's functional departments work together effectively. A hotel simply cannot run itself from the departmental level. Thus, a GM who is not a strong leader will be ineffective. The topic of leadership will be covered in detail in chapters ten and eleven.

CONCLUSION

Students often have little experience with managing organizations and even less with designing them. While understandable, this lack of exposure to the problems of organizing sometimes makes it difficult for them to fully appreciate the relevance of the material in this chapter. After all, the thinking goes, "when I go to work I'll have to fit into the business's existing organizational structure, and it could be years if not decades before I'm high enough in the company to engage in meaningful organizational design." While there are elements of truth in these statements, much of the material in this chapter will be useful fairly early in your career.

To begin with, understanding how and why hotels are structured the way they are will help you quickly fit into the organization. This means much more than being able to put names and faces together or develop familiarity with a hotel's routine. Fitting in means understanding how the hotel's organization gets things done. Fitting in means being able to use the organization's strengths to benefit your particular unit. Fitting in means knowing the organization's weaknesses and how to get around them when need be. Fitting in means understanding how the organization views chain of command, delegation, authority, and responsibility issues. In short, fitting in means performing effectively given the organizational parameters of the hotel. Clearly, your ability to get things done in any organization will be enhanced by knowledge of how it is designed and how it functions. So the material in this chapter on organizational design will be useful to you from the very first day you begin your management career.

Although you may not be able to make sweeping organizational changes in a hotel until you become a department head or GM, you will begin the process of forming an organizational structure the very first time you are made responsible for the supervision of a group of employees. When assigning tasks you will be confronted with issues of specialization, authority, span of control, coordination, and chain of command. Remember how quickly Chef Heidi had to confront issues of departmentalization in her small country restaurant. It won't be very long in your career before you will be engaged in organizing the activities of the workers under your control. It also won't be very long until you conduct the first meeting of your unit and form its first committee, thus beginning another important aspect of the organizing process. It's important to remember that as you progress up the organizational ladder you cease being a doer of things and become more and more an organizer of people. Since you will be measured by how well your organization performs it will be necessary for you to design it for maximum effectiveness.

The organizing principles presented in this chapter provide the foundation you will need to begin a hotel management career. These principles will become increasingly more useful as the scope of your organizational responsibilities and challenges expand.

REFERENCES

Aldag, Raymond J., and Timothy M. Stearns. 1987. *Management*. Cincinnati: South-Western Publishing Co.

Dann, D. and Timothy Hornsey. 1986. "Towards A Theory of Interdepartmental Conflict in Hotels." *International Journal of Hospitality Management* 5:23ff.

Pelletier, Ray. Fall 1988. "Overnight Success Takes Some Time." *HSMAI Marketing Review* 7(1):16–20.

Webber, Ross A. 1975. *Management: Basic Elements of Managing Organizations*. Homewood, Il.: Richard D. Irwin, Inc.

QUESTIONS

5-1.   Describe the basic elements of organizational structure.

5-2.   What factors will help you decide on the most appropriate span of control for your subordinates?

5-3.   In which ways can tasks and activities be linked together and how do these linkages affect a hotel's organizational structure?

5-4.   List and define the static principles of organizational design. Explain how these principles will be useful to you in your very first management job.

5-5.   How much should a manager delegate? Discuss.

5-6. Briefly list the principle functions of each of the major departments of a midsize, full-service hotel.

5-7. Discuss the strengths and weaknesses of a hotel's traditional, functional organizational design.

5-8. Let your imagination loose and try to develop an alternative hotel organizational design based on a criterion other than function.

CHAPTER 6

Coordinating the Activities of a Hotel

A hotel's organization chart is helpful in providing information regarding formal reporting and authority relationships. An organization chart alone is, however, insufficient when it comes to describing how coordination takes place between administrative units at the department or subdepartment levels. Chapter Five discussed some examples of intradepartmental coordination. This chapter examines some examples of interdepartmental coordination.

THE NEED FOR INTERDEPARTMENTAL COORDINATION

Suppose that the director of sales is under pressure to increase group bookings and does so without close coordination with the hotel's other departments. Here are some problems that may develop.

- If the reservations department is not consulted, the sales department might guarantee more rooms for a convention than are actually available, resulting in overbooking problems. The sales department might also book groups at low room-rates, thus making it impossible for the hotel to reach its average room-rate goals for the month.
- The sales department might book a group that has meeting-room needs the hotel cannot satisfy because of previous commitments. Touching base with the convention services' manager would have forestalled this problem.
- A similar problem develops with the food and beverage department if the sales department misrepresents the banquet capabilities of the hotel.

- Sales might find itself in conflict with the accounting department if, in its haste to book motor-coach groups, it offers credit terms more lenient than the credit manager's policies.

  Here are some things that could go wrong during a convention when departments fail to properly communicate and coordinate their activities.

- If convention services fails to inform food and beverage of all scheduled events, the coffee might be missing at a meeting's coffee break or hors d'oeuvre might arrive late for a cocktail party.
- If the hotel's laundry operation is unaware of an important banquet, there may be no clean waiters' uniforms available on the night of the big event.

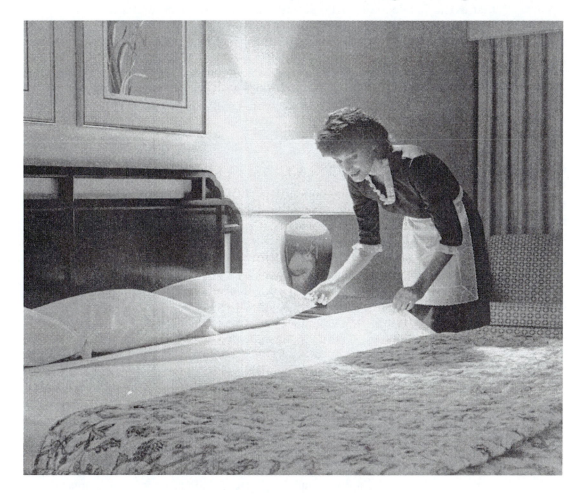

Turndown service at the Bethesda, Maryland Marriot adds a personal touch.

Courtesy: Marriott Hotels, Resorts and Suites

• The security department might schedule too few guards to handle the arrival of VIP guests.
• Front desk and housekeeping might be caught understaffed if they are not told that the arrival of a 747 charter jet has been changed from 6 P.M. to 2 P.M.

These examples, along with others in this and previous chapters, demonstrate the unending possibilities for service breakdowns in hotels. Call them miscommunications, glitches, lapses, or whatever, it's vital that service mistakes be kept to a minimum. A well thought-out set of standard operating procedures and systems can decrease the chances of many routine mistakes. Still, because of the amount of reciprocal interdependence that exists between departments, it's important that mutual adjustments and joint cooperation take place. Nowhere is this more important than at the department-head level where differences in functional specialties are most extreme (Dann and Hornsey 1986). Some specific organizational design response is needed to foster close cooperation between functionally specialized departments. The GM research revealed that a method often used for this purpose in well-managed hotels is the Executive Operating Committee.

THE EXECUTIVE OPERATING COMMITTEE

The executive operating committee (EOC) of a hotel is made up of the hotel's GM and its senior executives. There's no magic formula as to whom should be on the EOC, but usually it's those executives who report directly to the GM. Refer back to Figure 5-7, a typical departmental organization chart for a large hotel. The EOC for that hotel would consist of the GM and the eight department heads. For the midsize hotel shown in Figure 5-6, the EOC would be the five department heads and the GM. Table 6-1 summarizes the typical makeup of a hotel's EOC.

The first thing to note about the EOC is that it consists of the most senior members of a hotel's management staff: the heads of the major functional departments who report directly to the general manager. Executive Operating Committee members are also responsible for a hotel's major budgetary units. As such, each is responsible for the preparation of an annual budget by which his or her department will be judged. A subgroup of these executives, the GM, rooms manager, sales and marketing director, food and beverage director, and controller, pool their respective knowledge to produce the hotel's occupancy, revenue, and profit forecasts for each fiscal year. This forecast forms the basis for the hotel's overall annual budget, and it is the annual budget that determines executive bonuses.

The exact function of an EOC depends on how each hotel GM chooses to use the group, the GM's management style, and the structure of other management meetings in the hotel. Two important aspects of EOCs are: (1) the

TABLE 6-1   Make-up of a Hotel's EOC

	Medium	Large
	GM	GM
	Rooms Manager	Resident Manager (Rooms)
	Controller	Controller
	Food & Beverage	Food & Beverage
	Sales & Marketing	Sales & Marketing
	Personnel	Personnel
		Convention Services
		Engineering
		Public Relations

duties and responsibilities of the EOC itself, and (2) the extent to which the EOC serves as a means of communication between top-level hotel executives. The duties and responsibilities of groups can be spelled out in detail or left ambiguous. The Congress of The United States is a diverse group of people from every political persuasion. That it accomplishes anything is because many of its duties and responsibilities are spelled out in the Constitution. Consider, on the other hand, a group of neighbors who form a Great Books discussion group. No laws dictate this group's activities or function. Such a group may be lenient about meeting attendance, unable to agree on a book's interpretation, or might even find it difficult to agree on what books to read!

A hotel's EOC, therefore, could be a loosely structured group of unspecified function or it could be highly structured with a well-defined set of duties and responsibilities. The duties and responsibilities with which this discussion is concerned relate to decision making. Is the EOC usually a decision-making body or is it more likely to be an advisory group? The GM research revealed that the EOC is often rather loosely structured; it does not, for example, have formal authority for pricing, promotion, or capital budgeting decisions. The GM is held responsible for the success of the hotel and is granted the authority to make decisions to ensure that success. An important question all GMs need to answer is the amount of authority they wish to delegate, not only to individual subordinates but also to groups like the EOC. I found that the EOC in some hotels tended to be "involved" in decision making, but the degree of formality and structure was often ill defined. Depending on the GM's leadership style, the EOC may be drawn, more or less, into a group decision-making role. It really depends on the amount of authority a GM is willing to delegate to the group. Thus, one EOC might actually be structured to make certain group decisions, a second to play a strong though consultative role for the GM, and a third to have a weak or nonexistent group decision-making role within a hotel's organizational structure. How the ten GMs use their EOCs will be discussed in later chapters.

Quite apart from any formal decision-making role, EOC's act as a powerful communications vehicle within hotels. This occurs by virtue of the fact that EOC members meet regularly to discuss hotel business. It might at first seem that the meetings of a vaguely defined and structured group of executives would be a waste of time. That's not the case. Any time meetings are held, communications take place. Scott and Mitchell (1976) identify four functions of communications: (1) to provide information that helps executives in their decision making, (2) to be motivational by fostering a commitment to organizational objectives, (3) to act as a control device by resolving ambiguities regarding the role, responsibilities, and duties of executives, and (4) to afford individuals the opportunity to express their feelings and emotions. It's important to note that all four of these functions of communication may take place during meetings even when the exact purpose of the group is less than perfectly clear!

During the GMs study, some EOCs were observed to meet as frequently as twice each week, others met weekly, some bimonthly, and others monthly. Executive Operating Committee's that met less frequently were naturally less concerned with day-to-day operational matters. The stated objectives for monthly EOC meetings at one hotel were "to review policy, strategy, legal, and corporate matters." Monthly EOC meetings are also used to compare forecasted budgets with actual operating results, to discuss major operational problems, and to review special projects and programs. Financial performance is reviewed and intermediate term (one to six months) issues are stressed.

Biweekly and weekly EOC meetings, on the other hand, deal to a greater extent with day-to-day hotel operational problems ranging from daily function schedules to labor and food cost control. Of course, EOCs that meet frequently also address policy, strategy, legal, and corporate issues. More frequent meetings, however, allow the group to take up other, more detailed issues as well. Meeting frequency, agenda, and the amount of decision making delegated to an EOC will depend on a variety of factors.

- The more participative the GM's management style, the more likely the EOC will engage in joint decision making. Authoritarian GMs will find little need to foster a strong EOC.
- The greater the need for change within a hotel, the more likely it is that frequent EOC meetings will take place. A hotel that has been running smoothly in a stable environment will find less need for an active EOC.
- The less experienced the hotel's department heads, the more helpful frequent EOC meetings will be. Executive Operating Committee meetings can serve as a learning and training vehicle for relatively inexperienced department heads.

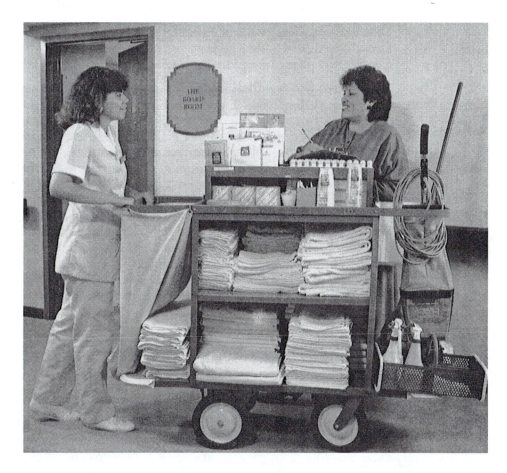

A room attendant and housekeeping supervisor getting ready to prepare rooms for incoming guests.

Courtesy: Best Western International, Inc.

Many variables affect how a GM decides to structure and use an EOC. Under the influence of a skilled GM, the EOC can be a valuable part of a hotel's organizational structure. Some of the ways it may be useful are:

• To foster group problem solving and decision making.
• To build a feeling of joint responsibility for overall hotel performance.
• To help instill common attitudes and beliefs among top executives.
• To foster top-down, bottom-up and horizontal communications among committee members.
• To assign duties, assess progress, and control activities.

• To build interdepartmental cooperation.
• To teach, coach, and build a responsive senior executive team.
• To ensure acceptance of priorities and decisions by senior management.

It's important to keep in mind that hotels are labor-intensive businesses organized along functional lines. Willing interdepartmental cooperation of large numbers of people is a necessity if quality service is to be provided. Thus, effective GMs must look for ways to get groups of people, as well as individuals, to work together toward common goals. If the GM only had to provide department heads with information, that narrow function could be efficiently carried out through memos, standard operating procedures, and one-on-one communications. The formation of groups, like the EOC, is an organizational strategy that goes far beyond the mere dissemination of information. At its best, GMs use their EOCs to foster collective responsibility for the hotel's success, to develop a group consensus regarding what is important, and to bring about a group commitment to interdepartmental cooperation. The end result is a hotel that overcomes the inherent disadvantages of its functional organizational design and really excels at quality service.

OTHER HOTEL COMMITTEES
AND MEETINGS

As important as the EOC is to a hotel, there is a lot more communicating and coordinating that must take place if a hotel is to function smoothly. Hotels address this problem organizationally through an elaborate complex structure of committees and meetings. Just like a hotel's organization chart, these committees and meetings constitute a formal part of a hotel's organizational structure. Just like the organizational chart, a hotel's committee and meeting structure is usually proscribed by the GM. Each group's responsibilities are spelled out (sometimes in great detail), regular meeting schedules are promulgated, and minutes are often taken and distributed to participants, as well as to higher level executives, including the GM. This committee and meeting structure of a hotel is anything but a casual affair. In fact, it is a well thought-out part of a hotel's formal organizational structure.

The Variety of Hotel Committees and Meetings

The purpose of these committees and meetings is as varied as the hotel itself. They regularly address a variety of concerns, including daily operational matters; intradepartmental and interdepartmental issues; hotelwide concerns; and financial, personnel, and marketing issues. Table 6-2 is a representative list of regularly scheduled hotel meetings, the participants, meeting frequency, and the general objectives of each group. Although Table 6-2 is not the meeting schedule for a particular hotel, it certainly could be. It will pay dividends to look over this list and spend a few minutes thinking

TABLE 6-2   Typical Meetings Structure for a Major Hotel

Meeting	Attendance	Frequency	Purpose	Meeting Length
Operations	GM, Department Heads, Front Office, Manager on Duty, Housekeeping, Security, Engineering, Executive Chef	1 to 5 Times Per Week	Review Upcoming Day's Activities Report on Previous Day's Results	15 to 30 Minutes
Staff	GM, Department Heads, all Subdepartment Managers reporting to Dept. Heads	Weekly	Review Last Weeks Performance, this Week's Activities, Next Week's Plans and Special Projects, Present Performance Awards	1 to 2 Hours
Executive Committee	GM, Department Heads	1 to 4 Times Per Month	Performance Review, Policy, Strategy Formulation	1 to 2 Hours
Sales Forecast and Marketing	GM, Resident Manager, Front Office, Sales, Reservations	1 to 4 Times Per Month	Review Room Demand for Upcoming 90 Days. Devise Strategies to Increase Room Nights, Average Rates or Both	1 to 2 Hours
Departmental	GM as needed, Department Head and all Subdepartment Heads, Managers, and Supervisors	1 to 2 Times Per Month	Review Departmental Issues	1 Hour
Subdepartment	Department Head as needed, Subdepartment Head, all Members of Management and Staff	Monthly Review	Subdepartment Department Issues	1 Hour
Credit	GM, Controller, Sales, Front Office, Reservations Catering and Credit Manager	Monthly	Review Accounts Receivable	1 Hour
Safety	Personnel, Food and Beverage, Housekeeping, and Engineering	Monthly	Review Safety Program and Safety Record	1 Hour

TABLE 6-2   **(continued)**

Meeting	Attendance	Frequency	Purpose	Meeting Length
Energy Conservation	Chief Engineer Resident Manager, Food and Beverage, Personnel, Rooms, and Housekeeping	Monthly	Control of Energy Costs	1 Hour
Super Staff Meeting	All Management and Supervisory Personnel	Bianually	Review Hotel Performance, Present Awards, Start New Programs	1 Hour
Annual Meeting	All Hotel Management and Employees	Annually	Year-end Review of Performance and Awards	1 Hour
Employee Meetings	GM and Selected Employees from throughout the Hotel	Monthly	Informal Communication and Discussion	1 Hour
Supervisor– Junior Manager	GM and Selected First-line Supervisors and Junior Managers	Monthly	Informal Communication and Discussion	1 Hour

about it. The kinds of meetings a hotel holds provides valuable clues about what it takes to manage a hotel.

One of the first thing to note is the sheer number and diversity of meetings. Surely, a critic might say that if a hotel were to hold all of these meetings there would be little time left over to actually do any work! In fact, the effective management of hotels requires frequent meetings. The meetings are part of the work of the hotel. Taking the midvalue of the meeting frequencies shown in Table 6-2, a hotel has 249 meetings dealing with interdepartmental issues each year! Also note that Table 6-2 has the GM attending 295 regularly scheduled meetings each year! In many hotels this is literally the case. Here are two examples.

• Jonathan Claiborne holds a daily operations meeting each weekday, chairs a weekly staff meeting, and a monthly EOC and credit meeting. Sounds simple enough, but when you add it up Jonathan attends 336 scheduled meetings each year!
• William Scully kicks off each week at his hotel with three separate Monday morning meetings: one dealing with weekly operations, one with cost control,

and a third with his EOC. He meets again with the EOC on Tuesday and acts as chairman of the Wednesday occupancy forecasting meeting. He is obligated to attend 260 meetings each year. Add in his biweekly and monthly meeting schedule and Bill's obligation is 330 scheduled meetings each year.

Meetings and Communications

Henri LeSassier was unhappy with the entire organizational structure of the Normandy Hotel. After making a complete reorganization, he drew up a revised organization chart. However, he still wasn't entirely satisfied. Next, he attached at the bottom of the new organization chart a list of all of the hotel's regularly scheduled meetings, the participants, meeting objective, and frequency. Then he devised a second chart that depicted lines of communication rather than lines of authority. By displaying the hotel's meeting structure next to its organization chart, LeSassier was recognizing the fact that decisions regarding a hotel's meeting schedule are an important part of its overall organizational design. As such, they must be thought out as carefully as chain-of-command and span-of-control decisions.

The communications chart followed his thinking about the hotel's meeting structure. He understood that lines of communication within his hotel were quite different from lines of authority (that is, those representing the chain of command). The communications chart did not, however, succeed in portraying what was really going on in his hotel. It failed because it is simply impossible to depict the full richness of communication that take place during meetings. Figure 6-1 depicts an "all-channels" communications network that would exist in an EOC meeting where all members participate in a discussion. In such a meeting each participant is able to communicate with every other participant so that each is linked by a line of communication. In a hotel with a meeting structure like that shown in Table 6-2 depicting lines of communication would be like drawing lines between nearly every pair of

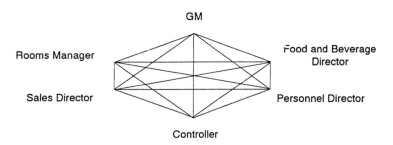

FIGURE 6-1.   All-Channel Communications at an EOC Metting

An elegant meeting room at the Springfield Marriott, Massachusetts.

Courtesy: Marriott Hotels, Resorts and Suites

executives. It is, therefore, wiser not to draw such a chart but simply to keep in mind that the powerful result of a well-developed meeting structure in a hotel is something akin to all-channel communications.

Communications within hotels will be covered more thoroughly in Chapter Nine. For now this discussion about meetings and committees should be understood in the context of organizational design. Management has the responsibility to structure a hotel's formal chain of command. It must also take care to also put in place a proper committee and meeting structure. There is no denying the fact that meetings are time-consuming. It's also true that some meetings are unproductive and inefficient. Even with these shortcomings there doesn't seem to be a better alternative to effectively manage a hotel (Conlin 1989).

One often finds frustrated, dissatisfied executives in hotels where there are too few meetings. These executives complain about not being kept informed of what is going on. These complaints operate on at least three distinct levels. One relates to managers simply not being informed of things that are happening: the success of the big convention held last week; the corporate V.P. of marketing is in town; the hotel exceeded budget last quarter; the Governor will be staying in the hotel next week-end. As elementary as it may seem, it is very easy for a hotel to fail to keep its managers and employees adequately informed. This shortcoming can have disastrous consequences with regard to the attitudes and morale of a hotel's staff. A second level of complaints relates to the lack of coordination that often is a consequence of too few meetings. Hotels are dynamic businesses subject to frequent, usually daily, changes. Meetings must be scheduled frequently in such an environment or their effectiveness will be lost. Quarterly meetings can't deal with situations that change weekly, nor can weekly meetings keep up with daily events. The final level of complaints resulting from too few meetings relate to confusion over the hotel's goals and objectives. As discussed, it is important that everyone clearly understands the hotel's mission, goals, and objectives. What is important to this hotel? What does it value most? What does it stand for? What constitutes good performance? Since hotels provide many intangible services, it is important that a constant effort be made, at all levels within the organization, to clarify and provide answers to these questions. Meetings provide an effective means of accomplishing this subtle but vital management function (Hosansky 1989).

CONCLUSION

Hotels are businesses that require an extraordinary degree of interdepartmental coordination. The functional organizational design used in most hotels was described in Chapter Five. This organizational form fosters efficiencies within each department of a hotel but is weak when it comes to coordination between departments. One of the organizing principles that hotels employ to overcome this inherent problem is a formal meeting structure designed to foster interdepartmental communication and cooperation.

The group most responsible for the overall coordination of a hotel's operations is its EOC. This committee is comprised of the GM and the heads of a hotel's major functional departments. Hotel EOCs are used differently by hotel GMs depending on the needs of the particular hotel. Some EOCs were found to play an important joint decision-making role within the hotel while others were not. They all, however, acted as a powerful vehicle for communication and coordination within the hotel. GMs use their EOCs to foster collective responsibility for the hotel's success, develop group consensus regarding what is important, and foster interdepartmental cooperation.

In addition to the EOC, excellently managed hotels usually have in place an elaborate and detailed system of meetings, both intradepartmental and interdepartmental, to cover the wide variety of issues a hotel faces. The typical hotel in the GM study conducted about 250 separate interdepartmental meetings each year. While this elaborate meeting structure never shows up on a hotel's organizational chart, it is vital to the success of any well-managed hotel.

Meetings can be time-consuming and are often criticized as being inefficient. They are, however, indispensable in that they make possible all-channel communication flows between each participant. It's difficult to measure the importance of frequent communications between hotel executives. It was typical, however, to find executive frustration and dissatisfaction with a lack of communications in hotels where meetings were few. Thus, an important part of management's organizing function is to design an effective meetings system that compliments the hotel's formal organization chart.

REFERENCES

Conlin, Joseph. June 1989. "Management Strategy: Get Control." *Successful Meetings* 38(7):37–42.

Dann, D., and Timothy Hornsey. 1986. "Towards a Theory of Interdepartmental Conflict in Hotels." *International Journal of Hospitality Management* 5:23ff.

Hosansky, Mel. April 1989. "Meetings Give You a Leg Up The Corporate Ladder." *Successful Meetings* 38(5):51–52.

Scott, W. G., and T. R. Mitchell, 1976. *Organizational Theory: A Structural and Behavioral Analysis*. Homewood, Il: Richard D. Irwin., Inc.

QUESTIONS

6-1.   Explain, with examples, why interdepartmental coordination is so difficult yet so important in hotels.

6-2.   List the variety of different uses to which a hotel's EOC can be put.

6-3.   Discuss how a GM might use the hotel's EOC differently depending on the needs of the hotel at the time.

6-4.   Draw up a list of the standing committees you would form if you were the GM of a 175-room roadside motel. Indicate the membership of each committee, the duties you would assign to each, the frequency with which they should met, and any other important details necessary to ensure their smooth functioning.

6-5.   While business committees and meetings are quite time-consuming they are, nevertheless, indispensable. In what important ways are meetings indispensable?

CHAPTER 7

Hotel Staffing

Staffing is one of a hotel's most important management functions. This can be quite a daunting job. Staffing a new 1,500-room hotel entails hiring about 1,000 employees and integrating each into the hotel's organizational structure. Most people would agree that this is no small task! Yet, it is repeated every time a new hotel opens. It is also repeated at seasonal resorts at the beginning of each new season.

Staffing is a major ongoing function in all hotels because of the relatively high rate of employee and management turnover. In many large cities an annual employee turnover rate of 33 percent would be considered low. This turnover rate means that in one year one-third of a hotel's employees will need to be replaced. At this turnover rate the entire hotel will have to be completely restaffed every three years. A 50 percent turnover results in a complete re-staffing every two years and a 75 percent annual turnover rate results in a complete restaffing every sixteen months! For a hotel with 450 employees and a 75 percent annual turnover, on average 28 new employees must be hired, trained, and integrated into its operations each month. Thus, a continual staffing pattern takes place in most hotels. It is, therefore, critical for a hotel to have in place an extremely efficient staffing process if it is to effectively integrate large numbers of new employees into its operation.

Because of its importance, many hospitality management programs have specific personnel management courses or, as they are more often designated today, human resource management courses. The theme of this book and space limitations make it impossible to spend more than a few pages on this important topic. This chapter will briefly review the major steps that comprise the management system a hotel must set up to discharge its staffing function.

Quality food, tasteful presentation and good service at The Ritz-Carlton in Naples, Florida.

Courtesy: The Ritz-Cartlon Hotel Company

FIGURE 7-1.   The Staffing System in Hotels

THE HOTEL STAFFING SYSTEM

Figure 7-1 depicts a hotel's management staffing system. The system begins with a job design where the requirements of each of a hotel's many different jobs must be thought-out. Next, employees must be selected for each of these jobs through a process of recruitment, screening, hiring, and placement. Once on the job, employees need to be trained properly for their current job and also developed for possible future jobs. Finally, the results of these efforts must be assessed through a performance appraisal system and compensation levels determined. This chapter discusses each step in this system in relationship to the ultimate goal of the process. For a hotel to be truly successful in its mission of providing quality guest service, it must employ large numbers of enthusiastic, productive, motivated, and guest-orientated workers. Properly designing jobs staffed by employees well suited to their work is an important first step in providing superior guest service (Mullens 1985).

Job Design

Chapter Five defined specialization as a fundamental issue of organizational design. One of the main issues in job design is the degree to which the efficiencies that accompany increases in job specialization are offset by employee boredom, apathy, and general job dissatisfaction. Considerable research has been conducted into which job characteristics tend to be motivating for employees (Hackman and Oldham 1974). Five aspects of jobs have been identified as motivating to employees. These motivating characteristics are: (1) the variety of skills, operations and/or equipment that an employee is required to use on the job, (2) the degree of autonomy workers have in carrying out their jobs, (3) the employee's ability to carry out an entire task or piece of work, (4) the significance of the job in relation to either the lives or work of other people, and (5) the ability of workers to receive feedback on how well they are performing their jobs. Management has some control over the degree of each of these characteristics that it builds into jobs. To the extent that management can increase these characteristics in jobs it should be possible to increase employee motivation, thus leading to greater job satisfaction, involvement and commitment to the organization.These characteristics should therefore be taken into account when management is deciding how to design jobs for workers.

It is not enough simply to write a detailed job description that pays attention only to which tasks must be performed. It is important that management seek to enhance as much as possible those job characteristics that give the greatest prospect for increasing employee motivation. The scientific management movement, which has come to be epitomized by the time and motion studies of Frederick W. Taylor (1911), has been criticized precisely because it stressed specialization and efficiency in job design while paying little or no attention to the psychological needs of workers. Today, that one-sided approach has changed. The concept of "productivity through people," has made management realize that good job design must take into account the needs of employees as well as the demands of the job. This is, to be sure, especially important in hotels where frequent employee–guest contact and the personal nature of the services provided magnifies the importance of employee attitudes.

Well-thought-out job design begins when management conducts what is called a job analysis (Lee 1987). A job analysis is a thorough statement of the specific tasks performed on a job and the time required to perform them. From a job analysis, job descriptions and job specifications can be written. A job description gives its title, pay, a brief statement of duties and procedures, working conditions, and hours. Job specifications outline the worker's qualifications necessary for a particular job. Finally, performance standards set forth the goals to be achieved on a job. Each of these steps is important to the overall hotel staffing function.

Employee Selection

The three steps in the employee selection process are recruiting, hiring, and placement. The process must take into account the hotel's needs based on job specifications, which are a by-product of proper job design. The

The Ritz-Carlton, Buckhead, doorman is often the first employee to greet arriving guests.

Courtesy: The Ritz-Carlton Hotel Company

employee-selection process must also be sensitive to the area's labor-market conditions and take into account the various federal, state, and local laws regulating employment practices (Sanson 1988).

Hotels recruit employees from a variety of sources. Most low or non-skilled hourly employees are recruited from newspaper advertisements, referrals from current employees, and in numerous cases, from educational institutions. Although newspaper advertising reaches a wide audience, a hotel has little control over the quality or qualifications of applicants it receives from this source. On the other hand, referrals from current employees have the advantage that employees are already familiar with the hotel, its operating philosophy, and the kinds of people that succeed there. Current employees, therefore, perform at least a minimum prescreening before suggesting to someone that they apply for a position. Educational institutions, from vocational high schools through colleges and universities, are excellent sources of employees for hotels. The growing number of hotel-related programs throughout the country add to the importance of this source, especially if the hotel is able to develop work schedules around the student's class schedule. Public and private employment agencies and, in some areas, hotel labor unions are additional sources of job applicants. Employees with technical skills, such as chefs, computer specialists, and managers, are recruited through personal contacts, employment agencies, educational institutions, advertisements in industry magazines and journals, and for chain hotels, from within the ranks of the company. The object of all of these various recruiting efforts is to have a sufficient number of qualified applicants available for positions as they come open. It's not an easy task; forecasting employee needs is often subject to much uncertainty because it's difficult to know when turnover will occur. A hotel can never have too many sources of good job candidates.

Hiring the right employees is critically important for hotels because they are more than service businesses, they are hospitality service businesses. This literally means the friendly reception of guests or strangers is much more than just efficient service. Figuratively, being hospitable means a willingness to entertain. So hotels are not just looking for employees to service customers, they are searching for hosts and hostesses to entertain guests! It's true, however, that many guest-contact jobs in hotels are at or close to entry level pay scales. Thus, although there may be numerous applicants for these jobs, most applicants will have minimal experience and skills.

In their best selling book on service management, *Service America!*, Karl Albrecht and Ron Zemke (1985) list three key personality factors that are important for success in high customer-contact jobs: (1) an adequate level of self-esteem, (2) a fairly high level of social skills, and (3) a fairly high level of tolerance for social contact. Clearly, these personality traits apply to hotels. Without reasonable self-esteem it would be difficult for an employee to be hospitable and friendly toward guests. Social skills and an ability for verbal communication allow for the kind of employee–guest interaction that results in the rapport necessary for a hospitable atmosphere. Finally, a high tolerance for social contact is needed so that the employee is able to treat the one hundredth guest checked into a hotel at the end of a shift with the same genuine warmth as the first. Albrecht and Zemke (1985) refer to these kinds of customer-contact jobs as "emotional labor." In their words, "The service personnel must deliberately involve his or her feelings in the situation. He or she may not particularly feel like being cordial and becoming a one-minute friend to the next customer who approaches, but that is indeed what front line work entails." (Albrecht and Zemke 1985, 114) They conclude, however, that these three personality traits are subjective and difficult to measure. They're correct, and this complicates the job of managing hotels.

Another prominent service management expert, James L. Haskett of the Harvard Business School, reviewed the research on employee attributes that lead to success in high-contact service jobs in his book, *Managing in the Service Economy* (1986). He found that success traits included "flexibility, tolerance for ambiguity, the ability to monitor and change behavior during the service encounter, and empathy with customers" (Haskett 1986, 123). One study of sales people by B.A. Weitz (1981) found that empathy with customers was more important than age, education, sales knowledge, training, or intelligence! Haskett, like Albrecht and Zemke, laments the fact that selecting people with these traits is far from a science. In fact, Joyce Hogan, Robert Hogan and Catherine Busch (1984, 168) reported in *The Journal of Applied Psychology* that they, ". . . could find no existing measures that adequately assess service orientation." So if empathy with customers is an important trait for guest-contact employees, but there is no adequate way to measure empathy, where does that leave us with regard to the hiring decision?

Hotels must try to make the best decisions possible under conditions that admittedly are less than precise. Hotels use a variety of techniques to help make hiring decisions. Having job applicants fill out application forms can be more valuable than it at first appears. In addition to obtaining important information about work history, education, and personal interests, how well an applicant follows directions and the neatness and completeness of the application can sometimes provide important clues about a person's potential for job success. References, although usually biased in favor of the applicant, is another way to learn more about an applicant. Personal interviews with applicants is another way for hotels to "size up" prospective employees.

Once an applicant passes initial screening by a hotel's personnel department, a personal interview is usually arranged with the manager whose department has the job opening. Personal interviews are often criticized on the grounds that they are subjective. This criticism is true; interviewers can be inexperienced, biased, or place undue weight on traits that are irrelevant to job success. Job applicants, in their desire to land a job, may be able to outsmart or mislead an interviewer. Still, if so-called objective tests of personality traits are of questionable predictive value, then the importance of personal interviews become apparent.

A variety of tests are used by hotels in their attempt to predict job success: ability tests are used to measure both mental and physical traits; personality tests attempt to measure characteristics such as independence, initiative, and leadership style; interest tests measure likes and dislikes; work-sample tests measure how well an applicant performs tasks required of a particular job. We know from the previous discussion that the predictive validity of personality tests is questionable. The same holds true for interest tests. Aldag and Stearns (1987, 365–366) report that research findings indicate good predictive success for ability tests and work sample tests.

The hotel hiring decision is far from simple. It takes effort, and it's expensive to recruit and to finally hire the large number of employees that hotels routinely need. It's especially difficult because of the inability of objective tests to accurately predict success in guest-contact jobs. This is where experience, intuition, insight, and persistence play an important role since hiring hotel employees is as much an art as it is a science. The more time, thought, and effort put into the hiring decision, the more likely it is that wise decisions will be made. In business, just like in sports, practice makes perfect. Outstanding hotels seem to take more time in their hiring decisions than less successful hotels, and successful GMs pay more attention to this process even though it is time-consuming. It is quite easy to lose sight of the importance of this process when a hotel is continually cycling one-third or more of its workers through the employee entrance each year. It should be remembered, nevertheless, that outstanding hotels can, and regularly do, provide high levels of guest service despite what may seem to be high turnover rates.

Matthew Fox has done an outstanding job for seventeen years managing one of the country's best known luxury hotels, The St. Charles. He may never have had a hotel career except for the insight and persistence of the hotel firm that first considered him for a job. Matt graduated from college with a degree in accounting and had been working for a CPA firm for three years. He was unhappy as a CPA, wanted to make a career change, but was unsure of exactly what he wanted to do. Matt's father had traveled quite a lot on business and sometimes brought Matt along on trips. Matt had always enjoyed the excitement of staying in hotels with his dad. In fact, while trying to decide on a career change out of public accounting, Fox would often sit in the lobby of a famous Washington, D.C. hotel watching the people go by while pondering his future. One day a friend told him that very same hotel was advertising for an accounting systems analyst and suggested that Matt apply. The idea of actually *working* in a hotel, for some reason, had never occurred to Matthew Fox until then. Once the idea crossed his consciousness, he seemed to know that this was the job for which he had been searching. In relating this story to me, Matt said that he exclaimed to his friend at the time, "Hotels! I've always loved hotels. That's a great idea. I'll apply for that job right away. I wonder why I've never thought of working in hotels before." When he applied for the job as a systems analyst, he had not worked a day in hotels, even during college, and could give no better reason for wanting to make a career change than the fact that he was unhappy working as a CPA and "had always liked hotels." As Fox tells the story, he was subjected to interview after interview by various executives of the hotel, including the personnel manager, the controller (in whose department he would be working), the resident manager, and the GM. Next, he was sent to the hotel's corporate office for further interviews and then reinterviewed by the controller. Even a quarter of a century later, his recollection of this month-long interview process is as vivid as when it happened. All this care, concern, and time was spent on filling a low-level management position. But how it paid off! Within a few short years Matt had risen to become the chain's best GM. He could easily have been dismissed as another unhappy, young CPA looking for a career change with little real interest or aptitude for the hotel business. Instead, by approaching this "minor" hiring decision carefully and thoughtfully, the company uncovered a superstar.

Training and Development

Every fall during the International Hotel Show in New York City, a unique alumni reunion occurs. Like all alumni reunions, it's accompanied by great fellowship and nostalgia. Old friendships are renewed, stories are retold about how tough their training had been, a banquet is held, and speeches about their shared experiences are made. Of course, these kinds of things take place at all alumni reunions. What makes this particular one unique is that it's not the reunion of the alumni of a traditional school, it's a reunion of hotel executives with one common experience—they all, at one time, had worked at the Waldorf-Astoria Hotel! The Waldorf has a well-deserved reputation in the hotel industry for the rigor of its training. Many ambitious young hotel executives feel that a tour of duty at the Waldorf is indispensable for their careers because of what they will learn there. Over the years, the Waldorf alumni have so valued their experience that they make special efforts to return each year for the reunion. What a wonderful testament to the training and development effectiveness of this hotel! Think of it; former employees returning each year to celebrate what they learned while working at a hotel! Something special has been going on at the Waldorf-Astoria Hotel for quite a long time. That something special, of course, is a single-minded dedication to the training and development of its staff, the Waldorf way. The Waldorf is a great hotel. What this story illustrates is one of the really important reasons for its greatness: the effectiveness of its training and development efforts.

Discussions of employee training and development often concentrate on training techniques without fully explaining what a business is trying to accomplish through training. Getting bogged down in discussions about techniques can be boring, especially if the reader has been provided only a narrow viewpoint of the training and development process. The first thing to understand about training and development is that it is not the responsibility solely of a hotel's personnel department. Rather, in outstanding hotels, all departments are involved in training and development. The second thing to understand is that employee training and development plays a vital role in implementing a hotel's strategic plan with regard to customer service. It's through training and development that employees learn how to provide improved customer service; periodic pep talks just don't work. Finally, employee training and development is not a technique or a one-time program (that is, for new employees). Rather, outstanding hotels understand that training and development is a continuing activity that activates employees and managers to reach organizational goals (Atkinson, Branch, and LaHatte 1987).

Training and development seeks to address a number of issues in hotels. One issue relates to imparting specific job skills that employees need to learn in order to perform their jobs. Making beds, waiting tables, checking in guests, and cooking omelettes all require certain technical skills that must often be taught to employees. It's here that the previous work of job analysis, job descriptions, job specifications, and performance standards comes in handy. Through these exercises a hotel will know, in detail, what an employee is expected to be able to do on a job. With this knowledge of outcome, it becomes much easier to devise a training routine to impart specific skills. The most effective training techniques will depend on the particular job and its skill requirements. Training may take place off the job in a classroom setting, through programmed instruction, or on the job where trainees learn by actually performing job-related tasks, or through a combination of all these methods. The job's complexity, variety, and the extent to which it requires worker–machine interaction (that is, front desk clerks who must learn a computerized checkin system) are all factors that affect which training technique(s) will be most effective. Remember that hotel employees learn most of their job skills while actually performing their jobs under close supervision. So while other training techniques are important and should never be neglected, it's important to remember that most of an employee's learning will take place on the job. Consequently, who does the actual training is an important issue for management. There is much to be said for a hotel involving its best employees, as well as its supervisors, in the training process. What better way to impress new employees with how to do things right than to expose them to the best of the hotel's staff. To be effective, however, a hotel's high-performance employees must consider their training duties as a reward for outstanding performance and not just extra work. Furthermore, the trainers must themselves be taught (trained) to be effective teachers as well as workers.

One of the by-products of having top-performing employees involved in training is that more than job-related skills get transmitted in the process.

Top performers cannot help but also pass along important organizational and personal skills to trainees in the process. Teaching employees organizational and personal skills is another important goal of training and development. Organizational skills means helping the employee understand what the hotel considers important in terms of employee behavior (that is, what it takes to be a successful employee). At the most basic level, organizational skills include teaching employees what a hotel values and shaping each employee's values to be in conformity with the hotel's.

Personal development of employees is yet another issue that must be addressed by hotels. Narrow job skills are not enough if a person is to grow and improve. Teaching employees such things as time management, stress management, interpersonal skills, value clarification, goal setting, and problem solving is a way of providing them with personal development skills that will also translate into improved job performance. The new food and beverage manager of a large, well-known hotel confided to me that he was shocked in discovering that most executives in his department were unfamiliar with goal-setting techniques. In consequence, the department had been run on a day-to-day basis for years with little thought being given to whether it was as successful as it should be. It was not that these managers were not highly trained technically, nor were they anything but conscientious and hard working. They simply had not been properly exposed to the management process of planning, goal setting, and evaluation that he took for granted. He took this lack of knowledge of "modern management techniques" as a training and development challenge. He felt that one of his most important tasks was to personally teach his managers goal-setting techniques so that they could then begin applying these techniques throughout the department.

An employee's personal development is one part of the development aspect of training and development. Another is preparing employees for advancement within the hotel. A policy of promotion from within, coupled with an efficient plan for qualified employees to learn new job skills, can be a powerful motivating force for employees, and just plain good business for a hotel. Promotion from within means that employees who are performing well in their current jobs and have the necessary qualifications will be given preference when job openings occur in the hotel. There are a variety of ways to structure individual employee development programs that allow employees to gain new job skills. Programmed instructional material along with competency tests is one way for an employee to learn new job skills. Another is to have employees engage in after-hours on-the-job training in new job skills under the supervision of a designated hotel trainer or manager. Many hotel chains have developed systems whereby qualified employees, if they desire, can begin an individual development program. Really excellent hotels make these programs work for large numbers of employees. Making individual development and promotion-from-within programs work is not as difficult as it might seem. Sometimes all it takes is a genuine desire to make it work.

When Frank Anderson took over as GM of The Napoleon House Hotel, it was notorious for high employee turnover and poor morale. Frank is known as an extremely demanding taskmaster, so morale certainly wasn't going to improve because he babied his employees. In looking around he noticed that job openings were being advertised in the local newspaper but that current employees were not being given prior notice so that they could apply. In fact, current job openings at the hotel were not being posted on the employee bulletin board or in the weekly hotel newsletter! Loyal employees with good work records were being given no information about job openings and advancement possibilities in their own hotel. Frank did two things. He started posting hotel job openings on the employee bulletin board and newspaper and he told his employees that these jobs would be filled from within if at all possible. He also instituted an informal, after-hours personal improvement program for qualified employees. These two initiatives were introduced with no new funds; that is, they were costless to the hotel. The result was a text book response from the employees. Turnover decreased, as did absenteeism. Morale improved, as measured by periodic employee surveys. In relating these changes to me, Frank's attitude was not the least bit self-congratulatory. Rather, he found it hard to comprehend why the previous GM had overlooked such a simple, elementary thing: reward good employees with the opportunity for advancement. As he put it, "Look after your family first."

Since people aren't perfect, not every employee will take advantage of opportunities, and a few might even abuse them. The point is that programs like these give a hotel's best employees a chance to improve and to grow—and to contribute more to the hotel's growth. It's often said that it's difficult to measure the "pay back" from dollars spent on employee training and development. Frank Anderson's answer is that in the first place it doesn't have to be expensive if you use your head. He also notes that within two years of initiating this costless employee-development scheme the hotel had promoted a total of twenty-three hourly employees into supervisory and management positions. Those numbers are a pretty straightforward measure of success.

Performance Appraisal

The problem of reliably predicting job performance of guest-service workers was discussed in the previous section. Chapter Two defined guest service as the factor that sets one hotel apart from its competition. Further, many of the services that hotels provide guests have an intangible component. For all of these reasons it is important for hotels to measure the performance of its employees as carefully as possible. Performance appraisal is important for two basic reasons: (1) it "completes the circuit" in that it is the ultimate test of a hotel's staffing process, and (2) it provides each employee, and the hotel, with valuable evidence of how well he or she is performing (Arnold 1989).

A major difficulty in performance appraisal is being sure just how to measure individual job performance. Some jobs, or parts of jobs, lend themselves to rather straightforward measurement. Examples of rather straightforward numerical measures of job performance are number of rooms cleaned, plates washed, guest checks processed, cars parked, or salads made during a shift. Whenever possible, objective performance measures should be established. Of course, these numerical measures would each have to take into account the employee's adherence to quality, accuracy, or safety standards. Still, it is relatively easy to measure performance in certain jobs based on objective, quantitative measures. Nevertheless, problems of performance measurement in hotels abound. A waitress may serve her designated number of guests but be rude in the bargain, or a desk clerk may properly, but mechanically, check a guest into the hotel, thus portraying efficiency but little hospitality. Generally speaking, the more nonroutine a job, the more difficult it is to measure performance. There are also evaluation problems to contend with. Bias, subjectivity, lack of observation of employee performance, or inadequate knowledge of the employee's job are practical real-world factors that complicate employee-evaluation systems (Herlong 1989).

The two traditional approaches to employee evaluation are the trait and the behavioral methods. The trait approach has a manager rate employees on traits thought to be indicative of good performance such as accuracy, dependability, speed, cooperativeness, and friendliness. Each employee is given some kind of score or rated along a scale for each trait. Clearly, when the traits rated lack an objective measure the rating can be criticized as no more than subjective judgments. In order to overcome this, the behavioral approach seeks to list specific employee actions that represent what is considered either good or bad performance. In fact, one approach actually provides a list of desirable and undesirable employee actions. This approach tends to be less biased in that it reports what employees actually do and it also gives employee feedback relative to the kinds of behavior the organization deems desirable. It may, however, make employees think of their supervisors as "big brother" snoopers who are continually compiling naughty or nice lists on their employees.

Another approach to performance appraisal attempts to measure desired outcomes rather than traits or specific behavior. The ultimate purpose of the hotel staffing process is to provide quality guest service. Thus, the criterion by which employees should be appraised is guest satisfaction. This kind of appraisal is in fact being done in some excellent hotels and will be discussed in more detail in later chapters. Outcome approaches to performance appraisal is a powerful concept because it gets directly at what is most important to the hotel (that is, satisfying customers).

If the desired outcome of each hotel job can be clearly stated and in some way measured, each employee can be led, through an appraisal of outcomes, to act in a way that leads directly to attaining the hotel's goals. Here's how Albrecht and Zemke view this issue when discussing employee attitude, which would be a trait factor rated by supervisors: "We can approach the matter of attitude on the job by encouraging employees to strive for measurable results that show up in terms of customer feedback. If we get high marks on the customer's report card, we can conclude that the service people have the 'right' attitudes" (Albrecht and Zenike 1985, 113). At the risk of being accused of a pun, it's worth saying that this quote displays a great attitude on their part. Why bother to measure employee attitude, which probably can't be done with any real accuracy in any case. It's guest satisfaction that counts, and if that rating is high (an outcome measure) then why bicker over employee attitude.

Employee Compensation

The roles played by job analysis, job descriptions, and job specifications have already been discussed. Recall that a job specification is a document outlining the qualifications that a worker needs in order to perform a particular job. That information, along with the job description, form the input for a job evaluation. In order to set compensation levels, job evaluations, which determine the value of the job to a hotel, must be performed. Knowing what a job is worth, and knowledge of wage rates in the hotel's labor market for each job category, allows a hotel to determine compensation levels for each job classification and to fashion an overall compensation policy. Such a policy is rationally determined by knowledge of the demands of each job, the qualifications that workers need to perform it, the value of the job to the hotel, and local labor-market conditions. Whether a hotel decides to set compensation levels above, below, or equal to prevailing market conditions will depend on its own evaluation of each job's value as well as its overall service and staffing strategies.

CONCLUSION

As soon as you have responsibility for managing people, staffing considerations will take on a completely new light. It doesn't take many hiring mistakes to make you realize the importance of employee selection. Similarly, consistent service delivery will only happen if employee training and development is an ongoing strategy. As a manager, you will look for feedback regarding your own performance and find appraising the performance of your subordinates one of your more difficult tasks. Finally, you will constantly need to balance employee compensation issues in light of what is equitable and competitive versus what the hotel can afford to pay.

REFERENCES

Albrecht, Karl, and Ron Zemke, 1985. *Service America! Doing Business in the New Economy.* Homewood, Il.: Dow Jones-Irwin.

Aldag, Raymond J., and Timothy M. Stearns. 1987. *Management.* Cincinnati: South-Western Publishing Co.

Arnold, John D., Feb/Mar 1989. "Performance Appraisals That Work." *Bottomline* 4(1):8-9ff.

Atkinson, Ann, Cindi Branch, and Greg LaHatte. May 1987. "Training For Excellence." *Cornell Hotel and Restaurant Administration Quarterly* 28(1): 15-17.

Hackman, J.R., and G.R. Oldham. 1974. "The Job Diagnostic Survey: An Instrument for the Diagnosis of Jobs and the Evaluation of Job Redesign Projects." *Technical Report No. 4, Department of Administrative Sciences*, Yale University.

Haskett, James L. 1986. *Managing in the Service Economy.* Boston: Harvard Business School Press.

Herlong, Joan E. January 1989. "How Am I Doing, Boss?" *Restaurants USA* 9(1):14-16.

Hogan, Joyce, Robert Hogan, and Catherine M. Busch. 1984. "How to Measure Service Orientation." *Journal of Applied Psychology* 69 (no. 1):168.

Lee, Mary Ann. April 1987. "How To Use Job Analysis Techniques." *Restaurant Management* 1(4):84-85.

Mullens, Laurie. 1985. "Job Analysis—Know the Job and the Person to Do It." *International Journal Hospitality Management* 4(4):181-183.

Sanson, Michael. April 1988. "How to Hire, Train and Retain Your Employees." *Restaurant Management* 2(4):41-45.

Taylor, Frederick W. 1911. *Principles of Scientific Management.* New York: Harper & Brothers.

Weitz, B. A. Winter 1981. "Effectiveness in Sales Interaction: A Contingency Framework." *Journal of Marketing* 45:85-103.

QUESTIONS

7-1. What are the major steps in a hotel staffing system?

7-2. What psychological needs must be taken into account when designing a job?

7-3. List the various personality traits you would like to see in a guest-contact employee.

7-4. Discuss how you would go about trying to identify the traits in a job applicant that you listed in Question 3.

7-5. Develop a training plan for an entry level job such as dishwasher, room maid, security guard, or cashier, in a hotel.

7-6. Specify the broad outlines of an employee personnel-development plan that would encourage ambitious employees to advance their careers.

7-7. Develop an employee appraisal form. Present it in class and justify it based on what you are trying to accomplish through employee appraisal.

CHAPTER 8

Motivation

Hotels employ large numbers of people who provide a variety of intangible personal services to guests. To be effective, these services must be provided hospitably. Many guest-contact jobs pay rather low wages, and consequently, hotel employees are sometimes inexperienced and minimally qualified. Finally, most employee–guest encounters take place away from the watchful eye of management.

The dream of every GM is to have the entire hotel staff *willingly* strive to accomplish the hotel's goals. If this can be accomplished, employees will perform at a high level. They will be satisfied in their jobs because by accomplishing the hotel's goals they will, at the same time, be fulfilling many of their personal goals. Nothing is more powerful than a motivated staff. With it a hotel has the potential to be great. Without it there is little chance of rising out of mediocrity. One of hotel management's great challenges is developing a highly motivated staff. This can only be accomplished with an understanding of what motivates people.

UNDERSTANDING PEOPLE

Eight of the ten GMs studied feel that understanding people is one of their main strengths. Furthermore, they considered their ability to develop people one of the major reasons for their success. The fifty-three hotel department heads interviewed ranked employee motivation as their greatest challenge. Some GMs seem to be naturals when it comes to people. William Scully feels that understanding and being able to deal with all kinds of people is one of his main strengths. It turns out that his subordinates feel the same way! They refer to him as fair, approachable, able to handle all kinds of people, caring, a friend, a strong leader with an easy manner,

A Marriott hotel concierge needs to be motivated to provide personal, friendly guest service.

Courtesy: Marriott Hotels, Resorts and Suites

and a person who makes you want to do a good job for him. Frank Anderson is an extrovert with a different saying for every occasion. Henri LeSassier feels that his flair and cleverness with people springs from an artistic mother.

For other GMs, understanding people did not come easily or naturally.

For many years, Matthew Fox and Curtis Samuels could not accept the fact that people make mistakes! Lawrence Wagner had to struggle to change the authoritarian ways he learned in Europe. Jonathan Claiborne is still struggling to make the transition from managing a hotel in the male-dominated Middle East to one in which half of his executives are young, female professionals.

Hotel GMs also admit to weaknesses when it comes to people. While most listed understanding people as a strength, they all mentioned some people-related deficiency as one of their weaknesses! One felt he was "long on criticism and short on praise," another could not understand why people were not all like him, and a few had to continually fight a dictatorial tendency. It was interesting going from one hotel to another and observing one GM struggling over a particular "people problem" that another GM had solved years ago. Two of the GMs studied, both of whom are now corporate vice-presidents, complained about the difficulty of motivating long-term employees. Three other GMs managed outstanding hotels that were noted for the longevity of their employees and managers. While they admitted to other shortcomings when it came to people, motivating long-term employees was not one of them.

Jonathan Claiborne had successfully managed another hotel but complained that it was hard "starting over" in his current assignment. He also felt that women were more difficult to manage than men. Having spent his last six years in the male-dominated Middle East, it's easy to appreciate his "problem." Half of his department heads now are women. Their reaction to him was equally interesting. One thought that he expected women to "hang on his every word," another felt that he viewed his pronouncements as "rumblings, like thunder from the clouds," while a third thought that he expected the female executives to "stand in awe" as he passed by. These modern, competent, female American executives had, of course, no intention of being intimidated by this GM, so it's no wonder he was finding the "transition" difficult. Poor guy! Unbeknownst to him, he was being broken in by these ladies to the realities of life in the United States. The fact that he really is a good fellow allowed these women to accept him in an understanding, one might even say, amused way. Each, in her own way, was in the process of "educating" him to the ways of modern American women.

Each of the GMs, and in fact nearly all hotel executives, spent the great majority of their day with people or talking to people. Thus, understanding people and being able to communicate with them effectively was for each a key skill that related directly to their success in the hotel business.

MOTIVATION AND WORK

During the planning for this book a friend who owns an oil drilling contracting business asked what topics would be covered. Upon mentioning motivation, he allowed that it would likely be quite a short chapter. Based on his experience in the oil drilling business and paraphrasing the children's fairy tale, his view was "people will work themselves into a spot of butter" if only you offer them enough money! His assumptions about people were: (1) they are motivated to work because of a need for money to live, and (2) since it's money they're after, they will expend more effort if offered greater financial incentives. To him, all problems of worker motivation can be solved through monetary rewards. Though it would be unrealistic to say that money is unimportant to workers (or executives), it would be equally unrealistic to say that money is their sole motivator.

Assumptions About People

The point of this story is that basic assumptions about people strongly influence managers' actions. The opinions subordinates held about their GM and the actions and statements of the GMs themselves are revealing in this regard. In some cases there was a close correspondence between a GM's basic assumptions about people and his behavior. Matthew Fox is a good example. He has been successfully managing the same first-class hotel for seventeen years. I interviewed numerous executives who worked for him, some for many years and others for just a few, and they all had him "figured out" in about the same way. One long-time associate said that Matt believes, "people are good and will do the right thing. He's been personally hurt when a long-time employee was found stealing." This same executive noted that over the years Matt had loaned money to hourly employees who were having personal problems. In fact, he is known around the hotel as a "soft touch." A recent associate spoke glowingly of watching Matt "work the room" at the hotel's anniversary party, likening him to a groom at a wedding reception. "He kept a list of the employees who had been with the hotel since it opened and he made a point of talking with each personally." Others described him as "generous to a fault; deeply concerned about people, sometimes to the detriment of the organization; he tends to procrastinate on personnel decisions, especially if they involve long-time employees—unable emotionally to come to grips with discharging a certain long-time executive." A few felt that the hotel had to "work around" maybe 20 percent of the older staff because Matt would not get rid of them.

While some of these remarks were meant as criticism, there was another side to their view of Matthew Fox. The younger executives especially viewed him as their trusted mentor. As one put it, "He hired me with little hotel experience; he saw some potential and was willing to take a chance on me. I'm sure in ten years I'll still feel the same about him." Another said that Fox was a person from whom he could learn and then, in a voice full of respect said, "Mr. Fox is my teacher." Most felt that "they worked for Mr. Fox and not the company." To me the most telling comment about him was, "Describing him as a *person* is the same as describing him as a *manager*."

There were numerous instances of consistency between the GMs' basic assumptions about people and their behavior. There were also some paradoxes and inconsistencies. Some subordinates described a GM as "cold and callused toward people; a person who loses sight of the human side of things; vicious at times and without compassion for the individual." Others said he was "very supportive of upward mobility; takes great pride in being a mentor; loyal to his people and recognizes that personal problems can affect performance and one's career." These differences of opinion can be explained by understanding that this GM felt that executives could be divided into two groups: those who were capable of performing at his extremely demanding level and those who could not. He was loyal and supportive of the former and quickly got rid of the latter. Viewed from this perspective his behavior was quite consistent with his basic assumptions about people.

Henri LeSassier was proud of his ability to "understand people and get the most out of them in rather untraditional ways." He admitted to playing "mind games" with them, purposely keeping them unaware of his intentions and practicing crisis management. It turned out that his subordinates agreed! They felt that he was upsetting, to say the least. Still, he did not come to the hotel, which was on the verge of bankruptcy, and "clean house" by firing most of the executive staff. Instead, he played his mind games with the existing management and, as they put it, had been domineering, pushing, insulting, and energizing them toward profitability ever since. While there was a certain love–hate relationship between LeSassier and his staff, he was true to his assumption about people's ability to adapt, grow, and change. As he put it, "When a person fails 90 percent of the time it's the company's fault."

These three examples illustrate different views about people held by different GMs. People develop views about human behavior through a subtle and complex life process. Some of these beliefs may be consciously held, others are subconscious. In either case, they affect the way in which people relate socially and on the job.

A Changing View of Workers

For many years, a broadly held assumption about worker behavior corresponded closely to that of my oil drilling friend who was quoted earlier. The assumption that people only work for money was held by the "scientific management" school of management, of which Frederick W. Taylor was the best known spokesman. In his *Principles of Scientific Management* (1911) he outlined a three-step management process that included: (1) time and motion studies to determine the one best way to perform a job, (2) scientific selection of employees with the proper physical traits to perform the job as designed, and (3) a compensation method (piece-rate) whereby workers received more money as their output increased. Under his system, workers were little more than another machine in a world of mass production. Many of the methods of Taylor and his followers did result in increases in output per employee during a period of rapid industrialization and technological change. In time, however, employee problems developed for a very simple reason: people are not machines and they refuse to be treated like them.

In the 1920's an industrial lighting experiment at the Hawthorne Manufacturing Works of the Western Electric Company turned up seemingly confusing results. Two groups of women assemblers were chosen to take part in a series of experiments concerning the influence of lighting on productivity. For one group, the control group, lighting was unchanged. For the other, the experimental group, illumination was varied. The output of the two groups was measured to see what effect lighting levels had on worker productivity. As the experimental group's lighting level was increased, their output increased. However, when the researchers then decreased the lighting level the experimental group's output increased once again. This strange trend continued even when the lighting was made quite dim! This startled the researchers but no more than the fact that the control group's output also increased even though there was no change in its lighting level. A group of researchers from the Harvard Business School, headed by Elton Mayo, were brought in to help figure out what was going on. They ran some additional experiments, including one where the experimental group's pay was increased while the control group's was not. Again both groups' productivity went up!

These now-famous experiments at the Hawthorne Works (Roethlisberger and Dickson 1939) attributed changes in productivity to psychological rather than physical or monetary factors. It was concluded that the women in both groups were proud to have been singled out to take part in these experiments. Both groups thought of themselves as special, and this feeling of being special motivated them to increase productivity. Even when the attention they received was to have the lights turned down, productivity increased. Even when nothing was done to the control group, productivity increased. These workers were saying, in effect, it doesn't make a lot of difference what you do, just pay attention and we'll work harder! The important conclusion drawn from this research is that workers are motivated by a complex set of psychological (that is, human) factors. People are not appendages to machines motivated solely by money. The Hawthorne experiments marked the beginning of the human relations school of management study, which focused on human behavior and its relationship to work.

People are complex, and each is a little different. It's not possible to treat all people the same. Lawrence Wagner is very careful never to criticize or pressure his director of sales, whom he feels is thin-skinned and a worrier. All it takes is a suggestion and the sales director, who is great at follow-through, will take it from there. On the other hand, he pushes and prods his public relations director, whom he considers thick-skinned and "likely to stop in her tracks" if not prodded along. Lawrence is more effective as a manager because he takes human differences into account and looks for different ways to motivate different people. Matthew Fox has come to accept people's shortcomings. He knows, for example, that sometimes it's impossible to get everything just the way he wants it. As he said during an early morning tour of his hotel, "If you want to slow things up, just give 100 different orders on a Monday morning."

The Motivational Process

A motivated person is one who senses a need, sets a goal to fulfill it, and then takes action to accomplish the goal, thus fulfilling the need. A motivated person is willing to *do something* to satisfy a need. Just wanting something is not enough. One may want to compete in the U.S. Open Golf Championship, but few are motivated to engage in the endless practice required to fulfill that dream. Motivation and positive action go hand in hand. Figure 8-1 depicts the motivation process. Needs result in goals, followed by actions, and then by comparison of results with original needs. When a need is satisfied, motivation (and action) will cease. If a need continues, action continues. Bobby Jones retired while still in his twenties after winning golf's four major championships in 1924, the first and only golfing grand slam. Jones said he had accomplished all that he could in golf. By so doing he lost his motivation for golfing competition. In contrast, Arnold Palmer, now in his sixties, continues to be motivated by a need for competition. While extremely wealthy and secure of his place in golfing history, he still plays in tournaments because of his continuing need for competition.

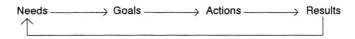

FIGURE 8-1.   The Motivation Process

INDIVIDUAL NEEDS

As a manager in the hotel business one of your challenges will be to develop a staff of employees and executives who are motivated to accomplish the goals of the hotel. In an ideal world each employee will be motivated to willingly work toward accomplishing these goals. However, people set goals in order to accomplish individual needs. Thus, to better understand how to motivate employees understand individual needs.

Theory *X* and Theory *Y*

Douglas McGregor, a professor at MIT's School of Industrial Management, summed up the different assumptions concerning human behavior held by the scientific management and the human relations school of management. He contrasted these two schools of thought as Theory *X* and Theory *Y* (McGregor 1960).

According to the Theory *X* view of human behavior, the average person dislikes work, will avoid it if possible, is not particularly ambitious, wants no responsibility, prefers to be directed, is uninterested in the goals of the organization, and is looking primarily for security. With employees like these, managers must closely control and direct their activities through the use of threats, punishment, and if necessary, coercion. Only in this way can the organization's goals be met.

McGregor rejected this view. Although people sometimes exhibit behavior consistent with the assumptions of Theory *X* he felt that it was due not to their human nature but rather is a result of mismanagement. His Theory *Y* is a much happier view of people. It holds that the average person is motivated by a variety of needs and that many of these needs can be fulfilled through work. The needs for social affiliation, self-esteem, and self-fulfillment are present in most people, and the opportunity to work toward fulfilling these needs on the job can be motivating to workers. For McGregor, the average person is not the passive dolt described by Theory *X*. Rather, most people have the capacity to assume certain levels of responsibility and, if treated (that is, led) properly, will willingly work toward organization goals. Thus, Theory *Y* suggests a more participative approach toward managing that attempts to unlock people's inherent motivations to fulfill a variety of their needs. Management's job becomes one of helping people achieve their personal goals *through* achieving organizational goals. Where Theory *X* proscribes authoritarian and controling behavior, Theory *Y* recommends participation and a degree of employee self-control and direction (Rinke 1989).

Frank Anderson believes in Theory *Y*. His approach to managing is to "delegate and let people make mistakes." While he wants to keep mistakes to a minimum, his basic assumption about human nature is positive. William Scully tried a Theory *Y* approach when he was an assistant food and

Waiters preparing for dinner

Courtesy: Radisson Hotels International

beverage director in a large convention hotel. On busy nights the dish-washers were unable to keep up with the amount of dirty china, crystal, and silver the hotel was producing. Something had to be done, and Bill was afraid that the solution might require a large capital expenditure for new warewashing machines. Before recommending more equipment, how-ever, he decided to see if the dishwashers themselves had any ideas to im-prove the situation. To his surprise the workers suggested relocating the existing dish machines and some changes in procedures that allowed the hotel to solve its problem at very little cost. In the process the dishwasher's productivity increased by 300 percent, and the hotel was able to use five fewer people in this area! This was a lifelong lesson for Bill. It taught him that all employees, even dishwashers, can contribute if only given a chance.

Things don't always work out that nicely, even for seasoned hotel executives. Henri LeSassier, who is quite proud of his people skills, is still learning to understand Americans. One of his complaints at the time of the GM research was that his sales executives had a poor work ethic: they would not stay after hours to enter sales data into the computer system. Was his assessment correct or was their unwillingness to perform this particular task the result of some other cause? While it's difficult to say, it seemed that LeSassier had already made up his mind and the subject was closed. These executives may forever be labeled lazy and treated accordingly. Some of his subordinates did, in fact, complain that he made snap judgments about people that were difficult to change.

The Theory X and Theory Y approaches to managing spring directly from basic assumptions regarding human needs and behavior. Understanding people's needs and behavior thus becomes an important skill all managers need to develop. The next section provides important insights into the question of human needs.

A Needs Hierarchy

One of the best known explanations of human motivation is provided by Abraham Maslow (1954). Maslow believed that people attempted to satisfy an *ascending* category of needs, as shown in Figure 8-2. His five categories of human needs, starting with the most basic, are: (1) physiological—food, shelter, and the basic bodily needs; (2) security—the need to feel protected, safe, and stable; (3) social/affiliation—the need for love, social interaction, and a feeling of belonging; (4) esteem—the need to feel that others recognize and respect one's accomplishments and self-worth, and (5) self-actualization—the need to be the best one can be, to reach one's potential through action. These needs are arranged in a hierarchy because Maslow believed that as a person satisfied lower order needs such as food, shelter, and some level of basic security, one's motivation toward those needs would diminish and be refocused toward accomplishing higher order needs.

This section discusses the relationship between Maslow's needs hierarchy and managing a hotel. Unmet physiological and safety needs, as anyone down on his luck will attest, are extremely motivating. Thus, considerations of pay, fringe benefits, and job security are obviously important and motivating to satisfy these lower order needs. However, once a worker has satisfied these lower order needs through some minimum level of job performance, they cease to be motivators for greater job-re-

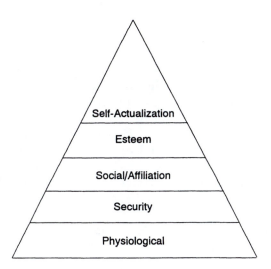

FIGURE 8-2.   Maslow's Hierarchy of Needs

lated efforts. If an employee is to bring forth more than the minimum level of effort required to keep a job, management must appeal to higher order needs (Goll 1989).

There are numerous ways in which hotels can fulfill a person's social or affiliation needs. The way in which jobs and work groups are organized can either enhance or diminish social interaction. Extracurricular activities (for example, a company softball league) may foster a feeling of being part of a team. Formal and informal groups form naturally in all organizations. Hotels that understand the need for group interaction can build strong group cultures where individuals identify with the organization, have a feeling of belonging, and consequently, are motivated to willingly act in ways that foster organizational goals. Being a little thoughtful also doesn't hurt. Although his hotel employs over 800 people, Bill Scully knew that one of his employees, a porter, managed a little league baseball team. When two ex-big league stars checked into the hotel Bill arranged to get their autographs on baseball cards so that the porter could give them to his players.

While people are social animals and need a sense of belonging, they also like to be singled out as individuals. It's nice for the entire unit to win a safety award, it's also fun to be individually honored for no lost-time accidents during the past year. Everyone wants to be a winner! Management's job is to provide the proper climate, incentives, and rewards so that people can think of themselves as winners. Give people a chance to be a winner and their natural need for self-esteem will motivate them to achieve. During the GM field research, Curtis Samuels introduced me to the executive responsible for safety at The Hotel Frenchman. Though an important job, few would characterize it as exciting, nor is it generally considered the best springboard for corporate success. I'd never have known this from listening to Curtis. He lavished praise on this executive for the great job she had done in a recent safety campaign and explained how her efforts had helped the hotel reduce accidents, thus lowering insurance premiums. Talk about self-esteem! When Samuels got through she knew she was the greatest safety officer in the company, that safety was of central importance to her GM, and that he recognized and appreciated the great job she was doing.

Maslow felt that people's ultimate need is achievement for its own sake: self-actualization. This idea is expressed in many ways: the U.S. Army wants to help you "be all that you can be," the marines are looking "for a few good men," adventurers climb mountains "because they are there," athletes devote their lives "in pursuit of excellence," artists starve while in "search of beauty," and even textbook writers plow on doggedly, often at the expense of their golf games! The self-actualization need often expresses itself as much in the striving as in the accomplishment. The late Malcolm Forbes once said that if a person isn't having fun trying to get to the top that the trip really isn't worth it. In other words, the game and the effort is as important and satisfying as the achievement itself. That's great news for hotels. It means that if management structures its goals, policies, and rewards properly, it can expect certain members of the organization to respond to the challenge because it's fun to try to be the best.

Curtis Samuels has devised all kinds of awards for his employees to strive toward, and he presents these awards at festive gatherings designed to celebrate achievement and build esteem. Two such awards ceremonies are called "The Roar of the Crowd" and "The Critic's Choice." It may sound a little corny, but the wide smiles and the pride of the employees being recognized clearly define its value.

Outstanding hotel managers realize that there are limits to what can be done by appealing only to lower order needs as motivators. Richard James understood this when he talked about the difficulty of keeping long-term employees motivated. These workers had security, were at the top of their pay grade, and were not interested in promotion. They could only be motivated by appeal to higher order needs. Jonathan Claiborne's problem was different. Because his hotel was losing money he was forced to freeze all wages for two years. At the same time he needed motivated, positive employees in order to run a high-quality hotel. He developed a variety of programs to keep morale high and his staff motivated, all of which *had* to appeal to higher order needs. Lawrence Wagner wanted his hotel to shoot for an extra "star" in a popular travel guide hotel rating system. In his desire to leave no motivational stone unturned, he initiated a program called Star Wars in which hotel executives and their spouses would check into the hotel as guests for the weekend. During their stay, the spouses would critique the hotel's amenities, physical condition, and service. While he was, of course, interested in the spouses' assessment of the hotel, he understood that the very process of involving them was motivating for his executives.

Subsequent research concerning Maslow's theory suggests there may not be five distinct needs and that people do not always move up the needs hierarchy in a predictable fashion. It's also likely that some people focus almost exclusively on one need while ignoring others. Also, the pleasure gained from fulfilling esteem and self-actualization needs may cause people to strive even harder to continue to experience these feelings. Further, needs are not progressive for all people. For some people needs may, for a variety of reasons, be truncated. It's been suggested (Alderfer 1972) that if people are continually frustrated in their attempts to fulfill higher order needs, they may quit trying and drop back to lower order needs. While some of the particulars of Maslow's ideas have been challenged, his basic insight has nonetheless had a powerful influence on management. Maslow opened up the prospect of examining individual human needs and designing management systems that appeal to higher order needs.

The Need for Achievement

Maslow's idea of self-actualization can also be thought of as a need to achieve. The need to achieve is a need to finish things successfully or to get things done. People with this need spend a lot of time thinking about how to improve a situation or how to do the job better. Some people seem to have the need to achieve from the day they are born. Others appear to lack it. People with high achievement needs are the results-oriented people of the world. They are extremely conscious of time; it seems to move faster for them than for other people because they are so concerned about getting things done. Achievement-oriented people like to set goals for themselves that are moderately difficult but attainable, enjoy the process of doing and accomplishing things, seek responsibility, and must have feedback to validate that they are accomplishing what they set out to do. While they do not shun monetary rewards, it's the doing and the achieving that turns them on the most. Some researchers (McClelland 1962) believe that the achievement drive is not an inherited trait but rather something that results from non authoritarian, warm, and encouraging parents who set moderately high but attainable goals for their children.

They further believe that the need to achieve, through proper training,

Conference rooms at the Indianapolis Airport Holiday Inn help attract group business

Courtesy: General Hotels Corporation

can be instilled in adults who may lack it. This can be done through an indoctrination into goal setting and the positive language and actions associated with achievement.

Achievement training holds the promise of improving the performance of both managers and employees. It's easy to understand how the need for achievement can be beaten out of someone who has tried many times and failed or whose background negatively influenced this trait. Teaching employees how to become achievers (winners) can make the difference between workers who are clock-watchers and workers who are actively trying to accomplish something.

Positive language and actions are something in which Frank Anderson believes strongly. Because of his background in football his speech is laced with sports terms. His feeling is that GMs should be *coaches* and *cheerleaders*; he hires *winning players*, and his philosophy is to turn *negatives* into *positives*. He sets the *game plan*. He and his team are "all in this together", and they move at "warp speed" to win the game of life! Words do make a difference, and Frank uses them to foster the achievement motive throughout his hotel.

He lives this attitude as well. I witnessed an incident that illustrated this. He had his public relations director set up a press conference to announce that the hotel had landed a particularly prestigious convention. When only one member of the press showed up, the PR director and Frank's senior executives who attended the press conference were noticeably upset. After the press conference, Frank immediately began to point out the positive things that had happened. As he talked to his executives he deftly deflected their negative reactions with positive statements. He simply refused to dwell on the negative and within ten minutes had his staff once again in a positive, winning mood.

Henri LeSassier tried to instill a winning attitude in his hotel by having its executives and staff organize a full-scale parade, complete with floats and bands, for a local festival. He also had his staff organize a trade mission to Paris for the city's mayor and some of it's leading business and civic leaders. Neither project had a lot to do with his hotel, but it sure was fun, and the entire staff derived a real sense of achievement and excitement from their efforts. After five years of losing money in the hotel, these executives were suddenly winners again!

Curtis Samuels wants to start his new employees off as winners. Each week when new hires go through orientation he drops by to give a little welcoming speech. It goes something like this.

> "I want you to go home this evening and tell your spouse, your family, and your friends that you are now working for the best hotel in the city. Tell them that this hotel interviews eight people for every person it ultimately hires, and that every position it fills is vital to its continued success. Tell your friends that you were hired because we see something very special in you that convinced us you will truly be of value to the hotel. Also thank them. Thank them because they had a hand in developing your positive qualities that resulted in your getting this job. Finally, when you get home congratulate yourself for having that something special that it takes to be part of an organization that strives to be the best."

One executive, when asked to describe some of the positive things Samuels had done since coming to The Hotel Frenchman simply said, "The employees think Curtis is God."

Worker Satisfaction and Dissatisfaction

What do you think you would find if you asked a group of workers to describe incidents that were particularly satisfying or dissatisfying about their jobs? Frederich Herzberg (1968) did exactly that, and what he found was rather interesting. The things that people reported as causing job satisfaction included achievement, recognition, the work itself, responsibility, advancement, and personal growth. On the other hand, the things that workers reported as dissatisfying included company policy and administration, supervision, relations with superiors, working conditions, pay, and fringe benefits. Herzberg designated satisfiers as motivators while he named dissatisfiers hygiene factors. He felt that if an organization could provide employees with the opportunity to experience satisfiers (that is, achievement, growth, recognition, and so on) this would result in motivated employees.

Low pay, poor working conditions, and unreasonable work rules can cause workers to be dissatisfied and are not to be neglected. Jonathan Claiborne surveyed his employees after becoming GM of The Riviera Hotel and found that 92 percent were basically pleased with their jobs. The only major complaint was the quality of the employee cafeteria food. He quickly improved the food and got off to a good start. But according to Herzberg, good pay, decent working conditions, and reasonable work rules only remove dissatisfaction. They do not result in the kind of worker satisfaction that is motivating! To Herzberg, you can't motivate employees through hygiene factors. People come to expect hygiene factors and, therefore, take them for granted. On the other hand, if management can structure an environment in which employees experience satisfiers on the job (that is, achievement, responsibility and recognition) this will result in motivated workers.

Here are some examples that illustrate Herzberg's point. Curtis Samuels had really driven his managers and employees for the first six months he was GM of The Hotel Frenchman. His executives told stories of 6 A.M. hotel walk-through inspections and 8 P.M. meetings that lasted till midnight. Once they got started with these war stories, I couldn't stop them. They were so proud of having lived through the experience and having become better managers because of it that they wanted me to know all about it! The hotel's personnel director proudly told me that Curtis had forced him to learn to read the hotel's financial statements and that he would never have done this without Samuels' insistence. It had opened his eyes to the business side of hotels, and he was proud of what he had achieved and how he had grown. Another example came from Richard James. After only three months as GM of The Hotel Apollo, he confided to me that his executives were beginning to feel the strain of his high expectations. He said that they would probably only realize that they were "having fun" when they had moved on to jobs in another hotel.

Herzberg's theory has had its share of criticism, especially the assumed cause-and-effect relationship that satisfaction leads to motivation. His ideas nevertheless have been quite influential in business. The basic idea that workers find satisfaction from a job's *intrinsic* rewards has led management to pay more attention to job design and job enrichment as legitimate methods of improving worker satisfaction, motivation, and productivity. Herzberg (1968) set forth a number of job-enrichment principles for management to follow. These job-enrichment principles and the motivating factors they affect are outlined in Table 8-1.

MOTIVATIONAL PROCESS

The next discussion involves a different approach to the topic of human motivation. The last section discussed human needs. This section will look at the way in which motivation takes place—that is, the motivational process. This approach to motivation is important to managers because it offers additional insights about how to go about the job of motivating employees.

TABLE 8-1.   Principles of Job Enrichment

Principles	Motivator Affected
Remove some controls over workers but retain worker accountability	Responsibility, achievement
Increase individual accountability for work	Responsibility recognition
Give workers a complete, natural unit of work to perform (not half a job)	Achievement, responsibility, recognition
Give additional job freedom and authority to workers	Responsibility, achievement, recognition
Give feedback on job and organizational performance directly to employees	Recognition
Introduce new, more challenging tasks to the job	Personal growth
Assign workers some specialized tasks, making them experts	Responsibility, growth, advancement

An Expectancy Theory of Motivation

Suppose that a student's grade point average (GPA) after two years of college is 2.5. His parents would like to motivate him to make higher grades so they offer a reward if he maintains a minimum *B* average (3.0) during the junior year. The reward, if family finances allow, is an all-expenses-paid vacation to Europe next summer. What thought process will the student go through in deciding whether the effort required to earn a *B* average is worth it? Questions he might ask himself would include:

1. Will additional study improve my academic performance to a 3.0 GPA?
2. If my GPA improved to 3.0, what are the chances I will get the European vacation?
3. How much pleasure will I get from a European vacation?

The student's level of motivation to study harder in this example will depend on the answers to these questions. Consider Fred and Rhett. Fred has been loafing through college while easily maintaining 2.5 GPAs. Fred's family is financially stable, and he's always longed to visit Europe. For Fred it's very likely that additional study will result in a 3.0 GPA, it's certain that his family will be able to afford the trip and he will get great enjoyment from it. All the ingredients add up to a highly motivated student. On the other hand, Rhett has been working very hard to maintain a 2.5 GPA and has serious doubts about his ability to raise it to 3.0. His family has had a history of financial ups and downs so there's only a fifty-fifty chance that there'll be money for the trip. Finally, Rhett would just as soon spend the summer playing baseball. Rhett, of course, will likely show little enthusiasm or motivation to make a *B* average. Table 8-2 summarizes these two cases.

This kind of thinking has led psychologists (Porter and Lawler 1968; Vroom 1964) to devise theories of motivation related to the mental processes people go through. An adaptation of one well-known process theory (Porter and Lawler 1968) is presented in Figure 8-3. Employees put forth *effort* which leads to certain *performance* outcomes. These outcomes result in *rewards*, which in turn lead to *satisfaction* and continued effort. In this motivation process the level of effort one exerts is affected by a number of variables.

Think of a motivated worker as one who willingly exerts effort on the job. In other words, motivation means willingness to try. But trying does not necessarily mean succeeding so there is a relationship between effort and performance that affects a person's willingness to try. When a person feels the chances are quite low that increased effort will result in improved performance (as did Rhett) there will be little motivation to increase effort. Suppose an employee is trying hard, but performance is low. This might be caused by (1) a lack of proper direction, (2) a problem of ability, or

TABLE 8-2.   The Motivation to Study Harder

	Fred	Rhett
The likelihood that additional study will result in a 3.0 GPA	High	Low
The likelihood that a 3.0 GPA will result in the promised European vacation	High	50%
The value one places on a European vacation	High	Moderate
Overall motivation level	High	Low

(3) an organizational obstacle impeding performance (Green 1972). Improper direction is a supervision and leadership failure. Workers must know what is expected of them and what constitutes successful performance. Curtis Samuels' favorite expression for this is knowing "what is good," and he says it probably ten times each hour to everyone he comes in contact with. Whenever a problem arises he wants to know "What is good?," In other words, what will success look like in this situation? He follows up

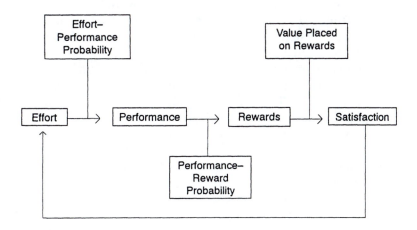

FIGURE 8-3.   The Motivation Process

just as persistently with his other expression, which is, "Talk to the customer and do it right the first time." A supervisory style that focuses on job tasks often will quickly clear up direction-related problems.

Problems of ability may be caused by lack of adequate job knowledge or skills, which can be remedied by training. The reasons hotels must deal with large numbers of relatively untrained employees and inexperienced managers were discussed in Chapter Two. A major link in the motivational process will be severed if workers are left untrained. Every now and then an employee may be unable to perform a certain job. When this happens there has been a recruiting or job placement mistake, which may require job transfer, job redesign, or in extreme cases, dismissal. The link between effort and performance will also be affected by organizational obstacles such as poor coordination, bureaucratic red tape, lack of sufficient resources and facilities, or improper delegation.

Thus, the relationship between effort and performance depends on a number of *intervening variables*, most of which are controled by management. Badly managed hotels inadvertently build obstacles to worker performance. Well-managed hotels find ways to facilitate worker efforts. They control intervening variables in such a way as to help employees believe that additional effort will lead to desired performance outcomes. All successful GMs view themselves as facilitators. Curtis Samuels feels that, "Being effective means getting the road blocks out of the way of my executives and staff so they can do their jobs. If I can do that then profits and guest service will take care of themselves." William Scully says that his job is to "give his managers and staff the opportunity to do their jobs as best as possible." Lawrence Wagner made many positive changes that helped people do their jobs better. One employee told him that although he liked the previous GM better, he would rather work for Lawrence!

Improved performance should lead to additional rewards. A person will be motivated to greater effort based on the degree of satisfaction that is derived from rewards. In the work environment a person may receive two kinds of rewards: extrinsic and intrinsic. Extrinsic rewards include money, fringe benefits, job security, working conditions, status symbols, praise, and recognition. These are the kinds of rewards that can be manipulated directly by the organization itself. Intrinsic rewards, on the other hand, include enjoyment of the work itself and a sense of accomplishment, achievement, and responsibility—the kinds of rewards about which Herzberg spoke. People get intrinsic rewards from doing the job; extrinsic rewards are set by the organization. The amount of effort a person exerts will depend on the extent to which he or she values certain rewards and the level of the rewards offered. For example, although a person may highly value money, little effort will be exerted toward a monetary bonus if it is perceived to be very small. Similarly, effort will not be forthcoming if the time lag between improved performance and rewards is excessively long, or if the relationship

Awards ceremonies at the Omni CNN Center, Atlanta, provide extrinsic rewards for employees who earn the most customer service commendations during the year.

Courtesy: Omni Hotels

between performance and rewards is ambiguous. Finally, a person's level of satisfaction will depend on the value placed on the extrinsic and intrinsic rewards received.

One of the nice things about the expectancy theory of motivation is that it makes clear just where and how managers can intervene in the motivational process. Figure 8-4 summarizes this. Management can help see to it that employee effort results in improved performance through good supervision, placement, training, and facilitation practices. Without these basics the link between effort and performance is broken and additional effort will, of course, cease. Nobody exerts much effort if he or she thinks it is useless. People lose faith in themselves or in the organization and revert back to some lower level of effort with which they were previously comfortable.

Motivational Linkages	Motivational Inhibitors	Management Actions to Strengthen Employee Motivaiton
Effort → Performance	• Lack of direction • Lack of ability • Obstacles of performance	• Better supervision/ goal clarification • Better training and placement • Better management facilitation
Performance → Rewards	• Lag between performance and reward • Unclear link between performance and rewards	• Alter reward schedule • Clarify relationship between performance and rewards
Rewards → Satisifaction	• Level of awards too low • Specific rewards not valued the same by all	• Increase level of rewards • Increase variety of rewards

FIGURE 8-4.   Management Intervention in the Motivational Process

Employees will also lose motivation for extra effort if the performance-rewards linkage is flawed. This can happen when the relationship between performance and rewards is unclear, bringing into doubt that rewards will be forthcoming if performance improves. A policy that rewards outstanding performance and average performance in the same manner may be demotivating. Why break your back when, in the end, everyone gets the same raise anyway? Motivation will also be weak if the level of rewards is perceived to be low. Motivation is also diminished if rewards don't follow performance within some acceptable time period. For example, workers under great pressure to reach weekly performance goals will be motivated best by a weekly bonus system rather than an annual bonus plan. It's management's job to devise equitable and understandable performance measures that are linked directly to rewards. It's also management's job to ensure that the reward schedule reinforces performance measures. Finally, rewards for improved performance will be satisfying to the extent that they are valued by the worker. Whether they are valued depends on both the type and the level of both extrinsic and intrinsic rewards. Management can raise the motivation level by increasing either the value or the variety of extrinsic rewards (Biagini 1988).

Goal Setting and Management by Objectives

The previous section discussed the possibility of motivating a student to improve his academic performance from a GPA of 2.5 to 3.0. If a student is prepared to make such an effort, then clearly he or she has set a *goal* to reach a certain performance level. There is quite a bit of evidence (Steers and Porter 1974; Locke et al. 1981) to support the contention that goal setting plays a positive role in motivation. Everyday experience also suggests that people without goals tend to be directionless while those with goals seem "to know where they are going." For example, athletes talk about the individual or team goals they are trying to accomplish.

In the world of business, firms need to translate the overall goals they set to measure organizational performance into goals for individual employees. As discussed in Chapter Three, this requires a translation of broad business goals into specific operational goals that each hotel employee can understand. These are the specific task goals that individual employees and groups are to accomplish in their jobs. Individual task goals are important for two reasons: (1) they direct behavior toward a specific end, and (2) they provide a standard for measuring, and therefore, rewarding achievement. Because goals clarify what the organization views as important, they help direct individual and group action. Goals also make it possible to measure performance. In fact, the very process of setting specific goals makes performance measurement easier (DeMicco and Dempsey 1988).

All of the excellent GMs excelled at goal setting. (For example, Henri LeSassier's 60 percent occupancy goal for The Normandy Hotel. Had he not done that the hotel would likely have gone into bankruptcy.) Curtis Samuels is particularly inventive in translating guest comments into operational goals for each department in The Hotel Frenchman. Frank Anderson says he likes to set goals and challenges for his executives. One of his many sayings, "Don't tell me how many storms you had to sail through, just that the ship is safe in port," gives some idea of how he views goal accomplishment.

How should managers set goals to ensure that the goals are as motivating as possible? A number of aspects of goal setting tend to be motivating (Steers and Porter 1974). The more specific goals are the more they are motivating. Imprecise goals do little to direct behavior. The previous section discussed a specific GPA goal of 3.0. Had a vague goal of "improved academic performance" been set by Fred's parents all kinds of outcomes would be possible. However, one either attains a 3.0 GPA or one does not. If a trip to Europe depends on a 3.0 GPA then presumably a 2.95 GPA will result in no trip to Europe. In this case Fred knew where he stood and could direct his effort accordingly. If "improved academic performance" will result in a trip to Europe one's actions will likely be less focused than when the goal is highly specific.

Reasonable, and therefore attainable, goals must be set for people to exert increased effort. A 4.0 GPA goal for a student whose average has been 2.5 would not be particularly motivating since it would be viewed as unattainable. Goal-attainment feedback is usually motivating, especially if the employee can receive it through actual job performance and relatively quickly. Feedback relates goals to extrinsic and intrinsic rewards and thus affects motivation positively through the performance–rewards–satisfaction system described in the previous section. Peer competition among employees or groups has the potential of being motivating but depends on how the competition is structured. Consider a rewards program in which there are few winners among many workers. Even if the rewards are highly valued, the stiffness of the competition may be demotivating to many. The trick is to set performance goals that can be reached by many in the organization, thus creating some competition and many winners.

It's not surprising that a strong positive relationship has been found between improved performance and the degree of workers' goal acceptance and goal commitment. Indeed, the attributes of goal setting discussed herein are, in a way, methods to ensure that workers will *accept* specific goals and *commit* to reaching them. If goals are accepted, and if they are reasonable, then they are likely to be met.

Since goal acceptance is so important to increased performance, management must pay particular attention to ensure that workers accept goals as their own. Management by objectives (MBO) is a goal setting technique that positively influences a person's goal acceptance. It is based on the premise that a person is more likely to accept a goal that he or she had some part in formulating. Peter F. Drucker, one of the most influential management thinkers of the last half century, was one of the first proponents of MBO. He argued that, "The only basis for genuine pride, accomplishment and importance is the active and responsible participation of people in the determination of their own work . . ." (Drucker 1954, 308). Management by objectives has evolved into a rather specific technique in which goals are set jointly by a subordinate (or a group) and a superior. The worker is given a degree of latitude regarding how goals will be accomplished, and rewards are based on goal accomplishment. The MBO process ties goals to a specific time period and is then repeated for the next time period. The idea is to gain goal acceptance and commitment by granting workers some responsibility for goal setting and task accomplishment. Management by objectives requires that subordinate and superior jointly engage in a planning process. They must agree on what will be accomplished (goals) and how they will be accomplished (methods). As Drucker put it, the MBO process helps give all workers a "managerial vision."

It's important to note how goal setting and MBO fit into the motivational process described in the previous section (Figure 8-3). The process of setting specific goals helps a person understand what is expected on the job and increases the certainty that added effort will lead to desired performance. Management by objectives, by allowing worker participation in goal setting and task accomplishment, also causes people to place a greater value on improved performance, thus increasing intrinsic rewards when goals are met. In other words, people will take pride in accomplishing something they set out to do. Note, finally, that the performance-feedback aspect of goal setting helps clarify the relationship between performance

A maintenance employee repairing a guest room bath sink—quick and courteous service is important.

Courtesy: Omni Hotels

and rewards. Properly conducted, MBO increases certainty that rewards will be forthcoming if improved performance results in goal accomplishment.

While doing the GM research, I watched Curtis Samuels conduct an MBO session with his chief engineer. The meeting began with a review of the just-completed month's "do list," the departmental budget, and the formal objectives set jointly by the two. It was a very detailed process. Every item was checked off and explained by the chief engineer, especially if not accomplished. When this process was completed the chief engineer and the GM both knew exactly which tasks had been accomplished, which goals had been met, which had not, and why. Curtis then explained to the chief engineer what was expected for the entire hotel during the next month. It so happened that actual revenues were likely to be below forecast so costs had to be kept in check if profit goals were to be met. The chief engineer then began to set objectives for the next month, and for the next fifteen minutes he and the GM jointly engaged in this process.

I chatted at length with the chief engineer the next day about MBO and Curtis Samuels. I was particularly interested in learning if the process worked like the books said or whether it was just a disguise for Curtis to tell the chief engineer what the GM wanted done! While admitting that his greatest challenge was "keeping the faith with Curtis Samuels" (that is, producing the results the GM wanted), the chief engineer went on to say that the MBO process had forced him to become better organized and had given him a better understanding of the big picture relating to hotel profitability. He felt that Curtis was demanding but fair and that, "We thought we were pretty good before he came, but he made us understand how good we could be." To me, however, his most telling statement about Curtis Samuels' version of MBO was, "I'd work for him anytime."

Equity as Part of the Motivational Process

How do workers decide if they are being fairly treated? In a study of hundreds of hotel employees making close to the minimum wage, I (Nebel 1976) found that their satisfaction with wages was really no different from workers in other industries earning considerably more! The reason is that people tend to base their satisfaction with pay (and other aspects of their jobs) on a relative rather than an absolute basis. College professors do not compare their pay with those of investment bankers any more than hotel front desk clerks compare their wages to plumbers. Rather, it seems that people have a well-formed idea of the relationship between the rewards from their job and what they put into it. This can be thought of as a ratio comparing job outcomes (O) to job inputs (I), that is, a O/I ratio.

To determine relative satisfaction people compare their ratio to some "other" person (Adams 1975). This other person may be an actual coworker, someone working in another firm, a composite of what the worker feels is a reference group, or even a comparison with his or her own past outcome input (O/I) ratios. Job outcomes include things such as pay, status, security, praise, working conditions, and promotional opportunities; in other words, both extrinsic and intrinsic rewards. Job inputs are what the worker brings to the job, including such things as effort, experience, education, seniority, social status, dedication, and intelligence. Each person makes a rough calculation of the outcomes he or she receives from a job compared to the inputs he or she brings to it, resulting in a subjective O/I ratio. People compare their O/I ratio to other peoples in order to judge if they are being treated fairly.

What happens when a person feels that his or her O/I ratio is below some comparison group? A number of worker actions are possible, some of which are quite unfavorable to the organization. A person can try to get outcomes increased (that is, ask for a pay increase) if it is felt that the O/I ratio is too low when compared to others. On the other hand, a person could lower inputs in order to bring the ratios into equality. Expending less effort on the job or producing lower quality work would be examples. This type of behavior is most likely to occur when a person feels that his or her inputs are roughly equal to others' but that their outcomes are greater. It's possible, however, that if the perceived inequality is caused by a lack of input a person might increase inputs (that is, effort) with the expectation that this will result in greater outcomes (rewards) and thus equalize the O/I ratios. What might happen if one perceives a *favorable* O/I ratio? It's possible that person would increase inputs in order to feel more worthy of the higher level of outcomes. It's unlikely, however, that one would want his or her outcomes reduced to be brought into equality with others. Generally speaking (Adams 1975) people who perceive an unfavorable O/I ratio are most likely to:

• First try to increase their outcomes,
• Resist increasing inputs that are difficult to accomplish,
• Resist changing the person or group with whom they compare themselves,
• Will terminate their job or resort to other kinds of withdrawal such as absenteeism only when the perceived inequality is great.
• Will resist changes in inputs or outcomes that adversely affect their self-concept or self-esteem,
• Will be reluctant to changing their perceptions regarding their level of inputs and outcomes.

Equity theory points out that employees continually compare their job outcomes and inputs with that of others. This comparison will result in feelings that they are being treated fairly or unfairly relative to how other people are treated. Feelings of unfairness may be motivating and spur a worker to greater efforts to increase job outcomes, but the opposite (unfavorable) result is more likely to occur. Workers may restrict inputs (that is, they can become less productive) in order to remedy a perceived imbalance. When designing jobs, evaluating performance, and dispensing rewards, management must be sensitive to this issue of fairness because imbalances can quickly result in undesirable worker behavior.

Behavior Modification

The task of leadership is to encourage workers to behave in ways that are favorable to the organization and to discourage them from detrimental behavior. The idea that people can be taught to modify their behavior in certain ways depending on how their behavior is reinforced was developed by B.F. Skinner (1969). Skinner held that people will tend to repeat behavior that is positively reinforced and will stop behaving in ways that are not positively reinforced or that result in noxious consequences. *Positive reinforcement* occurs when a person is rewarded for behaving or performing in certain ways. When performance is rewarded, a person's motivation to repeat the performance is strengthened. Management can also strengthen desired behavior through *avoidance learning*, where workers are taught to behave in certain ways in order to avoid or terminate some undesired consequence. Undesired behavior can also be changed by withholding positive reinforcement because people will not continue to do things for which they are not rewarded. Finally, of course, unwanted behavior can be suppressed if it is followed by some form of punishment (Norena 1987).

The prevailing opinion among proponents of reinforcement is that positive reinforcement is the most effective method of bringing forth desired behavior. William Scully states it simply by saying that he "gets more results with praise than with punishment." Curtis Samuels believes that most people would rather succeed than fail and, therefore, uses positive reinforcement as a technique to teach them *how* to succeed. Curtis preaches praise and rewards constantly and, to some degree, most of the outstanding GMs do. Frank Anderson says GMs should be cheerleaders, and he is constantly reminding his executives to praise good worker performance. The key is not to just tell people they are doing a good job, they must be praised for *specific* accomplishments. Frank suggested this at a staff meeting in which he instructed his managers to praise the employees who were responsible for a particularly quick turnaround of a large convention space. Some GMs realize they should use positive reinforcement more and admit to being "long on criticism and short on praise." Here are some practical rules (Hamner and Hamner 1976) for reinforcement techniques.

• All employees should not be rewarded the same, but rather should be differentiated based on their ability to meet or exceed predetermined standards. Equal rewards for all only fosters average performance from all.

- Failure to respond to worker performance or behavior has its own reinforcing consequences. Nonaction on the part of management will result in behavior modification just as much as action will.
- Workers must know exactly what kind of behavior will be reinforced. That's why performance standards and goals are so important: they let people know what constitutes successful performance based on objective criteria.
- Workers must know exactly what they are doing wrong. If a reward is withheld because of undesired behavior the worker must be made aware of exactly what he or she is doing wrong. Work is not a guessing game.
- If punishment is necessary, don't administer it in front of others because people will lose face.
- Make rewards (or punishments) equal to behavior. Praise work well done. Council and coach when things go wrong.

Avoidance learning, since people live in an imperfect world, is sometimes needed. An amusing example occurred while I was studying Richard James' day-to-day management style four months after he became GM of the Apollo Hotel. It seemed that four corporate executives were visiting the hotel to help implement a new purchasing system. One evening two of The Apollo's executives took the four corporate executives to dinner at a well-known (and very expensive) local steak house. They apparently ran up quite a bill, which was then submitted for the GM's approval as an "entertainment expense." Richard told the assistant controller who brought him the invoice that he had no intention of approving it. The corporate people could have been properly entertained in one of the hotel's restaurants for only a fraction of the cost, so the hotel's two executives would simply have to pay the bill themselves. The assistant controller swallowed hard and quickly left the GM's office. There was little doubt that the assistant controller would immediately be on the phone breaking the bad news to the two affected executives. After he left James looked at me with a sly grin and said that he "was teaching those guys a lesson" about fiscal responsibility and common sense. He intended to eventually approve the requisition but wanted them to "squirm" for a while. He would also subsequently issue a hotel policy regarding entertaining corporate executives but wanted to get the word out in a more dramatic way first. That day, I'm sure, a lot of avoidance learning took place.

JOB SATISFACTION AND JOB PERFORMANCE

Do workers perform at high levels because they are satisfied with their jobs? Are workers satisfied with their jobs because they perform at high levels? Is there any cause-and-effect relationship between job satisfaction and job performance?

These are very practical questions for managers because how one manages and motivates employees will differ depending on which of the above propositions is true. This discussion will view each side of this issue by following a review of this controversy by Green (1972).

Does Satisfaction Lead to Performance?

It would surely be nice if the saying "happy employees are productive employees" always held as a cause-and-effect relationship. If it did, then management's job would be simple: find some way to make employees happy (that is, satisfied) with their jobs and this will lead to high performance levels. Ever since the Hawthorne studies there have been proponents of the idea that employee well-being and productivity go hand in hand. And why not? This is such an appealing proposition that it's difficult to resist the vision of satisfied employees performing at high levels for the good of the firm. "Look after your employees and they will look after you" became a common saying in business. This view allows managers to deal with performance issues indirectly by first addressing satisfaction issues. This is a much more pleasant task than confronting employees directly with performance issues.

Alas, the pleasant way is not always the proper way. Here is a test regarding this proposition: suppose someone who values money highly is performing poorly. Suppose that despite this poor performance the person receives a significant raise. The test questions are:

• Will the worker's job satisfaction increase? Yes__ No__
• Will the worker's job performance improve? Yes__ No__

Most of the students whom I teach answer "Yes" to the first question and "No" to the second. Job satisfaction does improve because of the raise but performance does not! They refute the Satisfaction–Performance relationship by noting that while this person may be happier with more pay he or she has, after all, just been rewarded for nonperformance! In fact, various studies (Vroom 1964; Green 1972) confirm that there is little support to the idea that improved performance is caused by increased job satisfaction.

Does Performance Lead to Satisfaction?

There is more evidence to support the contention that improved job performance has a positive influence on job satisfaction. Figure 8-5 reproduces part of the motivational process of Figure 8-3. Note that the direction of

FIGURE 8-5.   The Performance → Reward → Satisfaction Sequence

the arrows show performance leading to rewards that in turn result in greater job satisfaction. Green (1972), Schwab and Cummings (1970), and others conclude that a cause-and-effect relationship exists between improved performance and greater job satisfaction because of the rewards associated with improved performance. The managerial implications of these research findings (Green 1972) can be summarized as follows:

- Increasing rewards increases employee satisfaction.
- Alone, increasing employee satisfaction will have little or no affect on performance.
- Tying rewards to performance increases the job satisfaction of high performers. It will also cause dissatisfaction for poor performers.
- If rewards are differentially administrated based on performance, management will have to defend its basis of performance evaluation to poor performers.
- Management will be forced to accept the inevitable tension that goes along with dissatisfied, low-performing employees until they either become more productive or leave the organization.
- By tying rewards to performance, management ensures that its most satisfied employees are also its high performers, thus increasing the chances of retaining its best workers.

Some Practical Considerations

This all sounds logical and perhaps even easy. In practice, however, these principles are often difficult to implement. To begin with, this motivational strategy is definitely not the line of least resistance: increasing rewards is! A motivational strategy that provides (differential) individual rewards based on performance is a more confrontational approach since it is certain to make some people happy and others unhappy. To succeed, management must be willing to confront the issue of performance and rewards head on and accept the fact that such a policy will create a certain amount of dissatisfaction. Management must also be able to fairly and accurately measure employee performance if rewards are to be based on performance. This is not always easy to do. It is sometimes difficult to distinguish individual from group performance. In addition, an easily determined quantitative measurment of performance may not be the best measure. It's also usually easier to measure output than it is quality. The difficulties of measuring

Charleston Place Ambassador Committee of The Omni Hotel is a quality circle representing each department of the hotel from housekeeping to banquets.

Courtesy: Omni Hotels

performance in hotels are compounded because hotels provide primarily services, many of which are intangible.

Two other practical management problems complicate the job of relating rewards to performance. While a worker may be motivated to exert greater effort, there are numerous reasons why greater effort may not result·in improved performance. Mentioned were problems of direction, ability, and a variety of other performance obstacles that can short-circuit the effort–performance relationship and thus the entire motivational process. Rewards can take many forms and they can be both intrinsic or extrinsic. Unless the type and magnitude of rewards are sufficiently attractive to employees, there will be little motivation to exert additional effort, and consequently, little affect on performance.

Views of Hotel GMs

What do successful hotel GMs think about the performance—satisfaction issue? While this question was not posed to them directly, their actions and answers to other questions leave little doubt about where they stand. While their individual characteristics and personalities will be discussed in detail in Chapter Fifteen, it should come as no surprise that these successful executives exhibited an extremely high need to achieve. As Curtis Samuels put it, "Every morning report gives me an opportunity to see whether I've done a good job." Richard James likes the "instant performance feedback" his job provides. William Scully enjoys the "immediate satisfaction and feedback of his performance." These people are action oriented: they love to compete, and they love to win. Furthermore, they have been judged all of their careers by bottom-line performance measures relating to efficiency, profitability, and guest satisfaction. They like being in charge, get pride out of their accomplishments, and love the instant feedback of daily achievement. In other words, their whole life is tied up with the intrinsic rewards they get from doing their job. They are so performance–rewards–satisfaction driven that the *reverse* process has probably never entered their minds. As will be shown in Chapter Ten, this drive for high performance is completely consistent with a high concern for the welfare of their employees. Still, as a group, they seem naturally to understand that performance comes first. While some of the GMs have been quoted as saying just about the opposite (that is, that happy employees make happy guests), I'm sure that they did not mean to suggest a cause-and-effect relationship but simply to recognize that in healthy, well-run hotels high performance and high job satisfaction go hand in hand. Outstanding hotel GMs are driven by performance goals, tend to be obsessive and are perfectionists. These are truly bottom-line-oriented people who are incapable of being satisfied except through high performance (Small 1987).

CONCLUSION

A truly great change in thinking began to take place when the assumptions, held by the scientific management school about human behavior, were challenged. The experiments at Western Electric's Hawthorne plant demonstrated that people are motivated by a complex variety of psychological factors. The human relations movement spawned by the Hawthorne experiments viewed people in a positive light. Rather than being unambitious, lazy, and passive when it came to work, the average person was viewed as basically ambitious, self-motivated, and capable of assuming a certain level of responsibility. Management's task is to unlock the inherent energies and motivation that most people brought naturally to the work place.

One of the keys to understanding motivation is human needs. A well-known theory divides human needs into five ascending categories; physiological, security, social, esteem, and self-actualization. According to this theory people first strive to satisfy the most basic needs for food, shelter, and a degree of stability and safety. As basic needs are satisfied, they cease to be motivating and people look instead to satisfy higher order needs such as social interaction, esteem, and finally, self-actualization. Two other views of motivation and needs were discussed: one concentrated on the need to achieve, the other dealt with factors leading to job satisfaction. There is evidence that the need to achieve can be instilled in adults who previously lacked it. This is reinforced by research which showed that workers listed factors such as achievement, recognition, responsibility, and personal growth as the things they found most satisfying about their jobs.

A common theme of these theories is that people have higher order needs and that many of these needs can be fulfilled through work. People do want to be winners. Of course, they want decent pay and job security, but in addition they want to be part of a first-rate organization. They also want to know that the job they do is important. People need recognition and respect, and they will often work quite hard to fulfill these needs.

The motivational process itself offers additional insights for managers. Expectancy theory looks at the relationship between effort, performance, rewards, and satisfaction. If a person feels the chances are good that added effort will lead to improved performance and that improved performance will lead to valued rewards, he or she will be motivated to exert extra effort. Management's job is one of intervention. Managers must see to it that increased effort results in improved performance, that improved performance is rewarded, and that rewards are both appropriate and valued by employees. Management's job is to raise worker's expectations of success throughout the motivational process.

The amount of effort a person exerts is related to the goals he or she sets. Goals that are specific, demanding yet attainable, relate to job performance, and are accepted by the worker usually result in improved performance. Without goals there's little chance that worker motivation and effort will be high. Goals must be accepted to be motivating. Management by objectives is a method to ensure that goals are accepted by those who have to carry them out. It is based on the idea that a person is more likely to accept a goal that he or she had some hand in formulating. Management by objective is a motivational process that includes goal setting, performance appraisal, rewards, and feedback.

The motivational process can be derailed if workers view their rewards as inequitable. Workers measure the inputs they bring to their jobs with the outcomes they receive from their jobs. Their satisfaction greatly depends on their perception of how they are treated relative to how others are treated. Fair and equitable treatment is a precondition of motivated employees.

Behavior modification techniques are based on the idea that people repeat behavior that is positively reinforced and stop behaving in ways that are not positively reinforced or that have noxious consequences. Positive reinforcement is generally considered the most effective behavior modification method. Behavior modification requires management to define what constitutes desired behavior, set performance standards, differentially reward desired behavior, and when necessary, dispense punishment for undesired behavior. Management nonaction is not without its behavioral consequences.

There's been a lot of confusion about the cause-and-effect relationship between job satisfaction and job performance. By itself, increasing employee satisfaction has little or no effect on job performance. A policy that concentrates only on improving employee satisfaction will not result in improved performance. In fact, top performers will become frustrated because of the lack of a linkage between performance and rewards. Tying rewards to performance will increase job satisfaction for a hotel's high-performing employees. This is exactly what management would like to do; keep top-performing workers happy. This policy will also cause poor performers to be dissatisfied. Thus, if rewards are differentially administered based on performance, management will be forced to accept the inevitable tension that goes along with dissatisfied, low-performing employees. This will continue until they either become more productive or leave the hotel.

Motivation requires that management clarify for workers exactly what is expected of them. In a business providing intangible services, this requires communication skills of a high order. This is the topic of the next chapter.

REFERENCES

Adams, J. S. "Inequality in Social Exchange." Reprinted in Steers, Richard M. and Lyman W. Porter. 1975. *Motivation And Work Behavior*. New York:McGraw-Hill Book Co. :138–154.

Alderfer, C. P. 1972. *Existence, Relatedness and Growth: Human Needs in Organizational Settings*. New York: The Free Press.

Biagini, David. May 1988. "Employee Awards: Powerful Motivation." *Hotel And Resort Industry* 11(5): 72–78.

DeMicco, Frederick and Steven J. Dempsey. Spring 1988. "Participative Budgeting And Participant Motivation: A Review of the Literature." *FIU Hospitality Review* 6(1):77–94.

Drucker, Peter. 1954. *The Practice of Management*. New York: John Wiley & Sons.

Goll, Gerald E. Spring 1989. "Management Misperceptions: An Obstacle to Motivation." *FIU Hospitality Review* 7(1):85-91.

Green, Charles N. 1972. "The Satisfaction-Performance Controversy." *Business Horizons* 15(5):31-41.

Hamner,W. C., and E. P. Hamner. 1976. "Behavior Modification On The Bottom Line." *Organizational Dynamics* 4:3-21.

Herzberg, F. January/February 1968. "One More Time: How Do You Motivate Employees?" *Harvard Business Review*: 53-62.

Locke, E.A. etal. 1981. Goal Setting and Task Performance:1969-1980. *Psychological Bulletin* 90:125-52.

Maslow, Abraham. 1954. *Motivation and Personality*. New York: Harper & Brothers.

McClelland, David C. July/August 1962. "Business Drive and National Achievement." *Harvard Business Review*: 92-112.

McGregor, Douglas M. 1960. *The Human Side of Enterprise*. New York: McGraw-Hill Book Co.

Nebel, Eddystone C., III. December 1976. *Manpower In Louisiana's Hotel and Restaurant Industries*. School of Hotel, Restaurant and Tourism Administration: University of New Orleans.

Norena, Jorge. October 1987. "How a Major Hotel Keeps Its Staff Motivated." *Executive Housekeeping Today* 8(10):13ff.

Porter, Lyman W. and Edward E. Lawler. 1968. *Managerial Attitudes and Performance*. Homewood, Il.: Richard D. Irwin, Inc.

Rinke, Wolf J. April 1989. Treat Your People Like Winners. *Restaurants USA* 9(4):13-16.

Roethlisberger, F.J. and W.J. Dickson. 1939. *Management and the Worker*. Cambridge, Ma.: Harvard University Press.

Schwab, Donald P.and Larry L. Cummings. 1970. "Theories of Performance and Satisfaction: A Review." *Industrial Relations* 7:408-30.

Skinner, B. F. 1969. *Contingencies of Reinforcement*. New York: Appleton-Century-Crofts.

Small, Robert. August 1987. Excellence and Employees. *The Cornell Hotel and Restaurant Administration Quarterly* 28(2):73-76.

Steers, R. M. and C. W. Porter. 1974. "The Role of Task-Goal Attributes in Employee Performance." *Psychological Bulletin* 81:434-52.

Taylor, Frederick W. 1911. *Principles of Scientific Management*. New York: Harper & Brothers.

Vroom, Victor H. 1964. *Work and Motivation*. New York: John Wiley & Sons.

QUESTIONS

8-1. Why are one's assumptions about people so important to a manager?

8-2. Describe the basic steps in the motivational process. How can knowledge of these steps help you be a better manager?

8-3. Do you fall under the Theory *X* or the Theory *Y* assumption regarding human nature? Where do you think a waiter, a room maid, a bartender, a receiving clerk, or an accountant would fall?

8-4. Is esteem important to you? For which hotel employees would esteem be unimportant? Explain.

8-5. List ten specific things you can do to foster the achievement motive in hotel employees. Is it worth doing?

8-6. What turns on workers? What turns off workers?

8-7. How can changing the requirements of a job affect employee motivation?

8-8. Explain how expectancy theory can help a manager diagnose a poor-performing employee.

8-9. Analyze the job of a kitchen dishwasher and develop an MBO program that will be motivating to the dishwasher.

8-10. Discuss the relationship between job satisfaction and job performance.

CHAPTER 9

Communication in Hotels

During the course of the GM research I spent many hours observing what these busy executives did during an average work day. Having read research studies of executive behavior by others (Kotter 1982; Mintzberg 1975), I anticipated finding the GMs spending a great amount of their time in verbal communication. Kotter (1982, 80), for example, found that, "Most of the GMs spent much of their work days talking and listening to others; a few spent up to 90 percent of their work time this way." Kotter's overall findings were that the executives he studied averaged only 24 percent of their time working alone, and this often occurred at home, while on an airplane, or while commuting. Mintzberg's (1975) findings were quite similar; he estimated that top executives spend 78 percent and middle level managers spend 89 percent of their time in direct communication with others.

THE INTENSITY OF COMMUNICATIONS IN HOTELS

Knowing statistics from other studies, however, is not the same as really understanding the implications of what they mean. As the GM research proceeded, I became more and more impressed with the terrific volume and intensity of the verbal communication that takes place in well-managed hotels. It's difficult to convey the amount of communication that is constantly taking place in hotels to someone who has not experienced it first-hand. Here are two examples that might help. Richard James seemed to be spending quite a lot of time on the phone one day, so that evening I counted his number of phone calls during my observations. It turned out that in six hours and twenty-four minutes he was involved in thirty-five phone conversations, or about one every eleven minutes. During that same

Good verbal communication keeps the 1,200-room Sheraton New Orleans Hotel humming.

Courtesy: Sheraton New Orleans Hotel

period he also had thirteen unscheduled face-to-face meetings with other hotel executives. In contrast, he spent only ten minutes on a written communication which, it turned out, was a strictly private matter. On an average day, Frank Anderson had personal face-to-face discussions with twenty-five people and phone contact with twenty people. Only about 10 percent of his time was spent alone, and he did not write a single letter or memo the entire day! In fact, one of his favorite sayings is, "GMs should be good listeners, not good readers."

These examples once again rely on numbers to make their point. A couple of nonstatistical examples may be helpful to appreciate the amount of verbal communicating that takes place in hotels and how successful hotel executives allocate their time. Lawrence Wagner and Curtis Samuels are in many ways quite different. Lawrence, fifty-two years old, is European and has been a GM for seventeen years. His apprenticeship-oriented European hotel school training and thirteen years of hotel experience on his way to becoming a GM makes him a seasoned veteran of hotel operations. On the other hand, forty year old Curtis Samuels is a classic example of a U.S. style manager: highly organized, hard driving, and quite sophisticated in his knowledge of management skills. He has been a GM for 9 years. Curtis is the kind of person who, his subordinates feel, could manage any kind of business. A science major as an undergraduate, his practical experience in the hotel business is modest compared to Lawrence. Curtis' first hotel job upon finishing his masters in hotel administration was as a resident manager! Finally, Curtis is a morning person, and Lawrence is an evening person, which affects their work patterns.

Notwithstanding their considerable differences, these two outstanding hotel executives share a common trait; they both spend nearly all of their 8 A.M. to 5 P.M. work day talking and listening to a bewildering variety of people. Being different kinds of people, they go about planning their days quite differently. Curtis likes a tight, highly organized schedule of pre-planned meetings, inspections, and interviews. On the other hand, Lawrence purposely refrains from too tight a schedule in order to be free to devote his time in "an unhurried manner" to the demands of the hotel as they arise. After spending most of the normal work day talking and listening to people, both executives still must find time for what each calls "paperwork." Because Curtis is an early riser, he does his paperwork in his hotel apartment from about 4:30 till 6:30 each morning. Consequently, his desk is cleared for the really important work of running the hotel when he arrives at his office at a little past 7 A.M. Lawrence, being more of a night person, reverses the process: his "quiet time" for paperwork begins around 6:30 in the evening and often continues through a light dinner in his office till around 9 P.M. Curtis rises in the dark to do his paperwork in the morning while Lawrence does his once the sun goes down. But both leave the day for talking and listening to people.

THE KEY ROLE PLAYED BY COMMUNICATIONS

The best contemporary books on management, and certainly those that concentrate on the service business, stress the key role of communications to a business's success. They also point out that the most important communication that takes place in businesses is verbal and face-to-face. Here are some quotes from best-selling works on management that make strong points regarding the importance of face-to-face communication.

- *Managing in the Service Economy* (Heskett 1986, 127–128)

  "If we can believe the message of many leading service firms, motivation starts not with compensation but with effective communication."

  Quoting Edward E. Carlson, former head of Westin Hotels and CEO of United Airlines: "If you're willing to get out and be a part of visible management . . . you learn how employees feel about their company. Then you can try to create a program where they believe in you."

  "Bill Marriott, Jr. still spends nearly half of his time in the field, listening and then talking to employees."

  "Sam Walton, Chairman and Chief Executive Officer of Wal-Mart, still spends the majority of his working time in the field. As he has said, 'The key is to get into the store and listen to what the associates have to say.'"

- *Service America* (Albrecht and Zemke 1985, 26, 116)

  In analyzing how Jan Carlzon, CEO of Scandinavian Airlines System, SAS, turned the company from an $8 million loss to $71 million in gross profits in just over a year: ". . . two key traits that made him the right man for the times: a creative mind and the ability to communicate his expectations clearly and dramatically."

  "We need to communicate the service strategy to front-line people in the first place, so they know what we want them to concentrate on."

- *In Search of Excellence* (Peters and Waterman 1981, 121, 248)

  When discussing characteristics of excellently managed companies: "the name of the successful game is rich, informal communication. . . rich, informal communication leads to more action, more experiments, more learning, and simultaneously to the ability to stay better in touch and on top of things.

  "The nature and uses of communication in the excellent companies are remarkably different from those of their non-excellent peers."

  Quoting Dana Corporation's one page statement of philosophy: "Nothing more effectively involves people, sustains credibility or generates enthusiasm than face-to-face communication."

It's particularly interesting to hear what hotel department and division heads have to say about the importance of communications. These executives are the link between lower level day-to-day operations of a hotel and the GM. From their prospective, they can see the importance of communication coming *down* from the GM and going *up* from the staff and lower management levels. One of the things they all agree on is that in large complex hotels GMs have little choice but to delegate quite a bit of authority to subordinates. As one put it, "GMs would drive themselves crazy" if they tried to do everything themselves. Furthermore, they feel that GMs cannot possibly know all of what is going on in their hotels. What is true for GMs is true for division and department heads as well; no manager can be everywhere. The simple fact is that whenever duties must be delegated to a large and diverse number of people in an organization, problems of communication are compounded. Thus, what we say about communications at the GM level is equally true for all management levels of a hotel (Shriver 1988).

To keep their "fingers on the pulse" of their hotels, GMs must continually be kept informed by their subordinates. Additionally, GMs need to be able to communicate downward to their immediate subordinates and all the way to the hotel's newest hourly employee. When describing the positive things the GMs have done, their key executives consistently mentioned these two vital aspects of communications. Many, for example, commented that by sharing financial information with all employees the GMs helped everyone better understand the hotel's business situation. The GMs often went to some lengths to explain to all employees the hotel's entire business strategy as if these employees were a part of the upper level management team. This included a detailed explanation of not only what was being done but also why it was being done. At the same time, subordinates constantly praised those GMs who were able to improve upward communications. Typical comments were: ". . . more open EOC meetings," "The GM is open to ideas," "He is a good listener," "He has an open-door policy," and "The GM encourages upward communication."

When subordinates complained about the level of communication it was never that there was too much communication but always that there was too little! Complaints usually dealt with either a feeling that the GM was somewhat inaccessible or that he did not meet often enough with his executives. Typical comments were: "He seems so busy one hates to interrupt," or "His days are so tightly scheduled it's difficult to get in to see him when I need to," or "I'm not really sure of what is going on because he never tells me," or "The GM does not know if problems are being corrected." One executive felt a GM did "not want to be bothered" unless the issue was really important, while another said, "The GM may not like something and will not tell you about it right away." Another said that he was allowed to run his department, but "never got any feedback" from the GM as to how he was doing.

In addition to complaints about one-on-one communications, others dealt with too infrequent group meetings with the GM. In one hotel, executives requested more frequent meetings with the GM. The request was granted and the executives felt that the additional meetings had increased "understanding, accountability, and awareness" over the past year. In another instance a GM had held regular meetings with department heads for a while but then had discontinued the practice. A number of executives suggested that he begin the meetings again, but he did not. The executives who related these incidents to me were upset, some were even a little bitter. They wanted to know what was going on and the GM's assessment of how they were performing. After all, they felt that they had quite a personal stake in how the hotel was doing.

The Fairmont, a famous and gracious New Orleans hotel.

Courtesy: Fairmont Hotel, New Orleans

TIPS FOR BETTER COMMUNICATION

Communication deals with the transfer of information, ideas, facts, opinions, problems, impression, and emotions. When people try to communicate with each other, their highest goal should be to convey meaning in such a way that each person understands the point of view of the other and each feels free to express his or her feelings to the other. A willingness to *express* and *accept* differences is an important aspect of communicating. This view of communications is quite different from getting someone to agree with what you say. While people try at times to convince others of their views, the process used to accomplish this often has the opposite effect. Rogers and Roethlisberger (1951) wrote a classic article on communicating entitled "Barriers and Gateways to Communication." Their formula for effective verbal communication is both concise and practical. It is also quite to the point concerning how to communicate effectively in hotels. Because their ideas are so relevant, this section contains a discussion of their theories.

Figure 9-1 depicts the conditions for effective two-way communication.There are a number of aspects of Figure 9-1 that are important. Note that A and B are both placed on the same level. While A may be B's superior within a hotel's organizational structure, they are depicted as equals for the purposes of effective reciprocal two-way communication. Figure 9-1 shows that one of the conditions for effective communication is A's and B's willingness to express their *feelings* to each other. While communicating factual information does, of course, take place, it's important to understand that when two people talk about ideas, opinions, problems, impressions, and emotions they are usually expressing their feelings. In fact, feelings are often involved in the recitation of so-called cold facts. Ask a person who has been battling an overweight problem if he or she has put on a few pounds and see

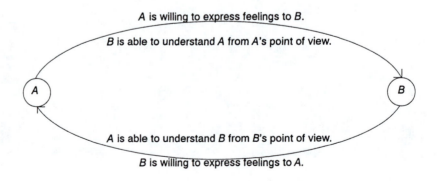

FIGURE 9-1.   The Condition for Effective Two-way Communications

how feelings can be put into a factual response (Ference 1989)!

In addition to a willingness to express feelings, another condition for two-way communication is an ability to understand what someone is saying from that person's point of view. In Figure 9-1 this means that *B* must be able to understand what A is saying *from* A's *point of view*. Similarly, *A* must be able to understand *B from* B's *point of view*. This condition of effective communication can be called the empathy requirement. Listening empathetically allows one to take another's viewpoint. One everyday way of expressing this characteristic is to say that a person is "a good listener." Another expression used to signal understanding is, "I know where you're coming from." While both give the appearance of describing empathy in communication, they fall short of a full enough explanation to be really helpful. The empathy requirement is very important because, as Rogers and Roethlisberger (1951) argue, one's ability to empathize during a conversation is the key that unlocks effective two-way communication!

Why is it so difficult to understand what someone is saying from that person's point of view? Carl Rogers, based on his experience as a psychotherapist, contends that the major barrier to interpersonal empathy "is our very natural tendency to judge, to evaluate, to approve (or disapprove) the statement of the other person or the other group" (Rogers and Roethlisberger 1951, 20). If one judges another's statements too quickly, the opportunity is lost to really *understand* what the other person is trying to communicate.

Good two-way communication requires an understanding that the process is probably more emotional than it is logical. Thus, we must look beyond "mere words" to feelings and perceptions. Remember, our purpose is for everyone to be willing to express themselves freely so that understanding may take place. This subtle process is accomplished by not rushing to judgment. Instead, asking questions will help us understand other points of views. If this can be accomplished the really important work of analyzing problems and devising solutions can begin. Table 9-1 summarizes some of these ideas (Alessandra 1989).

It's Easy to Get into Trouble

Suppose I say that *today's college students aren't like they used to be.* If you make a judgment about this statement you may have done so before fully understanding what I mean. If your evaluation is negative, you might respond emotionally by saying that neither are college professors! If I fall into the same trap and quickly judge (and disapprove) of your statement, our conversation could easily dissolve into one where you begin an emotional defense of today's college students while I do the same for college professors. Our assumptions about the meanings and motives of what was said have gotten us into trouble and our emotions have compounded the

TABLE 9-1.   **Assumptions Leading to Good or Bad Communication**

Bad Communication	Good Communication
• Communication is a logical process	• Communication deals with interacting feelings and emotions
• What a person says stands on its own	• The person, as well as what he/she says, is taken into account
• The purpose is for you to see things from my point of view	• The purpose is for me to get you to express yourself freely
• The purpose is to determine accountability	• The purpose is to solve a problem

problem. You evaluated my statement from your point of view and I, in turn, evaluated your statement from my point of view. At this rate it's unlikely that either of us will get the other's meaning completely right. Therefore, there's a good chance that a misunderstanding will develop. Whether this misunderstanding will lead to a complete collapse of communication depends on how we handle the next step in our conversation.

If I respond hotly with a defense of college professors while you do the same for college students, it won't be long before all communication ends. But what if we try, as Rogers and Roethlisberger (1951, 20) recommend, to listen with understanding. This means "to see the expressed idea and attitude from the other person's point of view, to sense how it feels to him, to achieve his frame of reference in regard to the thing he is talking about." What's needed to bring our discussion from the edge of argument back toward two-way communication? Either you or I, after hearing the other's first comment, must ask questions such as, "What do you mean by that," "Why do you feel that way," "In what way are college students (or professors) different," or "Can you give me an example of how they are different?" Of course, these questions must be asked in a nonevaluative tone of voice to be effective. By asking questions such as these we begin the process of trying to understand each other from the other person's point of view!

The really great thing about listening with understanding is that it need be initiated by only one person. Suppose that after my initial remark you had withheld judgment and asked me, "Why do you feel that way?" My response that today's college students seem to be more hard working and goal oriented than those of the 1960s would have increased your understanding of where I was coming from in my initial statement, and our conversation would have begun to be true communication.

Misunderstanding Slow Service

In a hotel, a food and beverage director receives a complaint about slow service at the previous evening's banquet. She calls in the banquet manager and begins the conversation by saying, "We've had another complaint about slow service; I think we had better initiate a waiter training program immediately to straighten out this problem." To which the banquet manager responds, "I'll do as you say, but it probably won't make any difference." Both parties have gotten off to a bad start in their attempt at communication. What each would like to do is solve the problem of slow service. Instead, their beginning comments may lead to confrontation instead of communication. The food and beverage director starts off with an evaluative statement. If she had begun by asking the banquet manager for his ideas as to why service was slow, the meeting may have gotten off to a different start. As it is, the banquet manager, predictably upset at being told how to do his job, reacts defensively with his own statement. What if the food and beverage director now assumes that the banquet manager is too stupid to understand the value of waiter training? She might try to convince the banquet manager of the benefits of waiter training. Since the food and beverage director has already judged the banquet manager's statement, her course of action is not to try to understand but to get agreement to a course of action.

Can the food and beverage director salvage the situation? Yes! Realizing that her initial remark upset the banquet manager, she might respond by saying, "Why do you feel that way," or "What do you think we should do," or even better, "What do you think is wrong?" These statements give the banquet manager an opportunity to respond to the problem from his point of view. They open up the possibility of trying to solve the problem and not set blame. They delay evaluation and judgment and allow the two executives to fully express their views from their own perspectives. With this opening the banquet manager may respond by pointing out that equipment breakdowns in the kitchen contributed to slow service, or that the menu was particularly difficult to prepare thus resulting in a food-preparation delay, or of course, any number of factors that caused the delays other than untrained waiters. Whatever the case, true two-way communication has begun (Slater 1989).

The Century City Marriott, California, sets the mood for an exciting banquet.

Courtesy: Marriott Hotels, Resorts and Suites

GMs CAUGHT IN THE ACT OF COMMUNICATING

The outstanding GMs I studied were, by and large, extremely good communicators. No one, however, always communicates perfectly. The following examples of both good and poor communications will help you to become a better communicator and manager.

Putting Yourself in the Other Person's Shoes

One day I watched Lawrence Wagner teach some communication principles to his food and beverage director. The local public health department had inspected the hotel kitchen recently and, for the first time in years, had written a negative report citing various minor violations. The food and beverage director felt that the inspector had been quite picky and that the citations were unwarranted. He was understandably upset over the negative report and wanted to vindicate his department by having the health department retract it. While being sympathetic with his food and beverage director's position, Lawrence also had a pretty good idea of the health department's reaction should the hotel decide to contest their findings. Rather than try to "fight City Hall" Wagner suggested that the two of them read the report, not from their prospective but rather "from the point of view of the health inspector," and in light of the specific sanitation regulations he is required to enforce. Lawrence knew that if they approached the problem by "thinking like the health department" they would be able to frame a proper response. The food and beverage director quickly understood Lawrence's suggestion. His anxiety lessened, and he was able, without any further help from the GM, to draft an appropriate response.

Rushing to Judgment

Communication breakdowns can occur quickly. While observing a GM in his office I heard him call the front office manager and complain that the proper flowers had not been placed in the room of an arriving VIP. As the front office manager began to explain the circumstances, the GM cut in quickly with an admonition that this kind of thing was not to happen again. It seemed to me that his mind was already made up concerning the facts of the incident. The next day I interviewed the front office manager and found her still angry over the incident. Her anger and frustration stemmed from the GM's not giving her an opportunity to tell her side of the story. She was convinced, she told me, that everything had been done properly and that she could have explained this to the GM if given half a chance. In her view he was not only wrong, he was unfair! In his view she was wrong and would only have made up an excuse. No matter who is right (or wrong) factually, on that day a GM failed to communicate with one of his key executives. Because of this incident they drew further apart rather than closer together, and a small seed of resentment and possibly distrust was planted. The phone conversation that caused this problem took all of thirty seconds.

No Such Thing as an Interruption

William Scully keeps a bowl of fruit on the conference table in his office. Even during most meetings, his door is open. Bill encourages his department heads, in fact all of his executives, to drop by whenever they want an apple or a bunch of grapes. One afternoon, while Scully was doing some paperwork, eight different executives stopped by his office for some fruit between 4:00 and 5:45 P.M. That's one "interruption" every thirteen minutes. In most cases there was a little small talk followed by a brief, seemingly casual, conversation about something going on in the hotel. It all seemed so relaxed and spontaneous until I remembered that Bill Scully had been named the company's outstanding GM two years running.[1]

Outstanding GMs don't consider interruptions as disturbances. Interruptions are nothing more than unscheduled important hotel business. In fact, one said that if no one came by his office for fifteen minutes he figured he was not doing his job! These busy executives expect to be interrupted and treat interruptions as a normal part of their job. It's not upsetting, they don't get grouchy, and they don't rush through unscheduled meetings to get to something important. They understand how important these "interruptions" are to managing a hotel. Outstanding hotel executives realize that if they are not approachable, they cannot manage (Feinberg 1986).

Frank Anderson got an idea one weekend to hire a well-known local chef for his hotel's most popular restaurant. Although his mind was made up, he wasn't sure of the reception the idea would get from his food and beverage director and executive chef. Some of the problems he anticipated dealt with what to do with the current chef and the difficulty of integrating an outside chef into the hotel's way of doing things. On Monday morning Frank met with his food and beverage director for four minutes to outline his ideas, promising to take his time with the decision. What followed for the next three days was more than a dozen seemingly random, unplanned meetings with the food and beverage director, the executive chef, and the resident manager about this idea. Each encounter was short. Some were only "informational," as when Frank dropped by the executive chef's office to mention that he had received a phone call from the local chef. All were seemingly unplanned. In fact, a very sophisticated communication and decision-making ritual was being carried out. Frank was letting these executives know what his ideas and feelings were on this subject. In addition, he was trying to find out what they felt and thought. He was willing to take a number of days and a dozen or more brief encounters in order to understand their points of view. In this regard Frank also used his resident manager as a go-between. The resident manager, after being told of the GM's idea, also talked to the food and beverage director and executive chef a number of times in an effort to understand their feelings. At the same time the resident manager communicated his interpretation of

---

[1] He is now senior corporate vice-president of the company.

the GM's feelings to the food and beverage director and the executive chef.

During the course of this "communicating," I interviewed all of the parties to this little dance. It was interesting that each understood exactly what was taking place! They knew that Anderson was trying to get them to understand why he wanted to hire the local chef. They further understood that he was also trying to get them to express to him their feelings and concerns about this move. The food and beverage director, for example, thought the move would cause a temporary disruption to his kitchen staff. Furthermore, developing a local following depended as much on hiring a well-known local maître d' as a chef. In his opinion, the idea had only about a 20 percent chance of success. The resident manager felt that his job was to sound out all parties and to delay the decision long enough so that everyone's ideas and feelings could be expressed. The executive chef had little use for the local cuisine and, therefore, thought that the idea was "much to do about nothing." Each subordinate, however, felt that the GM trusted and was loyal to them. They, in turn, trusted him.

Over the next few days information, ideas, opinions, impressions, emotions, and feelings were slowly communicated. Finally, a decision was made to hire the local chef. An attempt was made to interest the maître d' from the same local restaurant to join the hotel, but he refused even to meet with Frank. Everyone had their say. In their own way, everyone expressed their feelings. When it was all over, all parties felt good about moving forward and trying to make the move a success. Frank got his way, but he set up a communication and decision-making process in which everyone had an opportunity to clearly and honestly express how they felt.

There are certainly other ways to ensure good two-way communications. Frank Anderson choose to ease into the process with a series of quick, seemingly random encounters with each of the affected executives. He chose not to convene a formal meeting to make a decision. Presumably in such a setting people might be less willing to express themselves, even though the mutual trust between these executives was high. At first glance it might appear inefficient or unorganized to approach a decision in this manner. But recall that Bill Scully liked his executives to just drop by for a piece of fruit while he worked. When it comes to communications, efficiency is not the same as being effective. My feeling, having watched the process unfold, is that Frank Anderson would have backed down on the idea of hiring the local chef had his subordinates been strongly against the move. I think that his subordinates, after the communication process worked itself out, felt the same way. So, while not exactly euphoric over the idea, they were comfortable with the final decision. They had ample opportunity to provide input and were willing to give a good-faith effort to make the move succeed. In a world full of uncertainties, it's hard to hope for much more.

Chef preparing enticing fresh vegetable dishes at the Bethesda Marriott, Maryland.

Courtesy: Marriott Hotels, Resorts and Suites

You Can Learn Only When Someone Else Is Talking

One of the GMs had a logical mind and the ability to clearly express himself. He was, in fact, a master of one-way communication. In describing his strengths, he listed an innate ability of knowing how to do things. As long as he could remember he seemed to have a knack for getting things done and, after observing him for a number of days, it was obvious that he really did. He was a master of detail who could relate small matters to the big picture. His subordinates saw these traits in him and greatly admired him for them. They also admired his honesty, fairness, hard work, and a variety of other attributes. Still, they did express a reservation about him. The way they put it was that you could get along just fine with this GM as long as you did things his way. While they had little trouble understanding where this GM was coming from, they sometimes found it difficult to get him to view things from their perspective (Brownell 1987).

I saw an example of this while observing him training a newly appointed front office manager. The training took the form of extremely detailed inspections and critiques of the front office's operations. Day after day the GM went over front office operating problems with the manager, a person who was somewhat uncomfortable around the older, imposing GM. During the course of this training the GM would go into detail concerning how each problem should be solved. A minor crisis developed at the front desk during one of these sessions. The GM did a masterful job of resolving the problem in front of the front office manager and his two assistants. It seemed to me at the time that, had the front office manager handled the problem, the crisis presented the GM with a wonderful training opportunity.

Later that evening I talked to the GM about the incident, his training of the front office manager, and his communications in general. He felt that, since he was so good at knowing how to solve problems and get things done, his job was to "communicate" these traits to lesser skilled subordinates. He realized that he had a commanding presence and could be a rather intimidating person. Still, he felt he had logic on his side in pursuing that course of action. His method of communicating was entirely logical, from his point of view. His subordinates, however, felt that this approach thwarted their ability to express their feelings, ideas, frustrations, and problems. This GM was following a course that robbed him of vital knowledge. By assuming (correctly, it turned out) that he knew better than his subordinates how to get things done, he continually inhibited their willingness to express to him their points of view.

What is really important about this story? By inhibiting his subordinates from expressing their own points of view, the GM had difficulty understanding why their performance was often below his expectations. He could only puzzle, given his one-way communication, why it was so difficult for subordinates to pick up his way of doing things. Had he been more skilled at getting his subordinates to express themselves freely, he may have discovered why they were not performing up to his expectations and, of course, been able to do something about it.

The GM in this story is a man of considerable goodwill, who was sincerely trying to train his subordinates. In many cases his technique succeeded even though his job may have been made easier with two-way communication. He had analyzed his behavior and understood that his actions in part derived from an educational background that implicitly assumed an authoritarian management style was best under all circumstances. While discussing these issues, he put his finger on a personality trait that made two-way communication difficult for him. He admitted to being a perfectionist. It was impossible for him to accept anything but perfection from subordinates. He would rather do things himself, or direct exactly how they should be done, than accept any outcome that was less than perfect. This trait may have kept him from "listening with understanding" because of an underlying assumption that perfection could only be attained if things were done his way. Still, his abundant honesty, goodwill, and competence allowed him to succeed as an effective GM where a lesser man might have failed.

If You Do All the Talking
You'll Also Have to Do All the Thinking

While studying The Napoleon House Hotel, an example of extreme communication breakdown came to light in a rather interesting way. The current GM, Frank Anderson, was trying hard to develop his key subordinates to the point where they would be able to make decisions and run their departments on their own. His technique was to engage in intensive one-on-one coaching. This involved frequent face-to-face encounters during which the GM asked a lot of questions such as, "What do you think," "What would you do," "What are your feelings," and "Why did you suggest that?" I asked several of his subordinates to comment on the GM's coaching style of management. One of these executives, a division head, had worked under the previous GM, a man he described as having been legendary for his autocratic personality. The previous GM had no interest and little patience with conflicting views and had abruptly fired subordinates who dared express their own ideas. His actions quickly got the point across to the executives who remained; one-way communication became the rule of the day.

When asked about how executives who had worked for the previous GM were getting along with the new one, I was told that some were pleased with their new-found ability to express themselves, but that a few resented the new GM's communication style and fondly wished for a return of the previous GM. In fact, some executives viewed the departed GM as a great leader. When asked why, the division head allowed that by making all the decisions the previous GM made it possible for his subordinates not to have to think! To some, the new GM's communication and coaching style was upsetting because they were being forced to express their ideas and opinions. In other words, he was making them learn how to think for themselves!

CONCLUSION

Most of the communicating that takes place in hotels is one-on-one verbal communication. Outstanding hotel executives spend the majority of their days talking to and listening to people. There is literally no substitute for this kind of face-to-face verbal communication. It starts with presidents of large corporations, it's the way hotel GMs spend most of their time, and it's what first-line supervisors do—all day long.

It's something of a paradox to realize that while so many hotel managers spend their days talking, it's their ability to listen that's the key to effective verbal communications. Two-way communication takes place when each person is willing to express his or her feelings to the other. Communication is a process that entails emotions and feelings as well as facts. Because of this, it's important to understand what someone is saying from that person's point of view. This ability to empathize is the key to effective communication. Without empathy people tend to form judgments too quickly about what someone is saying. Once judgments are made listening often ceases. Instead of judging, communication is enhanced by questioning the meanings and feelings of the person you are trying to understand. Many managers are good top-down communicators. While this is better than having no communication skills at all, it misses the mark of what communicating is really all about. After all, how can a manager truly motivate subordinates if he or she is unaware of what their subordinates think and what they feel?

REFERENCES

Albrecht, Carl and Ron Zemke. 1985. *Service America! Doing Business in the New Economy*. Homewood, Il.: Dow-Jones-Irwin.

Alessandra, Anthony. March 1989. "Communication Involves More Than Listening to Words." *Lodging* 14(7):96-97.

Brownell, Judi. February 1987. "Listening: The Toughest Management Skill." *The Cornell Hotel and Restaurant Administration Quarterly* 27(4):65-71.

Feinberg, Mortimer R. October 1986. "The Accessible CEO." *Restaurant Business* 85:155.

Ference, Eugene A. August/September 1989. "Team Building For Quality." *Bottomline* 4(4):12-17ff.

Heskett, James L. 1986. *Managing in the Service Economy*. Boston: Harvard Business School Press.

Kotter, John P. 1982. *The GMs*. New York: The Free Press.

Mintzberg, Henry. July/August 1975. "The Manager's Job: Folklore and Fact." *Harvard Business Review*.

Peters, Thomas J. and Robert H. Waterman, Jr. 1982. "In Search of Excellence: Lessons from America's Best-Run Companies." New York: Harper and Row, Publishers.

Rogers, Carl R. and F.J. Roethlisberger. 1951. "Barriers and Gateways to Communication." Reprinted in "People: Managing Your Most Important Asset." 1987. Boston: *Harvard Business Review*.

Shriver, Steve. February 1988. "Don't Overstaff to Solve Problems that Can Only Be Solved by Better Communications." *Lodging* 13(6):41-47.

Slater,David. November 1989. "Coming to a Truce: Ways to Bridge the Gap Between the Front and the Back of the House." *Restaurants USA* 9(10):26–29.

QUESTIONS

9-1.   Why is verbal communication so important in hotels?

9-2.   Think of three or four jobs you have held. Make a list of the kinds of information you did not have about your job or the company that would have been important, helpful, or motivating to you. Explain why this is so. Keep the list for when you become a manager.

9-3.   What are the major barriers to effective two-way communication?

9-4.   What specifically must you do during a conversation to ensure that effective two-way communication takes place?

9-5.   Suggest ways that you might audit your organization to see if its members are communicating effectively.

9-6.   Why does communicating require listening?

CHAPTER 10

Leading People

This and the next chapter will give you the foundation on which to build your leadership skills. This chapter will present the findings of some of the most important social science research on the topic of leadership. You will learn the traits leaders possess and the sources and limits of their power. You will also learn the different kinds of behavior that leaders engage in and the various approaches they use in their roles as leaders. Further, this discussion will focus on how leadership behavior might vary depending on the particular situation in which a leader is placed. The concept of leadership will be expanded further in Chapter Eleven to include topics that relate not just to leading individuals but to leading organizations.

THE IMPORTANCE OF LEADERSHIP

In their book, *Leaders*, Bennis and Nanus (1985, 7) quote from a 1983 survey of American workers conducted by the Public Agenda Forum.

- "Fewer than 1 out of every 4 jobholders said that they are currently working at full potential.
- One-half said they do not put effort into their job over and above what is required to hold onto it.
- The overwhelming majority, 75 percent, said that they could be significantly more effective than they presently are."

Think of what this means. How would you like to be the manager of a group of front desk workers with these attitudes? Do you think you could exert the kind of leadership it would take to energize these employees to work up to their potential? Leadership is one of the main challenges you face in your hotel career. No less a hotelman than J. Willard Marriott had this to say about employee attitude (O'Brien 1978, 8): "Well, as I've often said, anybody—almost anybody *can't* run a hotel unless they have some great people to do it. I think one of the big problems in the hotel industry today, and in many other industries, too, is *indifferent employees*." (Italics added.) Mr. Marriott was talking from experience; he was nearly seventy-three years old when he uttered those words and had spent fifty-six years in the hotel and restaurant business! Peter Drucker (1954,144) has said that the purpose of an organization is to "make common men do uncommon things," and that leadership is "the lifting of a man's vision to higher sights, the raising of a man's performance to a higher standard, the building of a man's personality beyond its normal limitations." (Drucker, 1954, 159). These are lofty goals, ones to which Mr. Marriott would no doubt heartily subscribe. Under this kind of leadership there would surely be few of Mr. Marriott's "indifferent employees," and if effective leadership were common throughout America the findings of the Public Agenda Forum survey would surely be more heartening.

If the results of the Public Agenda Forum survey are representative of worker attitudes in general, America faces a "leadership crisis." If Mr. Marriott is to be believed, indifferent employees result in mediocre hotels, and if Mr.Drucker's definition of leadership is correct, management's job is to cause ordinary people to do extraordinary things.

Leadership in Hotels

The hotel department and division heads I interviewed had some very definite opinions about what makes a good GM, and leadership ranks high on their list. Considering all of the attributes they say makes an effective GM, leadership appears about 42 percent of the time! Division heads felt that as leaders GMs should

- develop their staffs,
- build a good management team,
- be motivators,
- be good delegators,
- be good communicators,
- be caring, trustworthy, and consistent.

Department heads did want their GMs to possess other traits. Other ideal GM traits, and the frequency they were mentioned, were: (1) understand guest needs (11 percent), (2) be good problem solvers (10 percent), (3) understand marketing (8 percent), (4) be well-rounded (8 percent), (5) understand budgets and have a profit orientation (7 percent), and (6) be good

The uncommonly striking San Francisco Marriott Hotel.

Courtesy: Marriott Hotels, Resorts and Suites

at both community relations (6 percent) and corporate–owner relations (6 percent).

Still, the leadership dimension dominated their thinking. As one department head put it, "Technical skills are not sufficient for the job." And another said, "The management and staff of this hotel *is* the product, the building is a given." An interesting comment regarding the leadership dimension was made by a senior division head who said, "A GM must be beyond reproach because he is always under a microscope." Another felt GMs must be "strong yet sensitive to people." These were typical of the kinds of comments made by these fifty-three senior hotel executives. Taken together one might say that a hotel GM had better be a combination eagle scout, football coach, teacher, and military general. That's quite a heavy load for anyone, but after all, hotel GMs are the chief executives of rather substantial businesses, and their subordinates look to them for leadership. Note that the first order of business for GMs is to be good at developing people and promoting teamwork. These traits are followed by the ability to motivate, delegate, and communicate. Finally, subordinates want caring leaders who are trustworthy and consistent. Note also that subordinates pay close attention to everything their superiors do. General managers had better pay attention to all of their actions since they are constantly "under a microscope."

It's likely that leadership would have headed the list of favorable management traits at all management levels within the hotel. In other words, the subordinates of division heads, department heads, and first-line supervisors would likely respond that leadership was the most important characteristic they looked for in their superior. The point is that people in organizations are always looking for leadership. When leadership is present and effective, organizations flourish. When it is absent organizations regress into mediocrity or worse (Worsfold 1989a).

What Is Leadership?

Chapter Eight dealt with motivation. It's obvious that the topics of human motivation and leadership are closely related. In fact, a good definition of leadership is the process of influencing people to willingly perform in ways that lead to the accomplishments of an organization's goals. This kind of leadership will result in self-motivated employees who choose to perform "up to their abilities." If coercion is necessary, as the Public Agenda Forum survey indicates, the average organization may have half of its employees exerting just enough effort required to hold on to their job.

Because leadership relates to people, it's subject to all the uncertainties, ambiguities, and paradoxes that surround human behavior. In consequence, being a leader is as much an art as it is a science; one can study the topic, but it takes practice to really get good at it. If you aspire to a career in the hotel industry, it's virtually impossible to have a managerial position where you are not responsible for the activities of a fairly sizable number of people. Being effective in your job will require that you exert influence over others who do not report directly to you. As soon as being effective in your job requires that you exert influence over others, you have been placed into a potential leadership role. Thus, the success you have in your career will depend on your ability to be an effective leader. Just as you need to develop skills in accounting, computers and purchasing, you must develop leadership skills to be an effective hotel executive. This chapter will introduce important leadership concepts and give examples of how successful executives in the hotel business lead. These leadership concepts and examples are much more than abstract theories or interesting stories. Think of them as guidelines to be used in developing your own individual approach to leadership. If you begin developing leadership skills now, you will be ahead of the game. Don't wait until you're put in charge of twenty employees to think about leadership. Too much on-the-job improvisation may damage your effectiveness and your career.

LEADERSHIP TRAITS AND SOURCES OF POWER

Are leaders born or are they made? Do circumstances thrust leadership roles on ordinary people or do natural leaders shape circumstances? By what power or authority do people lead? These important issues will be discussed in this section.

Leadership Traits

Are there any personal traits that make identifying leadership potential easy? For example, are most successful leaders physically imposing, masculine figures like a John Wayne? Apparently not. Leaders come in all sizes, shapes, and sexes. Napoleon barely exceeded five feet in height; Winston Churchill was short, fat, and in his sixties when he became Great Britain's prime minister during World War II; Liz Claiborne built her fashion empire into a $1.2 billion business in only thirteen years; while a grandmother named Margaret Thacher transformed British politics during the 1980s and earned the nickname "Iron Lady." Outstanding GMs also come in all sizes and shapes: Henri LeSassier is five feet four and prone to being overweight, while Lawrence Wagner and Curtis Samuels are tall, trim, and good looking. Generally speaking, however, most of the GMs would be hard to pick out in a crowd. Their interests also varied greatly: three are avid tennis players while two are golfers; one is interested in the arts while another is a real sports nut; one reads history, another spends his spare time fishing, and a third loves to get involved in civic causes.

If looks and interests can be deceiving, are there any other traits that clearly distinguish leaders? Leaders do appear to have a strong need for achievement and self-actualization. Additionally, successful business leaders seem to possess good supervisory skills and are intelligent, decisive, and self-confident. They do not, however, appear to place much value on job security (Ghiselli 1971). Hotel GMs seem to fit well into this profile. Additional GM traits that are readily apparent include a high energy level and a definite leaning toward being perfectionists (Worsfold 1989b). Still, these qualities can easily be found in a wide variety of people, many of whom would not be characterized as leaders. These traits, while often found in leaders, do not ensure that a person will be a leader. In short, the job of identifying leaders is not an easy one. It does appear, however, that leadership is a quality that can be learned as long as a person possesses certain minimum traits, abilities, and needs. That's good news because, while a few people seem to be "born leaders," most are not. If leadership can be taught, organizations can develop leaders rather than relying only on hiring them.

Sources of Leader Power

Because leading involves influencing it is important to understand the sources of power available to managers in their leadership role. It is commonly held (French and Raven 1959) that there are five basic sources of power: reward power, coercive power, legitimate power, referent power, and expert power.

Reward and coercive power refer to a leader's ability to administer either positive rewards or punishments depending on a follower's behavior. Recall the expectancy theory of motivation from Chapter Eight. The effectiveness of reward and coercive power will depend on a superior's ability to administer rewards or punishments, their level, the value placed on them by the follower, and the follower's assessment that rewards or punishments will be forthcoming. Further, positive reinforcement is generally considered to be the most effective method of behavior modification. Thus, rewards and punishments must be used in light of their behavior modification effects. Examples of reward systems include bonuses for increased output or sales, while typical punishments might include reprimand for tardiness or the threat of firing for substandard performance. Often, rewards and punishments are difficult to distinguish from each other. For example, is withholding a reward a form of punishment, or is stopping a punishment a reward? What is clear, however, is that the use of rewards will tend to attract the reward's recipient to its dispenser, while the opposite will be true for punishments. People like those who provide rewards and dislike those who punish.

Legitimate power is derived from our social and cultural norms, perceptions, and assumptions. When one feels that a superior has a right to exert certain power and, furthermore, that he or she has an obligation to conform to the superior's influence, then legitimate power exists. Within the family, certain members are able to prescribe the behavior of others based on commonly held cultural values. Acceptance of the prevailing social structure confers legitimate power as well. For example, British police do not carry guns, yet they are obeyed by the common consent of the people. By common consent, college students grant professors the power of assigning grades, and hotel workers grant certain powers to their managers. What people view as legitimate power changes over time. Revolutions redefine the legitimate power of citizens. Workers have redefined legitimate power through unions.

People who admire and want to be like their superior will likely grant the superior a degree of referent power over them. The more they desire to identify with a superior, the more they will tend to model their behavior after him or her. Thus, a superior's ability to influence a subordinate will be greater because of the subordinate's desire for conformity. Richard James confided to me that he had been tremendously influenced by a superior during the formative years of his career. This attraction extended past work-related behavior to include emulating the person's clothing and hair style. Referent power must be clearly distinguished from reward or coercive power. The extent that a person is attracted to another because of the desire for rewards (such as praise) or fear of sanctions (such as rejection) defines coercive power. On the other hand, referent power exists when a person is attracted to and wishes to identify with another regardless of that person's response.

Some of the GMs studied clearly had charismatic qualities that increased their referent power. Three in particular had this quality. Subordinates said of William Scully that he made them want to work hard for him; Curtis Samuels was described consistently as an inspirational leader who gave people purpose and pride and who was considered "a god" by the employees; Matthew Fox's subordinates trusted and admired him because they knew that he was fair, honest, loyal, and caring. Recall that some subordinates said they worked for Matt, not for the company.

Expert power refers to the perception of the amount of knowledge or skill a leader possesses relative to one's own. Thus, a hotel chef may command a degree of expert power over the kitchen staff because of superior culinary training and experience. If the staff wants to improve their culinary skills, they are more easily influenced by someone they perceive of as a master chef. While a chef may exert considerable expert power over the culinary staff, the range of that power will not extend very far from the kitchen.

There are a number of important points to make concerning the sources of a leader's power. In general, the stronger the sources of power, the more power one has. Thus, managers should cultivate as many sources of power as possible. Remember, however, that power depends on people's perceptions and, consequently, can change radically from time to time and from person to person. The range of influence one has depends on one's primary source of power. In some cases such as expert, reward, and coercive power, the range of influence is usually limited to the specific job circumstances. Attempts to use power outside of their normal range will be unsuccessful and may reduce one's level of power. With other sources of power, especially referent power, the range of influence may be quite broad. Power need not be used to be effective. Even though a boss may seldom use the power to discharge, it's still there in the minds of employees, and therefore, it is real. The more people see a source of power as legitimate, the more likely they are to accept the use of both reward and punishment. For example, the punishment for inattention metered out by an infantry drill sergeant is more likely to be accepted than that of a summercamp counselor.

Any leader must consider the sources, uses, and limitations of power in order to be successful. Power is rarely absolute, as former President of The United States Richard Nixon will readily attest. Power depends on people's perceptions, which can change. The political events during 1989 in Eastern Europe, which culminated in the destruction of the Berlin Wall, are dramatic examples of power crumbling in a matter of weeks. There are other organizational sources of power such as control of resources and information. As a leader you must learn to identify all possible sources of power and to apply them appropriately and wisely.

LEADER BEHAVIOR

Successful hotel executives pay close attention to their leadership behavior and that of their subordinates. Richard James laughingly described his leadership style as "a guided dictatorship." In a more serious vein, Richard indicated that his leadership behavior had evolved from when he was the GM of a 400-room hotel. In fact, he felt his "management style of four to five years ago would not have worked here, but I've matured." Lawrence Wagner was worried enough about his new chief of security, an ex-military type who was getting a reputation as somewhat of a "sledgehammer" around the hotel, that he met with his retired security chief to see if this behavior might adversely affect the hotel's relations with the local police.

This section discusses what people actually do in their role as leaders. In other words, what kinds of behavior constitutes leadership? How do leadership styles interact with each other, and how do the situations in which leaders find themselves influences their effectiveness.

Authoritarian Versus Participative Leadership

An authoritarian leader is someone who uses his or her power to enforce obedience, to control, to command, and to make decisions. Everyone has been on the receiving end of authoritarian leadership. Mothers forcing children to eat their carrots are engaging in authoritarian behavior. When the chef decides on all food-preparation methods by himself, he is engaged in authoritarian behavior. When an infantry sergeant orders his platoon to attack an enemy gun emplacement, he is engaging in authoritarian leadership. Participative leadership, on the other hand, involves both leader and fol-

An efficient reservations department at the San Diego Marriott Hotel and Marina

Courtesy: Marriott Hotels, Resorts and Suites

lower in a process of joint decision making. Everyone in the group has a chance to have a say. At the extreme, decisions can be made democratically on the basis of group consensus. When the whole family decides on the summer vacation together, when the GM allows the EOC to jointly decide on a rooms-pricing policy for the next year, and when waitresses are allowed to vote on the criteria for determining who gets specific tables participative leadership and decision making is being practiced.

These leadership styles, which at their extremes are referred to as autocratic and democratic, represent two ends of a continuum. At one extreme, the autocrat makes all the decisions, while at the other extreme majority vote rules. This means that for a particular decision a person cannot practice both authoritarian and participative leadership; behaving one way means not behaving the other way; becoming more authoritarian means becoming less participative, and vice versa. However, a person can make an authoritarian decision in one circumstance and a participative decision in another, so it's not necessary that one's leadership style be always authoritarian or always participative.

There is a common misconception that those who engage in authoritarian leadership behavior have little concern for people, while those who practice participative leadership are more caring about their subordinates. This is not necessarily true. Parents are perfect examples of benevolent autocrats who lovingly force children to eat liver, brussel sprouts, peas, and lima beans for their own good. On the other hand, it's also possible for a participative leader to have little actual concern for his or her followers. Concern for followers is generally considered to be another, separate, leadership dimension.

Pros and Cons of Authoritarian and Participative Leadership

What are some of the arguments in favor of authoritarian and participative leadership styles, and is one style generally more effective than the other? Some would argue that most people depend on work to satisfy lower order physiological, safety, and security needs, and that authoritarian leadership is preferable for the following reasons (Webber 1975, 185–187):

- It is predictable and effective in satisfying lower order needs through work.
- Many people expect their superiors to be authoritarian—to be otherwise would show weakness.
- Much work is unpleasant and would be avoided without directed leadership.
- Authoritarian leadership is fast: the leader need only tell the follower what to do, so little time is wasted on discussion.
- It's the easiest and most natural leadership style for most managers.
- It's honest and straightforward and does not attempt to meddle with people's personalities.

Proponents of participative leadership note that participation tends to satisfy higher order needs of affiliation, esteem, and self-actualization, and therefore, participative leadership is preferable for the following reasons (Webber 1975):

- People are not as dependent on one particular job as they used to be and will gravitate to the job that best fulfills higher order needs.
- Subordinates want to influence their superiors through participation and do not view their ability to do so as a superior's weakness.
- People are not lazy and will respond to the challenge of most jobs if given half a chance.
- Participative leadership can lead to greater creativity and, therefore, more effective performance.
- Both managers and workers are better educated today and have a better understanding of human behavior, including the need for people to fulfill higher order needs.
- Participative leadership is more honest because of greater mutual respect and communication between superior and subordinate.

Factors Affecting Leadership Style

Both sides of the argument make valid points. It's possible to cite cases where one or the other leadership style is obviously best. In the heat of the battle, an infantry sergeant must be autocratic. At the other extreme, a research team of scientists with different individual specialties will likely need to participate in group decisions. As might be expected, no one leadership style appears to be most effective in all circumstances. Two factors that influence the effectiveness of a leadership style are the personality of the follower and the nature of the task. Subordinates who are ego-involved in their work or who have a strong need for independence of action will tend to respond favorable to participation. Subordinates who are not ego-involved or who have dependent personalities often respond poorly to participation (Filley, House, and Kerr 1976). In general, participation seems to result in greater job satisfaction and improved morale among employees, while authoritarian leadership results in less job satisfaction. However, as previously discussed, there is no direct cause-and-effect relationship between job satisfaction and productivity.

A simple, routine job will lend itself more to authoritarian behavior. Experiments show that when presented with simple, routine tasks, groups voluntarily form themselves into centralized wheel-like communication networks that facilitate rapid, efficient problem solving. Simple tasks call for simple (authoritarian) leadership. On the other hand, when complex and ambiguous problems need to be solved, experimental groups voluntarily organize into all-channel communications networks, which facilitate joint decision making (Webber 1975, 110–112). Figure 10-1 demonstrates these tendencies.

Job time pressures affect the extent to which participation is possible. Many operational positions in hotels, such as banquet manager, have a very short time span between problem definition, solution and action. Often decisions must be made quickly or not at all, and therefore, there is only time for authoritarian behavior. As Henri LeSassier put it, "There's a true immediacy to problems . . ." in hotels. Extreme time pressures also require that the chain of command be occasionally broken. Most experienced hotel executives and workers understand that time pressures sometimes require authoritarian decisions and disregard for the chain of command. As one moves up in an organization it's usual for short-term time demands to diminish. It's also true that the nature of the problems managers' face become more complex. It's therefore common for a manager's leadership style to change from an authoritative emphasis during the early years of a career toward a participative focus in the latter years.

These findings reveal that an effective leader may have to be authoritarian in some circumstances and participative in others, since neither style has been shown to be superior in all circumstance.

GM Leadership Behavior: Authoritarian Versus Participative

The GMs varied individually in their tendencies toward authoritarian or participative leadership. Most were quite comfortable making decisions, had made them all of their careers, and had no problem making them alone if they felt it was in their hotels' best interest. Even though five of the GMs were only about forty years old, they were all extremely experienced executives who understood the ins and outs of the hotel business. Not only were they experienced when compared to GMs of smaller hotels, but their experi-

Simple Tasks   Complex Tasks

FIGURE 10-1.   Voluntary Communication Networks

Perceptions are important at this streamlined restaurant bar in a Le Meridien hotel.

Courtesy: Le Meridian Hotels, Inc.

ence relative to their key subordinates was also quite great. Only about five subordinates of these GMs had as many or more years' experience in the hotel business, and only a couple had experience in more than one functional department. In many cases these GMs knew what was best for their hotels and, therefore, could save time and effort by making an authoritarian decision themselves. Matthew Fox described this tendency well when he said,

"I've become more autocratic when it comes to the obvious things than I was ten years ago . . ."

Another aspect of leadership behavior was revealed when the GMs listed the areas of their hotels' operations in which they wanted to have decision-making input. Richard James wanted to be involved "in any decision that affects guest perceptions." In fact, he assumed total responsibility for refurbishing a large-night club at The Hotel Apollo. Jonathan Claiborne felt the same way about the new meeting rooms and the restaurant renovations that were under way at the 550-room Riviera Hotel. Bill Scully wants to be heavily involved in decisions relating to pricing and advertising, marketing, capital spending, and manpower.

Because hotels are such personal businesses, it's not unusual to see certain kinds of authoritarian behavior relating to tastes. Jonathan Claiborne personally decides on the placement of fresh flowers at The Riviera, and Matthew Fox decided on the exact location of a mirror in the Presidential Suite. Bruce Warren chooses his hotel's napkins and is quite proud of his choice of soap dishes. Lawrence Wagner makes the most minute decisions regarding the appearance of a restaurant menu and insists that he alone choose a pianist for the lounge. This kind of behavior, while authoritarian, is a natural consequence of the subjective nature of the hotel business. As Henri LeSassier puts it, "A hotel should reflect its GM's personality."

While there are certain circumstances where authoritarian decisions make the most sense in hotels, there are others where they do not. We quoted Matthew Fox as saying that when it comes to obvious things he has become more authoritarian over the years, but his full statement continues with ". . . but I'm willing to work with people and my executive committee on the really difficult problems." It turned out that by "work with" Fox meant participative decision making regarding some of the really key issues facing the St. Charles Hotel. So while in one way he is becoming more authoritarian over the years, in another important way he has become more participative concerning some decisions as well! In fact, his immediate subordinates all made the point that the EOC was playing a much greater decision-making role than it had five years before. This really is not a paradox, and successful hotel GMs are comfortable shifting from one form of leadership behavior to another.

Some GMs seem more naturally inclined toward participation while others are more comfortable as authoritarians. Each GM engages in both kinds of behavior as judged by their own statements, their actions, and the evaluations of their subordinates. It would be naive and overly simplistic to refer to these GMs as either authoritarian or participative. Of the ten, my impression is that two tilted toward authoritarianism, while another two leaned decidedly toward participation as their normal and natural way of behaving. The remainder were a mixture of both leadership styles, but on balance, they seemed to be trying to move their hotels in the direction of greater participation.

Consideration and Initiating Structure

The previous discussion focused on only one dimension of leadership behavior: decision making. Leaders behave in many other ways. Two basic kinds of behavior in which leaders engage (Stogdill and Coons 1957) are initiating structure and consideration, commonly referred to respectively as concern for task and concern for people. Leaders who exhibit strong initiating structure assign particular tasks to subordinates, clarify their expectations, schedule their work, and set a tone that values high performance and bottom-line goals. Consideration is characterized by a leader creating a climate of warmth and supportiveness by being friendly and by concern for subordinate welfare. We noted above that for a particular decision one cannot engage in both authoritarian and participative behavior at the same time; they're two ends of a continuum. With regard to consideration and initiating structure, this is not the case. It is possible for a leader to be high in concern for task and high in concern for people at the same time.

The Management Grid

A well-known representation of these two kinds of leadership behavior is the management grid (Blake and Mouton 1985, 12). The management grid does not measure actual behavior; it measures concern for people and concern for production, on a scale of one through nine (Figure 10-2), with one being low concern and nine high concern. Note that a person can score high or low on either leadership dimension. Let's step through various leadership combinations.

A (1,1) manager is a disaster, someone who cares neither for people or production. Under this manager a leadership vacuum exists, and the organization operates by virtue of its structure and systems. There is likely to be low subordinate performance and low morale.

A (1,9) leader is concerned primarily with maintaining harmonious subordinate relationships. Little concern is given to production or performance goals, and when a conflict between production and people arises, this leader sides with maintaining harmony over meeting production goals. Often referred to as country club management, organizations experiencing this leadership style will often have satisfied low-performing employees.

On the other hand, a (9,1) leader is only concerned with production, caring little for subordinate needs. While strong pressure to produce may for a time result in high performance, a lack of any subordinate consideration will ultimately depress morale and performance will suffer.

A (5,5) leadership style tries for a balance between production and morale. It's a middle of the road approach that will sacrifice high production

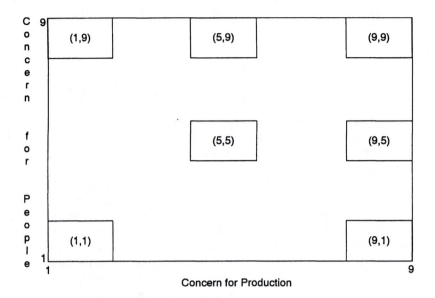

FIGURE 10-2. The Management Grid

levels in order to maintain an acceptable level of morale. It's the first kind of leadership behavior in Figure 10-2 that promises a degree of long-term success.

Blake and Mouton argue that the most desirable kind of leadership behavior is a (9,9), where a strong concern for performance is balanced by an equally strong concern for people. Under (9,9) leadership a highly motivated and committed team of managers and employees would attain high production levels through participation and involvement.

Factors Affecting Leadership Style

It's not altogether certain that a (9,9) leadership style is best in all circumstances. The kind of job tasks might influence the most effective place to be on the management grid. A group of employees engaged in low-level, routine, repetitive, and distasteful tasks may not perform well with a high level of concern for production. Some feel that too much task pressure under these circumstances would be resented (House and Mitchell 1974) and have little effect on performance. After all, if a job is routine and provides its own performance feedback, high pressure to perform may accomplish little. On the other hand, leader consideration and support in this circumstance becomes important. A friendly, sympathetic boss who is concerned with employee welfare may succeed if the job is repetitive and distasteful.

While a (9,9) management style under these circumstances may be too much task pressure, a (5,9) style, high in concern for people and moderate in concern for production, may be more effective over the long run. Take, for example, room maids in a hotel. They are usually assigned a quota of rooms to clean during an eight-hour shift. If objective criteria of what constitutes a clean room are clearly spelled out, and if the cleaning procedures are carefully taught, then it's fairly easy for the maids to assess their own level of production. A leadership style that's heavy on consideration and "reasonable" on production may have the best chance for long-term success. On the other hand, executives who are performing intrinsically interesting and challenging tasks have less need for leader consideration. If, however, certain ambiguities and uncertainties surround their jobs, a leader who provides structure and performance standards is welcomed because by so doing the leader helps clarify subordinate expectations. Under these conditions, a (9,5) leadership style may be most effective.

Subordinates' personalities may also affect the appropriateness of a leadership style. If subordinates have high achievement needs it's likely that they will respond best to a people-oriented leadership style or to a balanced (5,5) style. Using a primarily task-oriented approach will probably be resented since subordinates are already achievement oriented. On the other hand, subordinates with low achievement needs will probably not respond as well to a consideration-dominated approach. They need more direction and structure and will respond best to a balanced (5,5) or more task-oriented approach (Webber 1975, 198).

It's worth noting that while consideration may sometimes have little direct positive affect on production, it generally does no harm. When consideration is used in combination with initiating structure, it will often improve production. Effective leaders learn through experience to analyze task circumstances and spot subordinate personality traits when choosing the "best" combination of consideration and structure. Some managers appear to know instinctively when to stress one dimension over another. Many, however, learn leadership skills as they mature as managers.

GM Leadership Behavior: Task Versus People

One of the really interesting aspects of the GM research was observing these executives in their roles as leaders and trying to determine how best to characterize their leadership styles. As with the authoritarian–participative leadership dimension, it's not possible to precisely pinpoint each GMs task or people score. It is possible, however, to distinguish different tendencies among GMs along this leadership dimension. My assessment is that three of the ten were higher in their initiating structure–task orientation than in their consideration–people orientation. Three others seemed some-what higher in the consideration–people dimension than in initiating struc-ture–task, and the remaining four ranked about even in the two dimensions. While these evaluations are, of course, subjective, they are based on con-siderable evidence. Each GM was asked to discuss his leadership style. Key subordinates were also asked to describe their GM as a manager. The GMs were also observed continuously for three days during their daily work routine. These observations resulted in numerous follow-up questions regarding leadership behavior.

It was not surprising to find that most of the GMs ranked high in their initiating structure–task orientation. They could not have progressed to their present positions had they not been strongly achievement oriented. Remember that this dimension of leadership is concerned with bottom-line goals. A leader exerts pressure to perform, assigns tasks, schedules work, specifies procedure, and clarifies his or her expectations to subordinates. The GMs were quite insistent about the importance of this dimension of leadership. Furthermore, their subordinates did not hesitate to describe the GMs as highly task oriented. One GM said, "Performance and results are of primary importance—period." Another was in the process of "turning up the dials" on his EOC because he was unhappy with performance. A third was quite frank about "exerting tremendous pressure on his execu-tives and staff to perform." One GM readily admitted to being a perfec-tionist who wanted to be "number one" among his peers and described himself as "the kind of guy who would step in front of a 3-and-2 pitch" in order to get the job done.

This attitude came through loud and clear from the GMs' subordinates. The subordinates of one particularly task-oriented GM said this about how the hotel's environment had changed since his arrival: "The hotel is more controlled now; there's a more serious, work-oriented attitude now; there is more pressure to perform; he (the GM) sets and enforces standards." Another GM was described as "powerful and domineering" by his subordinates. Fur-thermore, that hotel's performance-oriented environment was described as "hectic." Another GM was described as "hard-nosed; a bottom-line guy; aggressive; a hard taskmaster on his department heads." It seemed to me that five of the GMs ranked very close to "9s" with regard to task orientation and that three of these five were probably "9s." Whether "9s" or not, all of these outstanding GMs were high in this dimension.

In terms of the GMs' consideration score, my subjective evaluation would place two right at "9," two at about "8," and the rest falling in the "5″ to "7″ category. The two GMs with "9s" for consideration also had slightly lower task scores. Most of the GMs appeared to be caring and loyal to their execu-tives and staff. While there were a few examples of mistrust and suspicion on the part of individual subordinates, the overall impression I got was that these successful GMs had a genuine concern for the people who worked for

GMs often attend to details, such as placement of flowers in the lobby of the Omni Melrose Hotel in Dallas, Texas.

Courtesy: Omni Hotels

them. This manifested itself in their assessment of the toughest decisions they had to make. Tough personnel decisions, such as having to fire an executive, lead the list at 37 percent. The GMs generally expressed a sincere sense of personal failure when an executive did not work out and had to be terminated. Each had, of course, fired executives and workers alike, but they did not like it and they usually considered it their fault when it happened. Chapter Fifteen will discuss this trait in greater detail. For now it's sufficient to say that most of the GMs were caring and sensitive when it came to the consideration dimension of leadership.

GMs Attention to Detail and Follow-up as a Leadership Trait

Two GM traits that led to their effectiveness with regard to initiating structure were: (1) their consistent attention to the numerous details of their hotels' operation, and (2) their equally consistent strength of follow-up. As a group, they were quite remarkable in this regard. All of the GMs regard the hotel business as one of details, and each enjoyed attending to detail. It is through attention to detail that GMs are able to specify procedures and clarify the expectations of subordinates. It is through consistent, unrelenting follow-up that GMs are able to exert continuing pressure for performance.

Some GMs, such as Lawrence Wagner, Richard James, Curtis Samuels, and Matthew Fox have devised fairly elaborate paperwork systems to ensure efficient follow-up. Wagner has his "trace" system. During meetings he carefully writes down "my actions, your actions, and deadline dates" for each subordinate. James maintains a large loose-leaf binder in which he keeps track of the multitude of activities each department has scheduled, as well as other projects he wants to initiate. James and Wagner are very careful to update their files daily whenever they issue an order or think of something that needs attention. Curtis Samuels keeps a file that reflects the monthly MBO sessions he conducts with each subordinate. Matthew Fox goes about it differently; he admits to being a "list maker." He keeps a number of separate piles of paper on his desk and around his office. On the top of each pile is a sheet of paper listing that pile's priorities. While explaining his follow-up system he pointed out a daily pile, a capital-budget pile, next year's operating-budget pile, and an advertising-campaign pile, to mention a few. The number and nature of the piles vary depending on what is important at the time. These piles don't make his office appear messy, and he has no difficulty keeping track of things. In fact, one of the qualities his subordinates marvel about is that with the help of his "list-and-pile system" he never forgets!

One of the qualities on which subordinates usually complement GMs is their ability to remember and to follow-up on hundreds of small details. This is how structure is initiated, how performance pressure is maintained, and how expectations are clarified—through attention to detail and unrelenting follow-up.

CHOOSING A LEADERSHIP STYLE

Leaders need to be flexible. A leader cannot always be effective by being participative (or authoritarian), any more than consideration (or initiating structure) is best under all circumstances. Knowing when to behave in a certain way and when to alter one's leadership styles is important.

Two approaches suggest how leadership behavior might be varied depending on circumstances. Each approach gives insights into what leadership really means and what people do in their role as leaders. Each will help define leadership behavior in different circumstances.

How Follower Maturity Affects Initiating Structure and Consideration

Leadership is the art of influencing others. Curiously, however, when one person *(A)* exerts influence over another *(B)* it's sometimes difficult to determine if it's *A*'s behavior that causes *B* to act in a certain way or just the opposite (that is, *B*'s behavior causes *A* to act in a certain way). For example, a football player who reports to training camp overweight and out of shape will be treated differently from other players by his coaches because of his unacceptable off-season behavior.

Choosing a Leadership Style

Hershey and Blanchard (1977) propose certain rules of leadership behavior that take into account important aspects of the follower. They define *job maturity* as the skill, training, and experience a follower brings to a job and *psychological maturity* as a follower's self-confidence and self-image. Followers can be high or low in both, or high in one and low in the other. A very immature follower would be inexperienced, untrained, and possess little self-confidence. A very mature follower would be highly skilled, well-qualified, and also possess considerable self-esteem and confidence. A variety of intermediate states of maturity are, of course, also possible.

The question Hershey and Blanchard ask is which combination of consideration and initiating structure is best given the relative maturity of the follower? Figure 10-3 summarizes their recommendations for effective leadership along this dimension. Leaders should exert a high level of initiating structure for followers of extremely low maturity (that is, those who lack both skills and esteem).

		Follower Maturity		
		High	Moderate	Low
Leader Behavior	Initiating Structure	High	Moderate	Low
	Consideration	Low	High	Low
		Low	Moderate	High

FIGURE 10-3.   Leader Behavior and Follower Maturity

According to Hershey and Blanchard, low-maturity followers desperately need structure; they need to be taught what to do and how to do it, and they need to know what is expected of them. For low-maturity followers, the need for structure is so pressing that for a leader to spend much time with consideration is simply inappropriate. The situation changes, however, as soon as follower maturity begins to develop. For followers with moderate levels of maturity, leaders should focus on a high level of consideration and only a moderate level of initiating structure. At this stage in the relationship, followers are developing adequate job skills and their self-confidence is rising. Initiating structure is becoming less important now, but if the follower is to continue to develop, consideration and psychological support become more critical. As follower maturity becomes high, the need for either form of leadership behavior diminishes. Followers become self-confident and are good at their jobs. They no longer need to be directed, nor do they need to be "stroked," although as discussed, a little consideration never seems to hurt.

Notice that a leader's goal is to try to move a follower toward a state of both job and psychological maturity. The leader, therefore, alters his or her leadership style depending on the maturity level of the follower. Clearly, there is mutual influence going on in a leader–follower relationship. While leader behavior influences follower behavior, the reverse is also true; follower behavior influences leader behavior. The Hershey–Blanchard approach allows for a wide variety of leadership behavior between a superior and a subordinate. A subordinate may be at a high level of maturity in certain job aspects but at a much lower level in others. Thus, a superior's leadership behavior might vary with the same subordinate depending on which aspect of the subordinate's job is under review.

How GMs Act

Skilled hotel managers are capable of making this kind of leadership transition without confusing a subordinate. They are also capable of different leadership behavior with different subordinates depending on the maturity level of each. When interviewing the GM's subordinates, it sometimes seemed that the subordinates of one GM were working for completely different people based on their assessment of their boss's leadership style. Subordinates who were experienced and had fairly long working relationships with a GM commented, "The GM let's me do my job; the GM gives me a lot of latitude; he is hands-on, but he let's me be my own manager; the GM trusts me and leaves me alone; I can argue with him but some department heads have a problem; the GM gives me independence but wants no surprises."

On the other hand, there were other situations where inexperienced subordinates, or those new to the job, felt quite differently. They spoke of being "coached and trained" by the GM. Two relatively young and inexperienced subordinates of Matthew Fox independently said that his leadership style "was a fine balance between hands-on and hands-off." One added that she was able to "run with the ball" but had to check carefully with Fox on what she was doing. The other noted that Fox often quizzed him to be sure that he was up-to-date on some issue or had the proper answers. Examples of GMs' coaching and providing structure to less experienced subordinates abound. I watched Lawrence Wagner spend two hours one evening teaching a subordinate how to analyze a problem; Frank Anderson took lengths one day explaining to a subordinate how to conduct a successful meeting; Henri LeSassier instructed his young food and beverage director in the subtleties of choosing the proper china to complement certain food and how to best prepare a memo to corporate headquarters; Bill Scully went to lengths to show two young executives how to set priorities; and Curtis Samuels spent an hour one day helping a subordinate organize his work. This is what initiating structure is all about. Really good GMs know how to switch between initiating structure and consideration, depending on the maturity of their subordinates.

It's been stated on a number of occasions that consideration on the part of a leader can rarely do any harm. This was frequently demonstrated during the GM research. When subordinate maturity was low, high structure and pressure to perform, accompanied by little or no consideration, often resulted in a tense and strained environment. When a little consideration was introduced, the work still got done, but things were a little more relaxed.

How to Choose Between an Authoritarian and a Participative Leadership Style

Vroom and Yelton (1973) have devised a procedure that has been used extensively to help executives improve their leadership and decision-making skills. Their method helps managers decide on the most appropriate amount of subordinate participation in decision making.

Choosing a Decision-Making Leadership Style

Table 10-1 describes five types of leadership behavior, with autocratic decisions (A-I and A-II) at one extreme, consultative decision making (C-I and C-II) in the middle, and democratic or group decision making (G-II) at the other extreme. It's fastest if an A-I decision can be made and probably slowest for a G-II decision. Speed, however, may not be the most important reason to choose a leadership style. Still, if more than one leadership style were acceptable, one might be inclined to choose the quickest method unless there was a more important reason to do otherwise.

Vroom and Yelton propose that leaders answer "yes" or "no" to the following questions before they choose a leadership style.

Table 10-1.   Possible Leadership Styles

A-I	Leader solves the problem alone with information at hand.
A-II	Leader obtains information from subordinates. Leader makes decision and may or may not share with subordinates the nature of the problem.
C-I	Leader shares problem with subordinates individually, gets their ideas and suggestions, and then makes a decision that may or may not reflect subordinate input.
C-II	Leader shares problem with subordinates *as a group*, gathers their ideas and suggestions, and then makes a decision that may or may not reflect subordinate input.
G-II	Leader shares problem with subordinates as a group and *together* they determine the most appropriate solution. Leader is willing to accept the group decision.

1. Is one decision likely to be more preferred to another?
2. Is sufficient information available to make the correct decision?
3. Is the problem structured or unstructured?
4. Is subordinate acceptance of the decision critical to effective implementation?
5. If the leader makes the decision, will it be accepted by subordinates?
6. Do subordinates share the organizational goals that will be met by solving this problem?
7. Is subordinate conflict likely over the best solution?

Questions 1, 2, and 3 are self-explanatory. Questions 4 through 7 relate to the importance of subordinate attitudes and their acceptance of a decision. The following discusses two situations where the model suggests the extremes of leadership styles (A-I and G-II).

It's obvious that a straightforward authoritarian leadership style (A-I) can be employed if the answers to questions 1 and 4 are both "no," and the answer to question 2 is "yes." A "no" to question 1 means that any one of a number of solutions to the problem are equally acceptable. A "yes" to question 2 means that the leader already has sufficient information to make a decision. A "no" to question 4 means that subordinate acceptance has no affect on the decision's implementation. Thus, the simplest and fastest course of action is for the leader to make the decision and move onto other concerns. An A-I leadership style would also be called for if the answer to questions 1, 2, and 5 were all "yes." In this case there is one preferred decision (Q-1), the leader has sufficient information (Q-2), and though subordinate acceptance is important (Q-4), they will accept the decision if it is made solely by the leader (Q-5). Once again, little will be gained by delaying. Generally speaking, if a leader has sufficient information to make a decision and need not worry about subordinate acceptance or attitudes, it's faster to follow an authoritarian style like A-1.

At the other extreme, assume a more complicated case for which a participative leadership style would be called. Suppose there is one preferred solution (Q-1), the leader has insufficient information to make a decision (Q-2), the problem is unstructured (Q-3), subordinate acceptance is important (Q-4), subordinates may not accept a decision made by the leader (Q-5), they do share organizational goals as they relate to this problem (Q-6), but there is a possibility of conflict over the best solution (Q-7). Because the problem is unstructured and information is scarce, a leader would be advised to involve subordinates as a group in the search for information and alternative solutions. The leader must also guard against making a decision that would not be accepted by the group. However, since subordinates share organizational goals, they can be expected to work honestly toward finding the best solution to the problem. Under these circumstances, a participative decision (G-II) is most appropriate. It helps ensure subordinate acceptance and guards against conflict after the decision since all subordinates have a say in the decision-making process.

What would be the best leadership style in the previous example if the answer to Question 6 were "no" (that is, subordinates did not share the goals of the organization)? In this instance it would be dangerous to allow subordinates who do not share the organization's goals to participate in a group decision-making process since there is doubt that a group decision would be in the best interests of the organization. In this case, the leader would be wise to adhere to a C-II style where the problem is shared with subordinates as a group, ideas and suggestions are discussed, but the ultimate decision is made by the leader, which may or may not reflect the influence of subordinates. The reason for this change, of course, is that a "no" to Q-6 means that subordinates cannot be trusted, in this instance, to have the organization's best interest at heart. Generally speaking, more participation is desirable when group acceptance is important, when problems are unstructured, when information to make a decision is lacking, and when followers accept the goals of the organization.

Research shows (Vroom and Jago 1978) that this model, while admittedly somewhat complicated, is useful in helping managers determine what leadership style to use. One study found that in about 85 percent of successful decisions managers reported using the leadership style prescribed by the model, while they used the prescribed leadership style in only 43 percent of their poor decisions. It was also found that managers are willing to alter their leadership styles, depending on the situation, rather than always being authoritarian or participative. However, managers were not found to be quite as flexible as the model would suggest, and they also tended to be somewhat more authoritarian than the model's prescriptions.

GMs and Decision Making

While some GMs tended toward authoritarianism and others participation, they all made both kinds of decisions and seemed to alter their behavior as required by the circumstances. The GMs with decided authoritarian tendencies were described as such by their subordinates. Henri LeSassier was described as autocratic, domineering, and a "pit bull" with regard to his determination. He had effected a complete reorganization of the hotel on his own initiative and set high sales goals over the strong objection of his director of marketing. Lawrence Wagner was described as "a prototype German personality" who "makes most of the decisions, even with respect to small details. Mostly, he is right." At the other extreme were GMs who had a decided tendency toward participation. Every key subordinate of William Scully commented that he allowed them to do their own thing. To be sure, Scully did not like surprises and expected subordinates to follow-up carefully. They also commented that he preferred discussion at EOC meetings, did not want its members to "roll over and give in," desired to have EOC concurrence, and in many cases, encouraged group decision making.

An example of this occurred during an EOC meeting I attended. Scully was trying to get the group to make a policy decision regarding merit pay increases. While he understood the issues involved very well, he had done a rather poor job of communicating some technical details of possible options to those at the meeting. After a long and sometimes confusing discussion the group was frustrated and still far from reaching a consensus. It seemed that the group was willing to let Bill make the decision himself. Instead, he chose to table the issue and bring it up again the following week. I'm sure by then he found a way to explain the technical details and, hopefully, move the EOC toward group consensus. While this process took time, it was entirely consistent with Scully's participative leadership tendencies.

Most GMs fell somewhere between the two extremes and tilted in one direction or the other depending on circumstances. Jonathan Claiborne say he believes in "controlled delegation." While some of his subordinates feel that he sides more toward "do it my way," others admit that if one is strong

Beautiful board room salon at the Radisson Plaza Hotel, Minneapolis, Minnesota.

Courtesy: Radisson Hotels International

willed Claiborne can be challenged on a decision, though not in public. A good example of his use of joint decision making was given by one of his marketing executives. The hotel was planning a major meeting-space expansion. It seemed that some of the meeting-space features that marketing felt were important to clients conflicted with the operational needs of the food and beverage department. Claiborne, an ex-food and beverage director himself, engaged the group in a joint decision-making process that resulted in a group compromise satisfactory to both sides.

Frank Anderson's subordinates feel that he is capable of changing his management style to fit the circumstances. One said, "He is democratic if you are prepared and autocratic if you are not." Recall from Chapter Nine on communications the incident concerning the decision to hire a well-known local chef. It is a good illustration of Frank's use of participation to gain group consensus in an important hiring decision.

A common theme among the GMs was that while they were certainly opinionated and strong willed, their opinions (and decisions) could be changed if subordinates could convince them that "a better way could be found." This usually had to be done diplomatically and in private so the GM didn't lose face in front of management or staff. Other common themes were their willingness to grant trusted subordinates substantial decision-making authority, their dislike of surprises, and consequently their desire to be kept well-informed.

There is, as one subordinate put it, a "fine line" between a GM's use of authoritarian or participative leadership. One division head criticized a certain "GM type" as having an "imperial" leadership style that tended to get more authoritarian the tougher times became. In his view, this type of manager had no concept of the meaning of "shared responsibility" for the success or failure of a hotel. He felt that shared responsibility among managers and workers could only be developed by a greater reliance on participation. In this regard, another division head commented, "Sometimes GMs must allow some decisions to be made differently than they would like" if, by so doing, the process of participation helped foster group acceptance and commitment.

CONCLUSION

Can a person be a manager and not a leader? Yes! The world is full of managers who are definitely not leaders. People will conform to certain standards of job behavior and will perform tasks at certain proficiency levels without leadership. They usually will not, however, go much further than "doing what is required of them" unless they are effectively led.

The work attitudes of the average American worker reported at the beginning of this chapter are, to say the least, not very encouraging. But aren't these underperforming workers the same people who, after work, are active in their church and PTA, participate in civic and charitable organizations, and take pride in their homes and neighborhoods? Too many of these people apparently turn into underachieving zombies when they punch a time clock each morning. This happens because too often they are over-managed and underled. Leadership was defined as a process of getting the willing cooperation of employees to perform in ways consistent with organizational goals. Drucker speaks of getting common people to do uncommon things and J. Willard Marriott understands that indifferent workers make indifferent hotels. While it's possible to manage people into indifference, it's only possible to lead people into willing cooperation and commitment. Only through leadership can uncommon results be produced by common people.

Leaders have a high need for achievement. While this comes as no surprise, it is worth pointing out the linkage between a strong need to achieve and the importance of persistence in effective leadership. McDonald's founder, Ray Kroc, was so convinced of this "secret" to success that he had his favorite inspirational message framed and hung in his office. His leadership philosophy was (Bennis and Nanus 1985, 45):

> Nothing in the world can take the place of persistence.
> Talent will not, nothing is more common than unsuccessful men with great talent.
> Genius will not, unrewarded genius is almost a proverb.
> Education will not, the world is full of educated derelicts.
> Persistence, determination alone are omnipotent.
> Ray Kroc

While leaders derive their power to lead in a variety of ways, it appears that referent power, the power one has over others because they admire and want to be like the leader, is the most potent. Referent power, while very useful, is also very subjective. A leader must earn referent power through deeds. It might be said that followers grant a leader power and influence over them. Remember that power is far from absolute. In a healthy, growing economy numerous jobs are always being created. Many workers and managers are quite uninhibited about changing jobs; in fact, job hopping has become something of an American tradition. Labor mobility diminishes some of the more traditional power sources available and puts a premium on noncoercive leadership behavior.

Authoritarian and participative decision making are two kinds of behavior in which leaders engage. Each represents extremes along a continuum of possible decision-making methods. The autocratic leader makes a decision alone without input or consultation from subordinates. The democratic leader allows the decision to be made based on majority rule. The most effective decision-making style will usually depend on a variety of circumstances, including the personality of the follower, the nature of the task, job time pressures, the amount of information available to make a decision, the importance of subordinate acceptance of the decision, and the degree to which subordinates accept the goals of the organization. Since no one leadership style is clearly superior, managers must have the wit and the wisdom to assess what is going on and to choose the most appropriate style.

A second form of leadership behavior discussed was consideration and initiating structure. These behavioral dimensions relate to a leader's concern for people and concern for task accomplishment. It is possible for a leader to be high (or low) in both consideration and initiating structure. It's unlikely that a single combination of these two leadership dimensions is best in all circumstances. Some situations call for a greater or lesser degree of structure, while at other times high consideration is best. Remember, however, that while circumstances may dictate a greater or lesser degree of structure, it does not appear that consideration is ever counterproductive. Don't be afraid to show a little concern and interest in people; being human will seldom cause problems. The way people react to structure and pressure to perform will be affected by the consideration they receive. Finally, the way a leader behaves with respect to these two dimensions will be influenced by the leader's perceptions of the subordinate's behavior and maturity.

Sometimes it is best to make decisions alone. Other times it is important to foster group decision making. Leaders must be able to sense when to provide close supervision and direction, when to allow subordinates greater freedom, and when stressing relationships and providing consideration is most effective. Each dimension of leadership has its place, but no single leadership mix will always be most effective. What works today may not work tomorrow under different circumstances. Leaders must be flexible, they must to be able to diagnose a situation and respond with the most appropriate behavior. That's why it takes most people time and experience to become effective leaders. It's also why leadership is considered an art as much as a science. It's also why you should have a healthy suspicion for simplistic prescriptions promising instant success as a leader. Finally, it's why successful hotel managers are often lifelong "students of leadership."

REFERENCES

Bennis, Warren and Burt Nanus. 1985. *Leaders: The Strategies for Taking Charge*. New York: Harper & Row, Publishers.

Blake, Robert R. and Jane S. Mouton. 1985. *The Management Grid III*. Houston: Gulf Publishing Company.

Drucker, Peter F. 1954. *The Practice of Management*. New York: Harper & Row, Publishers.

Filley, A. C., R. J. House, and S. Kerr. 1976. *Managerial Process And Organizational Behavior*. Glenview, Il: Scott, Foresman & Company.

French, John R. P., Jr., and Bertram Raven. 1959. "The Bases of Social Power." D. Cartwright, ed. *Studies In Social Power*. Ann Arbor: University of Michigan Press, pp. 118-49.

Ghiselli, Edwin E. 1971. *Explorations in Managerial Talent*. Pacific Palisades, California: Goodyear Publishing Company, Inc.

Hershey, Paul and K. H. Blanchard. 1977. *Management of Organizational Behavior*. Englewood Cliffs, New Jersey: Prentice-Hall.

House, Robert J. and T.R. Mitchell. Autumn 1974. "Path-Goal Theory of Leadership." *Journal of Contemporary Business*: 81-97.

O'Brien, Robert. 1978. *Marriott: The J. Willard Marriott Story*. Salt Lake City, Utah: Deseret Book Company.

Stogdill, R.M. and A.E. Coons. 1957. *Leadership Behavior: Its Description and Measurement*. Columbus: Ohio State University Press.

Vroom, V. H. and P. W. Yelton. 1973. *Leadership And Decision-Making*. Pittsburgh: University of Pittsburgh Press.

Vroom, Victor H. and A. G. Jago. 1978. "On The Validity of the Vroom-Yelton Model." *Journal of Applied Psychology* 63:151-62.

Webber, Ross A. 1975. *Management: Basic Elements of Managing Organizations*. Homewood, Il: Richard D. Irwin, Inc.

Worsfold, Philip. 1989a. "A Personality Profile of the Hotel Manager." *International Journal of Hospitality Management* 8(1):51-62.

Worsfold, Philip. 1989b. "Leadership and Managerial Effectiveness in the Hospitality Industry." *International Journal of Hospitality Management* 8(2):145-155.

FURTHER READING

Alessandra, Tony. 1987. "Mastering the Art of Influencing People Positively." *Lodging* November:54-61.

Caro, Margaret Rose. 1990. "Disney 'Magic' Sets New Industry Standard." *Lodging* January:32-33.

Kane, Joe. 1986. "Participative Management As a Key to Hospitality Excellence." *International Journal of Hospitality Management* 5(3):149-151.

King, Judy. 1989. "Solving Operational Problems In Groups." *Lodging* February: 57-62.

QUESTIONS

10-1. If you can get someone to do what you want by putting a gun to their head (that is, through threats) is this leadership?

10-2. Where does your power over subordinates come from in an organization? Which source of power is the "best" to have and why?

10-3. Describe the best and worst authoritarian leader you have ever experienced? Describe the best and worst participative leader you have ever experienced? Why were those people best and worst as leaders?

10-4. How could Matthew Fox become "more authoritarian over the years" and at the same time become more participative with his EOC?

10-5. How can a leader have a high concern for task completion and a high concern for people at the same time?

10-6. Explain how your leadership style might vary depending on the degree of experience, competence, and maturity of a subordinate.

10-7. What are some of the questions one should ask when deciding on an authoritarian or a participative leadership approach?

10-8. Is there one best leadership style? Explain.

CHAPTER 11

Leading Organizations

Interest in leadership has never been greater. It's necessary to review a little history to understand why this is so.

AMERICAN DOMINANCE CHALLENGED

The United States emerged from World War II in the most enviable economic position of any nation in history. It had incurred relatively few casualties and its entire industrial capacity was intact. In contrast, the war had devastated the industry of its major economic rivals. In 1945, the United States was the only advanced industrial nation in the world capable of quickly converting from a wartime to a peacetime economy. It did so, seemingly overnight, and for the next quarter century was the world's dominant economic power. With dominance came self-confidence, including the conviction that Americans knew better than anyone how to manage business enterprises.

In time the rest of the once powerful industrial world began to recover. First came the German "economic miracle," which was best symbolized by the appearance of those funny looking, beetlelike cars called Volkswagons. A trickle of cheap Japanese products, like transistor radios, followed. Soon, however, more and more high-quality Japanese products began to appear. By the mid-1970s it was obvious that America's postwar economic and industrial dominance had ended, and Americans were in a highly competitive battle with European and Asian nations for world markets.

Japan emerged during the 1970s as the United States' major economic rival and became a powerful symbol of business success. Many Americans began to doubt their ability to manage effectively in light of the frequent Japanese business victories. Interest in how the Japanese managed their businesses grew. Were there any "secrets of Japanese management" that Americans could profit from? During the late '70s and early '80s, efforts to understand why Japanese businesses were so successful were undertaken. More generally, the entire subject of why some businesses are excellent while others are just average was rethought.

One of the central conclusions is that Japanese businesses in particular and excellent companies in general are very good at getting involvement and commitment from most of their employees, and employee involvement and commitment is a very important reason for their success. This conclusion should come as no surprise. After all, the Hawthorne studies demonstrated the importance of the human element to productivity. Still, if the Japanese

Soaring atrium lobby of The Hyatt Regency New Orleans.

Courtesy: Hyatt Regency New Orleans

were beating Americans so badly, perhaps America had forgotten some of these basic lessons? Could it be that the Japanese were emphasizing certain human relations practices in their business while Americans had focused too narrowly on motivation and leadership? What emerged from these studies was a better understanding of the need for employee involvement and commitment as a crucial ingredient of business success. And since leadership is necessary to accomplish this, a renewed and more broadly based interest in leadership emerged during the 1980s.

This chapter will review two of the most influential "Japanese management" books written during the 1980s. The conclusions of a pathbreaking study of excellent U.S. businesses will also be presented. Finally, the leadership traits of outstanding American leaders will be discussed. These findings will be applied to leadership in hotels based on the GM research.

CHARACTERISTICS OF A JAPANESE BUSINESS

This section discusses how the Japanese view their own businesses. Mr. Hiroski Takeuchi is managing director of Japan's Long-term Credit Bank, advisor to its Labor Questions Research Committee, and author of numerous books on Japanese industry. In an article entitled, "Motivation and Productivity" (1985, 18–28) he outlined the major characteristics of Japanese businesses that affect employee motivation and productivity.

There is a strong tradition of lifetime employment in major Japanese businesses. When a young worker or manager goes to work for a Japanese firm, he or she can expect to spend an entire career there. As will be shown, this tradition places special responsibilities on both employee and employer.

A central theme of Takeuchi's article is that "Japanese businesses start with the belief that all people have about the same ability." Promotion is slower than in many U.S. firms, and people are not singled out for "fast track" advancements early in their careers. The Japanese reason that putting just a few people on a fast track early in their careers would be motivating to them but demotivating to the great majority who are not singled out. In Takeuchi's words, "Few are chosen for special promotion: there can be no heroes and elite people. Most people are promoted simultaneously through the same route. . ." Since promotions come later, Japanese firms are slower to evaluate and judge employees based on short-term performance, and employees understand that they cannot get ahead except by contributing to the long-term good of the company.

Job rotation is another central theme of Japanese firms. Takeuchi states, "All employees experience different jobs, understand relationships between different posts and come to see the interests of the company as a whole." In addition, group accomplishment and cooperation is valued above individual accomplishment. Since the Japanese believe that most people have about the same ability, it follows that little can be accomplished by an individual except through the cooperative efforts of others.

Takeuchi believes that, "An organization that trusts its employees and entrusts work to them has no need for supervisors." Furthermore, "The main goal of personnel management is to confirm the confidence of fellow workers in each other." This is reflected in the way Japanese managers supervise their subordinates. Japanese executives are hands on managers. While "Japanese executives have their own offices, . . . the offices are used for receiving visitors; the executives work with their subordinates in the same large office. They observe progress in the work entrusted to their subordinates, sense problems, and give advice in such a way as not to discourage their subordinates' will to work." It is considered a virtue for supervisors to defend and protect employees who make mistakes. In fact, the question of individual responsibility for a mistake is often left unresolved because of the strong feeling of shared group responsibility. Shared responsibility, in turn, stems from the practice of joint decision making. To quote Takeuchi: "If a president makes decisions by himself all the time . . . he will soon lose the support of his subordinates . . ." who will ". . . feel hurt, turn their backs on him, . . . and ignore his orders, although they may pretend to obey them."

Japanese companies also treat employees as if they were family members, providing for the lifetime welfare of an employee's family if he or she is disabled or dies. In addition to lifetime employment with the same firm, employees will not be laid off till the firm is on the verge of bankruptcy, and its president must be prepared to resign when this happens. In fact, Takeuchi states that, "Company presidents pay greater attention to employees than to stockholders."

Taken together, Takeuchi's description of Japanese management adds up to:

• Lifetime employment security based on a "family" atmosphere.
• The assumption of about equal ability among all workers.
• Slow promotion and evaluation based on long-term contributions.
• Frequent job rotation so that workers gain a broad prospective of the total company.
• Emphasis on group accomplishment rather than individual superstars.
• An atmosphere of trust that emphasizes building employee confidence.
• Group responsibility and decision making.

Clearly, some aspects of Japanese management are influenced by the broader social, religious, and cultural traditions of the country. This is especially true with regard to their emphasis on group accomplishments, the system of lifetime employment, and slow evaluation and promotion. While it would be unrealistic to expect that the entire Japanese management system could be transplanted to America, the following is true: (1) Japanese businesses have been successful in transplanting much of their management philosophy into their U.S. operations, and (2) some of America's most successful companies have independently developed a management style that is remarkably similar to that described by Mr. Takeuchi.

Theory Z

In *Theory Z: How American Business Can Meet The Japanese Challenge*, William G. Ouchi (1981), an American, compared the important managerial characteristics of Japanese and American firms.

TYPE Z ORGANIZATIONS

Ouchi referred to the typical Japanese firm as Type *J* and the typical American firm as Type *A*. He then looked for American businesses that had managerial characteristics similar to Japanese firms. He found that a number of U.S. firms had independently developed organizational characteristics similar to Japanese firms, and he named them Type *Z* organizations. Some of the American businesses that Ouchi classified as Type *Z* were IBM, Hewlett-Packard, Eastman Kodak, and Procter & Gamble. These firms developed their management style within the United States, independent of any Japanese influence. This suggests that many Japanese management ideas could be implemented in Western cultures as well. Ouchi studied a number of these American Type *Z* businesses. In particular, he studied the managerial style of a U.S. electronics company he referred to as Company *Z*. What he found is summarized in Table 11-1, which contrasts the managerial characteristics of Company *Z* with those of a typical American firm called Company *A*.

Employees and mangers typically find lifetime employment with Company *Z*. Everything possible is done to guarantee continued employment,

TABLE 11-1.   Contrasting Organizational Characteristics of Company Z and Company A

Company Z	Company A
Long-term Employment	Short-term Employment
Slow Evaluation & Promotion	Rapid Evaluation & Promotion
Nonspecialized Career Paths	Specialized Career Paths
Collective Decision making	Individual Decision making
Collective Responsibility	Individual Responsibility
Holistic Relations	Segmented Relations
Distinctive Management Philosophy	Vague Philosophy

avoid layoffs, and foster a paternalistic environment between company and employee. This has important implications not only for morale but also with regard to the way employees behave on the job. An employee committed to a business for the long pull had better act in its long-term best interest. Furthermore, it's unlikely an employee will be able to hide any selfish or self-serving acts over a long period of time. In effect, long-term employment tends to cause a convergence between the employee's interests and the company's interests.

Slower rather than fast promotion goes hand-in-hand with long-term employment. If employees are going to be with a firm for an extended period, time can be taken to evaluate and promote workers based on the sum of their contributions over time. Because of the nature of the American labor market, Type Z (American) firms cannot delay evaluation and promotion as much as Japanese firms for fear of loosing their most talented employees. Thus, more explicit performance reviews take place in Type Z firms, but they nevertheless tend to promote more slowly than typical Type A firms.

The common career path in Company Z has executives being transferred often into a variety of jobs in different functional areas of the business. This pattern of job rotation gives managers a varied knowledge of all aspects of the company. In the process, they also develop numerous personal contracts and relationships throughout the firm that would be difficult to do if they stayed in one narrow specialty. Thus, over time the managers of Company Z begin to understand and appreciate the totality of the business and, therefore, become more and more valuable to it. At the same time they become somewhat less attractive to other American firms because they have lost some of their specialist expertise. In this way the bonds of mutual interest between manager and company grow.

Collective decision making is another typical feature of Company Z, as is collective responsibility for both success and failure. Collective decision making fosters greater employee commitment and at the same time is a powerful form of mutual influence. Collective responsibility does not mean that individuals feel less responsible for the organization's performance; they just don't feel solely responsible. Decisions are made collectively, and group goals and performance are stressed. When something goes wrong, it's a group failure rather than an individual failure.

Company Z is also characterized by a holistic concern for its employees. The relationship is both economic and social. Workers stay with the same company for a long time and rotate into a variety of jobs. They therefore form numerous intimate relationships with large numbers of coworkers, both on and off the job. Over time "Values and beliefs become mutually compatible over a wide range of work and non-work related issues. . . thus intimacy, trust and understanding grow where individuals are linked to one another through multiple bonds in a holistic relationship" (Ouchi 1981, 54). Finally, Type Z companies also tend to develop rather distinctive philosophies of management, values, and goals that are generally agreed on by most of its employees.

Why Type Z Firms Are Top Performers

These then are the important characteristics Ouchi found in the American firms he called Company Z. As previously mentioned, the Z companies were some of the top performing companies in America. How did their management style contribute to their success?

Ouchi (1982) believes that in all organizations employees occupying even the most humble job possess some specialized knowledge about how to do it best. A firm can only achieve maximum efficiency if it grants its employees some degree of freedom to do their job as only they know best. Management will only be willing to grant this freedom, however, if there is sufficient trust that in so doing workers will not abuse it. Thus, there exists a relationship between *trust, freedom*, and *productivity* that must be developed if a business is to perform up to its potential.

Many of the characteristics of Japanese management tend to foster trust within an organization. An atmosphere of mutual respect, collective decision making and responsibility, and holistic relationships will foster trust, which in turn, makes it possible to provide managers and workers with the freedom necessary to be highly productive.

There is, to be sure, a degree of regimentation within Type Z organizations. One must either "buy into" the system or look elsewhere for a career. However, once an individual is willing to accept a Type Z managerial process, the end result is a degree of shared decision making and responsibility that enhances rather than diminishes freedom. While Type Z firms require a certain conformity of behavior and beliefs, so do other managerial systems. One need look no further than an autocratic, Theory X driven organization to see what can happen to individual trust and freedom and what is required in terms of individual conformity.

The simplest possible description of the Theory Z approach to management is, "Involved workers are the key to increased productivity." (Ouchi 1981, 4) Previous discussions in chapters Nine and Ten about motivation and leadership relate directly to this point. However, the context in which these concepts were discussed was somewhat narrower than that presented here. Ouchi's Theory Z firm reveals an organizational "culture" that encompasses many traditional aspects of personal leadership but is also broader in scope. This constitutes an enlarged concept of leadership in organizations. This enlarged view of leadership complicates a manager's task by expanding the number of variables that must be taken into account. It suggests that nearly every aspect of an organization, in one way or another, affects the attitudes, motivation, and productivity of its employees and its management. If it's trust and commitment that bring forth maximum voluntary effort, then there are few aspects of a business's overall culture that do not relate to leadership in one way or the other.

THE ART OF JAPANESE MANAGEMENT

The Art of Japanese Management, by Richard Pascale and Anthony Athos (1981) was published the same year as Ouchi's book. While many of the conclusions of these two books are the same, there are some important points stressed by Pascale and Athos that relate closely to leadership and therefore deserve mentioning.

Interdependence and Junior–Senior Relationships

Pascale and Athos feel that Japanese managers deal better than their American counterparts with the ambiguities, uncertainties, and imperfections that occur naturally in organizations and groups. American managers often strive for independence as a goal; in Japan interdependence is thought of as both natural and desirable. This shows up in the importance placed on the work group in Japan and the time and effort spent ensuring good group relationships and interaction. They note, for example, that, "The prime qualification of a Japanese leader is his acceptance by the group, and only part of that acceptance is found in his professional merits. The group's harmony and spirit are the main concern" (Pascale and Athos 1981, 199).

Interdependence also shows up in the relationship that exists between junior and senior managers. In Japanese businesses there is a close relationship between senior and junior managers, with the senior acting as a teacher and "godfather" to the junior. The senior manager's goal is to prepare the junior to be effective in the organization. Much coaching is required to do this. Since Japanese organizations place great importance on group performance, seniors must devote considerable effort to developing the human relations and people skills of their subordinates. This senior–junior relationship develops at the personal and emotional level as well as at the professional level. In the United States, according to Pascale and Athos, the relationship is often confined to the work place. Since management is an art as well as a science, junior managers in Japan are taught its subtle complexities through a process of ". . . experiencing, watching, feeling, sensing and imitating . . ." their superiors (Pascale and Athos 1981, 216). They believe that a boss's job is to help subordinates learn their job rather than to "test" how well they are performing (Pascale and Athos 1981, 233).

An American Example of Japanese Management

As Ouchi did in *Theory Z*, Pascale and Athos describe how an American executive, Ed Carlson of United Airlines, used a managerial and leadership style that is similar to "Japanese Management." The result was a dramatic turnaround of that company. Carlson had been president of Western Hotels before taking over at United and had no airline experience. Believing that the critical similarity between the two companies was people, he went to work. Carlson's management style at United (Pascale and Athos 1981, 252–270) can be described as follows:

- People Oriented—Subordinates had to be treated with trust and respect. They had to accept the boss's platform. "If they don't, you don't get their whole-hearted cooperation. In a service industry like this, if you don't have their support, you don't get the job done well no matter how tightly you try to control them."
- Visible Management—Carlson believed that "employees of the company ought to see the man who's in charge." He engaged in direct, two-way communication at all levels of United's 47,000 employee work force, spending 65 percent of his time in the field and traveling 186,000 miles in his first year as president.
- Decentralization—Carlson strived to have decision making pushed down in the organization to the people who were closest to the problems.
- Base Touching—Face-to-face informal meetings and consultation at all levels was a precondition for most decisions.
- Participative Planning and Control—Through the use of task forces, United devised the strategies, incentives, and control systems that turned the company from losses to profits.
- Support for Senior Executives—Long-time United executives were not dismissed but rather were rotated into a variety of jobs to broaden their perspectives, break down organizational barriers, and change the status quo mentality. Carlson was always accessible, did not play favorites, mixed pressure with praise, and was very sensitive to his executives' egos.
- Huddles—Through the effective use of two major decision making committees, Carlson was able to form a group consensus among United's top executives regarding both strategy and operations. He encouraged differing opinions and spirited debate, as long as it did not result in personal conflict. One could "disagree without being disagreeable."

Ed Carlson's management and leadership style bears striking similarities to Japanese management, and it was his leadership that caused the turnaround at United Airlines. It's a good example of leadership in a broad context.

Superordinate Goals

An important point made in *The Art of Japanese Management* relates to an aspect of leadership that Pascale and Athos refer to as *superordinate goals*. These are the basic beliefs, the shared values, and the significant meanings for which a business stands. Superordinate goals are the guiding principles of a business that allow its employees and its customers to understand and identify with it. Superordinate goals are also the principles that tie together the management functions of planning, organizing, directing, and controlling to form a unified whole. Superordinate goals are the enduring principles for which a business stands. They are a powerful aid to management and employees in their day-to-day decision making because superordinate goals continually remind all of what is really important.

One of the most quoted examples of superordinate goals are those of IBM. Thomas Watson, Jr., long-time head of IBM, places considerable importance on them. To Watson, "The basic philosophy, spirit and drive of an organization are more important than financial strength, technology, organizational structure, or anything else" (Pascale and Athos 1981, 296-297). Watson believes that a company must be willing to change everything except its basic beliefs. At IBM, these basic beliefs are: (1) respect for the dignity and rights of each employee, (2) the need to provide the best customer service in the world, and (3) the need to strive for excellence in everything the company does. That's it; these are IBM's superordinate goals. How much importance does Mr. Watson place on IBM's basic beliefs? To him ". . . the most important factor in corporate success is faithful adherence to those beliefs." Pascal, Athos, and Ouchi believe that Japanese firms do a better job instilling superordinate goals in a business than do average American firms, and this is one of the reasons for their long-term success.

Superordinate goals relate to: (1) the company itself, (2) customers, (3) employees, or (4) the company's relationship to society (Pascale and Athos 1981, 289-290). They are important to leadership because superordinate goals guide individual behavior and give purpose and meaning to employees.

Some consider Ellsworth Statler the premier hotelman of all time. He developed a code of service for guests of his hotels that is a good example of superordinate goals. Here are some examples (Lundberg 1979, 328) of Statler's superordinate goals:

- It is the avowed business of the Hotel Statler to please the public better than any other hotel in the world.
- Hotel service, that is, Hotel Statler service, means the limit of courteous, efficient attention from each particular employee to each particular guest.
- No employee of this hotel is allowed the privilege of arguing any point with a guest. He must adjust the matter at once to the guest's satisfaction or call his superior to adjust it.
- In all minor discussions between Statler employees and Statler guests, the employee is dead wrong, from the guest's point of view and from ours.
- Any Statler employee who is wise and discreet enough to merit tips is wise and discreet enough to render a like service whether he is tipped or not.

Superordinate goals that relate to the well-being and development of employees are particularly important because they define the relationship between a business and its workers. Superordinate employee goals might include a commitment to continual employee training, development, and promotion from within. They might relate to a commitment to job security or fair treatment, or a recognition of efficiency, innovation, or service. Whatever they are, superordinate goals must be fully accepted and shared throughout the organization if they are to be effective. If this can be done, Pascale and Athos (1981, 307) believe, superordinate goals are "probably the most under-publicized 'secret weapon' of great companies." In the opinion of Pascale and Athos (1981,327), United Airlines did not continue to prosper as effectively after Ed Carlson relinquished control because he was unable to instill a lasting set of superordinate goals that could sustain the business over hard times and through leadership changes.

JAPANESE MANAGEMENT IN THE HOTEL BUSINESS

Many attributes of Japanese management relate to the entire business organization. The GM research for this book was limited to the individual-hotel level and did not include study of corporate-level management policies. Seven of the hotels studied were part of large national and international companies, two were part of smaller companies, and one was an independent. An amalgam of both corporate and local management policies, practices, and philosophies were combined in the nine corporate hotels. Each hotel had its own "culture," which were composites of corporate influences and local influences. While this discussion will concentrate primarily on the local level, some comments will also be made about the relationship between corporate policies and the individual hotel.

Turnover and Its Consequences

In general, American hotels do not have the kind of long-term employment throughout the organization that is characteristic of Japanese firms. The GMs and their senior executives usually had considerable longevity with the corporation, but lower level executives and many hourly employees turn over quite rapidly. This causes a tremendous problem for some hotels. They simply do not have the depth of management and employee talent necessary to operate as effectively as management would like.

The fifty-three division heads interviewed complained about high turnover constantly. They reported that some of their greatest job challenges relate to training and coaching lower level managers in basic management skills such as supervision, employee motivation, goal setting, time management, and how to handle job pressure. The same kind of problems occur with hourly employees.

The hotels studied differed in this regard. Two had developed a strong middle- and lower-level management team and a rather stable hourly staff. In one hotel the depth of experience in its catering department was a major strength that contributed to its outstanding reputation. Matthew Fox attributed the St. Charles Hotel's reputation for consistent quality to the experience and longevity of its middle management and hourly employees. In fact, a highly competent middle management group gave Fox considerable flexibility regarding his top executives. He felt he could take a few more risks when hiring senior-level executives because his middle managers were so strong. He had easily taken on the temporary added duties of rooms, and food and beverage director at separate occasions in the past because of the depth of talent below him.

Rapid turnover and a relatively short-range planning horizon make it difficult for hotels to apply the principle of slow evaluation and promotion. There are quite a few "fast track" executives moving rapidly up the management ladder in hotels. All of the GMs fast tracked in their careers. With only one exception (that because a career change brought the individual into the hotel business in his late thirties), each of the GMs studied had been promoted to the GM level of substantial hotels while in their midthirties.

Specialized Career Paths

It's also quite common to find hotel department heads and GMs who advance up the corporate ladder through specialized career paths. While this tendency may run counter to what one would suspect in a hands-on operational business like hotels, it is nevertheless true and is characteristic of American business generally.

I did find individual cases of hotels rotating executives into a variety of assignments to broaden their prospective. For example, the resident manager and the rooms division manager of two of the hotels studied, who had both advanced through food and beverage, were now getting valuable experience in the rooms side of the business before being promoted to GM. Still, there is a tendency in American hotels for managers to advance through a single functional specialty. This makes coordinating different functional departments within a hotel more difficult. It also takes executives longer to begin to appreciate the "big picture." Willaim Scully made this point when he said that his entire management philosophy had to change after being promoted from director of restaurants to food and beverage director. The change was necessitated because, as a member of the hotel's EOC, he had to take a "total hotel view" for the first time in his career rather than a narrow departmental view. His specialized career path also caused him, after becoming a regional vice-president, to lament his lack of marketing knowledge. In another case, Richard James had been GM of two previous hotels and still complained that he was somewhat weak in front office knowledge.

Holistic Relations and Trust

It's unlikely that the same intensity of holistic relations found in Japanese firms could be duplicated in most American hotels. Turnover, transfers, cyclical demand, and the Western tradition of individualism all mitigate against it. Still, there were numerous examples of hotel GMs behaving in ways that illustrated their understanding and appreciation of the importance of holistic relations to the success of their hotels. Most of the GMs went to extraordinary lengths with executives and hourly employees to foster holistic relations and trust. Incidents from every hotel could be used to demonstrate this point, but the one I like best relates to Bruce Warren and The Vieux Carre Hotel's limousine driver.

Bruce Warren is big, a little gruff of manner, and somewhat intimidating. He manages an excellent independent hotel that's been a profitable business for many years. Warren likes to say that he tries to foster a family atmosphere, and there is a degree of casualness and informality around the hotel that's rather unusual. George, the hotel's limousine driver, had for years been its front office manager. Warren described him as "sometimes a good boy and sometimes a bad boy." After a number of years Warren finally got fed up with George's bad-boy side and decided to replace him as front office manager. Because of his long-time association with the hotel, however, George was offered a job as the hotel's limo driver. The offer was readily accepted and the former front office manager became a model limo driver. A bit of an entrepreneur, George wanted to start his own limo service during his off hours so he approached Bruce Warren with a proposition: would the hotel rent him its limo to use in his private limo business? Warren agreed and for some years now all parties have been happy with the arrangement. This incident, I think, sends a rather comforting message about holistic relations and trust to The Vieux Carre Hotel's employees who, like most of us, are probably "sometimes good and sometimes bad."

Collective Decision Making and Collective Responsibility

Chapter Ten discussed many of the issues relating to collective decision making. It was noted that some GMs had decided tendencies toward participation, others leaned toward authoritarianism, while the majority were a mixture of the two.

There were some differences in organizational climate in the hotels depending on the GM's tendency toward participation and the degree to which he had been able to fully implement his particular leadership style. It's perhaps easiest to explain some of these differences by looking at two extremes. At two hotels the extent of participation was quite high; the GMs were naturally inclined in that direction and they had been able to fully implement their ideas and leadership styles. Both hotels held many meetings.

A hotel's setting, such as the majestic mountain background of the Best Western Twin Peaks in Ouray, Colorado, sometimes makes all the difference.

Courtesy: Best Western International, Inc.

The executives at these two hotels commented that it had taken some time to make the meetings efficient and productive. "It just didn't happen overnight," as one executive said, "it took some time to get the meetings right." At both hotels there was a feeling of comfort and confidence among the executives. One had the sense that most people felt they really understood where the hotel was going. There was also a feeling of teamwork, group achievement, and responsibility that was more noticeable than in other hotels. This came through in the subordinates' assessments of their GMs' major accomplishments. Here are some typical statements:

- He brought EOC members together physically for better communication and it is functioning better as a group.
- Management morale is up, there's greater teamwork, the GM is approachable.
- The Monday morning sales, catering, and convention-services meetings have resulted in better communications.
- EOC concurrence and group decision making has been fostered.
- The GM is building a good management team and it's working.
- The GM developed a good executive meeting and communication system.
- The GM put together a good EOC team, and he is open to upward communication.
- Our EOC is the most competent I've ever worked with, and it has a single goal.
- The GM has established a recognizable structure for decision making.
- There is an esprit de corps at the hotel now and a sense of purpose.

These hotels were not without their problems, and certainly all decisions were not group decisions. Still, it was clear that certain favorable organizational characteristics followed directly from the GMs' participative leadership style.

Things were somewhat different in hotels whose GMs tended toward authoritarianism. Different, however, does not necessarily mean bad. In some hotels there was clearly a very high level of commitment, professionalism, and efficiency under authoritarian leadership. When the GM displayed a high degree of consideration, subordinate trust was also high. When differences did occur, they tended to revolve around issues such as direction, communication, collective responsibility, and group achievement. Subordinates working in an authoritarian leadership climate made the following kinds of comments.

- There is a problem of coordination between catering and convention services.
- We need more regular executive meetings, at least for communications.
- The hotel *seems* to be doing OK.
- There is rivalry and tension between EOC members.
- The environment is hectic.
- Changes are not accepted by many people.

- It's difficult to get people in other departments to understand what I do.
- There are often surprises, things are somewhat unpredictable.
- Organizational changes have caused disruptions, there is rivalry and lack of coordination between food and beverage and catering.
- It's hard to find ways to communicate with this structure.
- Although expectations are high, we do not have clearly defined goals and objectives.
- It's difficult getting people to learn how to adapt.
- There are many ingrained cliques in the hotel.
- The EOC does not meet and discuss things regularly enough.
- There are problems between the sales and reservations departments because sales is always overbooking the hotel.

These comments were drawn from a number of different hotels. Just as hotels where participation was practiced had weak points, those that tended toward authoritarianism had many strengths. Still, under authoritarianism there were problems regarding general direction, lapses in coordination and communication, and indications of departments sometimes working at cross-purposes. The difficulty of "building a team" and integrating the activities of different departments was expressed by one rather authoritarian GM who commented that his executives did not seem to be able to "grasp the big picture." The fault, of course, could lie in the GM's leadership style.

IN SEARCH OF (AMERICAN) EXCELLENCE

While *Theory Z* and *The Art Of Japanese Management* use examples of management excellence in U.S. businesses, both books come to their subject from a decidedly Japanese prospective. While it's important to understand what makes Japanese firms effective, U.S. firms cannot simply copy Japanese business and management practices; the two cultures are just too different.

But what about high-performing American businesses? Could some of them be held up as role models of management excellence? Understanding what makes America's excellent companies tick would help all American businesses striving to improve. Thomas J. Peters and Robert H. Waterman, Jr., did exactly that in their book, *In Search of Excellence* (1982). They chose excellent American companies based on a twenty-year record of outstanding performance in six financial categories. A total of sixty-two large U.S. corporations met their "excellent" criteria. The list reads like a Who's Who of American Business. Included are high technology giants such as IBM, GE, Hewlett-Packard, Boeing, and Digital Equipment and consumer goods producers such as Proctor & Gamble, Johnson & Johnson, Levi Strauss, and Maytag. Well-known general industrial corporations such as Caterpillar Tractor, 3-M, and Dana are on the list. Finally, the service industry is represented by the likes of Delta Airlines, Marriott, McDonald's, Disney, and Wal-Mart. Extensive interviews and research into the management of these sixty-two "excellent" companies lead Peters and Waterman to conclude that there are a number of characteristics of how the excellent companies are managed that distinguish them from ordinary, nonexcellent companies. Three of these characteristics are closely related to the previous discussions of motivation and leadership. These three"excellent company" characteristics are: (1) their attitudes toward people, (2) their values, and (3) how they go about day-to-day management.

Attitudes Toward People

There are four basic premises upon which the leadership conclusions found in *In Search of Excellence* rest. These assumptions regarding people's human needs in organizations are: (1) people need meaning in the organizations for which they work, (2) people must have some small level of control over their jobs, (3) people like to think of themselves as winners, ascribing success to themselves and failure to the "system," and therefore need positive reinforcement, and (4) actions (on the part of leaders) shape attitudes and beliefs and not vice versa (Peters and Waterman 1982, 102).

"The excellent companies treat the rank and file as the root source of quality and productivity gain" (Peters and Waterman 1982, 14). Excellent companies apparently *really* believe this, and therefore go to extraordinary lengths to develop, nurture, train, reward, praise, and develop their people. The language they use (employees are associates at Wal-Mart, crew members at McDonald's, cast members at Disney, and at Delta it's the "family-feeling") shows the closeness and special respect companies have for their employees. They spend a lot of time getting people to think of themselves as winners and they celebrate small wins much more often than ordinary companies. Workers are viewed as responsible adults and treated as partners in the business. Employees of excellent companies are given much more information about business performance than is the case in ordinary businesses. Open-door policies abound, as does a marked lack of organizational structure and formality. Great efforts are made to make work fun. To Peters and Waterman, excellent companies find ways to cause employee involvement in the enterprise and this, in turn, results in their attention to quality, productivity, and innovation.

Exactly these kinds of attitudes come through loud and clear with some outstanding GMs. Frank Anderson really keeps his staff up-to-date on the financial status of The Napoleon House Hotel. At his weekly management staff meeting he has his controller read *all* of the forecasted and actual operating and financial results for *every* department of the hotel. Each of the thirty executives at the meeting have copies of these data, but Frank still has the results read; no summaries, no shortcuts. It takes a full fifteen minutes.

To Anderson this is anything but a waste of time. It's done to stress an important point. Together, they are all working to make their hotel a successful business. If any part of the business is having trouble the whole business suffers. The hotel is each executive's business as much as the owner's. Everyone had better understand the big picture and pull together for the good of the total business or they will all be out of business. Frank feels that this same message is important to all employees, so these same operating results are then relayed down the line to everyone working in the hotel.

Lawrence Wagner has department heads invite ordinary hourly employees to sit in on the daily 9 a.m. executive meeting. The idea is for everyone to understand what the hotel is trying to accomplish, and how. William Scully has employee awards ceremonies as the first order of business at each of his weekly department head meetings. Curtis Samuels actually had an employees' parade down Main Street when their hotel was ranked first in the company in guest satisfaction. Following the Disney example, employees are called "cast members." Samuels really tries to make things fun, like having executives hand out instant cash rewards when they find an employee doing something right!

Values and Meaning

The second leadership attribute of excellent companies is their ability to give employees meaning in their work through the development of a unique value system. This characteristic is, of course, what Pascal and Athos refer to as superordinate goals. Whether it's McDonald's stressing quality, service, cleanliness, and value; Caterpillar Tractor's attention to reliability and an unsurpassed spare parts network; Delta's "special" relationship with its employees that results in their characteristic team spirit; or IBM's commitment to individual dignity, customer service, and excellence outstanding companies successfully translate business values into terms that are understandable to each and every employee, thereby giving meaning to what they do.

These values and meaning revolve around people's desire to be associated with something important, to be part of an organization that is special, to feel that the organization cares in a special way about them, or simply to be the best at something. Here is a simple, yet powerful, example of how leaders can instill values and meaning into an organization.

In the late 1970s a large addition, a separate building, was added to the National Gallery of Art in Washington, D.C. Known as the East Building, it was designed by world-famous architect I.M. Pei. It is a contemporary, modern building in contrast to most of the existing buildings along the mall of the nation's capital. Before construction began, Pei and the contractors held a special meeting with the construction workers who would build this museum. These construction workers were told they were involved in more than a

Marriott's Orlando World Center—a feeling of enchantment.

Courtesy: Marriott Hotels, Resorts and Suites

building project. They were involved in constructing nothing less than a public monument that would be a showcase for the nation's and the world's greatest art. Possibly never again would they have the opportunity to be part of such an historic and important building project. It was, in other words, the opportunity of a lifetime. Their leaders then asked them to do something incredible: they were asked to build a perfect building, a building without a flaw. These tough, hard-bitten construction workers were asked to spare no effort, cut no corner, and make no compromise in a single-minded obsession for perfection. They were challenged to work harder than they had ever worked before because the project's importance demanded it.

What was to be their reward for this pursuit of perfection? If they succeeded, their reward would be the pride of bringing their children and grandchildren to see the East Building of the National Art Gallery, and telling them that they'd had a part in building it. Their reward would be that at least once in their lives they could say they had been involved in building something that was fine, and grand, and important, and possibly, perfect. How would *you* have responded to this challenge? How do you think most people would respond? If you are wondering about what actually happened, go see the building the next time you're in Washington, D.C.; I think you'll find it's worth the trip.

Most of the hotels studied were part of larger corporations that themselves had their own unique values and culture. In some cases there seemed to be a close correspondence between corporate values and what could be observed at the individual hotel level. At other times there was clearly a divergence between the two. The conflict between short-term profits and the kind of outstanding customer service that ensures repeat business and long-run profitability was discussed in Chapter One. All GMs preach the twin themes of profits and service. Some, like Curtis Samuels, teach a service orientation through careful attention to guest comment cards. Others, like Jonathan Claiborne and Godfrey Bier, get this point across through the close personal attention they pay to guests. Lawrence Wagner, on the other hand, reinforces his values through constant attention to detail and incredibly thorough follow-up procedures. All GMs pay close attention to controlling costs on a daily basis to continually reinforce the profit motive. Each also attempts to give his hotel a feeling of being the best and most active hotel in its community. Matthew Fox does it through a web of personal contacts built over many years. It allows him to personally book $1.5 million in annual sales. Richard James requires his senior executives to be actively involved in a local civic organization, Lawrence Wagner is active in local educational efforts, and Curtis Samuels is a leader in the local tourist industry and the United Way. While these efforts do promote business for the hotel, they serve another important purpose: bragging rights. These strategies give each hotel's employees another reason to consider themselves the best, unique, or in some way special among their competitors.

Each GM in his own way tries to establish a special relationship between the hotel and its employees. No one uses positive reinforcement more effectively than Curtis Samuels, while Bill Scully and Matt Fox are masters at showing warmth, support, and understanding for their staff. Lawrence Wagner develops pride through professionalism, Frank Anderson coaches, and Bill Scully puts money and time into executive training and development. It's all a part of trying to develop values and meaning among employees.

Management by Wandering Around

The last aspect of *In Search of Excellence* that bears directly on this discussion of leadership is a form of managing found in excellent American companies called management by wandering around, or MBWA. This strange-sounding term, expanded on by Peters and Austin (1985)in a later book, is, in a way, central to the concept of leadership in excellent companies. Management by wandering around is nothing more (or less) than staying in touch throughout the organization. Mr. Takeuchi referred to it when he described Japanese supervisory methods. It's also called visible management, and certainly Ed Carlson was practicing it at United Airlines when he seemed to be trying to communicate personally to each of the airline's employees. Management by wandering around means spending more time out of one's office than in it; spending time with executives, employees, customers, suppliers, and every other kind of person that relates to one's business. In terms of leadership, MBWA means being in frequent touch with people throughout the organization.

In *A Passion for Excellence* Peters and Austin (1985,447) list three major activities that take place while practicing MBWA leadership: (1) listening, (2) facilitating, and (3) teaching and coaching. In a way, their idea is quite simple: a leader needs to be out among his or her followers if leadership is to be exerted. It can't be done through memos or speeches; it must be done day-to-day and it must be done one-on-one. In other words, people need to be engaged personally and often in order to create the kind of organization that strives for excellence. In this regard it's interesting to note that Pascal and Athos (1981,308) report that Japanese firms foster twice the contact between workers and foremen as U.S. firms by having fifteen employees reporting to a supervisor compared to the U.S. average of thirty.

Listening allows leaders to understand what is going on throughout the organization, and not just at the executive level. It involves two-way communication. Facilitating means getting the small impediments out of the way so that employees can do their jobs. In some ways this is the essence of a task-oriented leader in that facilitating behavior represents the "how-to" of task accomplishment. Because facilitation in hotels is a continuing necessity, it is a kind of leadership behavior that is continually reinforcing and, therefore, motivating.

The last aspect of MBWA is teaching and coaching. It relates to teaching in the broadest sense and might be better thought of as the kind of Japanese superior–subordinate relationship discussed earlier in this chapter. It means "teaching" values and goals, but not in the ordinary way of continually stating them to subordinates and workers. In effect, leaders teach by virtue of what they concentrate on while doing MBWA. If great customer service is what a hotel GM thinks really makes the difference, then customer service should be the primary topic discussed while doing MBWA. Paying too much attention to other (less critical) issues will simply confuse everyone. When leaders pay continuing attention to just a few things, they are teaching people what they consider is important—they are teaching values.

The more leaders focus on one, or just a few issues, the more everyone in the organization begins to understand what the leader really feels is important. Vince Lombardi told his Green Bay Packers that they simply could not be champions unless they could consistently gain yardage with the halfback power sweep. His teams never stopped practicing that play in an attempt to get it right. Ray Kroc always knew that his McDonald's concept could not succeed unless the thousands of restrooms in his restaurants were spotlessly clean, and he never stopped stressing this seemingly simple aspect of his business. Walt Disney knew that his amusement parks had to be based on fantasy, so that everything his organization did was based on maintaining that illusion. Here are some quotes from Peters and Austin (1985, 312–317) that relate to how attention while doing MBWA constitutes teaching, value setting, and leadership:

- "Attention is all there is."
- The only thing that a manager has to do is "to pay attention to what's important."
- "People pay attention to the obsessions . . . of managers."
- "What gets attended to gets done."
- ". . . It's a matter of the *quantity* of attention paid to the matter at hand rather than the quality, odd as that statement may sound."

What managers pay attention to while doing MBWA constitutes their teaching, their coaching, their value setting, and much of their leadership activities. This is where and how leadership is exerted in the real world, through repetition more than through brilliance. As Richard James says, "What I lack in brilliance I make up with hard work."

Hotel GMs Searching for Managerial Excellence

Outstanding hotel managers excel at MBWA. They really are into everything in their hotels and they literally wander around. Some GMs have daily routines that include wandering around their hotel as often as five or six times each day. They also wander around figuratively through frequent phone calls, meetings, and unscheduled conferences with dozens of managers and staff throughout the day. This is exactly why, with only one exception, the GMs purposely kept their calendars relatively unscheduled most days. This gave them time to wander around.

When asked what important things the GM had done to improve the hotel, subordinates often responded with commends such as: "a hands-on manager;" "very visible;" "heavy involvement, active and daily involvement;" "involvement and follow-through;" "hands-on from the beginning;" "attends to the little things." The GMs who were best at MBWA were able to do it in a way quite similar to Japanese-style supervision. Recall what Mr. Takeuchi (1985) said about Japanese supervisors: "They observe progress in the work entrusted to their subordinates, sense problems, and give advice *in such a way as not to discourage their subordinates' will to work.*" (Italics added.) The American way of saying this is that GMs get involved in a great variety of projects but do not take away "ownership" of the project from their subordinates. They do not do their subordinates' job nor do they solve their subordinates' problems or make decisions for them; the GMs helped subordinates do the job better. It's a process analogous to the Japanese senior–junior relationship previously described. Here are two examples of GMs doing MBWA, which will illustrate this form of leadership in hotels.

Curtis Samuels, if he is anything, is a decisive, fast-paced person. One morning two young female executives who worked in sales and marketing came to him to discuss a ticklish problem. A tour wholesaler had slipped $16,000 behind in payments to the hotel. There was also a disagreement regarding the terms of their relationship, with the tour operator contending that he owed the hotel a lesser amount. The executives were convinced that the hotel was owed the full $16,000 but were unsure their case could be proved in a court of law, if it came to that. To complicate matters, it was being rumored around town that the tour operator was close to bankruptcy.

The first thing Curtis did when they were seated was praise them on some other aspect of their jobs. He then asked them what *he* needed to know about the problem at hand. During their explanation he asked other questions to help clarify the issues. When this was done, he asked them to consider two questions: What was fair and reasonable for the hotel, and what was fair and reasonable for the tour wholesaler? He allowed them to define what fair meant and also to suggest a compromise solution. He did not agree or disagree with their decision, thanked them for keeping him up-to-date on the issue, and terminated the meeting, which took only eight minutes. During those eight minutes of MBWA Samuels had listened, coached, and taught. He listened to their problem, taught them a little about how to structure their thinking and decision-making process, and coached them regarding the need to look for a "fair and reasonable solution." He did not take ownership of the problem out of their hands by making the decision for them. In fact, he did not even give his approval of their decision. In this way he helped them understand that it was their problem to solve and that his role was to do MBWA.

Frank Anderson often says that one of his most important roles as GM of

The friendly welcoming of a bus tour group to a Best Western hotel.

Courtesy: Best Western International, Inc.

the Napoleon House Hotel is "to develop future managers" for his company. His relationship with Jeff Schaffer, who is today a GM himself, was an example both of MBWA and the Japanese superior-subordinate relationship. At the time I interviewed Jeff, he was resident manager at the Napoleon House Hotel working directly for Frank Anderson. Jeff knew that he would be promoted to a GM's position within the next year or two. Jeff had known Frank for about six years, having worked for him at another property before this one. After spending time with them both, I got the impression that at times their relationship was one of equals, at times Frank was clearly the superior, and at other times Jeff thought of himself as the person in charge.

There was, for example, an incident when Schaffer felt that Anderson was moving much too fast toward making a decision and that his (Jeff's) job was to slow down the process. Jeff wanted to keep the various parties involved "in the loop" long enough to have things proceed properly. He felt that he had a good appreciation for how the group dynamics and personal interactions should be handled, and that he was helping Frank by subtly orchestrating the decision-making process. Of course, it's possible that Frank Anderson consciously gave Jeff this role! In this role Jeff could practice the subtle art of persuasion and group consensus building in a situation where he had limited formal power. Any mistake Jeff might make could be easily corrected by Frank, who was ultimately responsible for the decision. Jeff, in effect, was being given a chance to practice his leadership skills in an environment where a mistake would not be threatening to his career.

Other aspects of their relationship had Jeff playing the role of subordinate. He often checked with Frank on how best to handle seemingly little things, how to approach problems and how to deal with certain individuals. At other times Frank could be seen giving Jeff advice about how to conduct his personal life. For example, Anderson advised Schaffer one day never to drink alcohol in the hotel or, for that matter, within two miles of it. Frank felt strongly that if he was to play his role as mentor properly it was important that he involve himself in certain aspects of his subordinates' personal lives. Many of the GMs felt the same way; it was quite common for them to talk long distance to former subordinates, as much about their personal lives as about their careers.

Outstanding GMs are classic practitioners of the art of MBWA: listening, facilitating, teaching, and coaching is mostly how they spend their days. It's worth noting that during the many days I spent with them, not once did they become upset because of an interruption, no matter how busy they were. As William Scully said, "If no one comes to see me for ten minutes, I figure I'm not doing my job."

SOME THOUGHTS ABOUT AMERICAN LEADERS

Warren Bennis and Burt Nanus (1985) wanted to know more about American leaders so they interviewed a total of ninety of them: sixty from the business world and thirty from a wide variety of other fields. Included from the business world were Ray Kroc of McDonald's, real estate developer James Rouse, and the CEOs of Atlantic Richfield, J.C. Penney and Times-Mirror. They interviewed university presidents, orchestra conductors, heads of major government agencies, famous athletic coaches, public interest leaders, and authentic American heroes such as Neil Armstrong, the first man to walk on the moon. Bennis and Nanus were looking for the common threads of behavior that distinguish and characterize leaders. They called these common themes strategies and identified four that the ninety leaders seemed to have in common (Bennis and Nanus 1985, 26–27). These strategies are:

- Strategy 1: Attention through vision
- Strategy 2: Meaning through communication
- Strategy 3: Trust through positioning
- Strategy 4: Self-development through:
    a. positive self-regard, and
    b. positive response to failure

Strategy 1: Attention Through Vision

Leaders usually have clear, focused ideas of where they are going and where they want the organization they lead to go. Their agenda is clear. Clarity of vision cannot fail to draw the attention of followers because it is the thing that leaders convey with a single-minded intensity not found in other people.

Most of the GMs studied exhibited this trait, but one epitomized it. In the military, Curtis Samuels would be said to have what's called "command presence." Tall and trim, Samuels strides through his hotel with an undeniable confidence and mission. Samuels has set up a system to measure the performance of each department based on guest satisfaction. Much of what happens in his hotel revolves around reaching the magic 92 percent guest satisfaction rating, which is Curtis's vision of "what is good." The way Curtis is characterized by EOC members will explain how he has instilled vision in the hotel. One executive said, "Curtis taught us direction; 'what is good.'" A number used the word vision, one saying, "He gave a sense of vision to the hotel by focusing people toward goals, especially relating to guest service." A third felt Samuels had "galvanized the hotel to be the best." One senior EOC member said that his major challenge was to "keep the faith" with Curtis Samuels. The best description, however, of this attribute of Curtis's leadership skills was given by his long-time friend and director of marketing who called him "a together person."

Strategy 2: Meaning Through Communication

Vision alone is not enough. Leaders must be able to communicate their vision to the average worker in such a way as to give meaning to them. To Bennis and Nanus (1985, 39, 43) ". . . *all* organizations depend on the existence of shared meanings . . . which facilitate coordinated action. The actions and symbols of leadership frame and mobilize meaning. Leaders . . . invent images, metaphors, and models that provide a focus for new attention." To them, "Getting the message across unequivocally at every level is an absolute key . . ." of leadership. Note that this is done both by the leader's actions (MBWA, for example) and by symbols. In fact, meaning must be communicated in the widest variety of ways because what the leader is doing in this regard is forming an organizational culture.

Joe Baum, who developed such famous restaurants as New York's Windows On the World and Four Seasons, once said that to be great a restaurant needed employees who understood the "romance, magic, and excitement of food." His message was that employees had to feel the intangible, abstract qualities of a restaurant if it was to be great. He's right, but how does a leader communicate the meaning of "romance, magic, and excitement" to employees? One will have to engage all five senses in this quest. Employees must be educated to the taste, the smell, the sound, and the look of quality dining. Deeds (a leader's actions) will often have to speak louder than words to make this point. Employees must be helped to develop a sense of "when it's working like magic." Like learning to appreciate great music or great art, learning to understand when a restaurant or a hotel is really working right requires a leader of great communication skills. It's not enough for the leader to know when it's right; it's important that a leader make everyone else feel it as well. Only in this way can the entire staff come to understand the meaning of why they are in the hotel or the restaurant business.

Some GMs, like Curtis Samuels, get their vision across through sophisticated performance and reward systems. Others rely on a variety of symbolic acts, which demonstrate what they are trying to accomplish. Matthew Fox and Godfrey Bier symbolize their concern for hospitality by the individual attention they pay to guests. It's really nice watching them move around a crowded dining room or lounge talking to guests. The way they treat guests as "old friends" is a powerful signal to the hotel's managers and staff. Actions like these are symbolic. By their actions these two GMs are conveying the kind of warmth, care, and concern for guests for which the hotel should stand. That's why, if Jonathan Claiborne wants to emphasize the importance of personal touches, he takes the time to personally arrange flowers in The Riviera Hotel's lobby and to hand write notes to VIP guests.

Strategy 3: Trust Through Positioning

Bennis and Nanus (1985, 44) call trust "the glue that maintains organizational integrity." Leaders must be trusted by their followers. The question, of course, is how to gain trust? Their simple (though not necessarily easy) answer is that trust is built through a leader's consistency and predictability. The more consistent and predictable a leader is the more followers will know where he or she stands and feels about things. In short, predictability leads to understanding, and understanding leads to trust.

While the idea is simple, the trick is in the doing. Being consistent and predictable, in words and in deeds, requires a togetherness, a vision, and an clear, well-set agenda. Leaders are "together people" who know where they are going. Once trust is earned, it gives leaders tremendous power over

Personal touches make The Garden Terrace of The Four Seasons Hotel, Washington, D.C., very inviting.

Courtesy: Four Seasons Hotels and Resorts

followers. Trust allows a leader to get away with things that a distrusted superior never could. It's often possible for a leader to get people to try things or to go along with a decision just out of trust. Though no leader would ever want to abuse trust, one of its great rewards is an enhanced willingness on the part of subordinates to give leaders the benefit of the doubt.

Some of the excellent GMs studied were not particularly liked by their subordinates, but they were trusted. This included GMs who exhibited quite different leadership traits. Authoritarian GMs were trusted as were those who practiced participative leadership styles. Those who were not particularly high in consideration were also trusted. In cases where a certain amount of distrust existed, it seemed to have two causes: erratic behavior and too little face-to-face communications. In one case it seemed that the erratic behavior was coming from the corporate level and that the GM was having difficulty insulating his subordinates from this problem. In another case it was the GM, himself, who was accused by subordinates as being erratic. In consequence, he was not totally trusted. He was described by subordinates as "changing his mind in midstream because he is going so fast," and as being "unpredictable." At another hotel the lack of both formal and informal communication between GM and subordinates caused an unsettled atmosphere that contained elements of misunderstanding and possibly distrust.

Strategy 4: Self-development

The fourth and final leadership strategy discussed by Bennis and Nanus is what they term the development of self through positive self-regard and a positive response to failure. They find that leaders are people who recognize their strengths and compensate for their weaknesses. Leaders continue to develop their skills, to grow, and to learn. They have a well-developed appreciation for what they are good at and what they are not. Leaders are people who understand and feel good about themselves. They are confident, have good self-esteem, understand their strengths, try to continually improve, and minimize their weaknesses.

The hotel GMs showed no false modesty when it came to self-evaluation. On average they listed about four strengths each in comparison to only one weakness. Some of the weaknesses they listed, such as too much empathy toward employees, being impatient to get things done, and being perfectionists, might even be considered strengths. They were all happy, self-assured people. They knew they were good, and as Bruce Warren put it, "enjoyed being part of a select group of people," and continued to improve all the time. One, in fact, admitted to no weaknesses!

These positive attributes of leaders, according to Bennis and Nanus (1985,62), have a "most astonishing result." The positive feelings of leaders tends to "rub off" on the people around them. Being around a leader helps others develop positive self-regard. People feel good when they are around leaders and, therefore, more willingly accept their direction. How do leaders develop other people's self-esteem to the point that they feel good?

Bennis and Nanus point to five important leader attributes that give them this power:

1. The ability to accept people as they are; to understand them on their terms rather than judging them.
2. The ability to approach relationships and problems in terms of the present rather than the past.

3. The ability to treat those with whom they work closely with the same courtesy and regard as strangers.
4. The ability to trust others, even in important things.
5. The ability to do without the constant approval and recognition of others.

A number of the GMs had to learn the trick of accepting people as they are. Frank Anderson and Matthew Fox made a point of saying that they had to overcome a tendency to expect people to be just like them. Jonathan Claiborne is still going through this in his evolving relationship with American female managers. Most GMs approach relationships in the present rather than in the past. This may be because there is always so much to do that there is little time to worry about the past. Only once did I encounter a GM who belabored a past mistake by one of his subordinates. Most GMs had terrific people skills. They had learned how to work closely and courteously with subordinates even under pressure, and their general tendency was to grant subordinates greater and greater latitude as trust develops.

Like all normal people, GMs appreciate praise. However, most don't seem to crave it because they're having such a great time at what they're doing! As Bruce Warren said, "Every day is wonderful!"

Leaders also appear to treat failures differently from most people in that they do not fear failure and setbacks. Leaders don't think much about failing and don't dwell on failure when it does occur. They also don't worry over decisions once made. In fact, failure is regarded as nothing more than a way to learn and a natural consequence of doing anything. If a failure can be thought of as something that happens while on the road to success, then it need not be equated to a personal defect or shortcoming. In fact, it's more useful not to use the word at all, and many leaders do not, preferring to use terms such as mistake, setback, false start, or error. Such terms allow everyone's ego and positive self-regard to remain intact in the face of difficulties. In this regard, problems are often referred to as opportunities to give them a less oppressive and more positive view. Leaders are able to build positive self-esteem in others. They treat failure as temporary setbacks that occur normally as part of the learning process. As subordinates begin to realize that "reasonable failure" is viewed by their leader as part of the learning process, real progress and change can begin to take place.

Hotel GMs are by nature optimists and as such view failure in a healthy way. Curtis Samuels does not use the word problem, nor will he allow his managers to use it. Everything that happens around his hotel is either an "opportunity" or, at worst, a "challenge." It was fun listening to Curtis and his executives find ways not to use the word "problem" in their everyday conversation. As for the word "failure," I'm sure it just did not exist for them. As previously noted, Frank Anderson's motto is turning negatives into positives. This sometimes includes simply pushing the negatives under a rug. It almost seemed as if he was willing to deny a failure in order to keep everyone in an upbeat frame of mind. Because large numbers of decisions are always being made in hotels, mistakes will happen, and sometimes failures will occur. Outstanding hotel executives realize this and learn quickly to take failure in stride as part of the job.

CONCLUSION

The relative decline of the U.S. economy and the spectacular growth of Japanese businesses caused a re-evaluation of American management practices as well as intensive scrutiny of how the Japanese manage. One of the principal conclusions was that the people-management and leadership skills of Japanese firms were better than America's.

The Japanese management practices discussed in this chapter include the leadership dimensions of participative decision making and consideration, which were covered in Chapter Ten. Additional leadership dimensions of Japanese management included such factors as long-term employment, slow evaluation and promotion, nonspecialized career paths, collective responsibility, as well as collective decision making, holistic concerns for employees, and superordinate company goals.

The distinctive characteristics of Japanese management go beyond what is traditionally covered under the topic of leadership. It is, nonetheless, important that you consider the influence these broader management issues have on leadership. Ouchi (1981, 4) views the Theory Z approach to management as: "Quite simply, it suggests that involved workers are the key to increased productivity." An amendment to this statement for the hotel business might read ". . . the key to productivity, quality, and service," it's hard to argue with its basic premise. Thus, if involved workers are the key, then leadership must be considered in the broadest possible context. Leadership must be thought of as involving all aspects of management to foster greater employee involvement. The test of leadership is the voluntary commitment and involvement of large numbers of employees. Any act of management that fosters voluntary commitment and involvement is an act of leadership. In fact, it's not an exaggeration to say that most of the activities that managers engage in involve at least some leadership component. For better or for worse, everything a manager does involves leadership and affects employee commitment, involvement, and performance.

It's comforting to learn that Ed Carlson, who developed his management skills in the hotel business, was able to have such a positive impact on United Airlines by practicing a style of leadership that bore striking similarities to "Japanese Management." It should also be remembered that Ouchi's (1981) Theory Z firm was, after all, a U.S. electronics business that was managed in a way that was much like a Japanese business. Much of what Peters and

Waterman (1982) found good about excellent American businesses reflected a style of management and leadership found in Japanese firms, including employee involvement, the need for meaning in work, and MBWA.

A widely acclaimed study by Bennis and Nanus (1985) of American leaders suggests that they succeed because: (1) their focused vision naturally draws people's attention, (2) they are great at communicating their vision and developing shared meanings, (3) they develop trust through the consistency and predictability of their actions, and (4) their own positive self-regard builds self-regard and esteem in others, and they deal positively with failure.

REFERENCES

Bennis, Warren and Burt Nanus. 1985. *Leaders: The Strategies For Taking Charge*. New York: Harper & Row, Publishers.

Lundberg, Donald E. 1979. *The Hotel and Restaurant Business*. Boston: CBI Publishing Co.

Ouchi, William G. 1981. *Theory Z: How American Business Can Meet The Japanese Challenge*. Reading, Massachusetts: Addison-Wesley.

Ouchi, William G. 1982. "Theory Z: An Elaboration of Methodology and Findings." *Journal of Contemporary Business* 11(2):27–41.

Pascale, Richard T. and Anthony G. Athos. 1981. *The Art of Japanese Management: Applications for American Executives*. New York: Warner Books.

Peters, Thomas J. and Robert H. Waterman, Jr. 1982. *In Search of Excellence: Lessons from America's Best-Run Companies*. New York: Harper & Row, Publishers.

Peters, Tom and Nancy Austin. 1985. *A Passion for Excellence: The Leadership Difference*. New York: Warner Books.

Takeuchi, Hiroshi. 1985. "Motivation and Productivity." In *The Management Challenge*, ed. Lester C. Thurow, 18–28. Cambridge, Massachusetts: The MIT Press.

FURTHER READINGS

Anon. 1987. "How To Instill 'A Passion For Excellence.'" *Lodging* September: 84–89.

Comen, Todd. 1989. "Making Quality Assurance Work for You." *The Cornell Hotel and Restaurant Administration Quaterly* November: 23–29.

George, R. Thomas. 1989. "Hospitality Managers as Caretakers and Change Agents: A Reconceptualization of the Position." *FIU Hospitality Review* 7(1):13–22.

Glover, W. Gerald. 1988. "Managing Quality in the Hospitality Industry." *FIU Hospitality Review* 6(1):1–14.

Haywood, K. Michael. 1988. "Managing Strategic Change." *FIU Hospitality Review* 6(2):1–7.

Orly, Christophe. 1988. "Quality Circles in France: Accor's Experiment in Self-

Management." *The Cornell Hotel and Restaurant Administration Quarterly* November:50–57.

QUESTIONS

11-1. What are the major management features of Japanese businesses? Contrast these features to the "typical" U.S. business.

11-2. What is the essence of the superior–subordinaterelationship from the Japanese prospective?

11-3. What management techniques did Ed Carlson employ at United Airlines and how did they resemble some of the principles of Japanese management?

11-4. Why are superordinate goals so important in a business?

11-5. What characteristics of excellently managed companies, in the opinion of Peters and Waterman, distinguish them from ordinary businesses?

11-6. How does MBWA relate to Japanese management?

11-7. What strategies did Bennis and Nanus identify as commonly found among American leaders?

CHAPTER 12

An Overview of Controlling Hotel Operations

One of Curtis Samuels disappointments during the past few years as GM of The Hotel Frenchman was not meeting the occupancy, revenue, and profit goals he had set for the hotel during one particular six-month period. To him, this reflected badly on his leadership and business skills. This didn't happen often to Samuels, and he did not like it one bit. Somehow, he had allowed his hotel to get out of control. To a bottom-line-oriented person like Curtis, this meant that all of the planning, organizing, and directing that had gone on day-to-day in the hotel over those six months had been to no avail. Curtis had failed in his last critical management responsibility of controlling the operations of his hotel. This and the next two chapters examine how outstanding hotel managers perform this last, important responsibility of their job.

The need for GMs to control the activities of their hotel represents a separate and important management function. The functions of management were defined as planning, organizing, directing, and controlling. In a perfect world things would always go according to plan. However, this is seldom the case. Devising a brilliant strategy, developing an organizational structure, and staffing the hotel with workers does not necessarily ensure that the hotel's goals and objectives will automatically be met. It's the management-control function that keeps a hotel moving satisfactorily toward its business and service goals. Without good control there is little chance that goals will be met. This chapter concerns the basic characteristics of control processes. Chapters Thirteen and Fourteen will give detailed examples of control processes in hotels.

FEEDBACK CONTROL

The intent of the control function in business is to ensure that goals and objectives are met. This means that controlling is a proactive, forward-looking management activity. Through its controlling activities, management engages in corrective actions whenever goals are not being met. The fact that many control strategies employ the use of accounting information has lead to the mistaken view that accounting information and the controlling function are one and the same. This is not the case. Many accounting reports, such as a hotel's annual financial statement or last month's food and beverage cost figures, are historical records of past activities. In contrast, the management-control function strives to get people in a hotel to do the necessary things to meet predetermined goals. Thus, the control function is action and futures oriented since its purpose is to ensure goal compliance.

Simple Feedback-Control Process

An example of a simple feedback-control process adapted from Merchant (1982) is described in Figure 12-1. The control process begins with a plan that includes the goals and standards for a business activity. A business plan also specifies the resources that are allocated to a business activity. As results are generated, they are measured and compared to goals and standards. If management concludes that the variance (that is, difference) between standards and results is unacceptably great, it must intervene with some form of

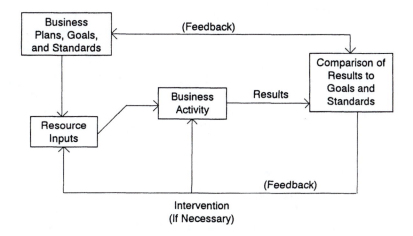

FIGURE 12-1.   A Simple Control Process with Feedback

corrective action. Management can intervene either with the business activity itself or with the resource inputs.

Management's control task is to make sure that actual results do not vary significantly from plans and, if variances are unacceptable, to take corrective action. In this sense control is futures oriented. Current results, of course, reflect past activity and cannot be changed. They can, however, be used to gauge the likelihood that future results will live up to expectations. The act of comparing results to standards and taking action if variances are unacceptable is called a feedback process. Feedback processes only work in situations that repeat themselves and where results can be measured and compared to goals and standards.

Where Feedback Control Cannot Be Used

Unique, one-time situations, such as the location decision of a hotel, do not lend themselves to control based on feedback because, once the results of a one-time event are known, it's too late to intervene. In the hotel-location decision, for example, by the time operating results (that is, the profits or losses) become available and can provide feedback to initial plans and goals, it's too late to do anything about the hotel's location.

Feedback control cannot be used when it is impossible to accurately measure some critical dimension of performance output. Generally speaking, this will occur whenever the tasks involved or the output itself can only be judged subjectively. The attractiveness of a hotel's remodeled guest rooms or the effectiveness of a public relations news release are examples of situations where results are inherently difficult to judge and measure objectively. Outside influences also make feedback control difficult. For example, consider the performance of a hotel's personnel department. The quality of workers in the local labor market is an environmental factor that influences a hotel's job applicants. This is a factor over which the personnel department has little or no control. Additionally, the quality of supervision and leadership in a hotel's various operating departments can confound or enhance the recruitment efforts of the personnel department. Thus, a "simple" output measure of a personnel department's performance, such as labor turnover, cannot be used exclusively as a feedback-control device (Flik 1988; Stephenson 1989).

Feedback Control in Hotels

There are numerous operational activities in hotels that lend themselves to feedback-control processes. Two tests of the applicability of feedback control are that activities must be somewhat repetitive and that the output of an activity must be able to be objectively measured. A great number of hotel activities repeat themselves, many on a daily basis. Guests are checked

All 630 rooms at The Omni Netherland Plaza, Cincinnati, have been renovated with custom-designed furnishings in subtle, contemporary color schemes to capture the mood of the 1930s.

Courtesy: Omni Hotels

in, beds are made, dinners are served, and complaints are handled every day. Less frequent but still highly repetitive activities, such as hosting a convention, serving a banquet, or staging special events like a New Year's Eve party, go on all the time. Hotels can and do develop a variety of control systems that incorporate feedback-control elements. All feedback-control systems incorporate three fundamental steps: (1) the establishments of standards, (2) the measurement of performance against these standards, and (3) corrective action and intervention if the variance between standards and performance is deemed by management to be unacceptable (Koontz, O'Donnell, and Weihrich, 1980).

Feedback-control systems perform a number of valuable functions in a hotel (Merchant 1982). In the first place, feedback provides valuable monitoring and oversight of a hotel's activities. The simple process of monitoring results often has positive motivational affects on employees, even without management intervention. What management pays attention to improves employee understanding of what the organization considers important. This helps employees direct their activities toward what is important. The monitoring, evaluation, and feedback that takes place in repetitive events often allows management to intervene quickly and decisively enough to affect an activity's results so that goals and standards are met. Finally, feedback can be a learning process as well as a control process. Remember that management intervention will take place whenever the variance between results and standards becomes unacceptably large. Management can only intervene in two basic ways: (1) by increasing or in some way reallocating the resource inputs into some activity, and (2) by changing the way the activity itself is done. In either case, the end result is a continuing examination of how intervention affects results. This is what organizational learning is all about. As learning takes place, it often becomes easier to determine the most appropriate levels of inputs, procedures, or employee actions that, in combination, produce desired results. In short, the feedback process allows experience to be the best teacher in repetitive situations. It's one of the reasons you will become a more effective manager over time (Gebhardt 1988)!

CONTROL TACTICS

In a feedback-control system, management attempts to control the results of a unit's activities. Controlling results is only one control tactic that a hotel may employ. Merchant (1982) classifies the various control tactics that a business might employ according to the particular object of the control. In addition to controlling *results*, hotels also exert control over the *specific actions* of employees. They also attempt to control employee actions by controlling their attitudes and motivation through what is called *personnel control*. Table 12-1 shows a number of specific control tactics for each of these three classifications.

Results Accountability Controls

Under this form of control, individual employees or groups of employees are held responsible for the end result of some activity. This requires that the activity's critical dimension(s) be defined and measured, that these measurements be compared to predetermined goals and standards, and that rewards or punishments be provided depending on the extent to which results meet standards. An example of a results-accountability control system is the bonus plan set up to reward a hotel's GM and department heads based on their ability to meet or exceed predetermined financial goals. At a lower level, results-accountability control would include the room service

TABLE 12-1   Control Tactics Classified By The Object of Control

Results Accountability	Specific Actions	Personnel

• Plans, goals, and objectives	• Behavioral constraints
	  Physical
	  (e.g., locks, guards)
	  Administrative
	  (e.g., separation
	  of duties through
	  job classifications
	  and descriptions)
		• Upgrade capabilities
		  Selection
		  Training
		  Assignment

• Budgets	• Action Accountability
	  Work Rules
	  Policies & Procedures
	  Codes of Conduct
		• Improve Communication
		  Clarify Expectations
		  Improve Coordination
		  Performance Reviews

• Standards	• Precompletion Review
	  Direct Supervision
	  Management by Wandering
	  Around (MBWA)
	  Approval Limits
	  Budget Reviews
		• Encourage Peer Control
		  Foster Work Groups
		  Develop Shared Goals

• Management by Objectives (MBO)		

Source: Adopted from Merchant, 1982.

department's ability to meet a service standard of fifteen-minute breakfast delivery, a room attendant's ability to properly clean fourteen rooms during an eight-hour shift, or a beverage manager's success in keeping beverage costs to no more than 18 percent of beverage revenues. Chapter Thirteen describes in more detail hotel results-accountability control systems.

Specific-Action Controls

Control of specific actions occur in hotels and, in fact, in all areas of our lives. "Don't Walk On The Grass" signs, "No Smoking" prohibitions on air-planes, and age minimums for the consumption of alcoholic beverages are everyday examples of specific-action controls (Zuckerman 1988) that are more or less effective. Keeping liquors and wines under lock and key in order to minimize the likelihood of employee theft is an obvious behavioral constraint, as is a prohibition against employees consuming alcoholic beverages during working hours on the hotel's premises. The sanitary regulations pertaining to food-production workers, the safety regulations that must be followed by hotel maintenance workers, and the procedures to follow in case of a guest accident are examples of holding employees accountable for acting in specific ways proscribed by the hotel. Specific-action controls define what a hotel considers acceptable behavior. Management can determine if employees are behaving in the proscribed manner, and rewards or punishments can be administered accordingly.

An example of an action-accountability control system that uses positive reinforcement is a policy that provided a "reliability bonus" to employees who have no absences or tardiness for a month. Such a control system clearly defines specific desired behavior (getting to work every day and on time), it can easily be determined if employees are behaving in the proscribed manner (from time clock records), and rewards in the form of a monthly cash bonus can be made to those who adhere to the standards.

Precompletion review is a form of specific-action control that entails review before an activity gets underway or before it is completed. The most common example of this is direct supervision of subordinates. One purpose of direct supervision is to detect problems of subordinate-specific actions as they occur and to make corrections immediately in order to keep employee actions in line with management expectations. This is one of the functions of MBWA. Although supervisory control and MBWA will often contain elements of both results accountability and personnel control, they are a powerful form of specific-action control.

Approved limits, such as the maximum guest check a clerk can cash without approval of higher management, restrict behavior by proscribing ranges of actions. Budget and other kinds of preaction reviews prevent potentially harmful behavior by requiring subordinates to clear in advance what they intend to do. This kind of control relates directly to the discussion of delegation in Chapter Five. The more control a superior desires, the less delegation will take place and the greater will be the level of preaction review.

Personnel Control

Personnel control differs from specific-action control in an important way. Whereas, specific-action control attempts to define explicit behavior, personnel control employs strategies whose purpose is to increase the likelihood that individuals can be trusted to do, *on their own*, what is best for the organization. This kind of control begins with effective personnel selection and training. Hiring the right person for the job and ensuring that person is properly trained increases the chances that employees can be trusted to do the right thing. Good communication is critical to personnel control for a number of reasons. The most important reason is that good communication helps workers understand what is expected of them. Knowing, as Curtis Samuels says, "what is good" must precede a control strategy that relies on individuals doing what is best for the hotel. In this regard, it's important to foster a group consensus about organizational goals if a hotel's personnel-control strategy is to be effective.

Employee-performance reviews take on added significance when viewed from the control prospective. Rather than a method of reviewing past performance, they become a control technique. By rewarding and praising desired behavior, management can use performance reviews to shape future behavior. The opposite, of course, will be true of undesirable behavior. Performance reviews are also a good time to consider training, reassignment, raises, and promotion decisions.

It is important to note the motivating influences of raises and promotions and how they act as a form of control. Granting raises and awarding promotions based solely on operating results criteria and desired behavior sends an important message to all of a hotel's ambitious employees. It says that performance and behavior is being carefully monitored and is the basis for personnel decisions. Employees who wish to be promoted or receive raises soon learn what kind of behavior will and will not be rewarded. In this way employee actions are controlled. Unclear or inconsistently applied criteria for raises and promotions only serve to confuse employees, making it difficult for them to understand the kind of behavior that is expected of them.

CHOOSING THE RIGHT CONTROL STRATEGY

It's generally not possible or wise to try to control a hotel's operations with only one control strategy. Excellently managed hotels employ an intricate web of overlapping and interrelated control strategies to ensure that the organization is meeting its goals. All hotels employ a variety of personnel controls, and in the best managed hotels these strategies can be quite effective. But control of results and specific actions are also needed. Thus, an important management skill is understanding the circumstances under which each of these three control strategies is most effective. The next section briefly discusses the factors that influence their use.

Specific-Action Controls

Specific-action controls can be useful whenever management has knowledge of the exact kinds of actions and behavior that are desirable in a particular job. The more management understands what constitutes desirable actions, the more it can simply proscribe that employees follow certain procedures. There are numerous examples in hotels where knowledge of desirable behavior is high. This is particularly true of repetitive jobs where feedback learning has taken place over time. The exact steps to follow in baking bread and the most efficient checkin or checkout procedures at the

Atrium lobby at the Indianapolis Airport Holiday Inn

Courtesy: General Hotels Corporation

front desk are examples where detailed job descriptions, work rules, and procedures that proscribe specific actions can be effective. The possibility of good control is particularly strong when it is easy to measure results along some important output dimension, such as the taste of the bread or the speed with which guests are checked in. In cases where it is not as easy to measure results management is required to exert direct supervision in order to ensure that specific actions are being carried out. Thus, specific-action controls often require some combination of direct supervision and/or a reporting system to ensure that the proscribed actions are being carried out (Zaccarelli 1990).

Specific-action controls are not without their drawbacks. Tight specific-action controls can often result in operational delays. Key control of food and beverage inventories is a desirable form of action control. It can, however, result in wasted time and service problems if storeroom issuing is delayed because of tight key access. Overly restrictive action controls can also cause a hotel to become bureaucratic, thus choking the spontaneity needed in organizations to adjust to novel or changing circumstances. During the GM study a food and beverage director complained that one of the problems he faced was getting employees to "use their minds and initiative" rather than "relying on the system" to solve operational problems. It's possible, of course, that the hotel's specific action controls contributed to the problem of a lack of employee initiative about which he complained. Complicated approval procedures, oppressive supervision and bureaucratic work rules can take all of the initiative away from employees and in the process remove all feelings of responsibility.

There are circumstances where management's knowledge of what constitutes desirable specific action is rather low. For most creative endeavors it's virtually impossible to correctly describe the proper steps that lead to success. It would be silly to try to write out a detailed job description and work procedures for a novelist, painter, or composer. It would be equally futile to try to control the inventiveness of a chef through strict action accountability. The same principle holds true, though to a lesser extent, when it comes to controlling the great variety of employee–guest interactions that take place every day in a hotel. While there are certain principles of behavior that experience tells us leads to desirable employee–guest service outcomes, there is reason to believe that it is neither possible or desirable to closely control every aspect of this kind of human interaction. Over-control along the guest-contact dimension can result in some of the more humorous and insulting forms of employee behavior. Everyone has encountered highly programmed order takers at the neighborhood fast-food restaurant cheerfully reciting a memorized speech. They often sound like a mechanical voice. The same can often be said of reservationists and telephone operators. While a waiter or waitress must be taught to adhere to certain procedures and standards of service, to try to "program" their every action would be both futile and counterproductive. Such behavior can be insulting to the guest being served and to the unfortunate employee who is forced to act more like a machine than a human.

Specific action control becomes increasingly difficult for executive positions, the more so the higher the position in the management hierarchy. A brief example will make this point. Most midsized and large hotels employ sales managers whose main job is to book group business such as conventions and business meetings. These groups often represent large pieces of business; a 1,000-room convention in a hotel for four nights could represent $500,000 or more in hotel revenues. There are certain kinds of sales-manager actions that are known to be desirable, such as number of sales calls made and the amount of time worked. Management can exert some control over its sales force by requiring that they submit reports of their specific activities, including such things as number of clients contacted by phone, letters written, personal sales calls made, and so forth. But as long as the relationship between the quantity of activity and sales effectiveness is less than perfect, management faces a situation where controlling of specific actions is a less than perfect control strategy. Thus, when knowledge of which specific actions are most desirable is poor, management's ability to employ specific-action controls is limited, and it may have to turn to controlling results.

Results Control

Controlling results can be effective if the following conditions can be met (Merchant 1982): (1) the correct areas of performance can be measured, (2) performance can be measured precisely, (3) performance measurements are timely, and (4) performance measurements are objective. Some areas of a hotel's operations meet all four criteria quite nicely. The next chapter describes a results-accountability control system for short-term revenue and cost control. Whenever performance results can be measured, it is desirable to consider a results-accountability system. This becomes especially important whenever management's knowledge of desired specific actions is poor, thus diminishing the effectiveness of specific action controls. As an example let's consider a hotel's nightclub entertainment acts. Knowledge of specific desirable actions is low as it relates to choosing the best acts. There is, however, a very straightforward results-accountability control strategy that can be employed. The number of patrons attending shows or nightclub revenues offers a precise, timely, and objective way of measuring results. Attendance and revenue goals can be set and control exerted (continuing or discontinuing the act) based on these performance measures. No knowledge of singing, dancing, or show business is required: the act is either good or bad based solely on its popularity.

To a lesser degree, a similar argument might be used with regard to a hotel's chef. While detailed control of a chef's specific actions are neither possible nor desirable, it is possible to devise output or results-oriented control strategies relating to meal counts, sales volume, food costs, and favorable customer comments. These measures can then be used through a feedback-control system to monitor the situation. Judging and controlling the chef's performance based solely on an assessment of the food's taste would not, of course, be wise since such an assessment would fail the objectivity test.

In general, it's possible to specify sales-results goals by stating the total number of room-nights a sales manager is expected to book in a year. If this were all there was to it, control could be exerted solely on the basis of results. It might be argued that management need not be that concerned with how its sales managers spend their time so long as they fill the hotel with guests. However, the purpose of control is to influence behavior. As such, a results-accountability control system must be able to detect deviations from desired results quickly enough to allow for corrective management action. Hotel sales managers, who solicit large conventions may, by the end of a year, have booked $5 million in sales. Though large in dollar value, this could represent only a dozen or two actual groups booked into the hotel. In any week, or possibly month, a sales manager who solicits large conventions like these could conceivably book no new business. This presents a dilemma from the control standpoint. In this example it's difficult for management to know if its sales managers are meeting their long-term sales goals by measuring output alone. When it's difficult for management to know precisely when to intervene based solely on results, it must resort to other control measures such as personnel or specific-action controls.

Problems can develop in results-accountability control systems when management specifies goals incorrectly or fails to fully specify all important goals. When this happens employees can be led into actions that are detrimental to the hotel. Suppose a hotel sets a goal of increasing food and beverage sales by 30 percent. Management designs a series of monetary incentives for its waiters and waitresses and institutes a number of food merchandising seminars to train them to accomplish this goal. There's no difficulty measuring performance along this single results dimension, and waiters and waitresses can be rewarded based on their sales performance. This is a results-accountability system with accurate feedback control. It may be a very poor system, however, if the customer-service dimension has been overlooked by management. If service quality is not also controlled, then the hotel's employees may compete vigorously for sales volume awards and neglect service quality. Sales may increase in the short term at the expense of repeat business and long-term profits. While it is easier to measure sales volume than customer satisfaction, this example demonstrates that a results-accountability system must be able to control all important dimensions of performance.

Personnel Control

Sometimes it is difficult to accurately measure the results of some activity, and it is also difficult for management to be absolutely sure what specific

"Camp Hyatt" summer activities checkin for kids at a Hyatt hotel—a special service.

Courtesy: Hyatt Hotels Corporation

employee actions are desirable. This is the most difficult control situation, and it can occur regularly in hotels where personal services and employee-guest contacts are such an important part of guest satisfaction. Try as they may, hotel management cannot completely control what happens during the numerous guest contacts that are always taking place. Nor can hotel management always accurately measure guest-service performance. Thus, no matter how hard hotel management tries to institute results and specific-action controls, they must also pay attention to a whole series of personnel-control strategies to ensure that their employees' capabilities, attitudes, and motivations are strong enough to do the right thing on their own. In a way, this is the ultimate test of management's leadership and control abilities. If hotel management can get its employees to want to do the right things, then it has developed the kind of positive organizational culture that will vastly increase its possibilities of attaining its goals and objectives.

Chapter Fourteen will discuss personnel control in more detail and review a number of the personnel-control strategies used by outstanding hotels.

CONCLUSION

Control is the final important management function that ensures a hotel's goals and standards are met. In this regard it is important to remember that control is action oriented and also oriented toward the future. A feedback-control process is useful in repetitive situations. As the results of an activity become known, they are compared to goals and standards. If the variance between results and goals is unacceptably large, management must intervene to bring the activity back into control. Feedback control can be an effective strategy when a particular business operation repeats itself and when results can be objectively measured.

Control tactics can be classified according to the particular object of the control. In the case of feedback-control systems, the object being controlled is the result of some activity. Another tactic relies on control of the specific actions of a hotel's employees. Finally, personnel control attempts to control employee actions by controlling their training, attitudes, and motivation.

Circumstances dictate what type of control strategy is most appropriate since each has its strong and weak points. When there is considerable knowledge of the kinds of actions that lead to desirable outcomes, specific-action controls can be effective. When it is clear what kinds of outcomes are desirable, and when these outcomes can be accurately measured, results control can be used.

In some circumstances it is difficult to accurately measure outcomes, and knowledge of the most desirable kinds of specific actions is low. This presents management with its most difficult control problem. In this case, personnel-control strategies must be devised so that employees, on their own, can be relied on to do what is best for the hotel. Well-managed hotels use combinations of these three different control strategies to ensure that they meet their goals and objectives. The next two chapters will focus on results, specific-actions, and personnel control strategies in hotels by reviewing examples of each.

REFERENCES

Flik, Julie Ann. 1988. "Focus Feedback, the Key to Success." *Food Management* 23(9):87088.

Gebhardt, Dennis C. December 1988. "Mini Internal Audits Can Help Control, Improve Operations." *Hotel & Resort Industry* 11(12):92–93.

Koontz, H., C. O'Donnell, and H. Weihrich. 1980. *Management*. 7th ed. New York: McGraw-Hill.

Merchant, Kenneth A. 1982. "The Control Function of Management." *Sloan Management Review.* 23(4):43–55.

Stephenson, Susie. March 1989. "Customer Relations: Feedback Techniques Tell 'How'm I Doin'?'" *Restaurants & Institutions* 99(8):20–21.

Zaccarelli, Herman E. January 1990. "Profit Guide: How to Implement Quality Control." *Cooking for Profit* 464:4.

Zuckerman, David. 1988. "Service: Righting the Wrongs." *Restaurant Management* 2(3):66–67.

QUESTIONS

12-1. Use the diagram of a simple feedback-control process to describe the principle of control for three different hourly hotel jobs.

12-2. Use the same feedback-control diagram to describe the principle of control for a department within a hotel.

12-3. Describe the three principal control tactics that relate to the object being controlled.

12-4. Under what circumstances would results, specific-actions, and personnel control be used?

CHAPTER 13

Controlling Results: Hotel Revenues and Costs

As discussed in Chapter One, GMs consider the fixed supply of hotel rooms at their command one of the key characteristics of the hotel business. Hotels cannot adjust to changes in demand by varying the supply of their product or through inventory-level adjustments. Since supply is fixed, hotels must pay particularly close attention to room demand and the variable costs they can control in order to be profitable. Controlling revenues and variable costs thus becomes a crucial issue for hotel profitability.

This chapter outlines a revenue-and-cost control system for The Regal Hotel, run by Lawrence Wagner. The chapter is divided into three sections relating to the time frame of the forecasting and control process: (1) the hotel's annual plan, (2) the hotel's monthly forecast, and (3) the hotel's ten-day planning-and-control cycle. This planning and control process is as important an example of a *results-accountability* control strategy as can be found in a hotel. It includes all of the necessary components of a results-accountability control system, including: (1) plans, (2) goals and objectives, (3) budgets, (4) standards, and (5) MBO. Results-accountability control will be illustrated by describing a system of control over rooms revenue, food-and-beverage revenue, and labor costs. It is beyond the scope of this book to explore all aspects of control in a hotel, so important issues such as food or beverage cost control and inventory control will not be addressed.

A diagram of this process is shown in Figure 13-1. Selling rooms is a hotel's obvious "reason for being," and forecasting and controlling room sales is a main focus of management. The number of occupied rooms and the number of guests in a hotel on a given day are the driving forces that

An attractive and comfortable guest room at the Raddisson Plaza Hotel, Minneapolis.

Courtesy: Radisson Hotels International

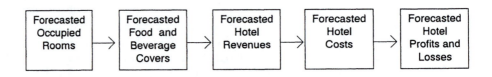

| Forecasted Occupied Rooms | Forecasted Food and Beverage Covers | Forecasted Hotel Revenues | Forecasted Hotel Costs | Forecasted Hotel Profits and Losses |

FIGURE 13-1.   The Revenue-Cost-Profit Results-Accountability Control Process

influence nearly every other operational aspect of a hotel. For example, rooms occupied and number of guests influences how many breakfasts room service will have to deliver and the number of dinners the hotel's restaurants must anticipate serving. Thus, accurately forecasting food and beverage covers requires accurate occupancy-and-guests forecasts. Once occupancy and number of guests are forecasted, revenues can be estimated by multiplying occupied rooms by expected average rates and number of covers by antici-pated prices per cover.

Certain costs vary with the activity level in a hotel, the most important two being labor, and food-and-beverage costs. A hotel's activity level (rooms occupied, number of guests and covers) will determine the number of maids that are required to clean rooms, the number of clerks to check in guests, the number of waitresses for the cocktail lounges, the number of chickens and fresh strawberries to order for banquets, and the number of bed sheets that will have to be laundered. Well-managed hotels pay ex-tremely close attention to the relationship between revenues and costs and especially to the two largest cost components in a hotel that vary with the activity level: labor costs and food-and-beverage costs. Through historical experience, staffing guidelines, receipt and inventory controls, and a wide variety of other control measures, hotels have developed specific goals with respect to labor and food costs as a percentage of revenues. These cost percentage goals constitute a form of *results control*. Once revenues have been forecasted, a hotel can apply these cost guidelines to forecast variable costs. Adding in fixed costs (that is, property taxes, interest on debt, in-surance, some items of maintenance) allows the hotel to project its profit and loss statement for the upcoming period (Schmidgall 1989).

It will become clear as this example progresses that this process is more than just a forecast. It is a process whose whole purpose is to make the future come out as the hotel's business plan intended. It is, in other words, an elaborate strategy to *control* the results of the hotel's business. Let's take a look, then, at this control process starting with the hotel's beginning forecast.

THE BEGINNING FORECAST

Each September The Regal Hotel begins the process of developing its annual plan for the forthcoming year.

Occupancy Forecast

The process begins with the sales and marketing department preparing an occupancy forecast for the next year. A review is made of two separate kinds of business: transient and convention. The Regal Hotel further subdivides transient guests into six categories, based on the pricing structure it follows. These transient guest categories and the room-rates associated with them are shown in Table 13-1.

The hotel's marketing strategy with respect to its transient market re-volves around these six categories. Some transient guests pay the full rack (published) rate of $150 per night. Tour wholesalers, on the other hand, pay as little as seventy-three dollars per night for the rooms they purchase

TABLE 13-1.   The Regal Hotel Transient Guest Categories and Room Rates (19XX)

Category	Average Room Rate
1. Full (Rack) Rate	$150.00
2. Business Travel	130.00
3. Corporate Rate	99.00
4. Wholesaler	73.00
5. Package Plan	87.00
6. Discounts	$109.00

for their tour customers. While the hotel would love for all of its transient guests to pay rack-rate, it knows that this is usually possible only during special events when the demand for rooms far exceeds their supply. Still, during a particularly busy month The Regal Hotel is often able to charge rack-rate to about 50 percent of its transient guests, while during the off-season it is lucky to get rack-rate for 20 percent of its transient rooms.

Variations in the percentages of transient guests in each rate category have a profound affect on the hotel's average room-rate. The average transient rate, for example, would fall dramatically if the number of guests paying rack-rate decreased and were replaced by guests paying wholesaler or package-plan rates. A numerical example will illustrate this. Suppose that half of the hotel's transient guests paid a rack-rate of $150, while the average rate of the other half was $100 per night. The average transient rate for this mix of business would be $125 ($150 x .5 + $100 x .5). If the guest mix were to change so that only 20 percent were paying rack-rate ($150) while 80 percent paid an average rate of $100, then the average transient rate would fall to $110 ($150 x .2 + $100 x .8), a 12 percent decline. To offset this fall in revenue the hotel would have to generate a 15 percent increase in transient occupancy just to stay even! This illustrates an important aspect of The Regal Hotel's results-accountability control system. The hotel must strive for the most favorable mix possible of transient room-rates, thus resulting in the highest possible *average* room-rate. Only in this way, for a given level of hotel occupancy, can the hotel ensure the highest possible room revenues. This example also illustrates that both the number of occupied rooms *and* the average room-rate must be forecasted if the hotel is to accurately forecast its total rooms revenue.

With just a few exceptions, such as special events and wholesaler room guarantees, most transient rooms at The Regal are booked no more than sixty days in advance. Thus, in September The Regal Hotel reservation system will show very few transient rooms reserved for most days during the next year. In effect, the hotel must begin its planning for the upcoming year with very little transient business on its books. Management must rely on a number of sources in order to forecast transient bookings. Among these are: (1) the historical pattern of transient bookings during past years, (2) its knowledge of what is happening in the local economy, (3) what it knows about competing hotels, (4) its assessment of the effect its marketing efforts will have, and (5) the extent to which its own convention bookings might affect the availability of rooms for transient guests. In other words, the marketing department must use its knowledge of past trends and its judgment regarding a variety of future variables to forecast transient rooms in each of the six categories. That, of course, is quite a tall order. It gets even more involved. Note that occupancy and average room-rates will vary considerably from one day to the next and season to season depending on the composition of demand. This has led many hotels to forecast occupancy and average room-rates separately for each day of the upcoming year. Only in this way can management get a picture of expected total rooms revenue. The Regal Hotel does exactly this. It forecasts, for each day of the next year, the number of transient rooms it expects to sell in each of the six room-rate categories listed above. As noted, this forecast is something of an educated guess because of the scarcity of actual transient bookings more than two months into the future. This is where knowledge of past trends and judgment based on experience plays an important role.

The second major component of occupancy that must be forecasted is convention demand. The Regal Hotel includes business meetings and seminars under the convention heading. Convention demand thus represents all group business in the hotel with the exception of group pleasure travel. The sales department is continuously working to book future conventions and business meetings into the hotel. It keeps detailed records of each group that has *definitely* reserved rooms as well as those groups who have given a *tentative* indication that they will book. The exact dates of these commitments, along with an estimate of the number of rooms that will be required, and the negotiated group room-rate is also carefully recorded. In September the hotel had 28,000 room-nights of convention business definitely booked for the next year and another 14,000 tentative room-night bookings, for a total of 42,000 total room-nights. This total is far from the total group bookings the hotel hopes to enjoy during the coming year. For the past three years The Regal Hotel booked 58,200, 65,800, and 58,500 convention room-nights, respectively. If, based on its detailed knowledge of the convention market, management decides that 60,000 room-nights is a reasonable goal for the upcoming year, then the hotel's definite bookings in September represent only 46.7 percent of what is required to meet next year's annual goal. Even if all of the 14,000 tentative bookings materialize (an unlikely event) the hotel will still only reach 70 percent of its sales goal of 60,000 room-nights. It must sell an additional 18,000 room-nights during the next fifteen months to reach a total of 60,000 room-nights. Once again, past experience of how tentative bookings are likely to convert to definite bookings is important. Also, certain groups book a year or less in advance. Knowledge of these and other factors must be combined with existing bookings in order to accurately estimate the amount of additional convention business the hotel can expect over the next fifteen months.

As with the transient component of demand, convention bookings are also forecasted for each day of the year. For The Regal Hotel, convention business varies seasonally. During the busy season conventions can represent 70 percent or more of the hotel's total occupancy. This drops to 25 percent or less during the off-season. For the year, 60,000 convention room-nights represent an annual occupancy of 32.9 percent for the 500-room Regal Hotel. Once room-nights are forecasted, room-rates for each convention must be estimated so that total room revenues from conventions can be forecasted.

The foregoing described how estimates are made for transient and convention room-nights and anticipated average room-rates for the next year. During this process the sales and marketing department will also forecast percentage of double occupancy so that an actual forecast of the number of guests in the hotel, by day, can be made. The actual managerial process that leads to these forecasts is more complicated then that described here. The key executives at The Regal Hotel that are involved in these forecasts are the GM, the director of sales and marketing, the rooms division manager, the reservations manager, and the controller. Recall that while sales and marketing is charged with the responsibility of filling the hotel with guests, detailed reservation records are kept by the reservations department, which is commonly part of the rooms division. The reservation department's access to detailed reservation statistics, both for the next year and historically, is invaluable for forecasting purposes.

These executives meet from time to time during September to review the preliminary forecasts made by sales and marketing with input from reservations. What eventually evolves is a group consensus of what the following year will look like in terms of both occupancy and average room-rates. This is a big job of "crystal ball" gazing into the future. Its accuracy depends on judgment, experience, and a determination to achieve good results for the hotel. The occupancy forecast that emerges from these deliberations is critical to the hotel. It influences all the other planning and control steps that eventually result in The Regal Hotel's annual plan, including its profit goals for the next year.

Departmental Forecasts

The hotel's occupancy forecast, which includes the anticipated number of guests for each day, represents the hotel's anticipated *volume* of business for the next year. This forecast is distributed to each department of the hotel. Each department, in turn, is responsible for preparing its own annual plan. In most nonrevenue producing departments such as housekeeping, accounting, and security, this means estimating operating costs based on the anticipated volume of business during the upcoming year. Labor and materials are the two largest costs in most departments. Each cost varies with volume of business, and they must be carefully considered. The problem faced by the food and beverage department is a little more complicated. Food and beverage must still forecast its level of sales before it can calculate its anticipated costs. The process entails forecasting the number of covers (meals) that will be served by the hotel's banquet department, room service, and its two restaurants, as well as the volume of business anticipated in its several lounges. While these forecasts depend heavily on hotel occupancy, they are also influenced by what is going on locally and by the department's own marketing efforts. Once covers are forecasted, revenues can be estimated by multiplying covers by anticipated sales price per cover. These forecasts are also made for every day of the succeeding year (Sill 1987).

Now that the hotel has forecasted business volume (occupancy, number of guests, and covers), it is a relatively straightforward process to estimate costs. The hotel's accounting department maintains detailed historical records of each department's costs and revenues. It regularly calculates major

Cafe International Buffet at the Indiana Airport Holiday Inn

Courtesy: General Hotels Corporation

cost items as a percentage of revenues. For example, Table 13-2 gives some historical cost ratios for The Regal Hotel's major labor and food cost categories. A wage and salary expense of 10.6 percent for the rooms department means that the wages and salaries of all personnel of that department, including its executives, were 10.6 percent of the hotel's total rooms revenue of about $15 million for the year. For the food and beverage department, wages and salaries of all employees and executives were 31.8 percent of total food and beverage revenues of $4.5 million. Furthermore, for every dollar of food revenues the hotel's food costs were 29.5 percent, and its beverage costs were 20 percent of each dollar of beverage revenues. These historical cost ratios give a pretty good indication of what costs might be next year if forecasted revenues materialize. Through experience and by comparison to industry and company averages, hotel executives are able to determine what cost percentages are appropriate for different types of hotels. So while the percentages shown in Table 13-2 were historical averages, some numbers quite close to these will probably represent The Regal Hotel's cost goals for the upcoming year. In fact, if a hotel were simply to use its historical cost ratios in calculating anticipated future costs, these historical relationships would automatically become operating goals for the forthcoming year.

By proceeding in this manner for each department, the hotel is able to put together an estimate of all hotel costs based on the volume of business it anticipates for the upcoming year. When all costs (both variable and fixed) are subtracted from anticipated revenues, The Regal Hotel can project its profit (or loss) for the next year. Such a projection is referred to as a *pro forma* (Latin for "as a matter of form") profit and loss statement.

What if this process results in a rather disappointing projection of profits for the upcoming year? Can anything be done about this or must the hotel simply accept the inevitable? As in all business affairs, The Regal Hotel has some, but not full, control over its fate. A forecast of falling occupancy and revenue may be offset by a strategy of more aggressive advertising or pricing. But what if these measures may not work! It might

TABLE 13-2.   **Historical Costs as a Percentage of Revenues**

Cost Category	Costs as a Percentage of Revenues
Rooms Division	
Salaries & Wages	10.6%
Food & Beverage Division	
Salaries & Wages	31.8%
Cost of Food	29.5%
Cost of Beverage	20.0%

be possible, through tighter personnel scheduling and purchasing controls, to keep costs down, thus cushioning the impact of lower revenues. The hotel could even cut its staff, delay certain maintenance expenditures, and lower purchasing standards in an attempt to lower costs. The point is that the process of forecasting a hotel's revenues and costs does not automatically ensure that profit levels will be high or that they will be acceptable to either management or owners. Thus, forecasting alone is quite different from developing an annual plan in which a hotel's revenue, cost, and profit goals are clearly and explicitly stated.

FORGING THE ANNUAL BUSINESS PLAN

To understand how The Regal Hotel's annual plan turns into a results-accountability control system, recall the managerial *process* that Lawrence Wagner has put together. Figure 13-2 depicts the revenue and cost forecasting process. The process begins with forecasts of occupancies, room-rates, covers, and check average. These forecasts involve input from the sales and marketing, accounting, food and beverage, and reservations departments. When these forecasts are completed, management makes a preliminary forecast of its volume of business (occupancy, number of guests, and covers) and its level of revenues for the upcoming year.

At this point in the process, Wagner allows each division head to develop his or her own annual plan *based on the volume and revenue forecasts that have already been made*. Each divisional plan includes forecasted revenues for those divisions that are revenue producers and forecasted costs for all divisions of the hotel. Together these plans result in a forecast of the hotel's overall revenues, costs, and profits for the next year. But what if this forecast is disappointedly low? How does the hotel react? How does this *forecasted* profit level get transformed into a *planned* level of profits that represents the *goals* toward which the hotel will work? In other words, how does this planning process evolve into a results-accountability control system (Coy 1990)?

Group Consensus at The Regal Hotel

At The Regal Hotel, the process is rather subtle, involving extensive communication and consensus building. To begin with, Lawrence Wagner does not set the revenue, cost, or profit goals for either the entire hotel or for any of its individual departments. Thus, the initial forecasts of business volume and price are based on the "best judgments" of the executives responsible for these forecasts. Recall that the forecasting process begins in September but that the annual plan is not submitted to corporate headquarters until mid-October. For about six weeks the hotel's executives are putting together the materials required for the final annual plan. Numerous scheduled and un-

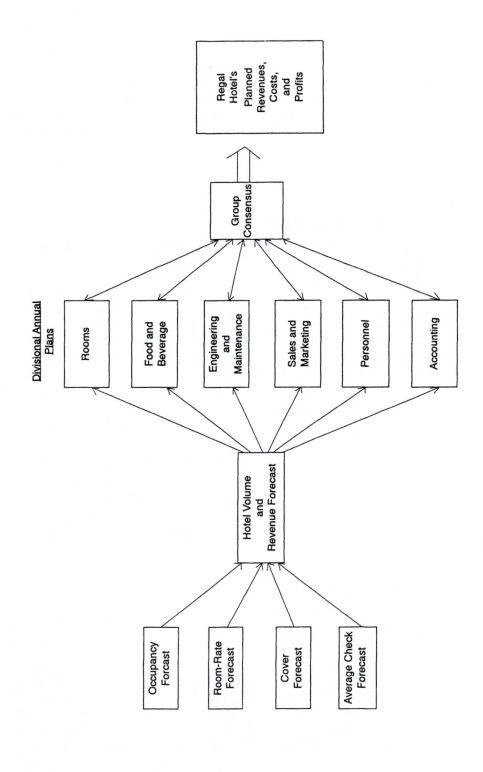

FIGURE 13-2. The Regal Hotel's Annual Revenue and Cost-Planning System

scheduled meetings are held during this time. These are often short meetings where one or two specific aspects of next year's plan are discussed. Here are two examples.

Lawrence Wagner met one day in late September with his department heads to discuss capital expenditure plans for the upcoming year. At that time preliminary volume and revenue forecasts had already been made and were familiar to everyone attending the meeting. These forecasts were not, however, brought up explicitly during the meeting. The meeting took place before the deadline for division heads to submit their annual plans to the GM. The issues discussed at this meeting dealt with capital expenditures. These expenditures were classified into those that had to be made, those that would be highly desirable, and those that were desirable but could be postponed until some future year. Each division head had prepared a list of capital expenditures based on this criterion and the entire group discussed the merits of the various proposals.

In some instances the need for the expenditures was so obvious that little discussion was necessary. For example, a manufacturer's recommended overhaul of the elevator breaking system. In other cases, the issues were less clear. The food and beverage director wanted to purchase some additional refrigerators to eliminate a storage problem in the kitchen. During the ensuing discussion it became apparent that cost saving for this expenditure had not been estimated. No decision was made at the time and the food and beverage director was asked to provide additional cost justification. In fact, most of the items discussed were neither approved or disapproved; they were just discussed. Remember, Wagner requires that each division head prepare his or her own annual plan. Each division head must ultimately make the final decision regarding his or her division's capital spending. Thus, the meeting was more a discussion than an attempt at group decision making. These executives were trying to develop a better sense of where the hotel was going in the upcoming year without being forced by the GM into hard and fast decisions.

The meeting then turned to a discussion of the need to update and refurbish some of the hotel's public spaces, including its lobby, patio, and lounges. These spaces don't really belong to any one department so it was appropriate for the entire group to discuss this issue together. The chief engineer had prepared two budget estimates: one a modest "freshening up" of the spaces by painting and minor improvements, the other a much more complete redecoration. The former approach would have only a minor impact on next year's profits but still leave the issue of a complete face-lift unresolved; the latter proposal would nearly wipe out next year's profits but settle the issue for a number of years to come. Lawrence prides himself in his ability to "shield his executives from the pressures imposed on him from corporate." Still, it was clear to all that this issue posed a dilemma in terms of corporate profit expectations. It would also impact their own bonus' for next year, which were based on overall hotel profits. They faced one of the classic dilemmas discussed in Chapter One regarding the tug of war between short-run profits and long-run quality.

These executives, being sensible people, came to a sensible conclusion: completely refurbish a portion of the public spaces for each of the next four years while maintaining the remaining spaces as attractively as possible without major expenditures. In other words, do a complete (and expensive) update of a fraction of the public spaces each year. The hotel's appearance would be upgraded and profit levels would also be maintained. A compromise decision to be sure, but one with which they were prepared to live.

In this way, and at numerous individual and group meetings during the

The lounge at the Radisson Resort's Jekyll Island Club Hotel—a cozy, inviting room in which to relax at the end of a day.

Courtesy: Radisson Hotels International

latter part of September and October, Lawrence Wagner and his senior executives continued the process of discussing, adjusting, and fine-tuning their ideas, estimates, and plans for the upcoming year. Lawrence met on a number of occasions with the director of sales and marketing to discuss the advantages of hiring an additional sales manager to concentrate on short lead-time group business. Numerous meetings took place with the food and beverage director and the public relations director about advertising and promoting the hotel's new fine dining restaurant, The Creole. A decision was ultimately made not to hire an additional sales manager. In the case of The Creole, it was decided to center much of the hotel's advertising for the upcoming year around the new restaurant. A decision was made to purchase radio advertising for the restaurant. In each case the effect of these decisions was factored into the estimate of the next year's volume of business and revenues.

As September turned into October, the senior executives of The Regal Hotel refined and adjusted their plans and forecasts for the upcoming year. While Lawrence Wagner's influence was always felt, it was not the heavy hand of authority. Rather, it was the guiding hand of an experienced hotel executive leading the group toward a consensus plan of action for the next year. Wagner's controller has worked with him for twelve years at two different hotels. They both respect and have affection for each other. Because of the controller's access to financial and cost data, he plays an important role in the process of developing the hotel's annual plan. He views the process as follows:

> "The Regal Hotel tries to reach a group consensus regarding our annual plan. The GM does not, on his own, tend to set arbitrary revenue or profit goals. Rather, we try as a group to make forecasts and set goals that are both aggressive but at the same time realistic. Once approved by corporate, this then becomes the annual business plan for the hotel against which its GM and executives are measured and by which executive bonuses are determined."

The last sentence of this quote is a clear-cut example of what has become, for The Regal Hotel and its executives, a results-accountability control system. The volume, revenue, cost, and profit figures that go to corporate in mid-October are now the *goals* that The Regal Hotel has set for itself. Corporate will hold these executives *accountable* for the operating *results* they attain based on this business plan. Bonuses will be granted or withheld, and raises and promotions will be determined based on these results. This is, without a doubt, serious business for everyone involved. Careers are often made or broken based on business plans being met. Once the business plan is in place The Regal Hotel's executives will try to do everything in their power to *control* the results of their hotel's operations in such a way as to meet or exceed the goals of the annual plan.

Making Difficult Choices at The St. Charles Hotel

An interesting example of hotel executives coming to grips with a difficult control issue occurred while I was studying Matthew Fox, GM of the St. Charles Hotel. Remember that corporate management and owners do not have to accept the business plan submitted to them by a hotel. They have the right to impose performance levels on the hotels they control. I watched Matthew Fox and his executives struggle with an imposed profit goal late one October during the final stages of preparing their annual plan. After a month of trying to develop revenue and cost goals that would meet the profit expectation of corporate, they were still $150,000 short. The atmosphere at the meeting to discuss this "challenge" can best be described as highly focused. There was no hostility or fear, but neither was there any small talk or joking. Try as they may, the hotel was still $150,000 short of corporate's profit expectations and some way had to be found to make up the difference.

The most pleasant way of resolving this problem would have been to find some way to increase the hotel's revenue estimate by $150,000. It became obvious, however, that the hotel's revenue estimates were already very aggressive, and the group felt uncomfortable raising them any higher for fear of not being able to deliver on the promise. They were left with no alternative but to reduce costs. It turned out that labor costs were the main target. Matt Fox realized that to take a little money from each division's labor budget was a bureaucratic and cowardly approach. The wisest approach was to cut labor costs in areas that would have the smallest impact on guest services and hotel efficiency, even if certain departments had to take proportionately larger cuts than others. Various strategies to reduce labor expenses were discussed for each department. Proposals included reassigning personnel, consolidating positions, changing job responsibilities, using more split schedules, and laying off employees. These were quite detailed and explicit discussions, and Matt's accounting background came in handy. He quickly calculated each idea's cost savings, while his controller kept a running total. As the meeting continued it began to appear that the rooms division would have to bear the brunt of these cuts. This conclusion evolved during the deliberations. Matt was in control of the meeting, but he was not bullying people toward a solution. They all understood, however, that Matt would be the final judge of which department took the hardest hit. These executives knew unpleasant decisions had to be made and, in the end, everyone suffered a little, but the rooms department got cut the most.

What emerged was a business plan that met The St. Charles Hotel's corporate profit goals. This was the plan by which Matthew Fox and his fellow executives would be judged. They felt that they could produce the intended financial results and hoped that they had wisely decided on cost cuts that would least impact guest services. The best was made of a difficult situation, and a group consensus had still been reached. Importantly, the rooms division manager emerged from the meeting, if not happy, at least satisfied that the cuts to his department were in the best interests of the hotel. He was also committed to a plan of action for his department for the next year.

The Final Business Plan

By early November The Regal Hotel's annual business plan was approved by corporate headquarters. All of the planning, forecasting, and decisions that were incorporated into it were now set, and the hotel's executives and staff were committed to achieving these goals. Their job now was to control events so that the goals of the business plan were met. In order to do this, The Regal Hotel shifted from its annual plan to a monthly planning and control cycle.

THE MONTHLY CONTROL CYCLE

Recall that the hotel's annual plan includes a forecast of business volume and revenues for each day of the next year. Generally speaking, the further into the future the hotel's executives look the fewer bookings they have for any one day, week, or month. As the hotel approaches the new year, reservations are continually accepted, conventions booked, and weddings and banquets scheduled. It was noted earlier that individual transient bookings only begin to build up about sixty days in advance. Also, in September only 46.7 percent of the convention business needed to meet the next year's goal had been booked. The hotel wants to *control* its operations in order to meet the goals of its business plan. To do this it needs to monitor its progress in a timely manner so that corrective action can be taken, if necessary.

The Thirty- To Ninety-Day Forecast

An important part of this monitoring process takes place every Monday morning at the weekly forecasting meeting. At this meeting executives from sales and marketing, reservations, and food and beverage update last week's activities and prepare a new forecast of occupancy and covers for the next thirty to ninety days. This exercise is truly a forecast, as opposed to a new set of goals in the business plan. The most recent information available is used to forecast business volume thirty to ninety days into the future. The results of this forecast are widely distributed so that executives at all levels can keep close track of how the hotel is progressing. Forecasts are compared with the goals that have been set in the annual business plan. Thus is established a feedback-control system. This forecast is an important part of the hotel's results-accountability control system because it provides *objective* and *timely* information about the future that can easily be compared to goals. Management still has time to make decisions and initiate actions that may influence the course of future events. The hotel still has some *control* over its own destiny.

There is, for example, still time to promote special room-rates in Houston and Dallas during periods when occupancy looks particularly low. A good offer can be made to the oil field service company that is considering the hotel for a training seminar. Food and beverage has time to plan a local food promotion if it has forty-five–days notice that cover counts will be down. For periods when the hotel looks like it is going to fill up, reservations can stop accepting tourist packages, anticipating a sold-out house. Management still has many options, especially with regard to its ability to influence the hotel's volume of business and revenues. Even while daily operating problems are being solved and conventions are being booked three years or more in advance, Lawrence Wagner and his executives are also talking, meeting, planning, and making decisions about how to make the hotel's thirty- to ninety-day future unfold as they would like.

It's worth repeating that The Regal Hotel's annual plan is set up for *each* day of the year and that the weekly thirty- to ninety-day forecast is made for *each* of those sixty future days. Management at The Regal Hotel not only worries about weeks that look bad, they worry about each of the sixty individual days in that future period that seem to be a problem. Because their rooms can't be inventoried, each day has to count. Any lost revenue on one day because of a foul-up or mistake, or simply because of lack of attention, can never be recovered in the future. As Curtis Samuels of The Hotel Frenchman puts it, "I determine how good a GM I am each morning when I read the previous day's daily report." Frank Anderson says that, "There's no such thing as a one-time author." Every day counts to outstanding hotel managers.

The Monthly Forecast

While Lawrence and his executives are trying to make sure that the future will come out as they planned, another, more formal part of the results control cycle takes place each month. In midmonth the hotel controller calls a meeting of representatives of the sales and marketing, rooms, reservations, and food and beverage departments to prepare the hotel's monthly forecast of business volume, revenues, costs, and profit and loss. The Regal Hotel's monthly forecast is a detailed six-page document. Table 13-3 lists the various components of the monthly forecast, which is usually completed by the third week of each month. The monthly forecast shows what the hotel actually expects to accomplish next month, how this compares to the same month last year, and more importantly, how the forecast compares to the goals set forth in the annual plan.

TABLE 13-3.   Components of the Monthly Forecast

• Monthly Rooms Occupancy Forecast

> For each day of the month
> By each market category
> Number of rooms sold and average rate, by category
> Room VARIANCE (FORECASTED-PLANNED) for each day

• Monthly Food and Beverage Forecast

> For each day of the month
> For each food and beverage outlet
> Number of covers by outlet
> Average check by outlet
> Revenues by outlet
> Comparison of FORECASTED, PLANNED, and LAST YEAR

• Profit from Operating Departments

> Revenues and direct expenses of Rooms, Food and Beverage,
>   Telephone, and Garage
> Comparison of FORECASTED departmental profits
>   to PLANNED and to LAST YEAR

• Hotel Profit and Loss Forecast

> Gross Revenue
> Overhead deductions from income
> Total house profit
> Other deductions and depreciation
> Profits before income tax
> All FORECASTED items compared both to PLANNED
>   and to LAST YEAR

Corporate executives are very interested in this document, especially the VARIANCE between FORECASTED and PLANNED results. A positive variance for revenue categories (forecasted revenues exceed planned) bring smiles to their faces since it looks like the hotel will make more money than had been anticipated. On the other hand a negative variance causes concern because it appears that actual revenues will fall short of planned revenues. The opposite holds true for cost items where a positive variance means that actual costs will likely be greater than expected costs. A positive profit variance (forecasted profits exceed planned profits) is a time for joy while a negative variance (forecasted less than planned) causes black clouds to gather.

A simplified monthly rooms forecast is shown in Table 13-4. For the first day of the month the hotel had planned to sell a total of 400 rooms but unfortunately the monthly forecast now anticipates selling only 300. This results in a negative variance of 100 rooms. For the 500-room Regal Hotel a -100 room variance is 20 percentage points below the 80 percent

TABLE 13-4.   The Monthly Rooms Forecast

Day	Planned				Forecast				Variance (Forecast-Planned)	
	Tran.	Conv.	Total	%	Tran.	Conv.	Total	%	Number	%
1	300	100	400	80	225	75	300	60	(100)	(20%)
2	325	125	450	90	325	125	450	90	0	0
3	350	150	500	100˙	360	140	500	100	0	0
4	250	100	350	70	300	160	460	92	110	22%
	•	•	•	•	•	•	•	•	•	•
	•	•	•	•	•	•	•	•	•	•
30	168	212	380	76	180	240	420	84	40	8%
Monthly Total	7,200	4,800	12,000	80%	6,800	4,450	11,250	75%	(750)	(5%)
Average Rates	$112	$98	$106.40		$117	$108	$113.44		$7.04	6.7%
Room revenue		$1,276,800				$1,276,200			($600)	nil

occupancy anticipated in the annual plan. On the second and third days, forecasted and planned coincided exactly for total rooms sold, even though on the third day the forecasted transient and convention booking differs slightly from planned. On the fourth day it looks as if the hotel will exceed planned by 110 rooms, or twenty-two occupancy points. For the entire month the hotel forecasts that occupancy will fall 750 rooms short of planned (see the second to last row labeled MONTHLY TOTAL), a deficiency of five percentage points. While somewhat disappointing, the forecast is anything but discouraging. Note that the second to last row in Table 13-4 shows the planned and forecasted average room-rates for both transient and convention rooms. It looks as if The Regal Hotel will increase both its transient and convention room-rates for the month resulting in an overall forecasted hotel room-rate of $113.44 compared to a $106.40 planned room-rate, or a 6.7 percent increase. This results in planned and forecasted rooms revenues for the month being virtually identical at $1,276,800 and $1,276,200 respectively.

A further examination focuses on how this monthly occupancy forecast acts as a control system. Since the monthly forecast becomes available only about ten days before the first of each month, there is less flexibility of action than was the case with the thirty- to ninety-day forecast. Still, The Regal Hotel is not without some options. What Lawrence Wagner and his managers want to do is cause the results to meet or exceed the goals they set in the annual plan. The monthly forecast tells them where to concentrate their efforts. One option open to the hotel, even at this late date, is to intelligently use the reservation system during the next forty days. Using actual and forecasted occupancies, the hotel's executives devise a plan for the next month that maximizes the chances of reaching or exceeding their goals.

Table 13-5 is an example of the reservations strategy used by The Regal Hotel for each day of the upcoming month. Note that different selling strategies are needed, depending on the circumstances. Look first at day seven. The hotel is overbooked by twenty-five rooms (not an uncommon occurrence in hotels because cancellations and no-shows will often reduce this number to zero) and the instructions are "sell nothing." On the other hand, day eight looks very bad, with 275 available rooms. The selling strategy is clear: reservationists should sell all types of packages, specials, and discounts. Since the hotel is unlikely to fill up, it doesn't want a potential customer to get off the phone without booking a room, even if that means a deep discount. Day ten is quite different; forecasted occupancy is 85 percent, so the instructions are to sell only at rack-rates. The hotel has decided not to discount rates because it anticipates a good occupancy (85 percent) on that day. For the time being, it would rather try to stick to its published rates than offer discounts. Of course, if occupancies do not build as expected, management may change its strategy in a few days and start discounting—but not just yet.

Now look at days one and twenty-three. While the actual occupancies on the two days are both 80 percent, the forecasted occupancies are dif-

TABLE 13-5.   Thirty-Day Reservations Action Board

Day	Actual Occupancy	Forecasted Occupancy	Rooms Available	Selling Strategies
1	80%	90%	100	Sell $125 rooms & up
•				
•				
•				
7	105%	100%	-25	Sold out, no room at the inn. Sell nothing!
8	45%	62%	275	Wide open, sell anything!
•				
10	75%	85%	125	Rack-rate only, please!
•				
•				
•				
23	80%	100%	100	Jazz Fest, $175 & up, sell those high rates!

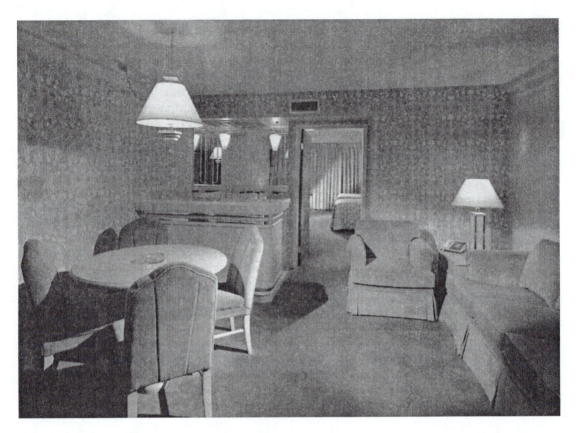

Embassy Suites customers get a two-room suite for the price of a single room at traditional upscale hotels.

Courtesy: Embassy Suites, Inc.

ferent: 90 percent on day one and 100 percent on day twenty-three. Day twenty-three coincides with a very popular local attraction, The Jazz Festival. For day one the hotel forecasts occupancy will increase to 90 percent, so they instruct reservationists to sell only rooms for $125 per night or more. This is an aggressive stance but one that experienced hotel executives are willing at times to take. This policy is a calculated risk, it may work or it may not. Let's look at the game of odds they are playing. If the hotel sells an additional sixty rooms by the first of the month at $125 each, it will garner an additional $7,500 in rooms revenue (60 X $125/room) and an overall occupancy of 92 percent. A more defensive strategy, which allowed for discounted rates, might result in an average rate of only one hundred dollars per room. If this strategy were adopted, the hotel would have to sell seventy-five additional rooms at one hundred dollars each (for an overall occupancy of 95 percent) in order to do just as well. In this example the hotel is willing to take the aggressive stance in hopes of making more revenue. Day twenty-three is another story altogether. Based on the experience of past years, Wagner and his executives are quite confident that the Jazz Festival's draw will eventually fill the hotel. Their business plan has predicted this outcome, and although actual occupancy is only 80 percent, they still confidently forecast 100 percent by the twenty-third. So what should their strategy be? Go for the maximum revenue possible, of course. Consequently, they take a very aggressive stance in which they only offer rooms at $175 or more per night. Their confidence level is high and they anticipate selling the remaining one hundred rooms, possibly at an average of $200 each, for a tidy $20,000 additional rooms revenue!

This is an example of an interesting game being played. The hotel is trying to *control* the demand for its rooms in order to meet its monthly revenue and occupancy goals. Their selling strategies are keyed into their goals, their forecasts, their current situation, and their best estimates of what is possible. This is a good example of a results-driven feedback-control system. It is a futures-oriented effort to cause events to come out as the hotel wants. If they succeed, the hotel will have controlled the situation rather than letting it just happen.

In a similar fashion, other income producing departments prepare their monthly forecasts. For example, the monthly food and beverage forecast includes the number of covers, average check, and total revenue for each of the hotel's outlets. Planned, forecasted, and last year's figures are given, as is the variance between forecasted and planned revenues. Because food and beverage volume is determined largely by occupancy levels, an unanticipated dip in forecasted occupancy will usually result in a downward revision of food and beverage revenues. While there is little time remaining to remedy such a problem, food and beverage is at least forewarned that its revenues for the upcoming month will be lower than anticipated. Once its volume of business is forecasted, the department applies staffing guides and carefully documented historical food–cost relationships in order to accurately estimate its departmental costs. Overhead items, such as advertising, repairs and maintenance, electricity, and administrative salaries, must also be estimated.

The Profit and Loss Forecast

Once these departmental calculations are made, the hotel prepares its profit and loss forecast for the next month. Table 13-6 is an example of such a forecast. This important report shows FORECASTED and PLANNED profits and the VARIANCE between the two.

TABLE 13-6.   The Regal Hotel Profit and Loss Forecast (June, 19XX)

Gross Revenue	Plan	Forecast	Variance	%
Rooms	$1,600,000	$1,350,000	($250,000)	(15.6%)
Food	416,000	337,500	(78,500)	(18.9%)
Beverage	220,000	200,000	(20,000)	(9.1%)
Telephone	49,000	40,000	(9,000)	(18.4%)
Garage	55,000	45,000	(10,000)	(18.2%)
Other	15,000	12,000	(3,000)	(20.0%)
Total Gross Revenue	$2,355,000	$1,984,500	($370,500)	(15.7%)
Departmental Profit				
Rooms	$800,000	$715,500	($84,500)	(10.6%)
Food and Beverage	104,000	100,000	(4,000)	(3.8%)
Telephone	7,200	6,500	(700)	(9.7%)
Garage	40,000	35,000	(5,000)	(12.5%)
Gross Operating Income	$951,200	$857,000	($94,200)	(9.9%)
Overhead Deductions From Income	$430,000	$380,000	$50,000	11.6%
House Profit	$521,200	$477,000	($44,200)	(8.5%)

In this example forecasted gross rooms revenues for June are considerably below planned revenues. Room revenues are forecasted at $1.35 million compared to $1.6 million in the hotel's business plan. The VARIANCE (FORECASTED - PLANNED) is a shortfall of -$250,000, or -15.6 percent below the hotel's goal. Reflecting less rooms business, the other revenue generating units (food, beverage, telephone, and garage) are also forecasted to be below plan. Overall, total gross revenue for the hotel is forecasted to be off by -$370,500, or by -15.7 percent. This is not a happy situation. Such a variance is considerable and will raise eyebrows at corporate. Management knows this and will try hard in the time remaining to increase revenues. Still, the hotel's ability to influence revenues at this late date are limited. Attention must turn more to cost reductions if profit goals are to be met. The next section of Table 13-6 shows departmental profit (gross departmental revenues minus departmental expenses) for the hotel's four revenue-producing departments. If expenses were to decrease proportionately with revenues, the hotel could anticipate a -15.7 percent variance between forecasted and planned profits. In order to cushion the impact of a -15.7 percent fall in gross revenues, The Regal must cut costs by more than the -15.7 percent fall in revenues. That they are trying to accomplish this is reflected in the departmental profit figures. For each of the four departments, the profit variance is *less* than the -15.7 percent revenue variance. The hotel is trying to cut costs so that profits can be maintained even in the face of falling revenues. Overall, management has done a credible job of this. The variance of gross operating income, which is the sum of departmental profits, is -$94,200. This is -9.9 percent compared to the -15.7 percent anticipated fall in revenues. The hotel's control process appears to be working! Departmental costs have been pared, and profits while down, are not down by as much as they might have been. The hotel is also working hard to cut overhead costs that are not attributable to individual departments. These expenses, such as advertising, electricity, human resources, and administrative are shown in Figure 13-6 as overhead deductions from income. Overhead deductions are often referred to as fixed costs reflecting the idea that they do not vary with the hotel's volume of business. Table 13-6 makes it clear that The Regal Hotel, in response to a revenue shortfall, is cutting even its overhead costs in an attempt to maintain profit levels. In fact, it is forecasting a $50,000 savings in overhead deductions for the upcoming month.

The Regal Hotel has, to some extent, succeeded in maintaining its planned level of profits. House profit, which is gross operating income less overhead deductions, is anticipated to have a $44,200 negative variance, or -8.5 percent. Had the departmental and overhead cost reductions not been made, house profits for June would have been down considerably more than $44,200. In fact, had departmental costs fallen proportionally to revenues, and had overhead costs stayed constant at $430,000, house profit would have fallen by $149,338 or -28.6 percent.

The monthly forecast in Figure 13-6 shows a hotel trying to control its operations in order to meet the goals of its business plan. It is future oriented because it represents what the hotel is trying to do in the upcoming month. It provides feedback, and therefore motivation, to Lawrence Wagner and his top executives. It allows corporate-level executives to anticipate next month's operating results and hold the hotel's executives accountable for them.

The Ten-Day Planning and Control Cycle

Every Wednesday a group of The Regal Hotel executives come together to prepare the last phase of a planning and control process that began in October of the previous year. The meeting is rather large. Most of the hotel's department heads are there, as well as the managers of the front office, reservations, each food and beverage outlet, banquets, and catering. The GM no longer regularly attends these weekly meetings. He did when he was setting up the hotel's operating routine, but now that it's firmly in place he is no longer needed. The purpose of this meeting is to forecast *everything* that is going to happen in the hotel for the next week, starting on Sunday and going through the next Saturday. Since the forecast is made on a Wednesday, the group also updates the previous week's forecast for Thursday, Friday, and Saturday, hence the name, ten-day forecast. In actuality, their major concern is with the upcoming week.

Forecasts are made for every possible aspect of the hotel's operations. The group forecasts rooms occupied; arrivals and departures; total guests in the hotel; covers for breakfast, lunch, and dinner in each food outlet; beverage volume by time of day in each beverage outlet; room service covers for breakfast, lunch, and dinner; and meeting and banquet function volumes for breakfast, lunch, and dinner. Each convention and group in the hotel, the number of rooms they will occupy, and the meetings and functions they have planned are all forecasted. The hotel's goal is to anticipate *everything* that is going to happen in the hotel during the next week, down to the 3 P.M. coffee break for a meeting of eight executives on Wednesday. This is very detailed and meticulous work; it is made easier by a well-designed array of reports, forms, and computer records that all fit together into a coherent system of records for each department and for the hotel as a whole.

Why this degree of precision? Surely the hotel has little influence over the actual volume of business that will materialize since the week in question begins in just four days. What, therefore, is the hotel trying to control at this late date? The answer, of course, is *costs*. While little can be done to influence the number of rooms that will be occupied, the number of banquets, or the number of covers in its restaurants, accurately forecasting business volume will help the hotel control its two most important cost categories: labor, and food and beverage. This is done through the use of detailed *staffing* and *purchasing* guidelines. These guidelines are based on past operating experience. They also reflect the hotel's cost goals for various volumes of business. Table 13-7 is an example of two staffing guides, one for housekeeping and one for the breakfast service staff in the hotel's dining room, The Creole.

The minimum staffing when the Creole restaurant anticipates serving fifty or less covers for breakfast is one manager working five hours, three waiters/waitresses working five and one-half hours each, one busman working five and one-half hours, and no hostess. The staffing guide shows the number of waiters/waitresses increasing steadily until ten are required when the number of covers reaches its maximum range of 281 to 320. Busmen also increase, reaching four at the restaurant's capacity. Finally, as volume picks up a hostess is added when 126 covers is reached, relieving the manager of that duty so he or she can supervise the overall activities of the service staff. Control is exercised by having exactly the right size staff on hand to serve breakfast. Too few staff results in poor service and unhappy guests; too many staff inflates labor costs. Lawrence Wagner wants the right number all the time. He runs a "tight ship" and does not suffer mistakes kindly.

TABLE 13-7.   Staffing Guidelines for The Regal Hotel

		Department:	Restaurant Creole			Period:	Breakfast		
	Hours Worked	Minimum to 50	51-100	101-125	126-160	161-190	191-240	241-280	281-320
Managers	5.0	1	1	1	1	1	1	1	1
Waiter/ Waitress	5.5	3	4	5	6	7	8	9	10
Busman	5.5	1	1	2	2	3	3	3	4
Hostess	4.0	0	0	0	1	1	1	1	1

	Department:	Housekeeping			Period:	Summer		
			HOURS					
Occupancy %	20%	. . .	50%	60%	. . .	80%	90%	100
Rooms Occupied	100	. . .	250	300	. . .	400	450	500
Day Maids	57	. . .	143	171	. . .	229	257	286
Night Maids	16	. . .	40	48	. . .	64	72	72
Housemen	24	. . .	48	48	. . .	64	72	72
Inspectress	24	. . .	56	56	. . .	64	72	72
Public Space	40	. . .	48	48	. . .	56	64	72
Linen Room	8	. . .	8	16	. . .	16	16	16
Seamstress	8	. . .	8	8	. . .	8	8	8
Night Cleaners	24	. . .	24	24	. . .	24	24	24
Administration	32	. . .	40	48	. . .	56	56	56
Morning Cleaners	24	. . .	24	32	. . .	40	40	40
Subtotal	257	. . .	439	499	. . .	621	681	718

Suppose, however, that management consistently misjudges the number of breakfast covers by only one volume category. For example, suppose that instead of scheduling for 126–160 covers the restaurant, because of poor control, consistently schedules its service staff for 161–190 covers. This mistake will result in scheduling one extra waiter/waitress and one extra busman, for a total of eleven unneeded man-hours. Since these employees share in a tip pool, their hotel salary might be only three dollars per hour. In that case the hotel has spent three dollars times eleven hours or thirty-three dollars more for breakfast than was necessary. One might be tempted to ask what's the big deal? In a hotel of this size is it worth worrying about an extra thirty-three dollars in labor costs at breakfast? An executive working for Lawrence Wagner at The Regal Hotel had better worry about thirty three dollars or look for work elsewhere. Wagner calculates that The Creole serves breakfast 365 days each year and that a thirty-three dollar mistake one day, when multiplied by 365 turns into a $12,045 mistake. Further, a similar "small" mistake at lunch and at dinner will cost the hotel $36,135 in a year, which is enough money to pay for an executive who will not make these kinds of "little" mistakes.

The situation is even more dramatic for housekeeping, whose staffing guide is also given in Table 13-7. Here volume is represented by the number of occupied rooms. The hotel has set staffing levels from a minimum of 100 occupied rooms (20 percent occupancy) up to a full house of 500 rooms (100 percent occupancy). Some categories, such as day maids, increase proportionately with the number of occupied rooms. Day maids work an eight-hour shift and are expected to clean fourteen rooms during a shift. As the number of occupied rooms increase, the number of day-maid hours increase proportionally. Other categories, such as seamstress, stay constant. Some, like housemen and inspectresses, jump only at intervals. Careful management and experience has taught the director of housekeeping how best to staff for different occupancy levels, and this experience is reflected in the staffing guide. Once again, a seemingly small mistake can have an unexpectedly large consequence. Calculating the cost of overstaffing by only one volume level (for example, staffing for a 90 percent instead of an 80 percent occupancy level) results in an error of a little more than 12 percent. As Table 13-7 shows, this error translates into an extra sixty man-hours (681 man-hours at 90 percent less 621 man-hours at 80 percent). The hotel has staffed too many day and night maids, housemen, inspectresses, and public space cleaners; in total, eight unneeded employees on that day. At an average hourly wage of five dollars per hour, the hotel has spent $300 more than was necessary. It is *out of control* and this is a serious problem. As a horrified Lawrence Wagner would quickly calculate, a mistake of this magnitude, repeated in the housekeeping department each day, would total $109,500 in unnecessary labor costs to The Regal Hotel in a year!

If these two examples of "small mistakes" in the housekeeping department and the restaurant were repeated every day, the result would be $145,631 of unnecessary labor costs in a year. How significant are costs of this magnitude? A 500-room luxury hotel might have total annual revenues of $20 million and pretax profits of about $2 million. Being out of control in these two departments alone will decrease pretax profits by 7.3 percent. This is no small matter. Think of the consequences if similar sloppiness occurs when staffing front desk clerks, cashiers, bartenders, and cocktail waitresses. Consider the spoilage problems if too much fresh produce is purchased. A hotel can waste money in hundreds of small ways. Over time these small mistakes add up to large amounts of money that can often be the difference between outstanding and average financial performance when times are good. It can also be the difference between making at least some profit or losing money when times are tough.

The final level of control, after the ten-day forecast is made, takes place

Festive Cafe Pierre in The Four Seasons' well-known Pierre Hotel in New York City.

Courtesy: Four Seasons Hotels and Resorts

during the actual day-to-day management of the hotel. Each manager is ultimately challenged to produce the results and reach the goals that this elaborate planning-and-control process has been set up to accomplish. Because of the systematic way in which this process has been developed, it would be impossible for any of The Regal Hotel's managers to be unaware of the results they are expected to produce during any week, day, or for that matter, during any shift.

The final group effort that Lawrence Wagner employs to ensure control takes place *daily*, when he convenes a fifteen-minute meeting of all department heads at 9 A.M. each morning. The activities of the hotel for that day are reviewed, and the previous day's results are quickly critiqued. Everyone focuses on what is expected during the day, the meeting is quickly over, and the day's work begins. Most of the GMs studied used this or a similar technique. Some held brief daily meetings like Lawrence, while others preferred longer meetings two or three times a week. All had the same purpose in mind: a final attempt to control the hotel's activities just before they were going to take place. Curtis Samuels, who has a catchy phrase for all of the management techniques he uses, calls his version of the morning meeting, "kick-starting the hotel."

Once a particular day's or week's activities have occurred, it's a simple matter to compare the actual operating results to what had been planned and forecasted. While this is looking backward rather than forward, it's nevertheless important. Reviewing past results gives a manager a scorecard by which to measure performance. Keeping score is important; it tells executives how they are doing, and it helps them figure out what can be done better. For example, while most of the ten-day forecast meeting at The Regal Hotel is spent anticipating next week's activities, some time is also spent reviewing the last week's results. The reason is obvious; not to do so would be like giving students a test and then never telling them how they did. As Jeff Harsha, Lawrence Wagner's long-time controller says, "Going over last week's results is used as a motivating device."

CONCLUSION

This chapter presented the outline of a results-accountability control system for a hotel. In this example the object being controlled was literally the hotel's revenues, costs, and profits. Well-managed hotels, like all well-managed businesses, do not passively accept whatever the future brings. Instead, they try to plan their strategies, organize their resources, and direct their efforts in such a way as to make the future turn out as they wish. In order to accomplish this, management needs to control the hotel's specific operating results.

A hotel's annual business plan is, in fact, part of a control strategy. The final revenue, cost, and profit goals that management sets for the hotel becomes the basis on which their performance is measured. Their efforts during the upcoming year will be focused on performing in such a way as to meet the goals of the business plan. Thus, their futures-oriented behavior is being controlled in a fundamental way. They are motivated to behave in this manner because the results of their efforts can be measured precisely and objectively. This control-cycle example also demonstrated how forecasts provided managers with timely measures of where the hotel was heading. The object is for management to be able to take appropriate action whenever variances between forecasted and planned outcomes appear to be seriously out of control. Management's response will vary depending on how far the forecast looks into the future. With sufficient time, efforts can be made to increase revenues. With little time, management must concentrate on cost containment. In either case, control is being exerted and efforts are being purposely directed toward goals.

The process of controlling results permeates throughout every subunit of a well-managed hotel, as was illustrated in this example of how occupancy and cover forecasts are used to determine staffing levels in housekeeping, and food and beverage. Seemingly small errors or management sloppiness in staffing could, if continually repeated, result in sizable cost overruns in the course of a year. Hotel managers, therefore, need to do two things extremely well if they are to discharge their control responsibilities. They must set up the proper control systems to focus behavior toward the hotel's goals. They must also be constantly vigilant of small mistakes, because it's a combination of small control mistakes that add up to major control problems.

REFERENCES

Coy, Jeff. Spring 1990. "Measure and Evaluate Your Hotel's Marketing Efforts to Reach Your Goals." *HSMAI Marketing Review* 8(2):7-12.

Schmidgall, Raymond S. April/May 1989. "Forecasting for Profitability." *Bottomline* 4(2):20-23.

Sill, Brian. May 1987. "How to Improve Productivity and Measure The Results." *Restaurant Business* 86(7):134-137ff.

QUESTIONS

13-1. Why is forecasting occupancy and room-rates an important element of a hotel's annual plan?

13-2. In what way is forecasting a hotel's occupancy for the next year wishful thinking?

13-3. Explain why a hotel's occupancy forecast must precede the forecasts of its individual departments.

13-4. Explain the concept of variance as it relates to profits, revenues, and costs.

13-5. What steps go into a hotel's monthly control cycle?

13-6. Describe in diagram from the various components of a hotel's annual planning-and-control cycle.

13-7. What can a hotel try to control sixty to ninety days in advance? What can a hotel try to control seven days in advance?

13-8. Why must hotels try to forecast occupancy for each day of the year?

13-9. How do hotels use their reservations system as part of their control process.

13-10. How do hotels use historical cost relationships and labor-staffing guides as part of their control process?

CHAPTER 14

Control: Getting Employees To Do Things Right and To Do the Right Things

Chapter Twelve classified control tactics according to the object that was being controlled: results, specific actions, or personnel. A results-account-ability control system dealing with control of a hotel's occupancy, revenues, staffing and costs was presented in Chapter Thirteen. This chapter presents examples of the other two types of controls: *specific-action controls*, where employees are directed and encouraged to perform in prescribed ways, and *personnel control*, where employees are relied on to do what is best for the hotel. Specific-action controls can be thought of as strategies that hotels employ to get people to *do things right*. Personnel control can be thought of as strategies hotels use to get people to *do the right things*. Examples of specific-action controls follow.

SPECIFIC-ACTION CONTROLS: GETTING EMPLOYEES TO DO THINGS RIGHT

People often do things a certain way or fail to do certain things simply because they don't know any better. Obvious examples come to mind from childhood experience; growing up is made vastly easier and less dangerous because many people teach children how to do certain things. The same is true of a hotel's staff. A hotel has an obligation to provide each employee with knowledge of the kinds of specific actions that will lead to success on the job and as an employee of the hotel. The next section presents an example of specific-action controls for new employees. As with nearly all the examples used in this book, those in this chapter are drawn from the hotels that participated in the GM research.

Introductory Training:
The "Dos" and "Don'ts" of Working for a Living

Starting one's first job or changing jobs is usually a rather stressful experience. All organizations, including hotels, need to establish certain ground rules of behavior for employees so that a minimum efficiency level will be ensured. Orientation programs begin this process the very first day a new employee starts work. Many of the hotels studied felt strongly about the importance of new-employee orientation programs. An example from one will demonstrate how quickly employees are confronted with specific-action controls. Table 14-1 lists some of the work rules, policies, and procedures contained in a hotel's employee handbook and explained to new employees during orientation. It's important to note that these rules apply to all employees of the hotel; they are not specific to the tasks required in a particular job. To better understand how these rules effect an employee's freedom of action, look more closely at one hotel's specific rules and procedures concerning absenteeism and personal telephone calls. The rules relating to these two policies are given in Exhibit 14-1.

Notice how specific and, therefore, controlling these two examples are. In the case of an absence the employee *must* contact his or her supervisor or department head. Simply leaving word if the supervisor is not available is not acceptable behavior. This hotel obviously wants the employee to talk directly with his or her supervisor, and not doing so is "not an acceptable form of notification." Furthermore, "failure to report an absence" in the manner proscribed "will be dealt with in a more severe manner." This is a

TABLE 14-1.   **Examples of Policies that Are Action Controls Placed on Employees in a Hotel**

- Absent–tardy procedures
- Conduct while working
- Use of employee entrance
- On premises after working hours
- Time card–paycheck policies
- Dress codes: uniformed–nonuniformed
- Conduct in guest areas
- Smoking
- Gum chewing
- Personal telephone calls
- Personal visitors
- Work rules
- Fire, safety, and hazards procedures
- Package passes

Absenteeism

The frequency of absences can be more damaging than the length of an absence. Excessive absences will result in disciplinary action and may result in termination. The usual procedure for handling unexcused absences is first a verbal warning; second, a written notice (usually indicating that the next offense may result in termination); and the third offense can result in termination depending on the consideration of all circumstances.

An employee should report as soon as he knows he is going to be absent. He *must* contact his Supervisor or the person in charge of his department to report any absence. If his immediate Supervisor is not available, he may contact the Personnel Office or the Assistant Manager on Duty to leave word. This does not excuse him, however, from calling back later to discuss the reason for his absence personally with his Supervisor. Leaving messages with the telephone department or another employee is not an acceptable form of notification.

Failure to report an absence will be dealt with in a more severe manner. Failure to report an absence for three or more days may be considered a voluntary quit.

Personal Telephone Calls

Employees are not allowed to receive personal phone calls while on duty. The operators are instructed to relay only *emergency* calls for employees to the Personnel Office.

They will take a message and then locate the employee and have him/her return the emergency call. If the Personnel Office is closed, the operators will route the calls through the Assistant Manager on Duty or the Night House Detective.

Telephones are placed in the employee cafeteria and at the employee entrance if an employee wants to make an outgoing call on his break or during his lunch period.

EXHIBIT 14-1.   Examples of Specific Action Controls

pretty clear policy; it tells an employee exactly how to behave when he or she is going to be absent, and it leaves little room for personal judgment (Weinstein 1989).

The personal telephone call policy is another example of a hotel policy that acts to constrain personal actions. Employees are simply not allowed to get personal calls, except for emergencies. Furthermore, emergency calls are not routed directly tothe employee but to the personnel office. Someone from personnel will then take the message to the employee, "and have him or her return the emergency call." This procedure allows the personnel office to monitor the emergency calls. It also constrains and dictates the actions of employees, even in the case of emergencies.

Doing Things Right on the Job:
Housekeeping Room Attendants

What's the most efficient way for a room attendant to strip and remake a bed? What sanitation procedures should be followed when cleaning a bathroom? What is the most efficient sequence of cleaning steps for a room attendant to follow? How many rooms should one attendant be able to clean properly in a Day's Inn, or a Holiday Inn, or a Four Seasons hotel? Would you allow the new room attendant you hire to determine on their

Room attendant using the correct and most efficient technique for making a bed at a Best Western Hotel.

Courtesy: Best Western International, Inc.

own how best to clean a room? Unless you've had experience in a house-keeping department you probably don't know the answers to these questions except, possibly, for the last one. Most people would be disinclined to allow room attendants to each clean rooms in their own way. Since this is a repetitive job, management has learned that certain techniques, procedures, and steps are more efficient then others. While it's true that any system can be improved upon, well-managed hotels will train their room attendants to follow a series of specific cleaning procedures and steps that experience has shown constitutes "doing things right." Recall from Chapter Twelve that this kind of specific-action control is appropriate in this case because: (1) there is excellent knowledge of which specific actions are desirable, and (2) the hotel can easily measure results along important performance dimensions.

Excellently managed hotels often go one or two steps further by trying to control employee behavior in areas that at first might seem unrelated to their job performance. Here is an example for the room attendants just discussed. In addition to their cleaning duties, one of the excellent hotels wanted to influence the behavior of their room attendants in the area of guest relations. In going to and from their rooms, guests often walk by a hotel's room attendants more than any other hotel employee. Thus, there are many opportunities for employee–guest interaction. This particular hotel, as part of its training, wanted to provide detailed instructions and procedures for room attendants to follow when interacting with guests. Exhibit 14-2 lists some of the specific forms of behavior that room attendants are expected to follow. Note that room attendants are expected to do a number of very specific things when it comes to guest interaction: greet guests by name, know the locations and hours of operation of the hotel's facilities, have knowledge of local attractions, and even be able to give directions around town. These are the kinds of extras that make the difference between an average and a really outstanding guest experience. Through experience, outstanding hotel executives know the kinds of things room attendants should be expected to do when interacting with guests (Lasley 1987).

While management cannot measure the results of these actions as easily as it can the cleanliness of a room, their best strategy is still to institute specific-action controls that outline in detail the kinds of behavior most likely to result in guest satisfaction. Hotels can indirectly measure whether the desired actions of their room attendants is working. This can be done through a results-accountability control strategy that revolves around careful analysis of guest-comment cards. Guest comments, subdivided by department, can give management evidence that its room attendants are, in fact, performing their intended guest-relations function. Curtis Samuels, of The Hotel Frenchman, regularly does exactly this. The system is not as precise or as immediate as room inspections, but over time a well-designed

Pleasing guests means more than providing clean and safe guest rooms. It means paying special attention to your guests, taking that extra step to anticipate their needs. A room attendant is often the first hotel employee that guests see in the morning. Your guests may not be familiar with the hotel facilities or with the local community. By anticipating your guests' needs, you should be able to answer many of the questions they may have. At the same time, you will be able to promote many of the facilities and services offered by your hotel.

Here are some helpful tips on how to establish good guest relations:

-Be polite and courteous to guests. Try to greet your guests by name, and particularly those guests staying for more than one night. Recognizing your guests by their names will make them feel that they are important and valued visitors at your hotel.

-Know the locations and hours of operation of your hotel's facilities:

• Ice and vending machines
• Restaurant, lounges, and room service
• Swimming pool, locker rooms, and health facilities
• Meeting, conference, and banquet rooms
• Valet and laundry services
• Limousine/shuttle transportation services

-Be familiar with local tourist attractions, recreation and/or entertainment opportunities:

• Golf courses and tennis courts
• Parks and public beaches
• Shopping areas
• Theaters, museums, and art galleries

-Be able to help your guests with directions. Know the primary roads, freeways, and major intersections in your area, and know directions

EXHIBIT 14-2.   Guest Relations Policies and Procedures for Room Attendants

guest-comment program can validate how well these specific-action controls are working.

Specific-Action Controls for Managers

It's not just employees who are subjected to specific-action controls in hotels. While managerial discretion and initiative should be encouraged, there are many occasions when detailed procedures and specific actions are called for. One example of specific controls in a hotel is the procedures that managers are required to follow with new employees. Experience has shown that the first few days and weeks of employment are a critical time for both the worker and the hotel. If a new employee gets off to a good start, the odds of that employee succeeding on the job are greatly increased. The control issue, then, is the extent to which a hotel should structure the procedures managers should follow with new employees. Many well-managed hotels have chosen to develop quite structured guidelines for managers to follow. The following are instructions, excerpted from one of the excellent hotels, for managers to follow when training a new employee.

- The manager will meet the new employee at the personnel office.
- The manager will then take the employee to his/her designated time clock and explain the appropriate procedures to follow. A tour will then be taken showing the employee cafeteria, the best way to get to the work area, and other areas related to his/her work. The employee should be introduced to his/her co-workers.
- The manager should then take the employee to his/her work area and give him/her a copy of the departmental work rules and regulations, job description and any other pertinent information, all of which should be explained in detail to the employee.
- As much of the actual on-the-job training as possible will be conducted by the manager, not a fellow employee. As much training as possible will be given before the area is open for business.
- As soon as the manager is confident in the new employee's grasp of the job, he/she should let the employee work alone with periodical checks. . . At the end of the shift the manager should talk to the employee to resolve any problems.
- The manager for the next few days should check with the new employee at least twice a shift to give any assistance the employee might need.
- At the end of each week for four weeks the manager should meet with the new employee to discuss any problems. . .

These are very specific instructions for managers to follow. The hotel that drafted these procedures feels strongly that this particular form of standardization increases the odds of new employee success. They go further in controlling their managers' actions by using a *First Day of Employment Checklist*, shown in Exhibit 14-3. It is the manager's responsibility to check off each of these thirty items. Both the manager and the employee sign the checklist and it becomes a part of the new employee's permanent record.

The process does not end here. Detailed follow-up procedures at two-, four-, and six-week intervals specify the exact meetings and actions that must be followed with each new employee. For example, after four weeks of employment a representative of the personnel department meets with the new

During the employee's first day on the job, the Manager is responsible for handling the following:

1. Introduction to Department and Division Head(s) as well as co-workers. (May vary depending on size of department.)

2. Lunch in the employee's cafeteria with someone from the department. Explain meal procedures, lunch breaks, etc. Lunch with:_____.

3. Tour of entire work area. Also explain location of supplies and equipment needed.

4. Explanation of how he/she should look in his/her uniform, when and where to get a clean one, etc.

5. Point out where schedules are posted and emphasize the importance of checking the schedule on a daily basis.

6. Explanation of actions which result in termination.

7. Reminder that he/she is on probation for 90 days and may be terminated at any time.

8. Stress proper appearance, conduct, personal service, and commitment to personal service.

9. Point out telephones for his/her use and remind him/her that these phones are for use *only* during breaks, lunch, or emergencies.

10. What the employee should do if he/she is going to be absent or tardy for work. "It is the responsibility of the *employee* to call *prior* to the beginning of the shift and notify the Supervisor or the assistant manager on duty. Do not leave a message with anyone else."

11. Visitors must remain at the employee entrance area when waiting for him/her to get off duty.

12. Point out where it is permissible to smoke.

13. Safety—point out in his/her work area where fire hoses, extinguishers and emergency exits are located, how to report a fire emergency, what he/she should do in an emergency, etc., and review fire procedures. Advise of required safety equipment.

14. Each department has a Hazards Communication Manual called Material Safety Data Sheet (MSDS). Please consult this manual before using any chemical; stress the importance of safety and hazardous materials that is "*Your right to know.*"

15. Explanation of open-door policy with regards to work problems, misunderstandings with fellow employees or management, etc.

16. An employee orientation is scheduled on _____. Explain the importance of this meeting. Attendance is mandatory.

17. Give the name of President and GM.

18. Remind him/her not to store valuables in lockers.

19. Explanation of which positions or departments he/she could be promoted into after probation period.

20. Where and when he/she should get his/her paycheck and what to do if there appears to be an error in pay.

21. Explanation of departmental policies.

22 Functions of the department.

EXHIBIT 14-3   First Day of Employment Checklist

23. Relationship of the department to other departments

24. The different kinds of jobs performed in the department.

25. Where his/her work originates and where it goes.

26. The importance of his/her particular job.

27. The quality and quantity of work expected—establish minimum production standards.

28. Give a copy of his/her job description.

29. Explanation of lines of authority (from whom he/she should and should not take orders).

30. To whom should he/she report in his/her manager's absence.

On-the-job training should begin! Good luck!

I have covered the 30 points outlined above on _____ with
                                                   date

_____ .
    Employee's name

The items listed above and also where to go if I have additional questions have been explained to me and I fully understand.

_____
    Manager's Signature

_____
    Employee's Signature

EXHIBIT 14-3   First Day of Employment Checklist (continued)

employee's departmental manager and supervisor to discuss the new employee's performance. The results of the meeting are documented by a performance review form used to assess the new employee's job performance.

This is an example of specific control of management action. While these controls do somewhat limit how managers perform their duties, their intent is to standardize new employee indoctrination and improve the chances of employee retention. As will be discussed in the next section, hotels also employ various results measures in the personnel area that help assess the effectiveness of specific-action controls.

Systems of Specific-Action Controls

Complex organizations like major hotels devise a number of control procedures that simultaneously engage large numbers of employees and managers.

All the right touches at the piano lobby lounge of the Hotel Inter-Continental, New Orleans.

Courtesy: Hotel Inter-Continental New Orleans

These systems of specific-action controls are needed because in many circumstances hotels must devise methods of coordinating the activities of a large number of employees, often from different functional departments. An example of a specific-action control system is the emergency procedures a hotel needs to have in place in case of a fire, one of the worst possible emergencies a hotel can face. The fire procedure for one hotel in the GM study is a detailed, seventeen-page document that proscribes the behavior of all employees and managers. The procedure begins with detailed instructions for all of the hotel's staff, employees, and management should a fire be discovered. Specific-action steps begin as follows:

- Any staff member suspecting or discovering a fire should immediately pull the alarm at the nearest fire alarm box and also call the telephone operator, giving your name and the exact location of the fire.
- Upon notification of a fire, *regardless of how small*, the telephone operator must call the fire department immediately.

• If the fire is small, secure a fire extinguisher and proceed immediately to put out the fire if you have been properly trained to use the equipment.

The document goes on to describe the makeup of the hotel's fire brigade, including its chain of command (very important during an emergency), the equipment to be used, and detailed instructions on how each member should react. For example, if the fire is large enough to require the hotel's evacuation, the fire brigade's commander is instructed as follows:

. . . The ranking member will advise the hotel's assistant manager and the telephone operator. He will then activate the public address or the general alarm of the Voice Evacuation System or sound the general alarm at the nearest fire alarm box.

Additional detailed procedures and instructions are proscribed for the telephone operator, the engineering department, the assistant manager on duty, the front office manager, the front office cashier, housekeeping, the bell staff, and all other departments. For example, the housekeeping floor supervisor is instructed to verify that guest rooms are empty and that doors are closed; the bell captain will direct bellpersons and doorpersons to be stationed at elevators and stair landings to help with the evacuation of guests and staff; the operating engineer will activate fire pumps, shut off boilers, air handlers, and the main gas valve, and stand by in the engine room for further instructions.

Fire procedures are a dramatic example of a situation where few would object to detailed specific-action controls. However, whenever management feels that it has excellent knowledge of which specific actions of individuals or groups would be in the best interest of the hotel, it should consider developing specific-action controls to improve performance. These types of controls will be particularly effective if performance can be easily measured, but even if performance measures are less than perfect, specific-action controls may still be useful.

Direct Supervision as a Form of Specific-Action Controls

From a control perspective, the object of direct supervision is, like all forms of control, to cause events to come out as the organization wishes. The supervisor's job is to anticipate problems and take corrective action in time to control outcomes. A future orientation directs management's attention to those aspects of employee behavior that will affect desired outcomes, even if these outcomes are not easily measured. Direct supervision requires diligence and, above all, patience. It is, as discussed in previous chapters, a form of teaching that, at its best, solves potential problems before they occur.

PERSONNEL CONTROL: GETTING PEOPLE TO DO THE RIGHT THINGS

While specific-action controls can go a long way, complex service organizations like hotels must rely on individual employees to do, on their own, the kinds of things that are best for the hotel. Outstanding hotel managers pay close attention to the techniques of personnel control. As learned in Chapter Twelve, personnel-control techniques include: (1) developing strategies for upgrading the capabilities of employees and managers, (2) being very good at communicating the goals of the organization, and (3) fostering shared goals and values throughout all groups within the hotel. This section describes a number of programs that do just that. These examples were excerpted from hotels that took part in the GM study.

Telephone Training: Simple Training for a Critical Skill

Everyone has a favorite story of rude, confusing, or unprofessional telephone behavior. Hotels have a particularly difficult problem in this regard because of the different ways guests and potential guests can access a hotel by phone. It is critically important that hotels do everything possible to control this aspect of guest-employee interaction. However, close control of either specific actions or results is difficult. In other words, hotels find it difficult to measure the results of this important service dimension in either a very accurate or a very timely way. Hotels must, therefore, rely on training, communication, and shared employee goals and values when it comes to ensuring proper telephone procedures (Feiertag 1988).

Many of the outstanding hotels studied have instituted telephone training programs as part of their overall control strategy. The preface to one such training program does a nice job of explaining the importance of proper telephone procedures within the broader context of guest relations and clarifying the hotel's expectations in this regard.

> Each of us holds down two jobs, the one for which we are employed and also a job as a public relations person for the hotel. Hotels deal with the public and, therefore, hotel employees are usually required to go through a training program to ensure the proper handling of customers and potential business. It's equally important for employees who deal with customers through another method of communication—the telephone.
>
> This program will help you develop good telephone habits. Remember, what you put into one end of a phone comes out the other! Your words and ways influence customers' feelings about you as an individual and about the hotel. Our customers will continue to count on you and feel positive about the hotel if your telephone manners are courteous and efficient, and if you take a personal interest in the caller.

A telephone training brochure explains the usual procedures to follow to handle phone calls efficiently, courteously, and professionally. Among the training tips are the following:

- Treat every message as important and not routine.
- Always identify yourself by name when answering or placing a call.
- Personalize calls by using the caller's name, preceded by Mr., Mrs., or Miss.
- When taking messages, be sure to include

  the caller's name (spelled correctly),

  the caller's firm,

  the caller's phone number, including area code,

  date and time of the call,

  your name.
- When the call ends, thank the caller before saying good-bye.
- When placing a call, stay on the line to be ready to greet your party. This avoids delay and resentment, and demonstrates respect and courtesy to the person you are calling.
- Answer the telephone promptly; on the first ring if possible.
- Speak in a courteous and interested manner.
- Hang up gently; slamming the phone down causes an unpleasant noise in the receiver.

Numerous other tips are given. They are all contained in an attractive brochure that includes a checklist for employees to grade their performance. Training sessions are held for new employees, periodic follow-up training is done for all employees who have access to phones, and managers are instructed to correct improper phone usage whenever observed. The latter strategy is an example of specific-action control supervision. With continual training, communicating, and follow-through the hotel hopes that its employees, on their own, will come to perform instinctively when it relates to correct telephone procedures.

Guest-Relations Training

No hotel can directly monitor or control the hundreds of employee–guest contacts that occur each day. Since a hotel must rely on its employees to do the right thing it must employ effective personnel-control strategies to accomplish many of its guest-contact goals. Most of the outstanding hotels studied had developed some form of guest-relations training to help in this regard.

The topics covered in a particularly good guest-relations program are shown in Exhibit 14-4. This training is given to all new employees and repeated periodically for all guest-contact employees. Training is conducted by operating department heads with heavy guest-contact exposure, such as

---

1. INTRODUCTION
   - What hospitality and service meant in the past.
   - Why it is important today.

2. WHAT WE ARE TRYING TO ACCOMPLISH
   - The kind of hotel we are.
   - Why *your* ability to provide outstanding guest service is so important.

3. KNOW YOUR PRODUCT
   - Review of our hotel's services.
   - Review of local attractions, restaurants, shopping areas, nightspots, transportation, and other hotels.
   - Know Your Product quiz.

4. GUEST SERVICE FILM AND DISCUSSION
   - The "Dos" and "Don'ts" of guest service.

5. OUR HOTEL'S ORGANIZATION
   - Knowing how the hotel works allows you to provide better guest service.

6. HANDLING GUEST COMPLAINTS
   - Turning negatives into positives.

7. OUR "ALL-OUT EFFORT" GUEST SERVICE PROGRAM

Exhibit 14-4.   Guest Service Equals Guest Satisfaction Training Manual Outline

food and beverage, and rooms—not by the personnel department. The GM personally covers topics one and two, "Introduction," and "What We Are Trying to Accomplish," with regard to guest service. His presence and involvement is meant to underscore the great importance the hotel places on guest service. Topic three, "Know Your Product," is meant to be educational. Employees are given a quiz to test their factual knowledge of the hotel and the community so they can answer typical guest questions. Employees are taught the answers to some unusual questions in this hotel. Over time it has been noticed that guests often have questions about the local food. All guest-contact employees are, therefore, taught the difference between Cajun and creole cuisine. That's a nice touch; it's something that guests will remember long after their stay. While it's a little thing, it demonstrates to the hotel's employees the kind of caring attitude for its guests that the hotel wants to

Helpful doorman giving directions to guests at the San Fransico Marriott Hotel.

Courtesy: Marriott Hotels, Resorts and Suites

foster. It's the attitude that's important, not the distinction between these two forms of cooking.

The guest-service film of topic four is a humorous account of a hotel guest encountering a series of ill-trained and unprofessional hotel employees. Each badly handled guest encounter is followed by an explanation of the correct way to handle the situation. Importantly, the film is presented from the guest's point of view, and the discussion with management that follows reinforces the importance of understanding the guest's viewpoint. It is pointed out that guests have insecurities and frustrations upon entering an unfamiliar hotel, and the hotel's employees can reduce these feelings through their thoughtful behavior. This portion of the seminar ends with employees and the seminar leader developing a list of "Do's" and "Don'ts" of employee behavior that are derived from the film, examples of which are given in Table 14-6. This kind of suggested behavior is then reinforced when the group is asked to develop a profile of the characteristics of an effective guest contact employee.

The overall organization of the hotel, including the specific functions of each department, is reviewed in topic five. This kind of basic knowledge improves each employee's ability to coordinate his or her actions and thereby provide better guest service.

Topic six deals specifically with how to handle guest complaints. Properly handling guest complaints is critically important to a hotel. It's inevitable that things will go wrong in any hotel. How problems are resolved, therefore, can make the difference between a satisfied and a dissatisfied guest. The seminar leader presents a step-by-step process for employees to follow when a guest makes a complaint. The process is based on transactional analysis ideas. The goal of the employee is to solve the guest's problem and at the

TABLE 14-6.   "Dos" and "Don'ts" When Interacting with Guests

DO

- Greet and welcome guest upon arrival.
- Offer assistance with luggage.
- Speak to guest by name.
- Use suggestive selling of the hotel's services.
- Acknowledge presence of guest when unable to serve him/her promptly.
- Apologize when unable to assist the guest promptly.

DON'T

- Ignore guest's presence when he/she enters the hotel or restaurant.
- Question a guest.
- Argue with a guest.
- Talk about other guests.
- Make personal jokes.
- Make excuses or blame others.
- Take complaints personally.

same time defuse any hostility or anger on the guest's part. The suggested steps are:

- Listen to the guest's complaint.
- Filter through to the real problem.
- Act immediately.
- Make no promises you can't keep.
- Refer problems beyond your authority to higher authority.
- Look for something in the guest's remarks
  with which to agree.
- Give the guest your undivided attention.
- Smile, be pleasant.

Examples of how to accomplish each step are given and the group is engaged in skits and role-playing practice sessions. It is, of course, impossible to completely script an employee regarding how to react to specific complaints, and this is not the intent of this training. Its purpose, instead, is to provide the proper guidelines so that employees, on their own, can do the right thing.

The final topic of this guest-service program introduces the employees to the current hotelwide guest-service program. It's called "All-Out Effort" and consists of a series of procedures that guest-contact employees are to follow to ensure rapid follow-up and resolution of guest complaints. All-Out Effort is, in effect, a form of specific-action control. Outstanding hotels are always looking for a new twist or technique to promote service and All-Out Effort is an example of one. The All-Out Effort program is explained, including how improved guest satisfactions will be measured, and how employees who perform particularly well will be rewarded. Employees leave the seminar with the motivation to begin immediately participating in an ongoing guest-service program and applying what they have just learned.

Total Employee Training

These two examples of employee programs were presented in relationship to a hotel's control function. The two, telephone training and guest-relations training, dealt with aspects of a hotel's operation that cannot easily be directly controlled. The hotel, therefore, had to rely on employees doing, on their own, the kinds of things that are beneficial to the hotel. Any well-managed hotel can think of literally dozens of training opportunities for its employees and managers. Technical skills need to be taught to new employees. Technology is changing, so even long-time employees need to be updated. In addition, basic-skills retraining is always needed to keep people from slipping into bad habits. Many excellently managed hotels prepare an annual training plan along with their annual business plan. It is developed with the same care and broadly based input as any other important hotelwide plan (Coward 1988).

William Scully was very disturbed with the quality of The Bourbon Hotel's managerial training for young managers. He immediately saw to it that a comprehensive management-training program was developed. How, he reasoned, could young managers do the right thing if they were deficient in basic management skills. Upon finding no training plan, Henri LeSassier ordered that a detailed training plan be developed immediately, even though The Normandy Hotel was suffering sizable losses at the time. Curtis Samuel,

The renovated Omni Parker House, Boston—the oldest continuously operating hotel in America.

Courtesy: Omni Hotels

who is very organized, proudly shows visitors the inch-thick training document for his 1,000-room hotel.

These efforts do not come cheaply. A 1989 article in *Lodging Magazine* reported that the newly renovated Sheraton-Carlton Hotel in Washington, D.C., spent $500,000 for training to complement the hotel's $16 million physical renovation (Keenan 1989, 25). The training was built around a guest-satisfaction theme entitled "Bringing the Guest Back." That's a major commitment to personnel but one that is often made by outstanding hotels.

Employee Relations Programs

There is another aspect of personnel control that differs from specific skills training that is also important. These are what is often referred to as employee-relations programs. The purpose of employee-relations programs is generally to foster a common set of values and goals among employees and to provide management with a means of keeping closely attuned to employee feelings and concerns. There is no one best way to accomplish this. Previous discussion focused on MBWA. Staying close to employees is the best way of keeping unwarranted behavior from occurring. But in addition to the importance of MBWA, most outstanding hotels institute a wide variety of employee-relations programs.

One particularly well-managed hotel that took part in the GM study employed a three-phase approach to employee relations comprised of: (a) employee programs, (b) employee surveys, and (c) measures of employee health.

Employee Programs

Table 14-7 lists the variety of employee-relations programs that were active at this hotel during the GM study. Briefly review these programs to get an appreciation of what the hotel was trying to accomplish.

The Cafeteria Communications Program recognizes the fact that the employee cafeteria has the potential of being much more than just a place to eat. While the purpose of this program included providing hot, nutritious meals, it also specified the following attributes that the cafeteria should have:

• An area where the hotel's staff can relax from daily pressures.
• An area to cultivate new friendships and renew old acquaintances.
• An informal atmosphere that provides a good setting for different types of discussion.
• The main area through which information is disseminated to staff members.

To accomplish these goals the cafeteria is open fourteen hours each day,

TABLE 14-7.   Typical Employee-Relations Programs

New Employee Orientation
Employee of the Month
Employee "Cafeteria Communications"
Lunch with the GM Program
Good Grooming Awards
Employee "Sound-Off"
Staff Newsletter
Monthly Anniversary and Longevity Program
Management–Staff Personnel Service Committee
All-Out Effort Committee
Safety Bingo Program
Employee Suggestions Program
Staff Flowers and Cards Program

serves a wide variety of hot meals, sandwiches, salads and fruits, and provides these meals free of charge to full-time and part-time employees. In addition, the cafeteria contains a bulletin board for information about various employee programs and events. A rack holds the hotel's weekly newsletter, and a photo board recognizes individual employees for things such as Employee of the Month, the Good Grooming Award, cost-savings ideas, guest-compliment winners, and employment anniversary recognitions. Boxes are provided for the hotel's "Employee Sound-Off" program and the "Employee Suggestion" program. Tables are arranged for group seating because management wants employees to interact and communicate with each other. By sharing thoughts and opinions in an informal and pleasant setting it is hoped that morale will be improved and that employees will better understand what is going on in the hotel. Much care is taken to ensure that this hotel's cafeteria plays the important role of fostering informal employee communication. In fact, as will be discussed in the next section, the hotel has a program to measure how successful they are in this regard.

Many of the GMs studied realized the importance of the employee cafeteria as more than just a place for food. Bill Scully had his entire executive staff eat all of their meals there; the only exception being when they were entertaining a client. Richard James made a point of sitting with different employees each day at lunch in the employee cafeteria. Jonathan Claiborne's first act as the new GM of The Riviera was to assess the quality of food in the employee cafeteria.

The Employee "Sound-Off" program has been around for quite some time. It provides employees with an opportunity to state grievances and complaints, to make suggestions, and to present ideas while remaining anonymous. Employees simply write down their comments and place them in the "Sound-Off" box in the employee cafeteria. The comments are reviewed weekly by management and responses are communicated to all employees via the weekly hotel newsletter and the employee bulletin board. The only ground rule is that personal criticism is not allowed; this is not a name-calling contest. Nearly any topic is fair game, including pay issues, dress codes, tip distributions, promotional policies, cafeteria food, scheduling and overtime policies, and much more. Employees are encouraged to participate and management prides itself with speedy and thoughtful replies. Management calls the program an "early warning system" that can often detect minor employee problems at an early enough stage to keep major problems from developing, which makes the "Sound-Off" box a form of personnel control.

The Suggestion Program, on the other hand, is not anonymous because cash awards are given for the best ideas. Employees drop their ideas into a suggestion box located, of course, in the employee cafeteria. Suggestions are evaluated weekly by a committee of all division heads. Accepted suggestions are published in the weekly hotel newspaper along with the employee's name and award. Each employee submitting an accepted suggestion gets a letter of congratulations from the GM and a twenty dollar award. The best suggestion of the year receives a one hundred dollar award. Employees whose suggestions are rejected are advised as to why. Employees who submit accepted suggestions are also singled out at departmental meetings and other hotel awards ceremonies. While the hotel would love to get great suggestions that vastly improve guest service or cut costs, its main goals for this program are to: (1) promote employee participation in the hotel's operations, (2) stimulate creativity among the staff, and (3) provide cash incentives for employees to improve their working environment. Home runs would be nice, but the program is really designed to produce a lot of singles.

Table 14-7 listed thirteen different employee-relations programs the hotel was actively using at the time of the study. Some of these programs are permanent fixtures in any well-managed hotel. Others come and go, depending on what is needed at the time. None of these programs are perfect. Programs that sound like good ideas sometimes fail. Programs that worked in the past sometimes lose momentum and have to be discarded. It's often difficult or impossible to measure the direct results of these efforts on employee performance. Really outstanding hotels don't let these obstacles bother them in the least! Outstanding GMs, like Frank Anderson, keep coming up with new programs all the time. Some work better than others and a few don't work at all, but things are never boring. The best hotels keep at it. If the goal is to have employees do the right thing on their own, it's better to overdo personnel control than under do it.

Employee Surveys

While a hotel can never be completely sure if its employee-relations efforts foster the desired behavior, the good hotels try hard to find out what they can. One method used is employee surveys. Employee surveys are by their nature imperfect measuring devices. What management would like to measure is the way employees are behaving on their own. Are they doing things on the job that are in the hotel's best interest? Because it's impossible to measure this directly, hotels resort to employee surveys as one strategy to keep abreast of what employees are thinking.

One outstanding hotel in the GM study relies on three different surveys to provide feedback on employee issues. It should come as no surprise that one of the surveys dealt exclusively with the employee cafeteria. The survey is conducted every three months, is very detailed and gives employees every opportunity to provide comments and suggestions for improvements. As Jonathan Claiborne knows very well, problems in the employee cafeteria can affect morale and attitude, and it's attitude that helps people want to do the right thing.

A common type of employee survey solicits opinions regarding a variety of job-satisfaction issues. One of the hotels in the GM study, for example, was interested in its employees' feelings on the following topics:

- Work requirements and expectations,
- working conditions,
- relations with supervisors,
- relations with other employees,
- satisfaction with salary and benefits,
- reason(s) for continued employment, and
- adequacy of training.

Employees were asked to fill out this general questionnaire annually. They were not required to sign it.

Another hotel was very interested in their employees' relationships with their immediate supervisors, so a detailed confidential survey of employee opinions about their managers was distributed. Employee morale, attitude, and performance will, of course, be influenced to a large degree by the supervisory skills of their managers. For a sensitive survey like this, employees were told not to give their names. This three-page survey tried to measure a variety of dimensions of supervision, including such things as whether employees judged their supervisor to be fair, straightforward, truthful, dependable, understanding, and complimentary. Additional questions related to work rules, equity, employee security, pay, adequacy of supplies and equipment, and work load. One question asked if the employee liked (or disliked) working for the hotel, and why. This particular survey was distributed to all employees annually, and the hotel's GM and

Employee morale and attitudes influence performance.

Courtesy: Radisson Hotels International

executives spent many hours reviewing the results and developing plans and programs based on what they found.

Employee Turnover

Excellently managed hotels pay close attention to employee turnover. There are a variety of reasons why employees leave a job: for a better job offer, to return to school, dissatisfaction with the job or with their supervision, and lack of advancement opportunities. Hotels also terminate employees for a variety of reasons, including excessive absenteeism, inability to perform assigned duties, unsafe practices, and dishonesty. Whether initiated by the employee or the hotel, a termination often constitutes a management failure. The time and money spent hiring and training an employee is wasted whenever a termination occurs, and the entire process has to begin again. In addition to the identifiable costs of an employee termination, there are less obvious but ultimately more important costs involved: the affect excessive turnover has on the operational efficiency and the quality of guest services. Inexperienced employees make mistakes, which lower operational efficiency and increase costs. They also make service errors that cause guest dissatisfaction.

While doing preparatory research for the GM study, I stayed at a hotel that was having obvious employee and operational problems. General housekeeping throughout the hotel was poor, service was uninspired, and even as a guest, I overheard employees on a number of occasions complaining about one aspect or another of the hotel's management. While meeting with the GM, I inquired about the hotel's turnover rate. He said that he did not know what it was and called his personnel director to see if he did. It turned out that the personnel director was not sure either, but when pressed by the GM, ventured a guess of around 75 percent annually.

This conversation would not have taken place with any of the excellent GMs. They keep close track of employee turnover because it is an important indicator of how well the hotel is performing its personnel function. Looking carefully at turnover is, of course, a form of control. Lawrence Wagner keeps detailed records of employee terminations. His hotel calculates turnover rates each month. In addition to calculating overall hotel turnover, they keep separate records of terminations in thirty-six subdepartments, starting with the executive office right down to the parking garage. Every month the hotel's computers prepare a report of the number of terminations and the turnover percentage (number of terminations divided by total number of employees) for each of thirty-six subdepartments. These statistics are reviewed monthly by the GM, the personnel director, and the manager of each department. Reports are prepared outlining the reasons for hotel-initiated terminations and the results of exit interviews of employees who voluntarily terminated. The Regal Hotel's management is always looking for trends that might indicate a potentially important problem. If terminations suddenly increase in the food preparation subdepartment or at the front desk, questions are asked, termination reports and exit interviews are scrutinized, and the results of employee questionnaires are reviewed. The idea, says Lawrence Wagner, is to "nip small problems in the bud" before they can cause the hotel big problems. The idea is control and, in this case, the measure of results is employee turnover (Giridharan 1987).

CONCLUSION

It's been aptly said that the art of management, like a cattle drive in the Old West, is to "get the herd generally moving in the same direction." (Peters and

Waterman 1982). People, to be sure, are not cattle, but the analogy rings true for all organizations, large and small. This chapter dealt with two important aspects of getting people in hotels to generally move in the same direction. One related to circumstances where management imposed specific rules, regulations, and procedures for employees to follow. This strategy was called specific-action controls. The other related to strategies whose purpose was to get employees, on their own, to behave in ways that are beneficial to the hotel's goals. This strategy was called personnel control.

Specific-action controls are appropriate when management is certain that it knows how best to accomplish something. In many instances, experience is a great teacher. When Matthew Fox said that he had become "more authoritarian" over the years he was expressing the idea that experience had taught him how to react in a number of different circumstances. Part of his job, therefore, was to teach others what he had learned regarding the best way to approach certain tasks or to solve certain problems. Hotel employees and managers perform a vast array of repetitive tasks and face an equally large number of recurring problems. Through experience, management has learned how best to perform certain jobs and how best to solve certain problems. Specific-action controls are a logical outgrowth of this experience. They keep a hotel's less-experienced employees and managers from having to "reinvent the wheel" at every occasion. They foster efficiency and consistency, and they impart structure and discipline within the organization.

Specific-action control strategies apply not only to individuals but also to more complex managerial systems. Specific-action control systems are developed to respond to recurring complex operational problems. Two examples of systems of specific-action controls described in this chapter dealt with fire procedures and new-employee orientation procedures. In these examples management developed specific procedures and guidelines that had to be followed by a variety of personnel from different departments. Well-managed hotels develop a wide variety of specific-action control systems. Examples are a guest-complaint control system, a guest-disturbance response system, a breech-of-security reporting and response procedure, and an accident-response system.

Organizations can sometimes set the limits of specific-action controls so tightly that all initiative and creativity is squeezed out of employees and managers alike. When this happens organizations become bureaucracies. The worker's main objective is centered only on complying with rules and regulations. During the GM research a common complaint of departmental managers who had instituted tight control systems was that employees lacked initiative and imagination. Employees were described as unwilling to bypass the "system," as was sometimes necessary, in order to solve a problem. In this regard, management must seek a balance between control and individual worker initiative.

That balance can only be maintained by programs that seek to get a hotel's staff to do, on their own, things that are beneficial to the hotel. This entails what's been described in this chapter as personnel control, whose goal is getting people to do the right things. Hotels rely on personnel-control strategies when it is difficult to specify appropriate behavior and also when it is difficult to measure behavior outcomes. In these circumstances, hotels must have the right kinds of employees, trained as broadly as possible, who understand and accept the goals and objectives of the organization. This requires intelligent hiring, training, and group consensus building.

Personnel control was illustrated by describing a number of specific initiatives taken by outstanding hotels. Two of these programs were telephone training and guest-relations training, areas where it is important for employees to do the right things on their own. For this kind of training to be effective, it's necessary for employees to accept the goals of the hotel and to behave accordingly.

In this regard a variety of employee-relations programs were described

Effective hotels stress employee awards programs.

Courtesy: Omni Hotels

whose purpose was to foster involvement and acceptance of organizational goals. Good grooming awards, employee cafeteria surveys, suggestion awards, and employee sound-off programs have at their core the goal of influencing employee behavior. It's not always easy to measure precisely the effectiveness of these kinds of programs. Even when quantitative measures like turnover are available, it's not always obvious how to interpret the numbers. These shortcomings simply reflect the basic ambiguities of dealing with people. This "sloppiness" is accepted as a fact of life in well-managed hotels. Rather than being a cause of frustration, excellent hotels respond with a wide variety of programs, training, contests, awards, and employee questionnaires. The goal is to cover all bases and to err on the side of too many initiatives rather than too few. A common saying in advertising is that a company usually wastes half of its advertising budget, but does not know which half of the budget is wasted. The same might be aptly said regarding a hotel's efforts toward personnel control.

It's important to remember that the employee programs discussed in this chapter dealt with a hotel's control function. When viewed from the control perspective these programs take on their proper focus. In this light, it becomes clear that the personnel programs discussed in this chapter represent management's continuing effort to meet the operational goals of the hotel.

REFERENCES

Coward, Jude. April 1988. "Six Banner Ideas in Recruiting, Training." *Lodging* 13(8):33–34.

Feiertag, Howard. November 1988. "Properly Handled Phone Calls Can Ring up Bigger Profits." *Hotel & Motel Management* 203(16):A-34.

Giridharan, Jiri. Fall 1987. "Managing Employee Turnover in the Hospitality Industry." *FIU Hospitality Review* 5(2):26–32.

Keenan, Kathleen 1989. "A Cool Half Million for Training Creates Warm Luxury." *Lodging* Vol. 15, No. 4:25–26.

Lasley, Del. June 1987. "Training Programs that Pay Big Dividends." *Executive Housekeeping Today* 8(6): 9–11.

Peters, Thomas J. and Robert H. Waterman, Jr. 1982. *In Search of Excellence*. New York: Harper & Row, Publishers.

Weinstein, Jeff. 1989. "Labor: Operators Work to Bring Absenteeism Under Control." *Restaurants & Institutions* 99(26):28–29.

QUESTIONS

14-1. Develop three separate specific-action control policies that direct employee behavior in areas where you feel you know best how employees should behave. Once you have finished this exercise, have it reviewed by at least three different people.

14-2. Go to a local hotel and secure copies of their employee manual, policies and procedures manual, and other documents relating to specific-action control. Evaluate these documents along the critical dimensions that pertain to the appropriateness of specific-action controls.

14-3. In what sense are personnel-control strategies the line of last defense in a hotel's control plan? On the other hand, in what sense is personnel control the obvious first strategy a hotel should consider?

14-4. Comment on whether there is an inherent contradiction between the concepts of specific-action controls and personnel control.

14-5. How will you know if you have gone too far with specific-action controls?

14-6. How do you control for the unexpected?

14-7. Outline three employee-development programs that you feel would be particularly important in hotels, as well as how you would try to "measure" their effectiveness.

CHAPTER 15

The GMs' Background and Personal Characteristics

One of the reasons why biographies and autobiographies of important and successful people are so popular is because of the insights these books give about their subjects. People are fascinated to learn about the backgrounds, upbringings, and personalities of important and famous people. More importantly, they form an important background that helps us understand how these people became what they were and why they acted and behaved as they did.

This book has as its major theme a description of what successful and effective hotel GMs do to manage their hotels. Just as your understanding of what Lincoln and Roosevelt did as presidents is enhanced by knowledge of their background and personality, your understanding of what successful hotel GMs do will be enhanced by knowledge of their backgrounds and characteristics. In reading this chapter, you should begin to make two important comparisons:

1. Compare the GMs' backgrounds and characteristics to your own, and
2. Analyze why they manage as they do in light of their background and characteristics.

These are two very important mental exercises to engage in if you want to be a successful hotel executive. By engaging in these exercises you will gain a better understanding of the kinds of people who succeed in the hotel business and why they manage as they do. You will also begin to form a role model of success that, when compared to what you know about yourself, will enable you to begin a self-development program that is critical to a successful career.

The chapter is divided into two major sections: a review of the GMs' backgrounds and comments on their personal characteristics.

The GMs' Backgrounds

The GMs' Basic Demographics

Table 15-1 summarizes the basic demographics of the ten GMs. The average age of these experienced GMs was just over forty-four. The two youngest were both thirty-nine and the oldest was fifty-two. Five of the ten were forty-two or younger. All were married; two have been married twice. They all lived very stable family lives. Each had children, but none had large families; only two GMs' had three children, and those were the two who had been married twice. Eight of the ten GMs' wives did not work outside of the home. In only one case did a GM's wife have a full-time career. Matthew Fox's wife owned and operated a number of women's clothing stores. In all other cases the GMs' wives were fully occupied with family matters.

Six of the GMs were Americans, two were French, one Swiss, and one German. Of the six who had served in the military, three were officers. Four of the GMs' fathers were college graduates, two being engineers, one a scientist, and one an M.D. Only Henri LeSassier's mother had finished college. Richard James' mother had completed two years of college, while all the others had completed high school. Two fathers owned their own businesses. Interestingly, only Jonathan Claiborne's father had been in the hospitality industry, having been a chef for 55 years. None of the GMs were only children, but only one had as many as three brothers and sisters.

The conclusion to be drawn from this profile and from numerous conversations with the GMs and their subordinates is that they are a group of stable, family-oriented individuals who were products of stable, middle-class families. In conversations with the GMs and their subordinates it was obvious that they were also devoted family men. They appeared to lead lives of moderation and had few vices. One did not drink at all and the others were light social drinkers. Only one was a smoker. None were particularly overweight.

Formal Education

Table 15-2 describes the GMs' formal education and extracurricular activities while in school. All ten were college graduates, the Europeans having all attended hotel schools in Europe. Three of the Americans majored in business: two in accounting and one in finance. Two of the U.S. GMs were science majors, while one majored in history and English. Five of the GMs

TABLE 15-1. The GM Demographics

Name	Age	Marital Status		Children	Wife Work	Nationality	Military Service	Parent's Education		Siblings
		Married	Times					Mother	Father	
Frank Anderson	44	Yes	2	3	Part-time	U.S.	No	High School	Grammar School, Commercial Artist	2
Godfrey Bier	45	Yes	1	2	No	German	No	No Answer		1
Jonathan Claiborne	40	Yes	1	2	No	French	Yes	High School	Technical School, Chef	1
Matthew Fox	51	Yes	2	3	Yes	U.S.	Yes	High School	Grammar School, Businessman	3
Richard James	42	Yes	1	2	No	U.S.	No	2 Yrs. College	High School, Farmer	2
Henri LeSassier	39	Yes	1	1	No	French	Yes	B.S. Music	Medical Doctor	2
Curtis Samuels	40	Yes	1	1	No	U.S.	Yes	High School	B.S. Science	1
William Scully	39	Yes	1	2	No	U.S.	No	High School	B.S. Engineer	1
Lawrence Wagner	52	Yes	1	2	No	Swiss	Yes	High School	B.S. Engineer	2
Bruce Warren	51	Yes	1	2	No	U.S.	Yes	No Answer		2

TABLE 15-2.   Formal Education

Name	Formal Education	Class Standing	Honors and Awards	Extracurricular Activities	Part-time Work While in School
Frank Anderson	B.S., Finance, Advance Management Program	Unknown	Not Given	Athletics	Not Given
Godfrey Bier	European Hotel School Degree	Probably Top 1/3	Not Given	Not Given	Extensive Hotel Work
Jonathan Claiborne	European Hotel School Degree	1st in Class	Valedictorian	Sports, Head of Band and Theater	Hotel and Restaurant Work
Matthew Fox	B.S. in Accounting	Not Known	None	Not Given	Various jobs Including Waiter
Richard James	B.A., History and English	Top 10%	None	Student Government President	None
Henri LeSassier	European Hotel School Degree, M.S. in U.S. Hotel School	1st in Class, "A" Average in M.S.	Best in Class	Not Given	Hotel and Restaurant Kitchen Work
Curtis Samuels	B.S., Biology M.S., Hotel Management	Top 1/2 First in M.S. Class	Graduate Honors Society	None as Undergraduate, Graduate Student Body President	Extensive Hotel Work
William Scully	B.S. in Physics and English	Top 5%	Excellence in Philosophy	Junior Class President, Student Council—4 years, Other Student Government Activities	Extensive Hotel Work
Lawrence Wagner	European Hotel School Degree	Top 1/3	None	Sports	Extensive Hotel Work
Bruce Warren	B.S. in Accounting	Not Given	Not Given	Not Given	Not Given

graduated in the top one-third of their class or higher; two were first in their class, one was in the top 5 percent and another in the top 10 percent. Those who did not know their class standing had attended top notch institutions and one had graduated from the advanced management program of a prestigious Ivy League University. While not knowing his class standing, Godfrey Bier had a *B+* average in college and was probably in the top one-third of his class. Two of the GMs, Claiborne of France and Scully of the United States, seem to have been model undergraduates. They both earned top grades, had extensive student leadership positions, won numerous awards and found time to engage in diverse part-time hotel work. Others, like Richard James, Matt Fox, Frank Anderson, and Bruce Warren, showed little or no evidence that they would end up as hotel managers.

All but one had either engaged in substantial extracurricular activities *or* had worked quite a bit while in college. The one exception, Bruce Warren, had declined to give specifics concerning this aspect of his background, but his record of important civic activities while a GM was truly extensive. While all of the European GMs had considerable hotel work experience while in school, only two of the six American GMs reported the same. Two of the GMs, Henri LeSassier and Curtis Samuels, had pursued masters degrees in the United States, both in hotel management.

What emerges from this profile is a group of bright, academically successful individuals who engaged in a variety of outside activities while in school. While some were top students, others had only average college careers. In discussing their college careers, none dwelled on their accomplishments or awards. Nor did any of them attribute their success as hotel managers to superior intellect, with the possible exception of Henry LeSassier. While they thought of themselves as bright, this fact alone seemed to have little influence on their assessment of their strengths as hotel managers. In fact, Richard James, who had an outstanding undergraduate record, commented that, "Brains alone will not get one very far in the hotel business."

Strengths and Weaknesses of the GMs' Formal Education

While the GMs did very little bragging about their educational accomplishments, they did have some rather revealing comments to make about the importance of what they learned. Generally speaking, the Europeans valued the technical hotel skills and the discipline they learned from their rigorous training. They felt deficient, however, with their training in business topics such as finance and marketing. They all praised the language skills they learned in Europe. Lawrence Wagner, however, felt that the "classic European assumption" of authoritarian management that he learned in school had not served him well. He felt that his schooling had neglected the human-relations and management skills that he needed to be an effective GM.

The Americans with business degrees felt that the analytical skills they learned in accounting and finance had benefitted them, but Matt Fox felt deficient in foreign languages. The three Americans with science or liberal arts educations felt that they had been helped by being broadly educated. William Scully, however, admitted to some gaps in business topics. Only Frank Anderson regretted that he had not studied harder in college but, nevertheless, felt that he had learned how to set priorities. Curtis Samuels, an American with an undergraduate degree in biology and Henri LeSassier, a Frenchman with a European hotel-school degree, both attended the same U.S. hotel school for their masters degrees. Samuels, who admitted to pushing himself in graduate school, thought his graduate education was great. LeSassier was disappointed, commenting that American students were only working for "grades and a good job."

Choice of a Hotel Career

All four of the Europeans made firm hotel-career choices before entering college and continued in that career after graduation. This is surely a consequence of their culture and the nature of educational choice in Europe. In contrast, only William Scully among the six Americans made a conscious career choice in favor of hotel management while in college, even though his majors were physics and English. The father of one of his friends was a hotel executive, and Bill had been working part-time in hotels while in college. He liked the work, and after talking with his father, grandfather, and his friend's father about a career in hotel management, determined that was what he would do. Throughout the remainder of his college years he systematically worked at various hourly hotel jobs to gain experience. Upon graduation he went with the same company he had been working for in college; he's been with them ever since and is now an executive vice-president.

The other Americans found their way into the hotel business partly by chance. Curtis Samuels, though he had worked in hotels while in college, never considered a career in hotels until he watched the movie *Hotel* on TV. Matt Fox liked hotels, was unhappy in public accounting, but had never thought of working in hotels until a friend mentioned that there was an accounting opening at a Washington, D.C. hotel. Bruce Warren had audited hotels for years as a CPA. In time he began to dislike public accounting and jumped at the chance of becoming a hotel controller. Frank Anderson went from an airline sales job to a hotel sales job without ever thinking that the move would result in a lifelong love affair with hotels. Richard James was not making enough money as a school teacher and took a hotel job primarily to better himself financially.

An attractive business center at a Homewood Suites Hotel

Courtesy: General Hotels Corporation

These Americans all finished college before the great expansion of hotel schools in this country took place and also before the widespread exposure to careers in the hospitality industry. It's likely that more young American men and women will decide on hotel careers early in life and pursue specialized college programs in hotel management. In that regard Americans may be moving somewhat closer to the European model of career choice. Still, it is important to point out that outstanding hotel GMs will probably always come from a wide variety of educational backgrounds. Success in hotel management will never be dictated solely by educational background nor will opportunities be limited only to those who pursue specialized training.

Types of Experience and Career Progression

It is important that ambitious young hotel executives get the kind of experience that will help them qualify for higher level jobs. Thus, the career paths of successful hotel GMs should provide useful knowledge to the ambitious. Table 15-3 provides a summary of the ten GMs' career paths. To

TABLE 15-3.   GM Career Paths

	Age at Which		Years to GM	Types of Hotel Experience	Resident Manager Experience	Years a GM	Number of Hotels Managed
	Hotel Career Began	Became GM					
Frank Anderson	25	31	6	Sales, Rooms, Housekeeping	Yes	13	5
Godfrey Bier	20	39	19	Nightclub, Food and Beverage	Yes	7	1
Jonathan Claiborne	24	36	12	Food and Beverage	Yes	4	2
Matthew Fox	27	34	7	Operations Analyst, Accounting	No	17	1
Richard James	25	36	11	Food and Beverage	Yes	6	3
Henri LeSassier	24	34	10	Food and Beverage	Yes	5	3
Curtis Samuels	30	31	1	Only as a Resident Manager	Yes	9	4
William Scully	22	33	11	Food and Beverage	No	6	2
Lawrence Wagner	22	35	13	Food and Beverage	No	17	3
Bruce Warren	35	40	5	Accounting	No	11	1

begin with, note that on average it took about 9.5 years of full-time hotel experience for these executives to land their first GM jobs. Godfrey Bier took the longest, nineteen years, but there were extenuating circumstances. For two of those years he worked as a cruise ship steward. He then immigrated to the United States and for five years worked primarily in nightclub operations. He began his full-time career at only twenty years of age, the youngest of any of the ten. Factoring these circumstances into his career path brings his years to GM into line with most of the others. The case of Curtis Samuels is, of course, unusual. He began his career after college as a resident manager and became a GM one year later! This exceptionally rapid rise can be explained by his five years as a combat officer in Vietnam, graduating first in his hotel management masters program, his considerable work experience in hotels as an undergraduate, and his natural aggressiveness and obvious capabilities as a leader. Bruce Warren's career history is also somewhat atypical. After a thirteen-year career in public accounting, specializing in auditing hotels, he took a position, at thirty-five, as the controller of an independent hotel. Within five years he was promoted to GM. For his last two years as the hotel's controller he was being groomed as its next GM.

In every other case these executives gained substantial hotel operating experience before becoming GMs. While Frank Anderson first became the GM of a small hotel six years after entering the hotel business, he later spent a two-year stint as the resident manager of his company's flagship hotel before being promoted to GM of a larger property. Although Matthew Fox rose to GM of a major hotel in only seven years, he had experience in three different hotels before that and, as an operations analyst, had gained considerable knowledge of the workings of each hotel department. Thus, it typically takes fast-tracking, extremely competent individuals eight to twelve years to becomes GMs. With the exception of Curtis Samuels, all had substantial experience as department heads before being promoted to GM.

It's also interesting to note the age at which these executives first became GMs. Except for Bruce Warren, who had spent thirteen years in public accounting and became a GM at age forty, the other nine became GMs while still in their thirties. Frank Anderson and Curtis Samuels were the youngest at thirty-one, while most of the others were in their midthirties. Hotel companies seem willing to confer the responsibility of chief operating officer (GM) of their primary profit centers (hotels) to relatively young executives who have proven themselves in the business for about a decade.

What is the importance of the job of resident manager in the career paths of these GMs? In particular, is the resident manager's job a critical step to becoming a GM? Six of the ten GMs had been resident managers during their careers, but two cases were exceptional circumstances. Remember that Curtis Samuels started as a resident manager and was a GM within a year. In the case of Frank Anderson, he had already proven himself as the manager of two hotels before his two-year tour as resident manager of a 2,000-plus-room hotel. Four other managers (Claiborne, LeSassier, Bier, and James) served tours as resident managers before being promoted to their first GM position. Excluding Curtis Samuels' atypical career path, five of the remaining nine executives had been promoted to GM without first having served as resident managers. Clearly, their qualifications to be GMs were based primarily on their performance as division heads.

This point is made even clearer by an examination of the four remaining executives who served traditional tours as resident managers. All four had advanced through the ranks in food and beverage positions. Three of the four (Claiborne, Bier, and James) stated that they had already been slated for GM jobs by their companies before being assigned positions as resident managers. Once Claiborne proved himself as food and beverage director of his company's largest food volume hotel, he was told that he would soon be promoted to GM. The same was true for Bier, who worked for a very small chain with limited GM openings. After success as a food and beverage director, he was groomed for one year in a variety of positions at the chain's flagship hotel. He then became resident manager for four years under the company's most senior GM, assuming his job upon the senior executive's retirement. Richard James was given the opportunity as resident manager to gain rooms division experience prior to becoming a GM. For Henri LeSassier, the resident manager's position appears to have been a proving ground after which his company decided on his qualifications to be a GM.

Thus, all of the GMs except one had already been chosen as future GMs before being rotated into the resident manager's position. They could, of course, have hurt or even ruined their prospects for promotion by subpar performances as resident managers. The important point, however, is that their companies had made the critical decision to promote them to GM based on their job performance as division heads! Proving themselves as division heads was, therefore, the key career accomplishment that lead to promotion to GM. The resident manager's job, while important, was only an intermediate step to broaden these executives' prospectives on the way to the top job. Their promotions to GM had been assured by outstanding performances as division heads.

Major Career-Decision Points

All executives face key career decisions. How these decisions are made can often make or brake their future. Each of the ten GMs could pinpoint important decisions in their careers that shaped their future. Understanding the kinds of decisions that are critical to a career will help you make the right choice when these important choices occur.

Frank Anderson quit corporate life for about a year. He became the owner–operator of a small country inn and restaurant. During that time he really "learned what it meant to run a business, worry about cash flow and meet payrolls." Since then he has never forgotten that he is running a business and that he is "out of a job" if the hotel he manages is not profitable. Bruce Warren was successful but unhappy in public accounting. Taking a hotel controller's job made all the difference in the world. Now, for him, "every day is wonderful." The turning point in Lawrence Wagner's career took place when, at age thirty-three, he became food and beverage director of a prestigious hotel in Washington, D.C. In that capacity he had many opportunities to stage banquets and receptions for some of the most powerful and influential people in America. Soon after going to Washington,

Lawrence met with the director of the FBI about a reception the Director was planning. By his own admission, Lawrence was "scared stiff" during the whole meeting. Slowly, his confidence began to build as he dealt with more and more Washington VIPs. Within a year, Lawrence was convinced that he was doing an outstanding job as food and beverage director. More importantly for his future, success in that job and his association with those powerful people in Washington gave him the confidence he needed to be the GM of a major hotel. This ambition had not in the past occurred to him. From that point on, he began preparing himself to become a GM. One year later he succeeded in that goal, and has been a GM for the last seventeen years! It's also worth noting that he moved directly from food and beverage director into a GM's job without a tour as resident manager.

Henri LeSassier's key career decision was to leave a company with which he had lost trust. After many years with the same company, he said that the decision was "like getting a divorce." While working in Africa, Henri got caught in a local uprising and for a while was a captive of one of the warring factions. The company never informed his wife, who at the time was on another continent, of what was occurring. The incident caused both husband and wife to loose faith in the company and led within a few months to his resignation. It was a tough decision because he had spent his entire career with that company. Once the bond of trust was broken, however,he felt that his ability to be totally committed had been destroyed forever. At the time he resigned he was on the verge of being promoted to his first GM's position.

William Scully's key career decisions have all involved consideration of other people. He turned down one promotion opportunity because it would have entailed extensive travel while his children were very young and nearly refused another promotion because of family concerns. In another instance he continued as food and beverage director of a hotel for a year longer than was best for his career as a personal favor to the GM. Turning down promotions for personal and family reasons is often considered a good way to end a corporate career. This was not so for Bill Scully. He was promoted to executive vice-president of his company at the age of forty-one. Contrary to popular belief, nice guys do not always finish last.

It's hard to fast-track much faster than Curtis Samuels, so obviously one of his key career decisions was to accept a resident manager's job right out of graduate school. He also changed companies a few years later in order to join what he termed "a high-quality company with a better reputation." While Samuels is certainly ambitious, he recently turned down a promotion to vice-president because the position entailed much travel, and his wife was going through a difficult pregnancy. He shrugged off the decision as an easy one "as long as you have your priorities straight." This sounds like something Bill Scully might have said.

After spending many years managing nightclubs, Godfrey Bier's big break came when he got a job as food and beverage director. Today he quickly admits that this was the turning point in his career. After two successful years as food and beverage director, his company began grooming him for GM. Had he stayed as a nightclub manager for another four or five years, where he was comfortable and where the money was certainly good, he may have forever been cast in that role.

Richard James was "making a lot of money and enjoying a great social life" as a single catering manager of a large convention hotel. For some time this seemed a good enough life. After a while, however, he tired of this comfortable life and decided to set his goals at GM. To do this, "I knew I had to prove myself first as a food and beverage director," a job he said he never wanted and to which he did not look forward.

Matthew Fox has made a number of interesting decisions that have affected his career. Since he became the GM of a famous hotel at age thirty-four he has been offered numerous attractive career opportunities over the years. At one time he turned down a lucrative opportunity to manage a very large hotel because, "It was not a luxury hotel." On another occasion he refused a position at one of San Francisco's most famous hotels that would have surely lead to the GM position because he wanted to be close to his son who lived with his former wife. Fox also turned down the position of chief executive officer of a well-known hotel chain because he preferred day-to-day hotel operations. At the time of the GM research, he indicated that a continuing key decision was whether to stay with the company that had recently purchased the St. Charles Hotel. He did not seem particularly happy with some of the policies of his new corporate bosses. He has subsequently chosen to sever his long-time relationship with The St. Charles Hotel.

This story illustrates that important career decisions keep occurring during one's entire career. Lawrence Wagner, for example, recently turned down a position paying twice his current salary because at his age, "I did not want to make a move, especially since I am quite happy working for this company."

Jonathan Claiborne faced a moment of truth when, after doing an outstanding job as a food and beverage director, he was not offered an opportunity to compete for the hotel's resident manager's position when it came open. He felt he was ready to move up to GM and wanted the resident manager's job to better prepare himself for the top job. This was particularly upsetting because he felt he had been promised a chance at the resident manager's job. Even though he did not want to change companies he quickly sought out other job opportunities and was offered resident manager positions in Hong Kong and on the French Riviera. With offers in hand he confronted his superiors: "get me quickly on the GM career track I've earned, or I'll sever my ten-year association with the company." The company immediately realized it had neglected a potential star, promoted him quickly to resident manager, and in seventeen months he became a GM.

Future Ambitions

The five oldest GMs (Anderson, Bier, Warren, Wagner, and Fox) expressed no interest in any jobs higher in their organizations than that of GM. Most had turned down opportunities to move up the corporate ladder and were comfortable with that decision. They were all happy in their jobs, well compensated, and apparently content that their career ambitions had been fulfilled. Some, like Fox and Wagner, had been offered opportunities to move into high corporate positions, while Anderson had opportunities for advancement in other kinds of businesses. All had refused with little regret.

The four youngest GMs (two were 39, two 40) were more varied in their ambitions. Scully clearly had aspirations for a high corporate position. Samuels had felt the same way, but during the past year or so had begun to question whether he would be happy in a corporate position. Claiborne felt he still had "something to prove as a GM" that included being successful in his current assignment and probably one more hotel. After that he was unsure of what his future ambitions might be, except that managing a first-class hotel back in France seemed a pleasant prospect. LeSassier had already turned down a move into a corporate position, but was tiring of moving around as much as he had been. He even indicated a willingness to consider a career change outside of hotels if that were coupled with the right living conditions. James, at age 42, fell in the middle between the older and younger GMs. He was definitely averse to the politics that he felt would be inevitable if he moved into a corporate job but also believed that running a hotel was "a young man's job." His plan was to continue as a GM for "the foreseeable future" and then, as his financial circumstances dictated, to retire from the hotel business and start a business of his own. Thus, with the exception of Bill Scully, these GMs had largely met their career goals in the positions they currently held.

PERSONAL CHARACTERISTICS OF THE GM

Sizing up people is not an easy task, nor is trying to describe "typical" characteristics of classes of people like successful hotel GMs. Over generalization can disguise real differences, but concentrating excessively on differences can often cause one to lose sight of important similarities. In an effort to describe the GMs' typical characteristics, this section focuses on the following: (1) their outlooks about their jobs, and their views about life and their families; (2) their evaluations about their strengths and weaknesses and their subordinates' evaluations; and (3) opinions about their common personal traits, especially those traits that are important to their success as hotel managers.

GMs' Outlook About Their Jobs

Something unexpected happened when the GMs were asked for copies of their resumes. Four of the ten did not have resumes. Two others looked around for a while and produced extremely brief one-page sketches of themselves. The remaining four had resumes available, but none were professionally done. This lack of resumes is a good metaphor about their feelings of job security. All of the GMs exuded confidence and a sense of security. This was evident to everyone in their hotels. By the time they had reached the GM level, each had experienced enough success and been tested sufficiently so that their confidence level was extremely high. Some of the hotels they were managing were having financial difficulties. While the GMs all took very seriously the difficulties they faced, none seemed to personalize these problems into a sense of insecurity. It's impossible to be sure if they had this same confidence level earlier in their careers but they certainly displayed it in their current positions. In fact, many of them felt that the abilities and skills required to be a top-notch hotel GM were in short supply in the industry. Possessing those qualities gave them a feeling of great security. This feeling of security freed them to go about their jobs dealing only with the issues at hand without worrying about their own personal prospects.

Tough Job Decisions

Most of the GMs ranked decisions concerning people the toughest they had to make. These personnel decisions mostly concerned situations where subordinate performance fell short of expectations and decisions to transfer, demote, or terminate had to be made. Because these decisions usually had an adverse affect on a subordinate's career, the GMs found them very difficult. When the GMs discussed this aspect of their jobs, they usually elaborated on it at some length. In most cases they related very specific stories of individual subordinates, recalling numerous details of what had taken place. It was as if they were rethinking the entire incident, including their attempts to salvage the person involved. While they did not blame themselves for what happened, many did consider that they had in some way failed when subordinates failed. Only one of the ten never expressed this kind of sentiment.

Another category of tough decisions related to strategic decisions. These decisions typically dealt with large capital expenditures or changes in the hotel's basic markets or service strategy. These fundamental decisions don't occur that often and, of course, were never taken lightly. Interest-

A romantic honeymoon at the Royal Sonesta Hotel in the historic French Quarter of New Orleans.

Courtesy: The Royal Sonesta Hotel, New Orleans

ingly, these GMs usually talked longer about making personnel decisions than they did about the strategic decisions they had to make. Richard James was typical in this regard. When referring to what he called "regular business decisions," including requests for large amounts of capital funds, he shrugged these off as not particularly hard to make, referring to them as "no big deal." His approach was to "do my best most of the time and sleep well with my decisions." Having said that, he returned to a discussion of how he deals with underperforming subordinates to lessen the possibility of their failure.

Most of the GMs, in one way or the other, had changed the strategy and direction of their hotels. Often this also included a change in the organization's culture as well. While the GMs did not usually consider these decisions difficult to make, they did find them difficult to implement. When they talked about difficult decisions, they often mentioned the difficulty of getting people and organizations to change their attitudes and to adapt to new ideas and ways of doing things.

Most of the GMs mentioned a career-related decision as having been difficult. For seven of the GMs this was a decision not to take a more lucrative higher lever executive position. The typical reason for refusing higher level executive positions was that the move would have taken them away from the day-to-day operational aspects of managing a hotel. Nine of the ten treated these kinds of career decisions as just one of many tough job-related decisions. One GM, however, only listed personal career-related decisions as being difficult. He gave no indication that other job-related decisions were ever difficult for him.

Recent High and Low Points in the GMs' Lives

In most cases, the pride of accomplishing things in their hotels and the recognition they received for these accomplishments formed the high points of the GMs' careers. Only one GM failed to list a specific operational accomplishment as one of the high points of his life over the last few years. Only two GMs mentioned as high points anything about their personal career advancement. When listing high points about their hotels the GMs tended to be quite specific. They often gave examples of individual banquets that symbolized the kind of service they were striving to provide. Other sources of pride came from meeting the revenue and profit goals the hotel had set. Interestingly, while many of the GMs were quite active in civic and industry affairs, only one mentioned accomplishments in this area as a high point. Also, only one mentioned any kind of outside social activity as particularly noteworthy.

Job-related lows were much fewer than highs and pertained mostly to failure to meet the hotel's operational goals. Falling profits, a bad occupancy forecast, guest complaints, and poor employee performance were the most mentioned causes of unhappiness. Two GMs explicitly mentioned relations with corporate as a source of unhappiness. I suspect that another three GMs were experiencing corporate-relations problems that constituted a source of concern. Excluding corporate-relations problems, it is interesting to note that six of the ten GMs expressed no low points relating to the operations of their hotels. Also, only one GM mentioned financial success as a high point.

While each GM mentioned something about his job as a recent high point in his life, only half mentioned a personal or family-related incident as a high point. Four listed lows relating to their family. When one adds up the number of job-related highs and compares them to personal highs it turns out that these GMs listed job-related high points 78 percent of the time.

Likes and Dislikes of Being a GM

These successful hotel managers get enormous satisfaction from being in charge of a complex organization. They also love having enough independence to be creative and to do things their way. They enjoy the fast pace,the variety of people they interact with, and the number of different activities they engage in each day. Because the results of their efforts can often be seen rather quickly, they also enjoy the instant gratification that comes with seeing success quickly. These considerations accounted for over 71 percent of their answers. Only three of the GMs mentioned financial compensation as an element leading to job satisfaction. These outstanding GMs like the power and prestige of their jobs and thrive on the daily challenges their jobs present. They know they are good and like it when their accomplishments are recognized. Really good hotel GMs would not be very suited to staff positions, no matter how high paying. Limit their freedom of action and power, and they will be unhappy executives. Limiting the variety of their activities would also lead to job dissatisfaction. Nor would they be happy in jobs where the time between action and results was very great.

These are some of the reasons why most of these GMs have refused promotions into higher corporate positions. Moving up the corporate ladder would have removed them from the day-to-day action and excitement they so love. Recall that only William Scully had a clear goal to move into a corporate position above the GM level. Even Scully had, at one point in his career, refused a promotion into a corporate staff position because, as he put it, it would be removing him from the direct operational aspects of the hotel business.

One of the things these outstanding executives savored about their jobs was the fact that they were responsible for running a total business. If the hotel succeeded, they could and did take credit for its total success.

Their dislikes were really trivial when compared to the things they enjoyed about their jobs. Two GMs said they disliked it when people didn't perform up to expectations. This can hardly be viewed in a business like the hotel business as much more than a passing lament. Other than that, a total of only five other complaints were voiced: (1) a lack of privacy living in the hotel, (2) fear expressed by the two Frenchmen that their children would lose their national identity, (3) company politics, (4) tough personnel decisions, and (5) moving too often. To sum up, many likes, few dislikes.

Views About Family

All of the GMs seemed to enjoy stable family lives. When discussing their family lives they expressed the traditional kinds of pleasures, frustrations, and disappointments typical of all married people. The comfort of family stability, the joy of a child's birth, and the relief of a wife's safety during a civil disturbance were the sentiments they expressed. Matthew Fox, who had married for a second time, spent every Sunday, all day, with his two young sons. Two GMs scheduled a weekend family vacation every month or so just to be able to "get away from the hotel" on a regular basis. Another often arranged to bring his wife along on business trips. A number regularly planned elaborate annual family vacations to compensate for the demands of their jobs.

Eight of the GMs did not feel that the demands of their jobs had adversely affected their family lives. Bruce Warren's sentiments are typical of the group. To him, it would have required dedication, hard work, and pretty long hours to be successful in any profession or business. In that regard the demands of the hotel business were no different than any other. Henri LeSassier did feel that for a time he had allowed his "ambition" to take precedent over his family, but had remedied that problem. One of the two GMs who had been married twice did feel that his divorce had been caused by the demands of his job, but the other felt that his divorce was not related to the hotel business.

Self-evaluation

How people view themselves can be a revealing window into their personalities. In assessing their own strengths these GMs sent a clear and consistent message: people skills and a few key personal traits made them the successes they are. They felt that they understood people, were good motivators, were sensitive to people's needs, and could evaluate people well. People skills accounted for 44 percent of their responses!

For some of the GMs, their people orientation seemed to be a trait with which they were born. This was certainly true of Matt Fox who was sensitive and caring. He had a reputation for being a "soft touch" around the hotel, which was exemplified by his habit of lending money to employees in financial difficulty. He also had a tough time removing long-time employees and managers from positions in which they were performing poorly. Henri LeSassier felt his people skills had been honed at home by the influence of his mother, who was an artist, and his father, who was a physician. Bill Scully's attitudes and outlook about people derived from his father's and grandfather's insistence that he follow the Golden Rule when dealing with people. Frank Anderson's participation in team sports seemed to be the spark that shaped his outlook and approach toward developing a winning team.

For other GMs, people skills definitely had to be acquired. Lawrence Wagner admitted to struggling to overcome his authoritarian predisposition. He credited a number of management courses with helping him in this regard. Even today he admits to being somewhat uncomfortable around people. Even though he evaluates himself as very effective in his people skills, he must constantly work at it. Curtis Samuels is an unexcelled motivator. He is also an extremely caring person. Still, his subordinates feel that he has quite a bit of trouble "loosening up" around people. Recall that Jonathan Claiborne is still working on his chauvinistic tendencies toward women.

There are a number of other personal traits that these GMs feel have contributed to their success, including confidence, a good work ethic, consistency, will power, predictability, and an action orientation. These traits constituted another 36 percent of their answers. Together, these personal attributes and their people skills accounted for fully 80 percent of their answers! Problem solving and analytical skills accounted for 10 percent of the responses and professional knowledge only 5 percent.

The GMs spent little time discussing their weaknesses. The few self-described weaknesses they admitted to also centered around personal traits, accounting for 56 percent of their answers. Impatience (19 percent) and authoritarian tendencies (12.5 percent) led the list. Only two GMs admitted to any weaknesses in their professional hotel knowledge.

Others' Evaluation's

How do the executives who work closest with the GMs describe them? This question was asked of 53 of the GMs' key subordinates. It is not surprising that their answers at times reflected some of the enigmatic, contradictory characteristics of their leaders. While their views did sometimes reveal differences of opinion, a number of common characteristics were also revealed. The 53 division heads made 142 comments about their GMs as people. In addition, the subordinates made 286 comments relating to the GMs' attributes as managers, many of which bore directly on the GMs' personal characteristics. In other words, the division heads had a lot to say about their GMs.

In sorting through these subordinate responses, the most mentioned positive personal characteristic was the GMs' basic fairness. Fairness, without a doubt, was the most important personal characteristic in the minds of the GMs' subordinates. It was mentioned about nine of the ten GMs. While the GMs were often described as opinionated and sometimes stubborn, their essential fairness was recognized by the majority of their subordinates. In general, the GMs were viewed as fair both in their approach to business issues and in their dealings with people. Fairness, of course, is central to the important issue of developing subordinate trust, without which it becomes difficult for a leader to lead. Subordinates rated GMs as fair even when they were also characterized as reserved, tough, and sometimes inflexible. In fact, fairness is a trait that could reside easily alongside other less-flattering GM attributes and still result in a high degree of subordinate trust.

A second personal attribute of GMs that was commonly mentioned by subordinates was their personal consistency, calmness, control, and even temperament. Only two of the GMs were not described in this manner. This characteristic, especially when coupled with trust, engendered a sense of GM predictability that subordinates found comforting.

A third personal characteristic that was commonly attributed to GMs was concern and sensitivity toward people. Concern for people was mentioned even when the GM was also characterized as reserved and, in a number of cases, difficult to get to know. In fact, only Bill Scully was characterized as a personal friend as well as a boss. Scully was described as a person who: (1) treats people with respect, (2) gets his hands dirty, (3) is fair, and (4) can be a true friend and also make the best decision for the company. To his subordinates this combination of traits made people want to do a good job for him. While this is a powerful combination of traits, it was not common among the ten GMs. Nor was it necessary for them to be effective.

Most of the GMs were described by their subordinates as good family men. Many were also characterized as being judicious and not given to rash or unconsidered decisions. While all were considered to be opinionated and strong willed, most were also judged capable of changing their minds if approached properly. Only one GM was generally characterized as inflexible.

PERSONAL CHARACTERISTICS
OF THE IDEAL GM

A good bit of time has been spent discussing the characteristics of these ten interesting people. This section attempts to piece together the different personal characteristics that would be found in what might be called an "ideal hotel GM."

Is it possible to specify each important trait that all outstanding hotel GMs should have? Probably not. People are not averages, they are individuals. There was considerable diversity among the ten GMs. The backgrounds and personal characteristics of Bruce Warren and Lawrence Wagner, for example, are totally different. Both, however, are effective hotel managers. One must, therefore, be wary about describing ideal characteristics of people in any kind of job. Still, the exercise is worth trying. No one manager will possess equal measures of each characteristic. But, characteristics that can be shown to be important to the effectiveness of hotel managers are important to know. So the process of trying to discern important, personal, success characteristics lends insight to what it takes to be successful in the hotel business.

The discussion will focus on five separate categories of personal characteristics: needs and drives, attitudes and values, interpersonal orientation, temperament, and cognitive orientation. For each category, characteristics will be assessed according to their importance to managerial success using the following classification: Must Have, Very Desirable, and Desirable.

Needs and Drives

Table 15-4 describes the needs and drives typically found in successful hotel GMs. Above all, successful GMs have a strong desire to achieve tangible results. The two GMs whose achievement needs were most obvious were Curtis Samuels and Henri LeSassier. Samuels would actually get excited talking about how much he enjoyed the daily "opportunities" to solve problems and achieve results. In fact, he and a number of the GMs like to evaluate their performance daily. Henri LeSassier is extremely bright and has a somewhat restless personality. He enjoys his role as a hotel turnaround artist, admitting that once things get on an even keel he tends to get bored. LeSassier also is an avid tennis player. He often bragged about his skills on the court and the big matches he won.

The best of the GMs also had a strong desire for independent action. In a few instances I was able to witness GMs caught in situations in which they felt corporate policies were unduly restricting their freedom of action. When this happened the GMs became visibly unhappy, sometimes ascribing not too flattering motives to their corporate bosses. It was not that they minded being measured or judged by their superiors, they just disliked any interference that restricted their freedom to manage their hotel. Also, when the GMs praised their corporate superiors it often had to do

TABLE 15-4.   Needs/Drives of Successful GMs

	Must Have	Very Desirable	Desirable
	Achievement	Varied Activities	Power
	Independence		Prestige, Recognition
	Quick Closure		Creativity

Entrance to the Homewood Suites Hotel in Lafayette, Indiana

Courtesy: General Hotels Corporation

with being left alone to do their job rather than the help and assistance they were getting. Finally, the need for quick closure (that is, to see problems solved quickly), is an important trait for outstanding GMs. Since so many problems in hotels must be solved rapidly, a personality trait that values rapid closure is a must.

The need to be engaged in a variety of activities is listed under the "Very Desirable" category in Table 5-4. Because a GM's job is so varied, a need to be involved in a variety of activities is a definite asset.

The need for power, prestige, and recognition are viewed as "Desirable" traits and certainly some of the GMs possessed them. While desirable, these qualities are not considered critical to success as a GM. The same is true of the creative impulse. While there are countless opportunities where creativity will pay off in hotels, lack of it will not necessarily keep a person from doing an outstanding job.

Attitudes and Values

Table 15-5 describes the attitudes and values that are important for GM success. A basic sense of fairness and honesty, while important in all walks

TABLE 15-5.   GM Attitudes and Values

Must Have	Very Desirable	Desirable
Fair Minded	Competitive	Strong Family Values
Honest		
Strong Work Ethic		
Goal Driven		

of life, is indispensable to long-term success in hotels. The large number of people who work in hotels, the intensity of their interaction, and the need for their willing cooperation to provide personal services makes any hint of bias, discrimination, or dishonesty heavy baggage for a manager. While a hotel might continue operating under an unfair or dishonest leader, it's unlikely that it will ever be outstanding.

The two other "Must Have" attributes of our ideal GM are a strong work ethic and a goal-driven attitude. The fast pace and heavy demands of a hotel require a person with a strong work ethic as well as a high energy level. Outstanding GMs just keep grinding it out. They like to set business goals and are willing to expend whatever effort is necessary to accomplish them.

It's very desirable for GMs to be competitive. A competitive attitude makes people want to win and to be the best at what they do. Frank Anderson was the GM who most typified a competitive attitude. In describing his desire to succeed he said that he was "willing to step in front of a three-two pitch in order to get the job done." Finally, strong family values are a desirable trait because of the stability they provide to a person involved in a long-hour, high-pressure environment like the hotel business.

Interpersonal Orientation

As Table 15-6 shows, the only interpersonal characteristic placed in the "Must Have" category for the ideal GM is care, concern, and empathy for people. A GM's true concern for people always comes through. Matt Fox was criticized by some subordinates because of indecisiveness regarding personnel decisions. Nevertheless, his obvious concern for the hotel's employees resulted in a degree of subordinate loyalty that overcame this deficiency. Curtis Samuels is anything but a warm and cuddly person, but everyone somehow seemed to know that he had genuine concern for the entire hotel staff. It would be better, of course, if a GM possessed all of the qualities listed under the "Very Desirable" category. GMs would cer-

TABLE 15-6.   Interpersonal Orientation

Must Have	Very Desirable	Desirable
Care, Concern, and Empathy for People	Understand People	Outgoing and Gregarious
	Good People Skills	
	Coaching Skills	
	Good Listener	

tainly be more effective if they understood people very well, had good people and coaching skills, and were good listeners. These are very valuable skills to have and nearly all outstanding GMs possess them. Still, a GM cannot run a really outstanding hotel if lacking in basic empathy.

Being outgoing and gregarious is a desirable trait in the people-oriented hotel business, but it is not indispensable to managerial success. For every outgoing Frank Anderson there is a Lawrence Wagner who still has to work at his social skills. For every team sport enthusiast like Bill Scully there is a Richard James who suffers pro football games with clients because it's "part of my job," but who would much prefer a good concert or art show.

Temperament

The ideal temperament for a GM would include the qualities shown in Table 15-7. While all of the qualities listed there were seen in varying degrees in the GMs, it seems to me that the six listed as "Must Have" are needed by

TABLE 15-7.   Temperament of an Ideal GM

Must Have	Very Desirable	Desirable
Confident	Not a Worrier	Personally Organized
Self-reliant	Decisive	Positive
Detail oriented	Direct	
Action oriented		
Stable, Even tempered		
High Stress Tolerance		

great GMs. Because they are the leaders of so many people they must display confidence. Because each hotel is a separate profit center, essentially responsible for its own success or failure, self-reliance is an important quality. Each of the ten GMs were great with details and enjoyed engaging in them. Each felt strongly that it was through their attention to details that the important work of the hotel took place. Only an action-oriented person can be a great hotel manager. This is no business for lengthy contemplation. The person with an impatience to set things right will succeed; the opposite personality type will quickly fail. Because the pace of a hotel is often hectic, a stable, even temperament goes a long way toward building subordinate confidence and trust. A high tolerance for stress is indispensable; people in the hotel business without this characteristic will usually experience burnout and failure long before becoming GMs.

It's impossible not to include attention to detail in the "Must Have" category of GM traits. The majority of the GMs studied paid great attention to the hundreds of details surrounding their hotel. Some bordered on the obsessive when it came to detail. A strong detail orientation must be present in any first-class GM. Having said this, it should be noted that two of the GMs who managed extremely large hotels seemed to be particularly effective because they managed the activities of others rather than by excessive attention themselves to all of the details of the hotel.

Other very desirable qualities in a great GM include avoiding excessive worry, and being decisive and direct. Personal organization and a positive attitude are assets, but not to the same extent as other attributes listed in Table 15-7.

Cognitive Orientation

The final set of personal characteristics, listed in Table 15-8, relate to cognitive orientation. Two "Must Have" characteristics are good memories and good concentration. General managers are involved in such a variety of daily activities and deadlines that they would be lost without good memories. It was quite common for the GMs' subordinates to compliment their bosses on their outstanding memories. Because of their memories, they were very adept at following up on things. General managers also need to quickly shift their attention from one task to another since the issues they face change so rapidly.

The final cognitive orientation in the "Must Have" category for great GMs deals with an ability to be somewhat introspective, to analyze their own managerial style. Of the ten, eight indicated they had spent considerable time over the years analyzing their managerial style. They had all made serious efforts to become more effective managers. Frank Anderson, for example, had recently been ill and was forced to take time off from running the hotel. During that period he made a methodical reassessment of the

Contemporary and chic design of Laurent, a Le Meridien hotel restaurant.

Courtesy: Le Meridien Hotels, Inc.

way he had been managing for the past twenty years. Based on that evaluation, he instituted a number of changes in how he managed. Richard James and Bill Scully had well-thought-out explanations of the differences between managing midsized and large hotels that showed they had spent some time thinking about this problem. Curtis Samuels was constantly looking for feedback regarding his managerial effectiveness. For example, he quizzed me repeatedly regarding my evaluation of his management style. In most cases, these outstanding GMs had grown and changed as managers over the years, and that was because, in large part, a special kind of introspection which made them students of their own managerial effectiveness.

Good analytical skills is a very desirable cognitive trait for a GM. All ten seemed to possess quite good analytical skills, and this had helped them over the years, especially in justifying capital expenditure decisions. Analytical ability is apparently in fairly short supply among hotel executives. The ten

TABLE 15-8.   Cognitive Orientation

Must Have	Very Desirable	Desirable
Good Memory	Good Analytical Skills	Good Basic Intelligence
Good Concentration		
Introspection Regarding Managerial Style		

GMs often expressed amazement at how few of their subordinates possessed this ability.

It's desirable that GMs have good basic intelligence, but it's not at all necessary for them to be brilliant. Some of them came right out and mentioned this, while it was implicit in the comments of most. Only Henri LeSassier, it seemed to me, thought of himself as unusually bright. He told me during the course of the research that I would find him "by far" the most interesting GM I would study! He also seemed the most restless of the ten, and he questioned his suitability to manage a hotel that was not having some major difficulty.

CONCLUSION

All of the GMs came from stable, middle-class backgrounds and led stable, hard-working, middle-class lives. They all went directly to college from high school and graduated without delay or difficulty. Some were top students, others were not. Some engaged in numerous extracurricular activities, others did not. Three did not work in hotels until after their college days. What they all demonstrated in school was a record of solid success. They went to college, finished on time, and moved on into the world of work. Only one regretted he had not studied more during college. The four Europeans all attended hotel schools and made their career choices before beginning college. Only one of the Americans did so. The other five Americans found their way into the hotel business a few years after finishing college. Since these GMs' school days this trend might be somewhat different with the growth of hotel schools in the United States.

On average, it took these GMs about a decade of work in hotels before their first GM job, at which time they were usually in their midthirties. (That's moving right along!) These individuals quickly impressed their superiors with their ability and fast-tracked right up the line to GM. This is not to say that the going was always easy; it definitely was not. What it does suggest is that their careers got off to a fast start and never slacked up. Most of the GMs moved up through one functional specialty in the hotel. They proved their worthiness to be GMs by outstanding performance as division heads. While six of the ten did gain broader experience as resident managers, in five cases this promotion occurred after their performance as division heads had earned them the ultimate promotion to GM.

Like all successful executives, each of the GMs could recount a number of critical decision points in their career. An important common theme is that each of these successful GMs actively managed his career in the hotel business. None attributed their success to luck or being in the right place at the right time. Instead, their explanations of the major decision points in their careers reveal well-thought-out goal setting and career planning.

It's interesting to note that as many as nine of the ten GMs felt that their career ambitions had already been met in their current positions. Many expressed an aversion to the travel and politics that promotion up the corporate ladder would bring. More importantly, they did not want to give up the day-to-day operational duties of being a GM, which they so loved and at which they were so well suited.

In a business as competitive and sometimes unpredictable as hotels, the GMs come off as extremely confident individuals who spend very little time worrying about either the decisions they make or about the possibility of failure. While they all make important decisions that affect the financial future of their hotels, most consider this just a natural part of their jobs and not an unduly burdensome part at that. What they do consider to be tough decisions are ones that relate to people, especially those that threaten the careers of subordinates. Time and again, GMs expressed how personnel decisions were upsetting to them and how they tried their best to salvage the individual involved.

It was the pride of some hotel accomplishment that represented the high points of these GMs' lives, while their low points occurred when their hotels failed to accomplish some goal. Promotions, pay, or civic accomplishments were seldom mentioned as high points. These ten people love hotel operations and operational success or failure accounted for their highs and lows. By and large, the highs far exceeded the lows; these were people really happy in their work.

GMs are turned on by having the independence to run a complex hotel. They also like to quickly see the results of their efforts. Most would make poor staff executives, which is probably why they often refused higher level corporate positions.

These GMs displayed a high degree of family stability. They were all loving husbands and fathers whose family stability seemed to be a source of strength to them in their demanding careers.

First and foremost, the GMs viewed themselves as possessing a variety of people skills that were critical to their success in the hotel business.

The Monteleone Hotel in the New Orleans French Quarter.

Courtesy: The Monteleone Hotel

Additional personal traits they attribute to their success included confidence, a good work ethic, consistency, predictability, and action orientation.

Subordinates valued the trait of fairness in their GMs above all others. Being fair, of course, leads to subordinate trust, without which a leader cannot long lead. Consistency of action was the second most valued trait listed by subordinates. Consistency reinforces fairness in the process of building trust. The third important trait was the GMs' sensitivity and empathy toward people. It wasn't the GMs' people skills that were being admired by subordinates as much as it was their concern for people.

This chapter ventured to propose a series of personal characteristics, or traits, that might be found in an ideal hotel GM. The list of "Must Have" needs and drives would include a strong need to achieve, a need for independence, and a need for results to follow quickly from actions. The ideal GM must be fair and honest, have a strong work ethic, and be goal driven. The ideal GM would really care about the people he or she led. He or she would be confident, self-reliant, stable, even tempered, action oriented, and have a high tolerance for stress. Finally, the ideal GM would have a great memory, terrific powers of concentration, and be interested in continually improving his or her management skills.

REFERENCES

Walker, Robert G. August 1986. "Wellsprings Of Managerial Leadership." *The Cornell Hotel and Restaurant Administration Quarterly* 27:14-16.

Worsfold, Philip. 1989. "A Personality Profile of the Hotel Manager." *International Journal Of Hospitality Management* 8(1):51-62.

FURTHER READINGS

Cichy, Ronald F. and Michael P. Sciarini. June 1990. "Do You Fit this Profile of a Hospitality Leader?" *Lodging* 15(10):40-42.

Cohen, Harlew and Eric H. Neilsen. May 1988. "Finding and Developing Tomorrow's Top Managers." *The Cornell Hotel and Restaurant Administration Quarterly*:34-41.

Guerrier, Yvonne. 1987. "Hotel Managers' Careers and Their Impact on Hotels in Britain." *International Journal of Hospitality Management* 6(3):121-130.

Koepper, Ken. December 1988. "Management Effectiveness: A Hotel Industry Appraisal." *Lodging*:53-57.

Wiederhold, Arthur. January 1987. "Executives on the Rise." *Hotel & Resort Industry* 10(1):36-42.

QUESTIONS

15-1. Meet with three hotel GMs and learn about their particular career progressions.

15-2. Develop three or four detailed career progression plans for your career assuming that your goal is to become a hotel GM. Develop a series of contingency plans that take into account unexpected developments in your career.

15-3. Why do you suppose that many successful hotel GMs may want to avoid, or possibly would be unsuited for, corporate-level positions?

15-4. Draw up a detailed statement of what you consider to be your important strengths and weaknesses, personally and professionally, at this time. Compare your assessment with those of the GMs. Map out a strategy to overcome your perceived weaknesses.

15-5. If you have not already committed yourself to a career in hotel management, state clearly and concisely what additional steps you will need to take in order to make a decision.

CHAPTER 16

The Day-to-Day Activities of Outstanding Hotel Managers

The practice of management is usually classified into the various management functions of planning, organizing, directing, and controlling. Management textbooks are typically organized around these four major activities. Indeed, this book follow this approach, while adding the prospective of the hotel GM. It would be reasonable to conclude that the GMs in this study could be observed planning, organizing, directing, and controlling. One might even speculate that executives such as hotel GMs might try to plan their work day in such a way as to provide time for these four activities.

When one does peek into the daily lives of executives, as I did during the GM study and as others have done in the past (Carlson 1951, Mintzberg 1973, and Kotter 1982), one finds something quite different. Managers do not usually divide their working days into blocks of time devoted to planning, organizing, directing, and controlling. Unfortunately for the student or the young manager, things are not as clear-cut or orderly as the textbooks sometime make them seem. It's often very difficult to say if a particular activity of a manager should be classified as planning, organizing, directing, controlling, or some combination of all four or something different from these four. In fact, what managers actually do sometimes bears little resemblance to these four activities!

This chapter takes a closer look at the daily activities of hotel GMs. This book is based on detailed analysis of observations of the daily work activities of the ten executives in the GM study. This analysis will try to answer a few basic questions: What are the challenges of the GM's job in terms of key job demands and key relationship issues? What managerial roles do GMs most often play? What is the effect of information flows on how GMs manage? How does the nature of their job affect what GMs do? What do hotel GMs actually do while on the job? How do these activities help them discharge their responsibilities? Why is the way they behave on the job the most effective form of behavior?

THE CHALLENGES OF THE GM'S JOB[1]

The demands of a hotel GM's job affect the kinds of personal relationships they need to develop and the managerial roles they must play in order to be effective. Understanding these demands, and the subsequent relationships and roles GMs must play, will add to an understanding of why they act the way they do in their daily lives.

Job Demands and Relationship Demands

The first brief description concerns the key job demands and relationship demands faced by a hotel GM. Table 16-1 lists key job and relationship demands according to whether they relate to a short-run, intermediate-run or long-run time frame.

Short-Run Demands

The short-run demands of a hotel GM's job revolve around the day-to-day operational issues of quality service and control of costs and revenues. Hotel GMs have direct operational responsibility for their properties. Like all operations managers, they are under tremendous pressure to produce short-term results. They therefore must devote much of their efforts toward operational control. To accomplish this requires intense downward communication within the hotel organization itself.

Because many day-to-day hotel operating problems have extremely short lead times, intense verbal communication and interaction with subordinates are required if a GM is to influence events. Major hotels are very complicated operationally and organizationally. Numerous activities are simultaneously and continuously taking place. Staying on top of such a complicated business is unquestionably the most demanding element of a hotel GM's job. In fact, the day-to-day operational demands of the job could easily become an all-consuming concern for a GM, leaving little time for anything else. Reflecting the intense pressure to manage day-to-day operational issues, Richard James indicated that he did not like to be away from The Hotel Apollo for more than one week at a time. Curtis Samuels,

---

[1] Kotter (1982, 10–33) discusses job demands and relationship demands as they affect executive behavior. Mintzberg (1973, 55–99) suggests ten separate work roles for managers. This section is organized around those two approaches to understanding managerial work.

TABLE 16-1.   Key Job Demands and Relationship Demands of Hotel GMs

Time Frame	Key Job Demands	Key Relationship Demands
Short-Run	Day-to-day operational control of service, revenues, and costs. Intense profit and service quality pressures.	Downward internal communications within hotel with subordinates.
Intermediate-Run	Develop, train subordinates; adapt service strategy to changing external conditions; develop management systems and build organizational structure.	Downward internal communications; lateral communications with the external environment; upward communications to corporate and owners.
Long-Run	Set basic service strategy; maintain physical plant; develop organizational stability.	Upward communications to corporate and owners; lateral communication with the external environment; downward communication to further organizational stability.

William Scully, Jonathan Claiborne, and others expressed similar views. If they were away for "too long" the control they had worked so hard to establish might begin to come apart. In discharging this aspect of their responsibilities, a hotel GM will be referred to as an *operational controller*.

Intermediate-Run Demands

A hotel's operational problems never end. To be more than a mere "reactor" to daily operating concerns a GM must also develop and train subordinates and put systems and programs into place to improve the operational consistency and control of the hotel. A GM must also adapt and fine-tune the hotel's service strategies to meet changing conditions of the marketplace. These initiatives constitute the bulk of the intermediate-run demands faced by a GM. In this role, the GM will be called an *organizational developer*. This role will also require intense, downward, internal communications with subordinates. This role, however, extends the GM's relationships and communications demands outside the hotel to include: (1) a network of industry and community contacts needed to better understand the marketplace in which the hotel competes, and (2) the cooperation of corporate staff specialists to help implement the GM's specific plans for the hotel.

Numerous examples have been given of specific plans and programs

GMs have developed in their hotels. Whether these initiatives were to exploit a new market segment, install a new control procedure, change the organizational structure, or develop a management-training program, they all took time to implement. When asked what he had done since becoming GM of The Napoleon House Hotel, Frank Anderson ticked off nearly two dozen major projects. Some had been completed in a few months, others took a year and a few were still in process after two years. These are the kinds of initiatives that an experienced GM like Frank Anderson would ordinarily be expected to take. All of the outstanding GMs did the same thing. Curtis Samuels, for example, had developed a detailed plan of what he wanted to accomplish during his first eighteen months as GM of The Hotel Frenchman, as did Richard James for The Hotel Apollo. In fact, James was explicitly pointing toward having his hotel in outstanding operational shape in time for a major national convention to be held in the city in two years.

Intermediate-run job demands, then, are concerned with putting into place a hotel organization that responds quickly to changes in external factors and efficiently meets the hotel's day-to-day operational demands. The GM is, in effect, fine tuning the hotel's strategy and refining its operations in order to ensure a smoothly operating business.

Long-Run Demands

An important long-run demand of the GM's job relates to the major capital expenditure decisions required to ensure the long-term viability of the hotel in the markets in which it competes. A further long-run demand is the need to develop a degree of organizational stability consistent with the hotel's strategy. On rare occasions a hotel may be forced by changing circumstances to completely rethink its basic marketing and/or service strategy. This might occur as a result of radical changes in transportation patterns, local tourist attractions, business activity, or competition. More often, however, major renovation and modernization capital-expenditure decisions will be made based on a fairly stable long-run marketing and service strategy. The key relationship issues for long-range job demands will be upward to corporate executives and/or owners and laterally to various industry and community sources for intelligence concerning the environment in which the hotel operates.

Developing organizational stability depends on a continued program of human resource training, development, and career progression. Many of the kinds of human resource programs that foster intermediate-run goals will ultimately benefit long-run organizational stability. In discharging these responsibilities, the GM will be referred to as the *business maintainer*.

The rich ambiance of the Presidential Suite at The Hotel Pierre in New York City.

Courtesy: Four Seasons Hotels and Resorts

The Roles a GM Must Play

The key job demands of a hotel GM are described herein as *operational controller, organizational developer,* and *business maintainer.* These roles depend on whether the GM is addressing short-run, intermediate-run, or long-run demands. The key-relationship demands the GM faces vary depending on the time frame of the job demands. In the short-run, most relationship demands focus downward within the organization. Lateral, downward, and upward relationships are all important to meet intermediate demands. Upward and lateral relationships are most important for long-run concerns. Each job demand and relationship demand has an affect on how a GM should perform his or her job. Each circumstance, in other words, helps to prescribe the particular role(s) a GM must play to be successful.

Based on his study of managers at work, Henry Mintzberg (1973) described ten separate work roles for managers. These roles are described briefly in Table 16-2. While the ten hotel GMs were observed performing

TABLE 16-2.　Mintzberg's Ten Roles for a Manager

Role	Description
Interpersonal	
Figurehead	Symbolic head of the organization. Required to perform certain legal functions and attend to various social activities.
Leader	Responsible for the staffing, training, direction, and motivation of subordinates.
Liaison	Develops a network outside the organization to gather information.
Informational	
Monitor	Seeks and analyzes a wide variety of outside information (from the liaison role) and inside information (from the leader role).
Disseminator	Transmits information received both from outside and inside the organization to other members of the organization.
Spokesman	Transmits information about the organization to outsiders.
Decisional	
Disturbance Handler	Takes corrective action whenever the organization faces unexpected, nonroutine disturbances.
Entrepreneur	Looks for ways to change the organization for the better. Seeks information internally and externally for improvement ideas. Initiates and supervises improvement projects.
Resource Allocator	Responsible for allocating all important resources of the organization, both financial and human, including how the manager schedules his or her own time, programs work, and authorizes actions.
Negotiator	Responsible for the organization's major outside negotiations.

each of these roles, those of figurehead, spokesman, and negotiator were found to be of relatively minor importance. The others, however, came into play regularly, depending on the particular job demands the GM was facing at the time. Table 16-3 contrasts GM job demands and the consequent role or roles they are required to play.

Managerial Roles as Operational Controller

As operational controller the GM is involved with the day-to-day and week-to-week operation of the hotel. Since the hotel's functions are many and varied, much of the GM's job must be involved with monitoring and disseminating detailed information pertaining to daily operational matters. During the course of the GM research, I watched William Scully and Godfrey Bier concern themselves daily with overbooking problems. While I was with them, their hotels were running very high occupancies because of large conventions booked into the properties. Time and again throughout the day they talked with a variety of subordinates, including the reservation manager, sales manager, rooms manager, and resident manager concerning the next few nights' anticipated occupancies. They needed to stay right on top of the problem so that the hotel could book to the fullest

TABLE 16-3.   Job Demands and the GM's Managerial Roles

Job Demand	Time Horizon	Managerial Roles
Operational Controller	Short-Run	-Monitor and disseminator of internal information -Disturbance handler -Resource allocator of own time -Leader
Organizational Developer	Intermediate-Run	-Liaison -Monitor and disseminator of both internal and external information -Entrepreneur -Resource allocator (own time, programs, funds) -Leader.
Business Maintainer	Long-Run	-Liaison -Monitor and disseminator of external and internal information to corporate and owners -Resource allocator (programs and funds) -Leader

yet not make the mistake of seriously overbooking. It was also clear from observing Curtis Samuels and Richard James that they were constantly monitoring the progress of the convention groups in their hotels. Matthew Fox personally acted as the convention coordinator for certain groups in The St. Charles Hotel.

GMs must also be available to handle disturbances that are not readily covered by the hotel's routine procedures. While at The Bourbon Hotel, the local fire department called the engineering department for permission to run a test on the main water supply to the hotel's fire sprinkler system. The test would disrupt the hotel's water supply for fifteen minutes and the chief engineer did not want to allow such a disruption on his own authority. He chose to phone Bill Scully for a decision. In order to play the role of disturbance handler effectively, the GM must have quick access to internal information and, in turn, be able to quickly disseminate information and orders. Thus, much of the GM's work as an operational controller involves collecting and processing a lot of information about the hotel's current status.

The GM's role as resource allocator revolves mostly around the allocation of his or her time to the various short-run demands of the job. It's true, of course, that a GM can allocate a certain amount of the hotel's financial and human resources toward solving short-run operational problems. Still, it's the way they allocate their own scarce time that is most important.

General managers perform the leader role through every contact with subordinates. Every question, comment, order, or suggestion of a GM will be analyzed by subordinates. Every time a subordinate is praised, reprimanded, questioned, consulted, or even ignored by a GM, some form of leadership is being practiced. Thus, every interaction between a GM and a subordinate provides the opportunity to exert leadership. That's why outstanding GMs realize that they are constantly on stage whenever they are in the hotel. A GM also exerts leadership by choosing the operational issues on which to concentrate. Subordinates are always looking for clues regarding what the GM considers important. Deciding which operational issues to spend time on is a clear signal from the GM regarding what he or she considers to be important.

Managerial Roles as Organizational Developer

As organizational developer, the hotel GM extends his or her managerial role beyond the confines of the hotel. The GM must become a liaison between the hotel and the outside world in order to monitor information about the community and the marketplace. This information must be analyzed and disseminated to subordinates in the hotel. Both external and internal information must be processed so the GM can play the role of entrepreneur or developer of specific plans and improvement programs. When Lawrence Wagner initiated his "Star Wars" program to ensure a continued four-star hotel rating, when Bill Scully decided to begin a series of management development programs, and when Curtis Samuels began using guest comments as a way of measuring operating performance, they were all embarking on specific programs to improve the operating efficiency or the service strategy of their hotels.

Decisions to pursue specific plans and programs has the GM playing the important resource allocator role. Whenever a new plan or program is begun, it imposes time obligations on both the GM and on subordinates. Funds may also have to be allocated, of course, and the GM must be the decision maker. Finally, the GM continues in the leadership role as organizational developer by virtue of: (1) continuing relationships with subordinates involved in specific plans and programs, and (2) choosing specific plans to pursue. In the leadership role, the GM must contend with the challenge of ensuring that subordinates fully understand and accept the agenda and strategy set forth for the hotel. This requires that special attention be paid to the role of disseminator of information.

Managerial Roles as Business Maintainer

The final job demand of business maintainer requires that the GM see to the long-run capital needs and the organizational stability of the hotel. In seeking capital, the GM's roles of liaison, monitor, and disseminator of external and internal information upward to corporate executives and owners is critical, as is the role of resource allocator of financial resources. This role will often require formal budget proposals and financial justification. This is especially true if the GM is proposing a major shift in the hotel's service strategy. As maintainer of organizational stability, the GM also plays the role of disseminator of important information downward to subordinates. The GM must also act as an entrepreneur with regard to human resource development programs and, as with all activities, continue as leader in the important role of developing management talent.

The GM as Information Focal Point

One of the common characteristics of the various roles a GM must play is the tremendous amount of communication that each role requires. An effective GM is the focal point of an incredible amount of information flow both within and outside the hotel. Figure 16-1 depicts the four major information flows with which a GM is involved. The *A* loop shows information coming from various subordinates, being processed by the GM, and returning to either the same or to different subordinates. This loop takes place continuously as the GM acts as operational controller and also as organizational developer. The *B* loop, with information coming from the

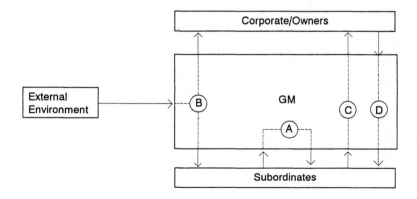

FIGURE 16-1.   A GM's Information Flows

external environment, is needed in order to properly perform the jobs of organizational developer and business maintainer, as are the *C* and *D* loops in which the GM filters and analyzes information coming both from above and from below.

Thus, the GM's job demands attention to the hotel's daily operational activities, sponsorship of specific plans and improvement projects, and attention to the business' long-term viability. To do this a GM must play a number of different managerial roles, the most important of which are leader, liaison, monitor, disseminator, disturbance handler, entrepreneur, and resource allocator. To meet these job demands, the GM must have quick access to a great amount of information from a variety of sources.

WATCHING A HOTEL GM MANAGE

Frank Anderson is the GM of the Napoleon House Hotel. While no two GMs in the study spend their days in exactly the same way, the description of what Frank Anderson did on one particular Monday is quite representative of what I found most of the ten GMs doing. The following description is Frank Anderson's actual day. It is not a composite of a number of his days or a

Exotic outdoor area of the Hyatt Regency Waikola, Hawaii.

Courtesy: Hyatt Hotels Corporation

number of different GMs; it is exactly what happened on that particular Monday. Please take the time to read it carefully. Try to get a feel for what it would be like to be Frank Anderson for that day. Try then to relate the particulars of what Frank Anderson did on that day to the ideas already presented in this chapter and the ideas that follow.

A Typical Day

Frank Anderson is forty-four years old. He has successfully managed hotels for thirteen years. In addition to managing five different hotels, he served a two-year stint as resident manager of one of America's most famous hotels. His undergraduate degree is in finance, and he graduated from the advanced management program of a world-famous eastern university. He has been managing The Napoleon House, a giant convention hotel of 2,000 rooms, for about two years. Under his direction the hotel has made great progress. Here is an example of one of Frank's typical days, a Monday.

7:45   Frank arrives at the office. It's just a brief ride down the elevator from the hotel suite he calls home. He checks the weekend's operating statistics and begins going through some paperwork on his desk.

8:05   Frank gets a call from Don Ranna, the company's regional V.P. and Frank's immediate superior. Don is more or less just checking on how things are going. Frank quotes weekend occupancy and revenue figures. They discuss a number of personnel moves, including a prospective marketing director for the hotel. Some corporate gossip is also swapped and there is a good bit of joking and laughing. Frank advises Don that he does not want the company's regional V.P. of marketing to accompany him to Memphis, where he will be trying to get a client to book a large convention into The Napoleon House.

8:24   David Smith, director of sales for the hotel, drops in to ask why Frank was lowering next month's revenue forecast. During the conversation Frank's secretary comes in with papers for him to sign, and he gets a phone call from the head of security. The conversation with Smith is not concluded because Smith has to leave for another engagement.

8:30   Larry Champagne and Dick Olano, junior executives who have been given responsibility for planning the upcoming employee picnic and golf tournament, drop by to discuss its details. Frank gets involved, makes suggestions regarding the courtesy food and beverage carts that will be stationed on the golf course.

8:48   Frank walks over to resident manager Bruce Horack's office to see what is going on about hiring a new chef. At the same time Frank shows Bruce the caps that will be given out during the golf tournament and mentions some of the things he talked over earlier with regional V.P. Don Ranna.

9:03 Jack Green, the hotel's convention coordinator, comes to Frank's office about a problem with a convention group that is currently in the hotel. Jack is visibly worried. Frank explains how he wants the issue handled but leaves it to Jack to work out the details.

9:06 While signing papers in his office, Frank gets a phone call from the hotel's chief engineer who brings up three or four matters.

9:12 Anderson goes to the eleventh floor to look over a rooms rehab that is in progress. While there he runs into Ed Burvant, the young executive in charge of the project, who fills him in on how things are going. Frank makes about five quick suggestions for Burvant to follow-up on.

9:33 The chief of security catches up with Frank and they talk while returning to his office. The conversation is about a guest's van that was stolen from the parking garage over the weekend.

9:45 Frank walks to the nearby office of the food and beverage director, Charlie Reeves, for what is a planned meeting regarding the decision to hire a new chef. Numerous aspects of the issue are discussed as are three or four other topics, including how well the Friday night charity banquet went. Charlie tells Frank some corporate gossip he learned from the V.P. of food and beverage that morning. They laugh and joke about corporate politics. The meeting lasts four minutes.

9:55 Frank gets a call from a local businessman who wants the address of football player Joe Montana. Frank has it in his file.

9:58 The hotel's attorney calls and updates Frank on a pending suit.

10:00 Frank attends the regular Monday staff meeting of all department heads. He congratulates everyone on the great Friday evening banquet, jokes with three or four executives, and then turns the meeting over to his controller while he signs papers and listens. Toward the meeting's end Frank tells everyone what went on at last week's owners' meeting and goes over the planning for this year's New Year's Eve events.

11:00 After the meeting formally breaks up, Frank has short, one-half minute conversations with five different executives.

11:05 Back in his office, Frank gets a call from the son of the hotel's managing partner, who is looking for some free rooms. He is refused because on the nights in question the hotel is approaching 100 percent occupancy.

11:08 Bruce Horack comes by to let Frank know that another hotel was chosen by the local tourist commission to house a group of wholesale travel agents who will be in town for a familiarization tour. Frank calls the city's director of tourism to try to get part of the business, even though the hotels provide the rooms free. He is assured that the next group will be housed at The Napoleon House.

11:23 Frank calls the chief engineer to check on an elevator problem. They also discuss the rooms rehab, the golf tournament and the Monday night football game.

11:45 The hotel's managing partner calls to ask a question about some expenditures listed on the previous months profit and loss statement. Frank looks up the information and explains the situation. The two discuss another six issues, including the outlook for the local economy.

12:02 Frank reviews an announcement about a reunion of his advanced management class, which will be held next year in Europe. He decides to attend and asks his secretary to check some details regarding the trip.

12:08 While reviewing a report, Frank calls the manager of the hotel's spa because he is concerned about excessive glass breakage.

12:15 The director of sales stops by to tell Frank that a competing hotel has offered a "ridiculously low" room rate of $80 to a large convention group for which they are competing. While they both complain about this irrational competitor, no decision about how to respond is made at the time.

12:18 Larry Champagne and Dick Olano bring Frank a copy of the pairings for the upcoming employee golf tournament. He studies them carefully and suggests some changes. There is much kidding and joking.

12:22 Frank's secretary steps in to tell him the mayor's office called about setting up a private dinner for about twenty people and for Frank to call the mayor upon his return from Washington tomorrow.

12:30 Frank goes down to the River View Restaurant for lunch with David Goodyear, owner of river boats, tour companies, and currently president of the local tourist commission. Their talk covers numerous topics relating to the local tourism industry. Still, their meeting had no real agenda, nor was any hotel business transacted. Frank is back in his office by 1:25.

1:30 A newly hired, young executive is brought by. Frank gives a short talk about how the hotel is trying to service small groups as well as large ones, and how important it is for even the smallest meeting group to get special attention, even in a 2,000-room hotel.

1:45 The controller brings the representative of a credit card company by Frank's office for an "unexpected meeting." There is some unusual-sounding new service being offered and before long there are five people in an impromptu meeting that lasts forty-five minutes. It comes to nothing, and afterwards Frank wonders ". . . why they brought this guy to me?"

2:30 Frank phones a prominent, local executive who heads up the city's PGA golf tournament to try to get some of their business. Nothing is resolved during their five-minute talk.

2:45 Frank asks resident manager Bruce Horack to come by so they can discuss six or so subjects. Topics include recent increases in the percentage of convention no-shows, a suggested room-rate policy for the next month, various plans to finish up the rooms rehab, and others.

2:59 The catering director brings by the rough draft of a bid proposal on an Italian–American Festival on which the hotel is bidding. Frank makes a number of suggestions and compliments the catering director on his efforts.

3:15 Frank reads two personnel-action forms from the human resources department. He calls its director to discuss both. Five or so other personnel issues are discussed during this ten-minute conversation.

3:33 Frank gets a call from a free-lance writer who is doing a story about tourism and economic developments. He answers her questions and asks her a number of his own during their twelve-minute talk.

3:45 Frank gets an unscheduled visit from the rooms manager about a guest who did not get a wake-up call and subsequently missed a meeting. The guest wants a free night's rent; they decide to offer him $59. The conversation goes on to malfunctioning message lights on guest room phones and finally to the trophies for the golf tournament. The rooms manager goes and gets the golf trophies to show Frank.

4:00 An assistant department head drops by to discuss a personnel problem. Frank takes time, asks questions, and outlines a detailed procedure to follow.

4:15 Frank does paperwork, and reads mail and memos for an uninterrupted twenty minutes.

4:35 Bruce Horack comes by with the hotel's operations analyst. The three discuss a number of technical questions relating to sales forecasts and reports to corporate.

4:40 Frank gets a call from the GM of a company hotel in Detroit. They talk company gossip, including possible corporate organizational changes. Other topics include Frank's health, the hotel's capital budget, their families, and his relations with the owners.

4:55 Frank calls the GM of the company's Miami hotel to express his sympathies over the death of his father. The GM had previously worked for Frank.

5:00 Frank returns to his apartment.

6:15 Frank meets about seven of the hotel's executives at the hotel's sports bar to watch some of the Monday night football game. He is introduced to a corporate engineering specialist who is in town for a few days. Frank asks him about various aspects of his job, but no local hotel business is discussed at the table. Mostly, it's a little football but much joking and kidding. Most of the executives drink beer; Frank drinks soda.

7:00 Frank Anderson says good night and returns to his apartment. It's been an average day at The Napoleon House Hotel for its GM.

Nearly any of the work days of the ten GMs would have revealed a similar pattern. Of the ten, only Curtis Samuels tried to structure a really tight schedule and stick to it, which often caused him difficulty. He often fell behind schedule, causing problems both for himself and the people on his schedule. He has also been criticized by his subordinates as being inaccessible because of his tight schedule, some indicating that they often had to "stand around" waiting for Curtis while he stuck to his rigid schedule. Each GM, of course, varied his activities and work schedule depending on his personality and what was happening in the hotel at the time. Whereas people just walked unannounced into Frank Anderson's and William Scully's offices, Lawrence Wagner, whose personality was more formal, liked to be informed by his secretary that someone was waiting.

One morning, while I was with Matthew Fox, an unannounced visitor dropped in about 9:30 for a "cup of coffee." He was Ed Murphy, a long-time liquor salesman who did a little business with The St. Charles Hotel. In truth, Ed was an old acquaintance of Fox's who had just stopped by to chat. Matt and Ed joked for a few minutes, but when the executive housekeeper stuck her head into Fox's office he began a conversation with her, which subsequently led to a couple of phone calls. During that time Murphy and I got acquainted while Fox did some work. A few minutes later Fox returned to the conversation until another interruption, this time from the resident manager, brought his attention back to hotel work. This shifting back and forth continued for about twenty minutes until Ed Murphy said he had to go. Fox just continued working. For a while Ed Murphy was just another ball that Fox was juggling, one of dozens. When Murphy left, Fox could shift his attention to another ball; there was certainly no shortage of balls at The St. Charles Hotel that needed a little attention.

An interior decorator forgot about a meeting one morning with The Hotel Apollo GM, Richard James. James, who was paying the interior decorator to oversee a major nightclub renovation, did not seem to be at all disturbed. He went on to other things and re-scheduled the interior decorator for the afternoon. Bruce Warren took a whole day to drive to the state capital for what he knew was largely a ceremonial meeting. The meeting did, however, give him an opportunity to see a lot of important people from around the state.

The remainder of this chapter will analyze GM behavior in light of other research findings concerning the nature of managerial work.

A "train car suite" at the Indianapolis Holiday Inn-Union Station. The hotel has twenty-six authentic Pullman cars made into hotel hotel suites.

Courtesy: General Hotels Corporation

Characteristics of Managerial Work

Two conclusions began to emerge from watching these hotel executives go about their daily work.

1.   It was often difficult to neatly categorize what the GMs were doing into traditional planning, organizing, directing, or controlling categories.

2. While they exerted some control over their daily activities, much of what they did seemed to depend on what was happening around them at the time.

Much of what the GMs did on a daily basis was quite consistent with the findings of other field research on executive behavior. The research of John Kotter (1982) and Henry Mintzberg (1973) both dealt with the day-to-day activities of North American business executives. Table 16-4 lists some of the characteristics of managerial work described by Mintzberg and Kotter, and attempts to correlate Mintzberg's "six characteristics" and Kotter's "twelve visible patterns" in order to point out the similarities in their findings. The next few sections briefly review these characteristics of managerial work and comment on how they apply to hotel GMs.

Hotel GMs Perform a Great Amount of Work (Mintzberg's number 1/Kotter's number 1)

Hotel GMs fall right in line with other findings regarding their workload and pace. There is never an end to what can be done in a major hotel. The GMs worked at a fast pace without letup. They took no coffee breaks, nor were their lunches long or leisurely. Four reported working seventy hours or more each week, three worked over sixty hours, two over fifty hours and one, who was recovering from a major illness, reported working forty-eight hours per week. After following the latter GM around for a number of days, I can certainly vouch for a fast pace during those forty-eight hours! Recall that Lawrence Wagner likened managing a hotel to pushing a large elephant up a hill, a rather unrelenting task, I'd think.

Hotel GMs Perform a Wide Variety of Activities (Mintzberg's number 2/Kotter's number 2, 3, 4)

Variety, fragmentation, and brevity of contact was characteristic of the way the ten hotel GMs spent their days. Except for scheduled meetings, most GM contacts lasted ten minutes or less. To report that GMs spend much of their time in short, disjointed conversations is not to imply that this time is poorly spent. Twenty minutes with Lawrence Wagner learning his ideas of what constitutes a good room inspection is an experience few young executives will ever forget.

Hotel GMs must be quick on their feet. When an owner calls looking for an explanation about a guest complaint, the GM must respond immediately. Two minutes later he will react just as quickly to a problem of soiled napkins in the hotel's laundry. Mintzberg found that managers preferred tasks of short duration. Furthermore, they encouraged interruptions. These were readily

TABLE 16-4.   Some Characteristics Regarding Managerial Work

Mintzberg's Six Characteristics of Managerial Work	Kotter's Twelve Visible Patterns of how Managers Use Their Time
1. The manager performs a great quantity of work at an unrelenting pace.	1. Managers work long hours.
2. Managerial activity is characterized by variety, fragmentation, and brevity.	2. The breadth of topics managers cover is extremely wide.
	3. The issues they discussed are often relatively unimportant to the business.
	4. Most time with others is spent in short, disjointed conversations.
3. Managers prefer issues that are current, specific, and ad hoc.	5. General managers rarely seem to make big decisions.
4. The manager sits between his organization and a network of contacts.	6. The people managers spend time with include many in addition to their direct subordinates and bosses.
	7. Managers ask a lot of questions.
5. Managers demonstrate a strong preference for the verbal media.	8. Managers spend most of their time with others.
6. Despite the preponderance of obligations, managers appear to be able to control their own affairs.	9. In allocating their time with others, the GMs often behaved in a "reactive" mode.
	10. Discussions with others typically contained a considerable amount of joking, kidding, and nonwork related issues.
	11. In these encounters, GMs rarely gave orders in the traditional sense.
	12. Nevertheless, GMs frequently engaged in attempts to influence others.

noticeable traits of the hotel GMs. Remember that hotels are businesses in which such a great variety of different services are performed that they are referred to as "a city within a city." Also, the "true immediacy" of many problems in hotels requires that they be dealt with quickly. Thus, effective hotel GMs have learned to deal with a great variety of issues (many of which are unexpected), to deal with issues quickly, and to deal with issues whenever they arise.

The issues hotel GMs deal with do sometimes seem to be relatively unimportant. General managers appear sometimes to get involved in too many minute details. While this trait could be a failing in some hotel executives, it was not in the ten highly successful executives in the GM study. Their attention to details, even of seemingly unimportant matters, must be viewed more broadly in light of their coaching and leadership roles. The work of a hotel is made up of thousands of small details. Miss the details and a hotel simply does not provide good guest service. It is absolutely essential that GMs impress on the entire hotel staff the need to be attentive to all manner of details. General managers must, therefore, behave in the same way they would have their subordinates behave. In this regard GMs must demonstrate their commitment to the principle of attention to detail to the widest possible audience. They must take every possible opportunity during their daily encounters with management and staff to concentrate on the "seemingly unimportant" details of running a hotel. This is a simple example of GMs' exerting leadership. Leadership depends on what leaders do more than on what they say.

Another reason why hotel GMs engage in varied, fragmented activity throughout the day is because only in this way can they truly keep their fingers on the pulse of the hotel's daily operations. General managers need rapid communications with a wide variety of people throughout the day to keep on top of what's going on in the hotel. That's partly why outstanding GMs tour their hotels. In large hotels, however, something can be going wrong in one area while the GM is in another. To restrict subordinate access would be cutting off the rapid flow of information GMs need to assess how the hotel is performing. A number of the GMs said that they could "feel it" when things were going well in their hotels. That feel, I suspect, comes directly from spending "most of their time with others, . . . in short and disjointed conversations (Kotter 1982, 81).

Hotel GMs Make Many Small Decisions on Current Issues
(Mintzberg's number 3 / Kotter's number 5)

Mintzberg (1973) says that management is practiced by a process of stimulus–response to live, concrete situations. That seems a fair description of hotel GMs. They readily admitted that most of their decisions were small ones. Frank Anderson called his job "ninety-day decision making." Although GMs must make major decisions, their days revolve around making a large number of small decisions.

Hotels develop detailed annual business plans that cover every aspect of their operation, so planning is not neglected. However, GMs often formulate their plans and strategies based on the broadest variety of information, including as Mintzberg says, gossip, speculation, and hearsay. The GM is the focal point of information flows in a hotel. Furthermore, planning does not take place as an isolated, separate task. It is, instead, something that takes place as a result of the GM's attention to current and specific issues. A GM's planning probably takes place at the subconscious level as much as at the conscious level.

Hotel GMs Have Extensive Dealings With the Outside World (Mintzberg's number 4/Kotter's number 6 and 7)

Hotel GMs are their organization's most important contact with the outside world. The two most important "outside" influences that they must interpret for their organization are: (1) the requirements, desires and culture of the corporate environment of which they are a part, and (2) the economic, social, and competitive environment of the geographic area and the markets in which the hotel competes. A hotel GM must, therefore, spend a fairly significant amount of time gathering information about these two environments. Most of the GMs studied spent about 10 percent of their week on community-related activities, in large part in order to be able to understand and interpret the local community and markets for their hotel. While much of this outside activity was hospitality-industry related, it also involved a wide variety of civic activities intended to keep the GM abreast of local trends and developments.

Contact with corporate executives and owners was also quite intense. The degree of intensity depended in part on what was going on in the hotel at the time. For example, during budget preparation time or before important corporate or owner meetings, it was not unusual for GMs to talk to various corporate-level executives five to ten times a day. It was also not unusual for three or more conversations to take place regarding a single issue. Richard James, for example, talked to his regional V.P. four times one day while trying to draft a response to a somewhat confusing letter from an important client. James was very concerned that he understand corporate's exact thinking on the matter before he committed a response to writing. William Scully acted the same way regarding a promotion decision. During numerous phone calls over a three day period to the regional V.P., he carefully explained his reasons for promoting someone into a particularly important position. Frank Anderson put a high premium on staying "in close touch" with regional headquarters because he wanted no surprises from them. He was also anxious to be sure that corporate staff would be available when he needed their help. He was forever alert that his hotel might be put in a bad light because of some confusion or because of corporate politics. He mentioned on a number of occasions not wanting to get caught in a misunderstanding like "the problem we had over that executive compensation issue last year."

Richly but subtly appointed board room of the Radisson Plaza Hotel, Minneapolis, Minnesota.

Courtesy: Radisson Hotels International

Hotel GMs Spend Their Work Days in Intensive Verbal Communication (Mintzberg's number 5 / Kotter's number 8)

As discussed, hotel GMs deal almost exclusively with verbal communication, either face-to-face or by telephone. This tendency was so strong that an entire chapter of the book was devoted to verbal communication. Further discussion centered around the informational roles that GMs must play and the fact that they are the focal point for information flows from outside and within the hotel. Finally, because many of the operational problems in hotels require quick action, only verbal communication is rapid enough to be effective.

Hotel GMs Allocate Their Time by Reacting to the Events That Take Place Around Them (Mintzberg's number 6/Kotter's number 9)

Both Mintzberg and Kotter reported that the managers they studied initiated less than half of their verbal contacts. The same was true of the hotel GMs I studied. This means that on an average day other people seemed to have more influence over how the GMs spent their time than did the GMs themselves. Superficially this would suggest that the GMs were unable to control the events that swirled around them and would probably benefit greatly from a time management course. How can this be? These GMs were some of the most successful and effective managers one could find anywhere. All except one behaved in the same way and the one who behaved differently had difficulty trying to structure his day. One must conclude that this form of reactive behavior is the proper response given the GMs' job circumstances and the challenges they face. To characterize these GMs as puppets being controlled by events around them is an improper interpretation of the facts. Nor is this the conclusion drawn by either Mintzberg or Kotter.

Remember that there are simply not enough hours in the day for a hotel GM to do everything. Thus, it is critical that they develop extremely efficient ways of behaving that allows them to accomplish as much as possible in the limited time that is available. Two of the critical functions they perform are: (1) to continually monitor what is going on in the hotel, and (2) to influence the activities of as many people in the hotel as possible. In order to monitor what is going on they must be in daily verbal contact with a great variety of people. In order to influence the widest variety of people they also need daily contact with a great variety of people. Since these two goals coincide, the only question is, "What is the most effective way of accomplishing this?"

On the one hand, hotel executives could tightly control their schedules. They could make detailed decisions regarding which subordinates to see and when to see them. If this procedure were followed, the GMs would be considered in control of their daily activities since they themselves would have initiated most of their meetings and contacts. On the other hand, daily contact with a large number of people could be accomplished by allowing subordinates to determine when they needed to see the GM. The GMs also regulated the number of people with whom they had contact by the amount of wandering around they did. The more MBWA, the more contact they had with subordinates.

Table 16-5 reviews some of the positives and negatives of tight versus loose control of a hotel manager's schedule, remembering all the while that, to be effective, the GM must have daily contact with a wide variety of people. General managers can increase control over their daily activities by scheduling a greater number of meetings and personally initiating a greater number of contacts. By so doing, predictability is automatically added to a GM's daily routine, interruptions are reduced, and a more controlled environment is the result. Presumably, the GM will also be able to schedule in such a way as to reflect the priorities he or she has set for the hotel, thus rationalizing his work day. Also, since the GM is the initiator, he or she can control the topics and the agenda of the contacts.

On the other hand, a tighter more controlled schedule is not without its problems. To begin with, just setting up a detailed schedule in an organization as busy as a hotel is no easy task. Most hotel executives face numerous daily deadlines. They also experience unexpected problems that demand their immediate attention, thus causing planned meetings to be canceled. In addition, a GM-initiated contact disrupts a subordinate's schedule. A GM-initiated contact or meeting also tends to add a touch of formality to the encounter, which could cause it to be less spontaneous and open than it might be. The encounter, because it is preplanned, will also tend to be longer than an unplanned or unscheduled encounter. Finally, to the extent a GM increases the structure of his or her daily activities, he or she automatically limits the access of other subordinates and automatically diminishes the possibility of nonroutine contact. One can't have it both ways.

Table 16-6 lists the pluses and minuses of a loosely controlled schedule.

TABLE 16-5.   Positives and Negatives of a Tightly Controlled Schedule for a Hotel GM

	Positive	Negative
	A predictable daily routine.	Scheduling problems requiring many schedule changes.
	Few interruptions.	GM-initiated contact disrupts subordinate's routine.
	GM sets the day's priorities.	A more formal, threatening procedure.
	GM sets the contact agenda.	Contacts may be of longer duration.
	A more controlled working environment.	Subordinates have limited access to GM.
		Fewer opportunities for nonroutine contact.

TABLE 16-6.   Positives and Negatives of a Loosely Controlled Schedule for a Hotel GM

Positive	Negative
Subordinates bring a wide variety of current problems to the GM.	GM subject to hectic, unpredictable daily activity.
Rapid information flow.	Little GM "quiet time".
Spontaneous, informal relationships fostered.	GM forced to deal with many minor issues.
Subordinates more receptive to general manager coaching and suggestions.	GMs less able to set priorities of daily contacts.
Less time-consuming than more formal scheduling.	GM less able to control topics during individual contacts.

The previously discussed negatives associated with a loose schedule are hectic days, little or no time for reflection, and a parade of numerous minor issues.

The last two negatives relate to GMs not having control over either who they have contact with during the day or the subjects that will be addressed during the contacts. On the surface these seem to be legitimate, serious concerns. If subordinates initiate the contacts, how will GMs know they are spending time with the " right" set of subordinates? Perhaps GMs' effectiveness would improve if they spent their time with different people. Also, since subordinates initiate the contact, they are more likely to control the agenda of what is discussed than if GMs made the first move. Therefore, how do GM know they are addressing the most important issues?

General managers have quite a bit of control over who has access to them. This control is exerted by the kinds of programs and projects they initiate and by the guidelines and instructions they establish regarding subordinate access. A GM who institutes a yield-management program will set into motion a series of actions that will, for a time, lead to greater contact and communication with subordinates in the reservations and the sales departments. Contact would be intense with engineering and rooms executives while a hotel is undergoing a major rooms rehab. In this regard, GMs are always making decisions that influence which subordinates will have the greatest need for interaction with them. As priorities change programs will change, thus automatically resulting in a different set of subordinates having first claim on GMs' time.

An example of this occurred when Henri LeSassier took over as GM of

The graceful iron grillwork and old spanish architecture of the Royal Orleans, the first major new hotel built in the French Quarter of New Orleans.

Courtesy: The Omni Royal Orleans

The Normandy Hotel. Occupancy and revenue were so low that most of his efforts had to be focused toward only two issues: (1) What could be done to quickly increase occupancies and revenues, and (2) what immediate cost savings could be instituted to avert financial insolvency? Numerous projects relating to each issue were immediately instituted by LeSassier, and he let it be known that he was always available to subordinates who were involved with them. By initiating these action programs he had clearly signaled *who* he wanted to see. By keeping a flexible schedule, he just wasn't exactly sure *when* he would see them. Like any good manager, he set completion deadlines and asked for progress reports. If schedules began to slip, LeSassier was prepared to quickly step in with corrective action. He also knew that success would likely depend on the quality of the close personal interaction he had with his subordinates. Like most of his fellow GMs, LeSassier chose to let his subordinates somewhat dictate the timing of this interaction. By his actions and programs he determined with whom he wanted to interact; by his availability he allowed subordinates to somewhat determine when this interaction took place.

What are the advantages of a loosely controlled schedule? By allowing broad subordinate access, GMs ensure that they are supplied with a wide variety of current information about their hotels' operations. It's unlikely, following this strategy, that a GM would be misled or uninformed about a problem since he would usually hear about it quickly and from a variety of sources. Division heads in 1,000-plus-room hotels say that GMs cannot know everything that's going on in their hotels and, therefore, must rely on their immediate subordinates to run their respective divisions. This is, of course, true. It is equally true, however, that outstanding GMs would never think of relying solely on their division heads for information about their hotels. Nor would they pass up an opportunity to interact directly with executives lower in the organization. General managers that loosely schedule their activities and encourage interruptions by subordinates are rewarded with rapid information flow. The research of Mintzberg and Kotter confirms that executives in a variety of different businesses have a strongly felt need for a wide variety of current information. Nowhere is this more true than in hotels, where problems must be solved quickly, often in a matter of minutes.

Another advantage to a loosely controlled schedule is that it tends to foster informal, spontaneous relationships with subordinates. Subordinates who feel comfortable bringing information, problems, and issues to their GM are likely to become more confident about their relationship with the GM. More contact means more familiarity and greater opportunity for developing the kind of personal relationship that leads to trust and understanding. It's also likely that when subordinates initiate contact they will be more receptive to GM coaching and directing than if the initiative came from the GM.

A loosely controlled, more reactive style of managing may be less time-consuming for busy GMs than any other strategy. Because the demands on a GM are so great, this is an important point. From the standpoint of the efficient use of time, it may be best for a GM to adjust his or her schedule to the needs and demands of subordinates than the opposite. Following this mode of behavior the GM becomes a reactor to the needs of members of the organization. In a narrow sense, the GM becomes a servant responding to the needs of his masters, his subordinates! In what sense can this be efficient behavior? To be effective a GM must constantly attend to the problems of a great variety of people. The more urgent the problem, the more important it is to resolve it quickly and correctly. Since part of a GM's job is rapid problem identification and solution, a management style that encourages subordinate interruptions is indeed appropriate. To get the same amount of information by GM-initiated encounters would be quite difficult. The GM would have to initiate communications with a wide variety of subordinates, many of whom were encountering no problems requiring input from the GM. There's an expression that captures the spirit of this: "If it's not broken, don't fix it." Since their time is limited, GMs must spend it on things that are broken or on things that they deem need fixing. General managers who are clever about their relationships contrive to have subordinates bring to them the problems that most need to be fixed. In this sense GMs are acting very efficiently and very rationally. Like doctors, they are not wasting their time dealing with well people.

There is another positive aspect of this kind of behavior. The wider the variety of subordinates a GM has contact with, the more people the GM is in a position to influence. Limit the contacts, limit the potential influence. Increase the contacts, increase the potential influence. Whenever GMs have contact with subordinates, the possibility of a favorable outcome exists. General managers who have no agenda or who have no real message to impart can easily miss these precious opportunities. Those who do know where they are going use each of these opportunities to make things better. Mintzberg (1973, 51) eloquently expresses this idea by saying that, "All managers appear to be puppets. Some decide who will pull the strings and how, and they then take advantage of each move that they are forced to make. Others, unable to exploit this high-tension environment, are swallowed up by this most demanding of jobs."

Additional Aspects of Managerial Work

Kotter's tenth point relates to the amount of kidding, joking and nonwork-related discussions that went on during the course of the work day of the subjects he studied. While this form of behavior was observed with each of the ten GMs, it was not so noticeable that I would have included it as a typical characteristic of their behavior. Most of the hotels operated in a fairly relaxed atmosphere but could not be characterized by the amount of joking and kidding that took place. Joking and kidding did take place and nonwork-related issues were discussed, but if I were to characterize the encounters between executives it would be a rather serious focus on hotel issues.

In just a few instances I discovered, after the fact, that something had occurred that might have been "staged" mostly for my benefit. The most humorous took place when one GM (who, by the way, was truly admired and in many ways loved by his subordinates) finished a particularly intense EOC meeting by inviting everyone to lunch in the hotel's fine dining restaurant. The lunch was great, the GM was charming, but the conversation could have been a little more spontaneous. Over the next few days more than one EOC member noted that this lunch had probably been "in your honor" since they could not remember a similar occasion in many years.

Kotter also found that the executives he studied rarely gave orders in the traditional sense of the word, but that they definitely did try to influ-

The beautifully decorated Festival Restaurant in the Radisson Plaza Hotel, Minneapolis, Minnesota.

Courtesy: Radisson Hotels International

ence the behavior of others. Hotel GMs did give direct orders. This book contains a number of examples where GMs went to some lengths to explain exactly what they wanted subordinates to do. Further discussion has centered around how GMs vary the direct and explicit control they exert over subordinates depending on subordinate experience and maturity. All of the executives Kotter studied were at a much higher level in the organizational structure than hotel GMs. While a few of Kotter's subjects did have operational responsibility, they were still higher in their organizations than the individual operating unit such as a hotel. Hotel GMs face more severe short-run operational pressures than Kotter's subjects. Hotel GMs also have to contend with less experienced subordinates than executives who are higher in the organizational structure. Thus, circumstances dictate the need for more detailed order giving and structure on the part of hotel GMs.

CONCLUSION

This chapter took a close look at how successful and effective hotel GMs go about their daily jobs. Some of the findings about their work routines may be surprising, but these findings are quite consistent with other studies of managers at work.

The demands of a job will determine the roles that must be played by a manager. In the case of the hotel GM, the key job demands were described as: (1) operational controller, (2) organizational developer, and (3) business maintainer. These job demands required the GM to play a variety of managerial roles, especially those of leader, liaison, monitor, disseminator, disturbance handler, entrepreneur, and resource allocator.

In order to perform these roles successfully, the GM must have access to a great amount of current information from a wide variety of sources. A hotel GM is the CEO of a semiautonomous profit center. This position requires the GM to be the focal point of information flows from within the hotel, from the outside environment, and from owners and corporate superiors.

A key issue regarding how GMs should spend their work days revolves around how best to process the great amount of information that is vital to performing their jobs. There are a number of common characteristics about the GMs' day-to-day activities.

- Hotel GMs work long hours at an unrelenting pace.
- Their activities are characterized by both brevity and variety. They address important and seemingly unimportant issues alike.
- Hotel GMs deal primarily with current, specific issues.
- Hotel GMs process large quantities of information from inside and outside the hotel.

- Hotel GMs prefer verbal communication because it is fast.
- While hotel GMs normally spend their days in a reactive mode, they do in fact have control over their activities.

During the GM research, I observed Frank Anderson at work one very busy morning. People were continually coming and going and Frank

The Four Seasons' Hotel Pierre on Fifth Avenue, New York City—a place where magic is made.

Courtesy: Four Seasons Hotels and Resorts

seemed particularly happy. During a short break in the action he turned to me and said that he liked to manage in an "act, react, and act again" mode, and that he liked to do it at "warp speed." On another day I watched Lawrence Wagner decide on the exact location of the door knobs on the front doors of the hotel's new restaurant. Later that day Lawrence discussed with the director of housekeeping the number of coat hangers he wanted in each room. One day he said that GMs make many small and very few large decisions, but that it was important that all of the small decisions be consistent with the GMs' vision for the hotel. As time went on and I studied more of these GMs at work, a certain purpose and design began to take form in my mind. What at first seemed to be random, reactive behavior began to take on a certain regularity and purpose. What, for a number of the GMs, seemed to be controlled chaos began to make more sense. What at first appeared to be obsessive interest in minutia began to take on purpose.

Each of these successful GMs had devised routines to cope with the demands of their jobs. In most cases their strategy was to remain rather unstructured in their daily routine, to encourage rapid verbal communication even if that meant considerable interruptions, and to deal reactively with both large and small issues as they came up.

These GMs were effective working in this manner because they were, in fact, following an agenda. They had initiated various plans and programs to improve their hotels and they were continually receiving feedback from a variety of sources concerning their progress. They took every opportunity to exert leadership with the large number of subordinates with whom they came in contact. They moved their hotels forward by dealing with small immediate issues in a way that was consistent with their long-run goals and dreams for the hotels they so loved.

REFERENCES

Carlson, Sune. 1951. *Executive Behavior: A Study of the Working Methods of Managing Directors*. Stockholm: Strombergs.

Kotter, John P. 1982. *The General Managers*. New York: The Free Press.

Mintzberg, Henry. 1973. *The Nature of Managerial Work*. New York: Harper & Row.

FURTHER READINGS

Anthony, Carmen. September 1986. "Managing Megahotels." *Hotel & Resort Industry*:34–40ff.

Arnoldo, Mario J. 1981. "Hotel General Managers: Profile." *The Cornell Hotel and Restaurant Administration Quarterly* November:53–56.

Eder, Robert W. and W. Terry Umbreit. 1989. "Measures of Managerial Effectiveness in the Hotel Industry." *Hospitality Education and Research Journal* 13(3):334–41.

George, R. Thomas. 1989. "Hospitality Managers as Caretakers and Change Agents: A Reconceptualization of the Position." *FIU Hospitality Review* 7(1):13–22.

Hales, Colin and Michael Nightingale. 1986. "What Are Unit Managers Supposed to Do? A Contigent Methodology for Investigating Managerial Role Requirements." *International Journal Of Hospitality Management* 5(1):3–11.

Iaconetti, Joan. October 1985. "Making the 'One-Minute Manager' Principles Work for You." *Hotel & Resort Industry*:62–67.

Ley, David A. November 1980. "The Effective GM: Leader or Entrepreneur?" *The Cornell Hotel and Restaurant Administration Quarterly* 21(3):66–67.

Umbreit, W. Terry. 1986. "Developing Behaviorally-Anchored Scales for Evaluating Job Performance of Hotel Managers." *International Journal of Hospitality Management* 5(2):55–61.

Umbreit, W. Terry and Robert W. Eder. 1987. "Linking Hotel Manager Behavior With Outcome Measures of Effectiveness." *International Journal of Hospitality Management* 6(3):139–147.

QUESTIONS

16-1. Classify and discuss the various job demands and relationship demands faced by hotel GMs.

16-2. Explain the different roles a GM must play as operational controller, organizational developer, and business maintainer.

16-3. Discuss Mintzberg's six characteristics of managerial work as they relate to hotel GMs.

16-4. Discuss Kotter's twelve visible patterns of how managers use their time as they relate to hotel GMs.

16-5. Discuss the positives and negatives of a tightly controlled schedule.

16-6. Discuss the positives and negatives of a loosely controlled schedule.

16-7. Explain how a loosely controlled, reactive style of managing can be a very efficient strategy.

APPENDIX

GENERAL MANAGER QUESTIONS

1. Describe the key characteristics of the hotel business.
2. Describe your job. Being effective in your job means what?
3. Chronologically, what are the key things that have happened to you since taking the job? What did you do and why? What effect did it have? What problems developed? How did you handle them?
4. What are the toughest decisions you have made in the past few years?
5. What are the high and low points in your life in the past few years?
6. How effective have you been in your job? Specifically, why? How do you measure success and why? What has led to this level of effectiveness? What could you have done better? Why?
7. Describe the management style? How has it changed over the past five to ten years?
8. What are you trying to achieve in your career? In your life?
9. What are your strengths and weaknesses?
10. Has any particular event or experience in your life influenced your management philosophy or style?
11. What were the major decision points in your career? How do you feel about them now?
12. What percentage of your time do you devote to community activities? Why?
13. What are the major constraints of your job?
14. What was your formal education? How was it helpful to your career? Were there any gaps in it?
15. Was any work experience particularly helpful to your career?
16. Hours worked:
    number hours/day
    number days/week

17.   Do you live in the hotel?
18.   Have the demands of your career adversely affected your family life?
19.   What do you like *most (least)* about being a hotel G.M.?

DIVISIONAL HEAD QUESTIONS

1.   How long have you been with the hotel, and what is your background? How long have you known your GM? What are the biggest challenges you face on the job?
2.   Key things I need to know about the hotel business and this hotel to understand the context in which your GM works.
3.   What key things has your GM done, good or bad, in his job. Why? What was the impact?
4.   How do you interact with the GM? How often? How long? Why? Examples of what he does.
5.   Describe the GM as a manager. As a person.
6.   Rate his performance. Why?

INDEX

Albrecht, Karl, 162-163, 170, 213
Athos, Anthony, 268-271
Austin, Nancy, 281-282

Bennis, Warren, 229, 285-291
Blanchard, K.H., 249-250

Crison, Ed, 268-271
Communications, 210-227
  assumptions affecting, 217-219
  GMs communicating, 220-226
    taking time to communicate, 221-223
  importance of verbal communication,
    213-215
  tips to better communication, 216-217
  verbal communication in hotels,
    210-212
Competitive environment, 18-24
  forecasting demand, 22-24
  hotels are commodities, 19-20
  hotel overbuilding, 20-21
  rooms are perishable products, 21-22
Control of personnel, 349-361
  employee surveys, 359-360
  employee relations programs, 356-358
  employee turnover, 360-361
  guest relations training, 350-354
  telephone training, 349-350

Control of results: revenues and costs,
  309-337
  annual business plan, 317-323
  departmental forecasts, 314-317
  forecasting revenues and costs, 309-311
  group consensus, 317-321
  monthly control cycle, 323-331
    monthly forecast, 324-329
    profit and loss forecast, 329-331
    ten-day control cycle, 331-336
    thirty-ninety day forecast, 323-324
  occupancy forecasts, 311-314
Control of specific actions, 338-348
  direct supervision as a form of, 348
  introductory training, 339-340
  room attendant training, 341-343
  specific action controls for managers,
    343-346
  systems of specific action controls,
    346-348
Control overview, 294-307
  control tactics, 298-301
    personnel control, 300-301, 305-307
    results accountability, 298-299,
      304-305
    specific actions, 299-300, 301-304
  feedback control, 295-296
    in hotels, 296-298

Coordinating hotel activities, 144–156
  executive operating committee, 146–150
  GMs and meetings, 152–153
  meetings and communications, 153–155
  need for interdepartmental coordination,
    144–146
  typical hotel committees and meetings,
    150–153
Cycles, in hotels, 10

Dedication to job, 18
Drucker, Peter, 68, 93, 196, 230

Employees, 39–45
  attitudes, 41–44
  employee-guest dichotomy, 40
  productivity, 40
  turnover, 44–45, 157, 360–361
  wage rates, 40
Excitement, in hotels, 4–6
Executive operating committee, 146–150

General managers at work, 406–427
  characteristics of GM managerial work,
    412–425
    GMs allocate their time reacting to
      events, 418–423
    GMs have extensive dealings with the
      outside world, 416
    GMs make many small decisions on
      current issues, 415–416
    GMs perform a great amount of work,
      413
    GMs perform a wide variety of
      activities, 413–415
    GMs spend their days in intensive
      verbal communications, 417–418
    a typical day, 407–411
General managers' backgrounds, 367–378
  basic demographics, 367–368
  career-decision points, 375–378
  choice of a hotel career, 371–372
  experience and career progression,
    372–375

  formal education, 367, 369–371
  future ambitions, 378
General manager ideal characteristics,
    385–392
  attitudes and values, 387–388
  cognitive orientation, 390–392
  interpersonal orientation, 388–389
  needs and drives, 386–387
  temperament, 389–390
General manager job demands, 398–406
  information focal point, 405–406
  intermediate-run demands, 399–400
  long-run demands, 400
  short-run demands, 398–399
General manager roles, 401–405
  business maintainer, 405
  operational controller, 402–404
  organizational developer, 404
General manager: personal characteristics,
    378–385
  job likes and dislikes, 382
  others' evaluations, 384–385
  outlook about jobs, 378
  recent high and low points, 381–382
  self-evaluation, 383–384
  tough job decisions, 379–381
  views about family, 383
Guest needs, 37–39
  anticipating needs, 38
  needs vary, 37

Hawthorne experiments, 178–179, 205
Hershey, Paul, 249–250
Herzberg, Frederich, 187–189
Heskett, James, 89, 163, 213
Hilton Hotels, 66–68
History in hotels, 3–4
Holiday Inns, 71
Hotel functional organizational design,
    130–142
  accounting department, 135–137
  food and beverage department, 133–134
  large hotel organization, 137–139
  mid-size hotel organization, 130–131

personnel department, 135
rooms department, 130–133
sales and marketing department, 134–135
strengths of functional design, 139
weaknesses of functional design, 139–141

Japanese management practices, 263–276
an American example of, 268–269
characteristics of, 263–265
in hotels, 271–276
junior-senior relationships, 268
superordinate goals, 269–271
Theory Z, 265–269

Kotter, John P., 210, 398, 413–418, 423–425
Kroc, Ray, 257

Labor intensiveness of hotels, 36–37
Leading organizations, 261–292
attitudes toward people, 277–278
management by wandering
around(MBWA), 281–282
GMs doing MBWA, 282–285
strategies leaders follow, 285–291
attention through vision, 286
meaning through communication, 286–287
trust through positioning, 287–289
positive self-regard, 289–291
values and meaning, 278–281
Leading people, 229–258
choosing a leadership style, 248–256
for decision making, 251–254
follower maturity and leadership,
249–250
defined, 232–233
importance in hotels, 230–232
leader behavior, 236–247
authoritarian versus participative,
237–243
GM tendencies, 240–243, 254–256
task versus people, 243–247
GM tendencies, 245–247, 250–251
GM's attention to detail, 248
personal traits of leaders, 233–234
sources of leader power, 234–236

McGregor, Douglas, 180–182
Managers, 46–48
job pressures, 46–48
training, 48
turnover, 47–48
Marriott, J. Willard, 230
Maslow, Abraham, 182–185
Mayo, Elton, 178
Merchant, Kenneth A., 295, 298–301, 304
Mintzberg, Henry, 210, 398, 401, 413–418
Motivation, 173–207
behavior modification, 200–201
and equity, 198–200
GM's understanding of people, 173–174,
176–177
individual needs, 180–189
Hawthorne experiments, 178–179
need for achievement, 185–187
and positive language, 186–187
needs hierarchy, 182–185
theory X and Y, 180–182
worker satisfaction and dissatisfaction,
187–189
job enrichment, 189
job satisfaction and performance, 201–205
views of GMs, 205
motivational process, 179, 189–201
expectancy theory, 190–195
management by objectives, 195–198

Nanus, Burt, 229, 285–291
National Gallery of Art, 278–280

Organizational design, 112–130
authority, 118–119
chain of command, 125–127
coordination, 122–125
delegation, 128–130
degrees of, 129
departmentalization, 115–118
functional design, 115–116
line versus staff, 118–119
spans of control, 119–122
factors affection, 121
unity of command, 127–128

Organizational design *(continued)*
  work specialization, 112–115
Ouchi, William G., 265–268
Owners, 48–53
  absentee, 48–49
  attitude toward profits, 49
  management companies, 50

Pace of hotels, 9–18
  hotel cycles, 10
  unpredictability of problems, 14–16
  immediacy of problems, 16–18
  need for quick decisions, 17
  a 24-hour per day business, 10–12
Pascal, Richard, 268–271
Peters, Thomas J., 213, 276–278
Planning in hotels, 84–109
  an aggressive strategic plan, 100–105
  determining markets to serve, 90–91
  GM's role, 87–89
  goals and objectives, 89–98
  human resource goals, 95
  productivity goals, 93–95
  profitability goals, 95–96
  reason for, 84–86
  retrenchment and turnaround, 105–109
  service and quality standards, 91–93
  SWOT analysis, 74–76, 98–99
  time horizon, 86–87
Profits, 52–55
  in bad times, 52–53
  in good times, 52

Roethlisberger, F.J., 216–218
Rogers, Carl R., 216–218

Service, 28–48
  attitudes toward, 36
  consistency of, 35–36
  intangible nature of, 31–32
  personal nature of, 31
  standards, 32–35
    GM's responsibility to set, 34
Service versus profits, 50–52
Scope of operations, 8, 12

city within a city, 8
many different businesses, 12–13
Sheraton Hotels, 61
Strategic planning, 57–79, 84–109
  defined, 57–58
  distinguishing characteristics of, 58–59
  planning hierarchy, 59–63
    business level, 61–62
    corporate level, 60–61
    functional level, 62
    hotel level, 62–63
  planning process, 63–80
  evaluation, 78–79
  formulating a plan, 70–76
    goal setting, 66–70
    SWOT analysis, 74–76, 98–99
    implementation, 76–78
    overview, 64–66
  time horizon, 79–80, 86–87
Skinner, B.F., 200
Staffing, 157–171
  compensation, 170
  employee selection, 160–165
    employee success factors, 162–163
  job design, 159–160
  performance appraisal, 168–170
  training and development, 165–168
  and turnover, 157
Statler, Ellsworth, 270

Takeuchi, Hiroski, 263–265
Taylor, Frederick W., 160, 177–178
Theater and hotels, 7–8

United Airlines, 268–271

Vroom, Victor H., 251–254

Waldorf-Astoria Hotel, 165
Waterman, Robert H., Jr., 213, 276–278
Watson, Thomas, Jr., 270

Yelton, P.W., 251–254

Zemke, Ron, 162–163, 170, 213